Shannon T. Bischoff, Carmen Jany (Eds.)
Insights from Practices in Community-Based Research

Trends in Linguistics
Studies and Monographs

Editor
Volker Gast

Editorial Board
Walter Bisang
Hans Henrich Hock
Natalia Levshina
Heiko Narrog
Matthias Schlesewsky
Amir Zeldes
Niina Ning Zhang

Editor responsible for this volume
Volker Gast

Volume 319

Insights from Practices in Community-Based Research

From Theory To Practice Around The Globe

Edited by
Shannon T. Bischoff
Carmen Jany

DE GRUYTER
MOUTON

ISBN 978-3-11-068537-4
e-ISBN (PDF) 978-3-11-052701-8
e-ISBN (EPUB) 978-3-11-052481-9
ISSN 1861–4302

Library of Congress Control Number: 2018934494

Bibliographic information published by the Deutsche Nationalbibliothek
The Deutsche Nationalbibliothek lists this publication in the Deutsche Nationalbibliografie; detailed bibliographic data are available on the Internet http://dnb.dnb.de.

© 2019 Walter de Gruyter GmbH, Berlin/Boston
This volume is text- and page-identical with the hardback published in 2018.
Typesetting: Integra Software Services, Pondicherry
Printing and binding: CPI books GmbH, Leck
♾ Printed on acid-free paper
Printed in Germany

www.degruyter.com

Contents

Shannon Bischoff and Carmen Jany
Introduction —— 1

Keren Rice
Collaborative research: Visions and realities —— 13

Elena Benedicto
When Participatory Action Research (PAR) and (Western) Academic Institutional Policies do not align —— 38

Ewa Czaykowska-Higgins, Xway'Waat Deanna Daniels, Tim Kulchyski, Andrew Paul, Brian Thom, S. Marlo Twance, and Suzanne C. Urbanczyk
Consultation, relationship and results in community-based language research —— 66

Colleen M. Fitzgerald
Creating sustainable models of language documentation and revitalization —— 94

Gabriela Pérez Báez
Slowly, slowly said the jaguar: Collaborations as a goal of linguistic field research over time —— 112

Bertney Langley, Linda Langley, Jack B. Martin, and Stephanie Hasselbacher
The Koasati Language Project: A collaborative, community-based language documentation and revitalization model —— 132

Ardis Eschenberg and Alice Saunsoci
Full collaboration of native speaker and linguist, working together for language revitalization —— 151

Marie-Odile Junker
Participatory action research for Indigenous linguistics in the digital age —— 164

Mizuki Miyashita, Jackelyn Van Buren, Rebecca Goff, S. Megan Lunak, Annabelle Chatsis, and Scott Schupbach
Implementing collaborative research in Blackfoot language instruction —— 176

Shannon Bischoff, Amy Fountain, and Audra Vincent
100 years of analyzing Coeur d'Alene with the community —— 194

Natasha Warner, Quirina Geary, and Lynnika Butler
Creating learning materials and teaching materials for language revitalization: The case of Mutsun —— 212

Raina Heaton and Igor Xoyón
Collaborative research and assessment in Kaqchikel —— 228

Julie Velásquez Runk and Chenier Carpio Opua
The collaborative process in a Wounaan meu language documentation project —— 246

Pius W. Akumbu
Babanki literacy classes and community-based language research —— 266

Philip Mutaka
Exploring new research perspectives on African cultures through language documentation —— 280

Joshua R. Meyer, Nicholas Kloehn, Andrew Carnie, Diana Archangeli, Ian Clayton, Muriel Fisher, Michael Hammond, Adam Ussishkin, Natasha Warner
The field is not the lab, and the lab is not the field: Experimental linguistics and endangered language communities —— 296

Margaret Florey
Transforming the landscape of language revitalization work in Australia: The Documenting and Revitalising Indigenous Languages training model —— 314

Index —— 339

Shannon Bischoff and Carmen Jany
Introduction

Abstract: Here we present the working definition of *community-based research* (CBR) that served as the starting point for this volume. We discuss how we began with notions of CBR as a practice and how such notions shifted, without abandoning the outlined tenets within the working definition, as chapters developed to include notions of CBR as a *tool* and *ideology* as well as an *orientation* and *philosophy*. We then turn to a review of the chapters presented in the volume. We conclude with a brief discussion of some important questions raised during the process of developing the volume that we believe demand future consideration.

Keywords: community-based research, field work, community engagement

1 Introduction

In recent years there has been an increasing interest in the emerging subfield within linguistics and anthropology often referred to as *community-based research* (see Himmelmann 1998; Rice 2010, this volume; Crippen and Robinson 2013; among numerous others). This volume on the topic brings together the work and ideas from academics, community members, and those that find themselves in both academia and the community working in a community-based approach. In addition, the volume brings together perspectives on community-based research (CBR) from a number of linguistic subfields and numerous geographical locations from the Americas, Australia, India, Europe, and Africa. The goal of the volume is to build on the emerging literature and practices in the field to arrive at a better understanding of how CBR is theorized and practiced in a variety of environments, communities, and cultures. We begin with a working definition of CBR and then move to a discussion of the contributions. We conclude with reflections on some of the challenges and limitations that arise when defining and implementing CBR that have come to light in the process of putting the volume together

---

Shannon Bischoff, Department of English and Linguistics, Purdue University Fort Wayne, 2101 E. Coliseum Blvd. Fort Wayne, IN 46805, bischofs@ipfw.edu
Carmen Jany, Department of World Languages and Literatures, California State University, San Bernardino, CA 92407-2393, cjany@csusb.edu

https://doi.org/10.1515/9783110527018-001

and what that means for future work implementing and theorizing CBR within linguistics and linguistic anthropology.

The starting point for each contributor was that notions regarding CBR are diverse; thus we, the editors and contributors, employed the phrase in the spirit of Rice (2011) and Czaykowska-Higgins (2009) foundationally. Rice notes the following:

> "[c]ommunity-based research has at its core community involvement through all stages of the research [...] Similar definitions are found in other places. The Centre for Community Based Research (http://www.community basedresearch.ca/Page/View/CBR_definition.html; accessed 20 July 2010) identifies three major aspects of this type of research, summarized below.
> – Community situated: research begins with a topic of practical relevance to the community (as opposed to individual scholars) and is carried out in a community setting.
> – Collaborative: community members and researchers equitably share control of the research agenda through active and reciprocal involvement in the research design, implementation, and dissemination.
> – Action-oriented: the process and results are useful to community members in making positive social change and promoting social equity." (p. 189–190)

The above definition embodies what at first blush appears to be solely a *practice* or *methodology*, but Benedicto, Bischoff et. al., Pérez Báez, and Fitzgerald, in their chapters of this volume, illustrate how CBR is itself an *ideology*, as well as a practice, for confronting, defining, and making sense of both the past and present for practitioners of CBR without abandoning the principles above. For Mutaka, CBR is seen, in part, as a *tool* for reshaping and redefining linguistic field work while embodying the principles above. We indeed see that notions regarding CBR are diverse. Rice suggests CBR be construed, in part, as an *orientation towards research*. In her chapter she explores the above definition elucidating a number of characteristics and challenges common within discussions theorizing and describing CBR in a way that allows us to make sense of the seemingly diverse *notions of CBR* (many within the pages of this volume) without losing sight of what the volume suggests is at the core of CBR: *community situated*, *collaborative*, *action-oriented*, and *community involvement through all stages of the research*.

2 The volume

The volume comprises a total of seventeen chapters. Most chapters represent a case-study with the first five chapters including discussions of broader issues and theoretical perspectives while exploring CBR as an emerging subfield within linguistics. These first five chapters focus on theorizing CBR, locating

CBR within the field of linguistics, and defining key elements of CBR such as: *research*, *products*, and *community*. The first chapter by Rice explores ways in which CBR is defined and construed in academia and in the community. Rice argues that CBR is *research* and not *simply service*. Significantly for Rice, CBR is not only research but an important element in the research process and essential to maintaining productive relationships and outputs in the research setting. She begins by tackling the challenges of defining CBR and examines how CBR has *unfolded* especially in terms of language documentation and revitalization. Rice concludes that CBR is an *orientation* or *philosophy* not simply a methodology. In later chapters we see the tension between the idea of CBR as a methodology (e.g. working directly with the community in prescribed fashion as illustrated in the various case studies within the volume), and this philosophical idea of approaching work in a community, as Rice puts it, employing the R's commonly discussed in Canadian indigenous communities: respect, relevance, responsibility, and reciprocity on the part of the participants. However, as Bischoff et al. suggest, the apparent tension is perhaps illusory, that in fact, the methodology emerges out of the philosophy and thus while the specifics of the perceived methodologies may differ across communities they share the core of principles outlined above as they are grounded in the same philosophy or orientation.

In the following chapter Benedicto continues this exploration of CBR in academia and the community. For Benedicto a crucial challenge in theorizing CBR is what she identifies as a *misalignment* between Participant Action Research, which has CBR at its core, and academic institutional policies (a theme echoed in the chapter by Velásquez Runk and Carpio Opua and elsewhere in the volume including in Mutaka's contribution). She argues that this misalignment is grounded in the types of requirements on initiation, definition, processes, and output of research that academic institutions and participatory methodologies impose: things that might determine what *counts* as *academic research* or *academic service* and what counts as *meaningful to the community*. In the end Benedicto outlines what can be identified as a system of ideologies, or in the spirit of Rice what we might refer to as philosophies, that underlies the academic world in the hopes of initiating a conversation about how we as academics define academic work and what that means for CBR practitioners.

Drawing on their experience of working on a CBR project on a southern Vancouver Island in Canada, Czaykowska-Higgins et al. invoke what they term *countable outputs* and *intangible outcomes* to illustrate that in order to develop mutually beneficial partnerships, a community-based research project needs to ensure that consultation amongst participants is meaningful, involving a genuine conversation where participants feel heard and responded to within the project.

The authors go on to argue that *intangible outcomes* (e.g. defining governance structures and protocols, agreeing upon memoranda of understanding), are more significant than *countable outputs* in their experience. They then demonstrate how consulting meaningfully, and thus productively, requires development and continual re-evaluation of consistent, clear, mutually-agreed-upon, and concrete lines of communication. Thus, like Benedicto, Czaykowska-Higgins et al. draw our attention to a shift in scholarly productivity, the shifting nature of what it means to conduct field research in the age of CBR, and the challenges that this poses for both communities and academic institutions in determining what constitutes meaningful research, meaningful results, meaningful products, and meaningful relationships. Further, they explore what it is to be a researcher and what it is to be a community within the emerging context of CBR. In this way Bendicto and Czaykowska-Higgins et al. provide real world examples of what happens, as Rice notes, when we have learned "that community-based models help deepen our knowledge of language, and that collaboration with communities can bring about new kinds of research questions." Further, they reveal the challenges, struggles, and rewards related to when community-based work shows a need to, and begins to, as Rice further notes "transform the discipline, bringing new types of students into the academy, introducing new lines of inquiry, re-examining methodologies and what they can tell us, introducing a more overt focus on ethics, and valuing different kinds of knowledge."

In the next chapter Fitzgerald explores the role of training within a CBR framework. Specifically, she presents case studies involving the University of Arlington Native American Language Lab and language communities in the Oklahoma and Texas. Fitzgerald argues that training leads to a pool of experts, both indigenous and academic, that can draw on a variety of resources for shared goals that include long-term capacity building, where no one person is the cornerstone, while simultaneously ensuring long term grassroots academic-community collaborations in the context of CBR. Further she argues for what she describes as "essential properties of sustainable models of community-based language research" grounded in the notion that revitalization and documentation are often blurred, which emerges from viewing CBR from the lens of training. Fitzgerald provides further examples of the complexity of CBR, as discussed in the previous chapters, in terms of the various types of relationships, outputs, and outcomes that academics and community members need to somehow quantify for the purposes of funding agencies, community leaders, and academic institutions, a subtext of many of the chapters in the volume. Additionally, Fitzgerald's work clearly demonstrates that conceptualizing CBR as an orientation or philosophy allows for the consideration of methodologies and practices described in the chapter to fall under CBR without dimensioning or divorcing CBR from the primary tenets listed above, thus giving us further reason to conceive of CBR, at least in part, as Rice describes an orientation or philosophy in research.

In the fifth chapter Pérez Báez emphasizes the importance of time needed to establish a successful collaboration as researchers need to gain the trust of the community and identify "viable opportunities for collaboration." The author advocates an approach whereby CBR is set as a goal of linguistic research rather than as a condition, which is possible, and necessary, in situations of long-term collaborations. Pérez Báez draws attention to the fact that much of the work conducted in CBR by seasoned fieldworkers began as linguistically focused work. This again suggests that rather than conceptualizing CBR simply a methodology, researchers can go to the field with a CBR philosophy or orientation that allows for the possibility of later collaborative projects. This would, it seems, provide a means to reconcile notions of the so called "lone wolf" approach to field work (Crippen and Robinson 2013) and CBR approaches as described in Bowern and Warner (2015). With CBR as an orientation or philosophy a researcher can go to a community with a specific direction and goal in mind, but end up in a completely different place, with unexpected collaborators, and with different, but entirely meaningful, outcomes, as Junker's work in this volume clearly illustrates—just as is the case, as Rice notes, when academic scholars work with other academic scholars.

The remaining chapters of the volume each focus on a specific case study from different parts of the world. These case studies in collaborative language revitalization, documentation, and experimentation focus on lessons learned from a variety of CBR projects and partnerships and shed light on the reality of CBR in action and how that may impact theorizing CBR for these practitioners. Because CBR occurs in different cultural, socio-political, and geographical settings, the following chapters are sequenced by geographical areas that also reflect, to varying degrees, different cultural and sociopolitical realities at the macro-social level: North America, Latin America, Africa, Europe, and Australia, and the Pacific. The papers all represent case studies from early and long-standing CBR practitioners that reveal not only the promise of CBR but also demonstrate many of the challenges and pitfalls of such endeavors. They provide insights into successful CBR practices while simultaneously raising questions touched on in the previous chapters regarding how we define such activities in terms of research and service, institutional and community requirements, and countable outputs and intangible outcomes.

The remaining chapters represent case studies from different parts of the world. The first six case studies focus on work in North America. Drawing on their experiences working on a long-term CBR project involving documentation and revitalization of the Koasati language, Langley et al. identify how CBR, in the case of language documentation, differs from traditional documentation by an outsider. With this case study, Langley et al. contribute to emerging notions of how CBR should be defined and how CBR differs from previous approaches to research involving communities. In addition, the chapter illustrates how intangible outcomes facilitate the development and production of meaningful countable outputs. Specifically, Langley et al. clearly articulate how the different outcomes impact not only scholarly outputs, but how those outputs do or do not impact the community. Further, they show how a CBR orientation and approach cannot only lead to meaningful products for the community, but can also, as Rice describes, shift the power dynamic of community research and transform the discipline by bringing different perspectives, priorities, and participants to the field.

In a similar vein Eschenberg and Saunsoci describe their ten-year collaboration developing pedagogical resources and teaching the Omaha language. The chapter explores the nature of the collaboration and how it was extended beyond the language classroom into the domains of theoretical linguistics and pedagogical studies. Eschenberg and Saunsoci provide a model of collaboration that ties to native values of knowledge acquisition and relationships. Thus they offer a theoretical basis for the strength of such collaboration in terms of the community. This chapter also demonstrates how the CBR projects described "resulted in a deep interpersonal relationship and tie that endures distance and upholds a common humanistic interest." Such interpersonal connections are a natural outcome of research collaborations that have at their core "trust in the collaborative process and one another, flexibility in making changes, and transparency among all." These themes emerge throughout the volume.

The next three chapters, still within the context of North America, focus on the increasing role of technology and the creation of, and access to, digital resources within CBR and how collaborative relationships can foster the development of such resources that benefit and meet the needs of all involved. The chapters also share an emphasis on how CBR can lead to new ways of imagining language documentation, maintenance, and revitalization. In the first of these three chapters Junker describes how an orientation toward participatory action research shaped her collaborative work with Cree and Innu communities and led to the development of a series of digital resources that were meaningful to community members in terms of language maintenance, as well as to academics and their research agendas. Junker explores how the process of developing these resources was not only productive and meaningful but also empowering to the community members. Junker's work over the past twenty years illustrates well how an orientation or philosophy of CBR can impact how a researcher approaches community-research, research more broadly, and how that can lead to unexpected and fruitful collaborations that yield meaningful outcomes to the academic community and the communities involved in the actual research. It also demonstrates how CBR can shape the discipline in the spirit of Rice's chapter. The work outlined in Bischoff et al. was directly inspired by a 2005 talk given by Junker related to work described in this volume and thus, in part, inspired the volume itself. Therefore we can trace Junker's engagement in CBR directly to the shaping of the discipline.

Next, Miyashita et al. describe a project that demonstrates how CBR can draw on the expertise of all participants, not only linguistic and cultural experts, in the development of meaningful and accessible digital resources. In their work the authors describe the development of digital storybooks for classroom use in the community. The authors touch on themes seen in earlier chapters regarding the importance of developing trust between partners through open dialogue and ongoing relationship building. Similarly to Langley et al., they demonstrate that a contribution to the community does not have to occur after the modern linguistic research (e.g. analysis) has already been undertaken but can occur before as well. This is followed by Bischoff et al., who describe a project that brings together resources collected over four generations of collaboration in the Coeur d'Alene community in digital formats accessible to the community members and academics alike via the internet and mobile applications. The authors present a description of the resources created while also exploring the history of the resources and the nature and evolution of the collaborative efforts involved in the collection and dissemination of these resources. They argue that CBR can be more than just a methodology, process or approach; in fact it can be a tool, and ideology or philosophy, to assess the work and relationships of earlier scholars and communities. These three case studies demonstrate the increasing importance of technology and the development of digital resources for those communities that have access to such resources within the CBR framework. Given the significant technological divide between many community members and non-community members, especially in the USA context (see Tventen 2016, among others), CBR is crucial in terms of understanding what technological resources are useful but also possible given the various states of infrastructure and access to technological resources. Like the other chapters, these emphasize the importance of community agency and strong interpersonal relationships grounded in trust and respect. Further, they demonstrate that viewing CBR as a philosophy or orientation allows one to connect the various projects in the chapters of the volume to the notions of CBR outlined at the start while acknowledging what might be construed as potentially different methodological approaches.

Next, Warner et al. illustrate how CBR allows for the reimagining of revitalization practices and the resources necessary for awakening dormant languages. The authors emphasize the importance and value of creating *learning opportunities* where learners are allowed to practice open conversation and teaching how to stay in a language when one does not know a specific word. Warner et al. emphasize the importance of transcending the traditional classroom experience and the importance of going beyond a focus on written teaching materials. The chapter demonstrates how CBR can lead to broader, and different kinds of, thinking when it comes to revitalization and the creation of opportunities for language learning inspired by a rethinking of power relations and allowing for community perspectives to shape the research and research goals.

The following two chapters represent case studies from Latin America. Some of the challenges and pitfalls of CBR are the explicit topic of the chapter by Heaton and Xoyon. The authors explore the consequences of the formation of *Maya for Maya* in Mayan areas of Guatemala. *Maya for Maya* is an organization that outside researchers are expected to consult in order to ensure researchers demonstrate solidarity with Maya socio-political concerns (England 1996, 2003; Cojti Cuxil 1997; Maxwell 1996; Barrett 2008). Heaton and Xoyon argue that this innovative and unique situation can serve as an important precedent for all research done in Mayan communities with which current researchers must comply. It can be used as an example and model for other communities as well. Following, Velásquez Runk and Carpio Opua present a CBR project documenting language from 60 years of Wounaan oral history recordings. They discuss the challenges and opportunities faced in such international CBR projects, with multiple theoretical perspectives and goals, and conclude by addressing differing discourses of *power* in collaborative anthropological and linguistic research. The authors explicitly touch on many of issues discussed in Rice, Benedicto, and Czaykowska-Higgins. Specifically when it comes to outcomes, the authors illustrate the challenges of satisfying funding agencies and academic institutions when focused on community-driven products. The chapter illustrates how the discipline has not fully been changed in such a way that the community-driven tangible outcomes of CBR projects are equally valued in the community and traditionally academically aligned institutions such as most funding agencies. The work by Fitzgerald (discussed above) suggests a way forward when it comes to making community driven tangible outcomes meaningful to funding agencies. Further, the number of projects discussed in the volume funded by major funding agencies suggests that the discipline is indeed changing but may have a ways to go yet.[1]

---

[1] It is important to remember that many funding agencies turn to experts in the field when it comes to evaluating research projects for funding. Therefore, it might not be so much an issue of changing funding agencies within the discipline alone, but also changing our colleagues and how they view meaningful research.

The following two case studies are from Africa. In the first one, Akumbu draws our attention to the missed opportunities when collaborative research focuses primarily on the interests of the academic linguist. Drawing on his experience in Northwest Cameroon, Akumbu argues that in addition to the need to have contemporary understanding of linguistic phenomena and the need to utilize the most up-to-date technology, one area of great importance for communities are resources for adult literacy in the language of the community. He goes on to discuss how building literacy among adults can have a positive impact not only on the community and the health of the language but also on those types of goals most associated with academic linguistic research. In the spirit of rethinking what constitutes meaningful research and the relationship between scholar and community, in the next chapter Mutaka presents a project in lexicography that emphasizes the important link between language, culture, and linguistic documentation from an *African* perspective. Building on this relationship between language, culture, and linguistics, Mutaka argues that CBR in Africa provides an opportunity for documentary linguists to examine what it means to be human from an African perspective thus expanding our understanding of what it means to be human in the broadest sense. The chapter explores the complex relationship between language, culture, and documentation while also emphasizing the importance of literacy, identity, and the human experience: key elements that often drive CBR. What Mutaka argues for is a CBR that not only allows for a significant role in the process by community members but also a significant role for CBR to reshape the process itself in new and meaningful ways or as Rice puts it, for CBR to shape the discipline. Crucially, both chapters reflect again Rice's notion of an orientation or philosophy rather than simply a methodology.

The next two chapters each represent a case study from Europe and from Australia, respectively. Meyers et al. explore how experimental research can be made more scientifically rigorous and of value to a community when elements of CBR are embraced in a European context. The authors discuss the challenges of conducting experimental research in language communities and the challenges of making such research valuable to community members themselves. The authors draw on their experience working with Scottish Gaelic speakers on the Isle of Skye to explore these issues and reflect on how their research was perceived by the community of Gaelic speaking collaborators. They conclude that careful work done in collaboration with community members is critical to successfully creating an experimental research program that is both scientifically rigorous and of value to the community, thus echoing the claims of earlier chapters of the volume. Along with Fitzgerald's contribution, this chapter challenges the notion of CBR as simply a methodology. Further it illustrates an interesting contrast, perhaps intersection, between the lone wolf approach (Crippen and

Robinson 2013) and what we might call a strong CBR approach related more to Bowern and Warner (2015), Rice (2010, this volume), and Czaykowska-Higgins (2009, this volume). Meyers et al. describe a research project that appears to be grounded in academic pursuits but that is implemented in a way that attempts to embody the notions of CBR presented at the start of the paper. This suggests that the authors were attempting to fit their research agenda into a CBR philosophy or put another way, orient their research in terms of CBR.

Finally, the chapter by Florey describes the Documenting and Revitalizing Indigenous Languages (DRIL) training program, a flexible grassroots training model for Aboriginal people in Australia. The author discusses the challenges of the program and how it has been adapted to the needs of the communities. Special attention is given to the methods used for growing the program and including the next generation of non-Indigenous linguists into these endeavors. The chapter touches on all of the major themes that emerge throughout the volume regarding methodology, philosophy, orientation, products, and community. As in earlier chapters the notions are embedded in the work described but the work described goes beyond those elementary elements and allows us to imagine CBR as a philosophy or orientation that embraces different methodologies and approaches grounded in those fundamental notions of community situated, collaborative, and action-oriented.

3 Conclusions

The present volume is meant to provide the starting of a framework for CBR and offer insights into how CBR is being implemented in communities around the world. The contributors present perspectives on how academics and community members are articulating CBR for themselves and within the field. As a result, we see that the core of what we began with as our definition of CBR at the outset is at the heart of the theorizing and practice presented in this volume and therefore the definition is grounded, at least in part, in the reality of practice. However, the volume also draws our attention to a number of important questions yet to be addressed. We briefly discuss two of these questions here.

The most important perhaps is the issue of *community*. Rice provides a glimpse of how the term is construed within CBR and provides reference to others who have discussed the issue, but she also recognizes the challenges of defining community within the context of CBR. That is perhaps due to the challenges of defining and identifying *community, communities,* and *community membership* in general, let alone within the context of CBR. Community at its core is a concept that describes social organization, but that connotes a wide range of meanings. In the work of this volume social groups identified as communities often represent communities based on *geography, identity,* and *interest or solidarity* (Aggarwal n.d.). In the chapters presented here the three converge in that the contributors represent peoples from specific geographic areas who may come together at times in one specific geographic area or focus on one such area, who have multiple identities grounded within characteristics or attributes associated with different groups of people, and who share the stated interest of maintaining, documenting, and/or preserving a language or languages. However, it is not always clear how an individual sees him- or herself within a community or within multiple communities nor how others see that same individual within a given community or given communities. This is perhaps illustrated best when we ask the following questions: a) *Who has the authority to speak for a community?* b) *Who represents a community?* c) *Who gets to make decisions about a community's language use?* or d) *Who gets to define what is or isn't in a community's language?* This holds for academics and non-academics alike. Pursuing notions of community within the context of CBR is fraught with challenges, but what we see from this volume is that the contributors see themselves as representative of the described and implied communities revealed within the volume with the authority to share their stories.

Another question, raised by an anonymous reviewer, was one of policy and planning or rather a lack of fuller discussion regarding policy and planning issues. The majority of contributors to the volume are academic/community linguists, community/academic anthropologists, teachers, and activists and not necessarily planning or policy experts. Planning and policy experts are needed in CBR, along with technologist, healthcare professionals (see Whalen et al. 2016), politicians, and numerous other experts and stake holders. In fact, CBR practices are a natural fit, perhaps uniquely so, for the development and implementation of diverse and inclusive projects that adhere to the competing, shared, and complementary values and goals of the various partners and communities necessary for such projects to be successful in the immediate and long-term future (as many of the chapters demonstrate).

References

Aggarwal, Pramila. n.d. Understanding the community. UNESCO Educational Resource. http://www.unesco.org/education/aladin/paldin/pdf/course01/unit_06.pdf

Barrett, Rusty. 2008. Linguistic differentiation and Mayan language revitalization in Guatemala. *Journal of Sociolinguistics* 12 (3). 275–305.

Bowern, Claire and Natasha Warner. 2015. 'Lone wolves' and collaboration: A reply to Crippen & Robinson (2013). *Language Documentation and Conservation* 9. 59–85.

Cojtí Cuxil, Demetrio. 1997. *Ri Maya' Moloj pa Iximulew: El Movimiento Maya en Guatemala* [The Maya movement in Guatemala]. Guatemala City, Guatemala: Cholsamaj.

Crippen, James A. and Laura C. Robinson. 2013. In defense of the lone wolf: Collaboration in language documentation. *Language Documentation & Conservation* 7. 123–135.

Czaykowska-Higgins, Ewa. 2009. Research models, community engagement, and linguistic fieldwork: Reflections on working within Canadian Indigenous communities. *Language Documentation & Conservation* 3 (1). 15–50.

England, Nora. 1996. The role of language standardization in revitalization. In Edward Fisher and R. McKenna Brown (eds.), *Maya cultural activism in Guatemala*, 178–194. Austin, Texas: University of Texas Press.

England, Nora. 2003. Mayan language revitalization and revitalization politics: Linguists and linguistic ideologies. *American Anthropologist* 105 (4). 733–743.

Himmelmann, Nikolaus. 1998. Documentary and descriptive linguistics. *Linguistics* 36. 95–161.

Maxwell, Judith M. 1996. Prescriptive grammar and Kaqchikel revitalization. In Edward Fischer and R. McKenna Brown (eds.), *Mayan cultural activism in Guatemala*. Austin, Texas: University of Texas Press. 195–207.

Rice, Keren. 2010. The linguist's responsibilities to the community of speakers: Community-based research. In Lenore A. Grenoble and N. Louanna Furbee (eds.) *Language documentation: Practice and values*, 25–36. Amsterdam: John Benjamins.

Rice, Keren. 2011. Documentary linguistics and community relations. *Language Documentation and Conservation* 5. 187–207.

Tveten, Juliane. 2016. On American Indian reservations, challenges perpetuate the digital divide. *arsTechnica* http://arstechnica.com/information-technology/2016/01/on-american-indian- reservations-challenges-perpetuate-the-digital-divide/?comments=1 (accessed 25 August 2016).

Whalen, Doug, Margaret Moss, and Daryl Baldwin. 2016. Healing through language: Positive physical health effects of indigenous language use. *F1000Research* 5:852 https://f1000research.com/articles/5-852/v1 (accessed 20 May 2017).

Keren Rice
Collaborative research: Visions and realities

Abstract: This chapter provides a perspective on community-based research in linguistics, examining the range of variation in this work. I seek to broaden the definition of community-based research so as to better accommodate the different kinds of situations that arise over both time and space, taking as the foundation that community-based research is an orientation towards research, not a methodology (Ferreira and Gendron 2011).

Keywords: community-situated, control, collaboration, action orientation, empowerment, social justice, equity, relevance, community-of-practice, relationships

1 Introduction

Recent years have seen an explosion of literature on community-based research in linguistics, with collaborative work becoming a hot topic in linguistics and in other disciplines as well. For linguistics, see, for instance, Bowern and Warner (2015) (in response to Crippen and Robinson's 2013 work on lone-wolf models rather than addressing community-based research per se), Czaykowska-Higgins (2009), Dobrin and Berson (2011), Dwyer (2006, 2010), Grenoble and Whitecloud (2014), Leonard and Haynes (2010), Penfield et al. (2008), Rice (2009, 2010, 2011), Vallejos (2014), Yamada (2007), the chapters in this volume, and many others. For overviews of other disciplines, see, for instance, Israel et al. (2005), Minkler and Wallerstein (2011), and Schensul et al. (2015). See also Ferreira and Gendron (2011) for a very interesting overview of the historical contexts and future directions of community-based participatory research with traditional and indigenous communities of the Americas. There is a list of resources, including websites, journals, and books, available at http://communityresearchcanada.ca/ resources.[1]

---

[1] Terms for this orientation towards research include community-based research, community-engaged research, community-based participatory research, participatory action research, community-centered research, and transformational research. Schensul, Schensul, Singer, Weeks, and Brault (2015) examine these and other terms used in anthropological research, differentiating between different kinds of collaborative research. I use the term community-based research, following the title of this book.

Keren Rice, Department of Linguistics, University of Toronto, 100 St. George Street, Toronto, Ontario, Canada M5S 3G3, rice@chass.utoronto.ca

https://doi.org/10.1515/9783110527018-002

This chapter provides a perspective on community-based research in linguistics, starting from a basic definition and examining, in very broad strokes, some variations on the theme. I begin with characteristics of community-based research written to introduce a broad audience to this type of research. I then examine how such research has unfolded in linguistic work, focusing on language documentation and revitalization, a topic taken up in detail in the chapters in this volume and elsewhere, and I attempt to broaden the understanding of this type of research.

It is important to keep two points in mind in reading this chapter. First, I write as an academic linguist who has been involved in community-based projects. Second, I draw examples largely from the Americas, where some variety of community-based research has a deep history in the social sciences, and where there has been considerable attention paid to such a model in both linguistics and other disciplines.[2]

2 What is community-based research? A definition and some characteristics

There is a wealth of literature on community-based research broadly defined, under various names. I draw on the characterization of community-based research provided by the Centre for Community-Based Research Canada (http://communityresearchcanada.ca). This centre, as well as a number of other organizations, has long been an advocate of community-based research. Such organizations provide an interesting starting point to understand what community-based research is and what principles underlie it. I begin with the Centre for Community-Based Research Canada's three-part definition: it is community-situated, collaborative, and action-oriented. These terms are expanded on as follows, quoting from the Centre for Community-based Research Canada (http://www.communitybasedresearch.ca/Page/View/CBR_definition) and Community-Based Research Canada (http://communityresearchcanada.ca/cbr).

---

2 See Dobrin and Berson (2011: 211) for comments on the geography of collaborative research in linguistics, and Ferreira and Gendron (2011) for discussion of the development of the collaborative model more generally. Ferreira and Gendron (2011: 155) point to its origins, noting that it arises from action research (termed the Northern Tradition) and participatory research (the Southern Tradition, in Latin America, Asia, and Africa), and they stress the important role of Paulo Freire. For discussion of collaborative research outside of the Americas, see, for instance, Good (2012), discussion in some of the articles in Essegbey, Henderson, and McLaughlin (2015), and chapters in this volume on Africa, and Wilkins (1992), among many others, on Australia. See also the recent collection edited by Pérez-Báez, Rogers, and Rosés Labrada (2016) on language documentation in Latin America.

First, community-based research begins with a research topic of practical relevance to the community and is carried out in community settings. Second, community members and researchers equitably share control of the research agenda through active and reciprocal involvement in the design, implementation, and dissemination. Finally, the process and results can transform and mobilize diverse ideas, resources, and experiences to generate positive action for communities.

Hallmarks of such research are also given by the Centre for Community-Based Research, and include the following (http://www.communitybasedresearch.ca/Page/View/CBR_definition):
- The relevance of the research topic is identified or verified by community members.
- The resources of research (financial, expertise, etc.) are shared with community members, particularly those most affected by the research topic.
- The research process recognizes and utilizes the expertise that community members have.
- The research process recognizes and addresses power imbalances between researchers and community members.
- The research process is driven by values, including: empowerment, supportive relationships, social change, learning as an ongoing process and respect for diversity.
- The research process and results are accessible and understandable to community members.
- The research process and results consider and adapt to the context in which the research is conducted.
- The research leaves a legacy, both in terms of the utilization of research results, as well as in the future collaboration among partners.

Successful partnerships are described in the following ways:
(http://communityresearchcanada.ca/res/download.php?id=3382)
- have mutual trust and mutual respect
- agree about goals and strategies
- share power
- communicate clearly and listen carefully
- understand and empathize with one another's circumstances
- share a worldview
- remain flexible
- strive to ensure that partners' primary interests and needs are met
- strive to ensure that partners' organizational capacities are enhanced
- understand and agree to the long-term commitment

In general, the idea of community-based research, at least in a North American context, tends to start from these perspectives. The characteristics provide a broad overview of community-based research, but, as I stress throughout this work, they may not work well in all settings or at all times in a particular setting, and may not be viewed by everyone as being definitive of community-based research. See, for instance, Holton (2009) and discussion that follows in this chapter.

Underlying community-based research is a fundamental principle: community-based research is grounded in social justice and responsibility. Social justice is a complex concept, and a presentation of its nuances is beyond the scope of this chapter. In discussions of social justice, phrases such as equitable, fair, safe, respect for basic human dignity, and good of the society (not just the individual) are found. See, for instance, Dolan-Reilly (2013) and Novack (2000) for general discussion. See Bowern and Warner (2015), Czaykowska-Higgins (2009), Dobrin and Berson (2011), and Dobrin and Schwartz (2016) for some perspectives on community-based research in linguistics with reference to social justice.

In the next section, drawing on the ideals of community-based research outlined in this section, I relate them to the realities of such research as it has been carried out in language work in recent years.

3 Community-based research and language work: How well does it fit these definitions?

The groups that developed the above statements about community-based research are well aware that this research is complex, and that definitions, hallmarks, and indicators of successful partnerships should not be interpreted as prescriptive, but rather provide a broad overview of the foundations of such research. While a characterization of community-based research such as that presented in section 2 was not intended to be taken simplistically, it is easy to interpret such lists as recipes for success. Thus, in this section I introduce some of the ways in which the definition, hallmarks, and indicators of success have worked out in community-based research with language documentation and revitalization as its goal.

3.1 Community-based research as beginning with research of practical relevance to the community and carried out in community settings

The first part of the definition of community-based research, community situated, states that community-based research begins with a research topic of practical relevance to the community and is carried out in community settings. There are several parts of this statement that are worthy of further discussion, namely "begins with," "practical relevance," "community," and "community setting."

3.1.1 "Begins with"

Is it the case that community-based research begins with a research topic of practical relevance to the community? I focus first on the "begins with" portion of this. In a narrow sense this is probably true, but in fact, much precedes what might be regarded as the "official" start of a community-based project. I briefly examine a few cases of community-based language research to give an indication of the kinds of things that precede what the authors define as community-based research.

The project described by Czaykowska-Higgins (2009) and Czaykowska-Higgins et al. (this volume) had its formal inception as a grant from the Social Science and Humanities Research Council of Canada, awarded in 2001, for community-based research in Vancouver Island Salish communities. However, the research in fact began far before the team applied for the grant. Given the complexities of preparing a grant proposal, the fact that the project was grant-funded suggests that much preceded the formal beginning of this community-based project. As the authors describe, prior to applying for the grant, there was interaction between the Salish communities involved with a number of linguists — the authors write that the project grew out of these relationships, common goals, and aspirations. This process itself took around two years before a grant proposal was submitted, and that grant then led to the formal research project. See Czaykowska-Higgins et al. (this volume) for detailed discussion of this project.

Langley et al. (this volume) write about the inception of the Koasati Language Project in Louisiana. This project, like the Salish project described above, began with community members approaching a university in order to be able to apply for a grant. Much had already gone on in the community prior to this, and the grant-funded research grew out of work that had begun some time previously.

The community-based work that Yamada (2007) describes with the Kari'nja in Suriname arose out of her having been a Peace Corps volunteer in Suriname. While perhaps not involved with language work at the time, Yamada had established relationships with people in the Kari'nja community that served as a foundation for this research.

Penfield et al. (2008: 190), in an article on defining best practices for community-based language documentation in North America, identify several projects that set the stage for a collaborative project involving linguists from the University of Arizona and community members from the Colorado River Indian

Tribes reservation in Arizona. These projects focused on technology training and the development of on-line dictionaries. The authors do not discuss the earliest stages that led to the idea of a partnership, but the work that they discuss grew out of already established relationships.

Pérez-Báez (this volume) elaborates on how her own research with speakers of Diidxazá in Mexico evolved into a community-based project, although it did not begin as one. She lays out the many stages that the research went through on its way to becoming what she identifies as community-based research. She writes of the kinds of conditions that are necessary for community-based research to be effective for all involved. She is explicit about beginnings — without some knowledge of the community involved and its language(s), it is difficult to imagine community-based research involving community and academic researchers.[3]

Thus, while in some formal sense community-based research might begin with a research topic of practical relevance to the community, it is very often, and perhaps always, the case that such collaborative projects grow out of relationships that have been previously established in some way, whether they be traditional research relationships or relationships established in other ways, as with the Peace Corps work that Yamada describes. As Pérez-Báez (this volume) discusses, community-based research tends to be "grounded on a significant infrastructure of community relations and resources which take time to assemble."

3.1.2 "Practical relevance"

Next I turn to "of practical relevance." The word "practical" is defined as follows in Merriam-Webster: of, relating to, or manifested in practice or action — not theoretical or ideal (http://www.merriam-webster.com/dictionary/practical), and "relevant" has the following definition: practical and especially social applicability (http://www.merriam-webster.com/dictionary/relevance). In language documentation and revitalization work, one tends to think of revitalization as the part of the pair that is of practical relevance. It can be difficult, however, to disentangle documentation and revitalization. For instance, developing materials for revitalization often depends upon there being documentation, and documentation is of relevance in this sense. Langley et al. (this volume) discuss the need for language research beyond the existing grammar of Koasati in order to develop pedagogical materials, focusing in particular on the necessity for deeper knowledge of conversation. As Bowern and Warner (2015: 67) and others discuss,

---

3 See Bowern and Warner (2015) on various models that involve hiring a linguist to do a job. These models may become collaborative, but do not necessarily start out with collaboration as a goal.

practical goals (e.g., creating a dictionary, videotaping) can yield material that is of interest to different parties in different ways. Some (see for instance Crippen and Robinson 2013) are critical of the materials that might be considered to be of practical relevance, essentially limiting them to classroom materials. However, as stressed by Bowern and Warner (2015) and Langley et al. (this volume), for instance, practical research is fed by academic research and vice versa.

What makes something part of community-based research is that the research is of interest to members of the research team, with each member seeing benefit in what they do. This might involve somewhat different methodologies than one might use if the research were not seen as community-based — for instance, Langley et al. (this volume) discuss staged production, and remark on the production of a topical dictionary followed by a small dictionary followed by a larger dictionary with audio. As an academically-driven project, one might prefer to begin with the goal of as complete a dictionary as possible. "Practical relevance" can be interpreted in a range of ways, and allows for a range of types of outcomes and products.

3.1.3 "Community"

Turning to "community," this word too is a challenging one: as Schensul et al. (2015:206) point out, "communities are complex entities, with many different sectors." The Merriam-Webster provides the following two definitions (http://www.merriam-webster.com/dictionary/community):
- a group of people who live in the same area (such as a city, town, or neighborhood)
- a group of people who have the same interests, religion, race, etc.

The first of these definitions is likely what comes to many people's minds in thinking about community. In considering collaboration between a language community and a university, no one would think that in such a collaboration the entire university would be engaged, or even an entire unit within the university, but it is often assumed that, in some way, a substantial subset of a language community should be engaged in the research. However, as Linn (2016) and many others discuss, there are different ways of defining community. In community-based linguistic research projects, the second definition of community is generally more appropriate — such research engages a group of people who have a common interest in their language.[4] Penfield et al. (2008), in their work on best

---

[4] See Dobrin and Berson (2011) for interesting commentary on the types of people who tend to engage in such projects. That there are different sectors within a community with respect to

practices for community collaborations in North American Indigenous language documentation, explicitly note as a recommendation that the team(s) be chosen carefully, and that the team forms the community at least at the start. Communities often shift over time, and the participants who begin a community-based research project and those who finish it may well be different.[5]

3.1.4 "Community setting"

What does it mean to be carried out in a community setting? While it is perhaps by definition the case that community-based research is carried out in speaker community settings, in fact the people in the research community need not necessarily be physically in the same room, or even in the same geographical location. Communities may be geographically dispersed, with people working with each other from a distance. Penfield et al. (2008) note the challenge of geographic separation of the community and university researchers, and advocate the importance of academic researchers spending time in the speaker community, especially at the beginning of a project. Some aspects of the research may be better carried out in the university setting; for instance there may be better access to certain types of materials in the university community than in the speaker community. Valued speaker community researchers may live outside their community, but be important contributors to a project. Academics likely have responsibilities in their universities, not allowing them to be in the community setting for much of the time (see Langley et al. this volume for some comments on this). Frequent contact and close communication may be necessary for such research, but it need not be bound tightly to a single location.

---

issues of language conservation and revitalization can be a challenge in implementing language revitalization broadly.

5 A reviewer raises some questions regarding communities: Does a community have to all speak the same language? What about language diasporas — do they belong to the same community as the home country? Do speakers of a language in a geographically widespread area count as one community, even though it is unlikely that they will have the same interest or goals in language work? There is no simple answer to these questions. Communities are defined at different levels, and individuals may be part of a community for one purpose and not part of that community for another. The term community-of-practice is perhaps a better one than community. A common definition of community-of-practice is as follows: "Communities of practice are groups of people who share a concern or a passion for something they do and learn how to do it better as they interact regularly" (http://wenger-trayner.com/introduction-to-communities-of-practice/), similar to the second definition given in the text above.

3.1.5 Summary

While the notion of community-based research beginning with a research topic of practical relevance to the community and carried out in a community setting is useful, in fact beginning with practical relevance, community, and community setting all raise questions, and should not be taken as rigidly definitional.

3.2 The collaborative nature of community-based research

Having examined the definition of community-based research as beginning with a research topic of practical relevance to the community and carried out in the community setting, I now address the word that is perhaps at the heart of community-based research, collaborative. This is elaborated in the characterization of community-based research discussed in section 2 as follows: community members and researchers equitably share control of the research agenda through active and reciprocal involvement in the design, implementation, and dissemination.

The meaning of collaboration is reasonably clear on the surface — working jointly. Again, questions arise. What does "equitable" mean? The Merriam-Webster dictionary gives the following definition: "just or fair, dealing fairly and equally with everyone" (http://www.merriam-webster.com/dictionary/equitable). In collaborations within an academic setting, collaboration does not mean that each person in a team is fully engaged in every aspect of the research. This is also the case with community-based research. "Fairly" and "equally" do not require that all are in lockstep with each other, with identical responsibilities.

Collaboration is sometimes considered to involve two-way training and joint decision-making as a way of reducing power imbalances. Leonard and Haynes (2010) stress the importance of collaborative consultation in defining research roles and goals. It is difficult to judge whether research is equitable and collaborative independent of some understanding of a culture. Dobrin (2008) and Holton (2009), for instance, discuss cases in which, from an outsider perspective, research might seem to be driven totally by the academic researcher, but this was, the authors argue, what was valued and expected by community members, and, in this sense, such research too can be viewed as collaborative, as it is appropriate to the values of the community. Pérez-Báez (this volume) discusses how community members expected that she would provide leadership and direction, although she advocated at the start a model where these were shared amongst team members.

"Active and reciprocal involvement" may transparently involve creating a community-defined plan as a team (e.g., Penfield et al. 2008), but there might be involvement that does not appear to an outsider to be active and reciprocal, but is with respect to the culture of the particular community. As above, these notions, as those who write about community-based research are the first to acknowledge, should not be regarded as prescriptive, but are worked out depending on the individuals and communities involved. What matters is that there is communication, with different parties being engaged in ways they choose to be, and having the sense that their contributions are valued. See Leonard and Haynes (2010) and Bowern and Warner (2015) for discussion of some of the ways in which research can be collaborative, and Dobrin and Schwartz (2016) for a critique of a somewhat narrower definition of community-based research.

3.3 Action-oriented

The third part of the definition of community-based research involves action-orientation: the process and results can transform and mobilize diverse ideas, resources, and experiences to generate positive action for communities. We can ask what action-oriented means in language work. One sometimes sees the term "give back" to the community used, where the academic researcher has in mind that they will leave copies of their field notes or give a copy of their thesis. This, while perhaps valuable, is not what would generally be considered to be action oriented, at least in a North American setting — giving back in this sense is a choice by the giver without necessarily taking into account what the speaker community's values and needs are. Speaker communities often do want field notes, dissertations, and the like (see, for instance, the articles in this volume by Langley et al. and by Bischoff, Fountain, and Vincent), but providing such resources will not, in many places and at some times, be viewed as providing something needed by the community at that moment in time. Collaborative research in the action-oriented sense suggests that the work is of benefit to all those engaged in the research in a way that is valued by the communities. This could be the contribution of materials, but whether this is or is not viewed as action-oriented in the sense described is not easily determined by the academic researcher alone.

In collaborative work in language documentation action-oriented research is often considered to involve capacity building, with training people to record, transcribe, and translate.[6] Sustaining and revitalization is almost always a goal,

---

[6] There may well be ideological differences between the goals of the academic linguist and the goals of community members, and such differences may go unrecognized by the members of a

and is an explicit goal in most community-based research that I am aware of that starts with the community researchers. This type of research is discussed in the references in this chapter; see also Gerdts (2010) and many other sources. There are other goals as well for many engaged in collaborative research, including valorizing languages, understanding the language ecology of the community, contributing to understanding the basics of what the core values of a community are through language, contributing to the health of communities, and, in general, addressing issues of social justice. See Bowern and Warner (2015) for detailed discussion of a range of types of collaborative projects. The action may also turn out to not be based on the academic knowledge of the linguist, at least for a time. For instance, as I discuss in Rice (2011), it could involve cleaning roads, cooking, baby-sitting — these might not be viewed as action-oriented or transformational by some, but may be what is of the greatest value to members of the community at a point in time.

Action orientation involves having a shared notion of what action means. Dobrin and Schwartz (2016) examine a number of cases where the stated goals and the actual beliefs are at odds, making proposed and on the surface agreed upon action difficult. To give just a few examples, in fieldwork in Papua New Guinea, Dobrin found that people talked about the need for a preschool, but then, when it opened, they did not send their children to it. Dobrin came to understand that the preschool was valued to the degree that it was supported by outsiders; when this support was not available, the villagers were not interested in it. Dobrin and Schwartz (2016) use this example to show the value of ethnographic research; I take it to show that it is easy to become involved in what one takes to be action when in fact that action is not what is of interest, with disappointment in the end on the part of those involved due to this type of misunderstanding. Dauenhauer and Dauenhauer (1998) address ideological differences in language revitalization in Alaska, asking why projects that people appeared to be excited about did not work out. They note a "broad gap between verbally expressed goals, on the one hand (generally advocating language and cultural preservation) and unstated but deeply felt emotions and anxieties on the other (generally advocating or contributing to abandonment)" (Dauenhauer and Dauenhauer, 1998: 62–63). See Kroskrity (2009) for detailed discussion.

---

research team, with each implicitly thinking that the goals as agreed upon are actually the same. See below for some examples.

3.4 Summary: community-oriented, collaborative, action-oriented

Summarizing the three key words that characterize community-based research — community-oriented, collaborative, action-oriented — each is complex and requires careful consideration for a particular situation. What is probably at the core, as articulated by Leonard and Haynes (2010: 288), Czaykowska-Higgins et al. (this volume), and many others is time and trust, with the awareness that things can change over time and space, and that there are peaks and valleys.

3.5 Hallmarks of community-based research

The characterization of community-based research introduced in section 2 includes a number of hallmarks of such research. These too are more complex than one might initially think. In this section, I remark briefly on a few of them.

3.5.1 Relevance

One of the hallmarks given is that the relevance of the research topic be identified or verified by community members. As discussed in section 3.1, such projects may grow out of research that is not community-based in the sense discussed in section 2. In some cases, the presence of a linguist in a community might lead to an interest in the language, and the realization that things like documentation and revitalization exist and are possible. With a project defined by community linguists, it might take time for an academic linguist to understand what the questions are that the community researchers want to address. Once a formal project is identified, relevance is an important hallmark, but, as discussed earlier, what this means can vary over space and time.

3.5.2 Power imbalances

Another hallmark that is worthy of comment is that the research process recognizes and addresses power imbalances between academic researchers and community members. It is in large part these power differences that led to community-based models. Dobrin and Berson (2011: 202) point out that in language documentation, "the act of creating documentary and descriptive linguistic objects as traditionally understood reproduces the suspect power hierarchy that linguistics-in-recognition-of-indigenous-rights is intended to dismantle." There are not imbalances in terms of knowledge, but different participants bring different types of knowledge to the project, and documentation, as Bowern and Warner (2015), Dobrin and Berson (2011), Leonard and Haynes (2010), and others argue, tends to favor that of the academic researcher. One way in which the awareness of this imbalance has played out, Dobrin and Berson suggest, is through collaborative models that involve negotiations between the parties. Penfield et al. (2008), for instance, note that all the community collaborators in their project were language activists who received training to document the language by doing data collection and organization and learning the technology, and Czaykowska-Higgins et al. (this volume) discuss in detail the work that they did to address power imbalances. Leonard and Haynes (2010) stress the importance of spending the time to create trust in relationships.

Pérez-Báez (this volume) provides interesting insight into the value of not interpreting the notion of power imbalance too narrowly. She planned to undertake a community-based project through listening, based on advice in work by Leonard and Haynes (2010: 287) and others, although she felt uneasy about this based on her knowledge of Mexican societies and cultures. She quickly learned that listening was not appropriate, and that, in fact, she was expected to take a leadership role and provide direction; other team members took on leadership roles with respect to workshops and printed materials, but not more broadly. What it means to address power imbalances is something that needs to be thought through on a continuing basis; it would be possible, with all good intention, to unwittingly reinforce rather than reduce them.

3.5.3 Accessibility

A third hallmark of community-based research discussed in section 2 is that the research process and results are accessible and understandable to community members. "Accessible" and "understandable" are complex terms. I have recently been involved in a research project on caribou (see Polfus et al. 2016 and Polfus et al. 2017). The overall goal of this project is to use multiple knowledge sources to interpret patterns of biodiversity in order to develop effective conservation strategies for caribou. The team involved members of a Dene community in the Northwest Territories, Canada who are native speakers of the language of the community with deep traditional knowledge as well as experience with outside researchers. The team included two non-Dene partners who live in the community and have background in resource management. It also involved non-Dene wildlife biologists and a linguist. Many of the members of this team had worked closely together before the project started. It is unlikely that any single member of this team controls a deep understanding of all aspects of the research. A major piece of the research involved a study of caribou DNA. Although much was done to make the technical aspects of the DNA as clear as possible, the deep knowledge of DNA is controlled by just a small subset of the team, perhaps only one person. In some way this research is accessible and understandable to all members of the research team even though all the details are likely not understood by any individual member of the team.

3.6 Criteria for successful partnerships

In section 2 I introduced a number of criteria that are recognized as important in determining the success of a partnership. These include mutual trust and respect, agreement about goals and strategies, sharing of power, clear communication, understanding and empathizing, flexibility, striving to ensure that partners' needs and interests are met and that their organizational capacities are enhanced, and understanding and agreeing to a long-term commitment. I address one of the criteria for successful partnerships here, sharing a worldview, and discuss a few of the others in section 4.

One suggested characteristic of a successful partnership is that the partners share a worldview. In a discussion of successful partners, the document CBR & Partnerships (Office of Community-Based Research, University of Victoria) notes the following:

> Although differences in points of view are extremely important, there needs to be a basic worldview shared by the researchers, specifically philosophical understanding of people, communities, and society. Questions regarding what humans are capable of (such as governing themselves, or understanding their situations), as well as what "community" is, must have similar, workable answers if a project is to proceed. Otherwise, partners will find that their basic assumptions about how to do things are at odds.

I take this notion of some kind of shared perspective as a given. Setting this aside, perhaps what is most rewarding, and also challenging, about community-based research is precisely that collaborators do not necessarily share a worldview on the topic of interest. Mithun (2001: 53) discusses this from the perspective of linguistic work:

> But if the research is limited to eliciting translations of English vocabulary and syntactic constructions, collecting grammaticality judgments, and checking off known typological diagnostics, we may miss what is unexpected about the language under study. In so doing we risk depriving descendants of the speakers of what is special about their heritage and

lose opportunities to expand our own theoretical horizons. If speakers are also allowed to speak for themselves, creating a record of spontaneous speech in natural communicative settings, we have a better chance of providing the kind of record that will be useful to future generations. The search for what is special in a language does not necessarily entail a rejection of the quest for language universals. It can provide the opportunity to arrive at finer and deeper generalizations that are grounded in real language rather than conjecture.

Grenoble and Whitecloud (2014) address directly what they learned about the different perspectives that Western scientists and community speakers in Greenland brought to what is science, what counts as data, and what analyses are appropriate. They were particularly interested in reconstructing plant knowledge in Greenland. As the authors discuss, the Western-trained scientists began with wanting to learn and understand local knowledge systems, beliefs and ideologies. But they learned that they had to take care not to impose their own conceptions of scientific inquiry. They conclude "that the differences in ideologies and beliefs are not insurmountable but rather can provide valuable points of entry into new ways of thinking and seeing the world, and new ways of packaging knowledge" (p. 353). It is not the shared view that makes a successful partnership, but the willingness to enter into a world where views are not necessarily shared.

As Dobrin and Berson (2011: 207) note, "respecting the interests of speakers [...] demands a willingness not only to build relationships across difference, but to approach those relationships analytically." Perhaps this interest in thinking analytically is part of what must be shared between participants in the research, in addition to the philosophical understanding of people, communities, and society noted above. Thinking analytically does not mean agreeing on conclusions — different participants may propose very different analyses based on the same evidence — but perhaps it is that ability to analyze and find where the source of the different conclusions lies that leads to some kind of resolution. See, for instance, Dobrin and Schwartz (2016) and Kroskrity (2009) and the references therein for discussion of cases where the perspectives and ideologies of different participants were very different, and the kinds of challenges that this introduced.

3.7 Summary

As the very existence of this book demonstrates, community-based research has become a valued model in linguistic research in recent years, and this type of model is increasingly commonly referenced in language documentation and revitalization work. I have examined some of the underpinning of community-based research, reminding us that there is not one simple way of defining such research — much depends on the time, the people and their experience together, their history, and the place. A rigidly defined model of community-based research could easily be divisive; what is important is to find something that works, is beneficial to those involved, and that makes a positive difference. There is no single way of defining what it means for something to work, to be beneficial, to make a difference. The understanding of these will evolve over time such that what seemed to be beneficial and making a difference at one point might not at a later point; organizational models will change as relationships develop. Penfield et al. (2008: 199), in developing a working model for community partnerships in linguistics, point out that "best practices for this type of work [...] will always depend on how our recommendations play out in any context. We do not claim to be providing a fool-proof blueprint as to how such projects are conceived and actually implemented."

4 Some additional challenges

I have discussed some of the challenges in defining community-based research, and I address some additional types of challenges in this section. Section 4.1 briefly lists some of the kinds of practical challenges and section 4.2 addresses deeper-rooted challenges, particularly involving the building of partnerships.

4.1 Some practical challenges

I start by introducing some of the practical challenges that arise in community-based research. Funding is frequently an issue, as community-based research (like much other research) often relies on grants and other short-term funding. Finding time can be difficult — both academic and community researchers are often very busy, with other commitments that make it difficult for them to give the time to the project that they would like and to find common times at which they can work together. The time required to build relationships often cannot be factored into a grant proposal, as grants tend to be result-oriented, presenting another challenge to this type of research.

The technology of current language documentation, while simpler than it once was, can still be a barrier, even to the technologically sophisticated. This can lead to disagreement about appropriate software, for instance. Dobrin and Schwartz (2016) discuss an example where a decision was made to use Microsoft Word for a dictionary rather than FLEx. While the latter is generally considered to be best practice in documentation today, it was not appropriate at the time in the community. In documentation, expectations of community and academic researchers may differ as to what is important in annotating a documentary corpus, with different degrees of depth expected. On the one hand, community members may simply be uninterested in the technology as well; see Vallejos (2014: 56) for discussion. In situations where there is an interest, Dobrin and Schwartz (2016: 270) discuss cases where linguistic best practices are not met, suggesting that such decisions represent a type of 'linguistic social work', and conclude of such cases that "a conscious investment in "linguistic social work" contributed to the development of positive social relations from the perspective of our community interlocutors, and these in turn led to follow-on opportunities that could not have been foreseen, let alone negotiated, at the initiation of the research." While such issues often resolve themselves in the positive way that Dobrin and Schwartz note, they present additional challenges in community-based research.

Another type of challenge involves the development of pedagogical materials. Academic and community linguists working on revitalization often do not have background in culturally-appropriate language teaching and learning, and this knowledge often must be developed from the ground up. This too can present a serious challenge for sustainability of a project.

Pérez-Báez (this volume) addresses a number of other challenges to community-based research, focusing on the conditions needed for such research to be successful, including external conditions such as government regulations. See also Franchetto and Rice (2014) and many other sources for additional discussion of these kinds of challenges.

4.2 Deeper-rooted challenges

Beyond these practical challenges are deeper-rooted ones. These are perhaps most easily seen when considering the principles that are given for successful partners introduced in sections 2 and 3.6. Recall that these include having mutual trust and mutual respect, agreeing about goals and strategies, sharing power, communicating clearly and listening carefully, understanding and empathizing with one another's circumstances, sharing a worldview, and remaining flexible, among others. I have discussed many of these and in this section I briefly return to building trust, sharing power, and agreeing about goals and strategies, topics discussed in almost every work on community-based research.

It is easy to say that it is important to build trust, agree about goals, and share power, but doing this is not necessarily straightforward or easy. As noted earlier, there is simply no single recipe for success: what works in one place may not work in another, what works at one time may not work at another and what works with one group may not work with another. Stenzel (2014: 290) makes this point clear in writing about her experience with community-based research. Referring to Dobrin (2005), Stenzel writes that "We should always keep in mind that ideals and guidelines appropriate and possible in one setting may be at odds with conditions and cultural values in another." We learn from all that we undertake, but the lessons are broad and the details must fit the place, time, participants, and history.

Considering building of trust, Leonard and Haynes (2010: 288–289) point out that "We do not pretend that true collaboration is an easy model to implement. The continuous negotiations inherent to collaborating with others can be both time-consuming and emotionally demanding." This is reinforced by all who write on the topic of community-based research.[7]

Stenzel (2014: 302–303) comments on the different perspectives that participants bring to collaborative research in conjunction with relationships:

> When it comes to participatory research, we have to recognize that no matter how positive our relations are and how much we envision and work toward a project in partnership with the community, the 'project' and the ideals in the researcher's mind and the 'project' in the minds of our community partners are most likely (or perhaps most *certainly*) quite different things, as indeed are some of the goals each of the stakeholders hopes to accomplish [...] The point I want to make is that participatory projects are, by their very nature, *multiple* projects in which we work toward negotiating shared goals and hope to leave everybody reasonably satisfied.

Stenzel goes on to say

> [...] though we may try our best to identify and respond to differences, there will inevitably be aspects of the endeavor that remain unknown and unknowable to the parties involved and that these may lead to points of frustration and dissatisfaction that are hard to put one's fingers on [...] there were moments in which I felt quite insecure as to what extent my partners and I were 'on the same page' regarding the projects and its ideals. We worked through those moments, listened to each other, laughed, regrouped — shifting directions when necessary — and found our way back to common ground, but grains of uncertainty nevertheless remain.

This sense of multiple projects and insecurities is likely part of working collaboratively. Relationships bring complexities with them, and in intercultural relationships, these are compounded. As discussed in section 3.6, the ability to analyze what is going on, and discuss it, is of value; see, for instance, Dobrin and Schwartz (2016) and the many references therein for numerous examples.

---

[7] Many also comment that community-based research may be very fragile, affected by other things going on in the lives of the people involved.

Overcoming these challenges involves dialogue, with patience and persistence, and a belief on the part of the participants that, at the core, there is something worthwhile to accomplish in the project that is best achieved through collaboration. At the same time, there is a time for action beyond dialogue, and it can be a balancing act to determine what the priority at a particular point in time is.

5 Conclusions

Community-based research originated outside of linguistics, and many people who have engaged in community-based research in linguistics first knew it as a model articulated by social movements. Dobrin and Berson (2011: 203) write that this is not "the first time that linguists have made overtures toward non-canonical research relations as a mode of scientific possibility and social responsibility." But, they go on to say,

> [...] the thematicization of collaboration that we find emerging as a central methodological issue in documentary research today knows no precedent in the discipline. Language documentation is now conceived by many in the field to be an activity that not only can but *should* be equally responsive to both the technical questions posed by linguists and the more immediate practical interests of speakers. Issues of rights and power are no longer mere afterthoughts, or even cause for hand-wringing. They are taken to be fundamental matters for negotiation between researchers and speakers [...]

What are the lessons learned from community-based research as it has been carried out in recent years in linguistics? The discussion in section 2 provides a basic framework for community-based work, as articulated by the Centre for Community-Based Research Canada, who draw on various sources and experiences. They define community-based research as community-situated, collaborative, and action-oriented. Perhaps the two most important lessons that have been learned since discussion of community-based research began in linguistics are as follows.

First, this model narrowly defined is not appropriate everywhere; it is not appropriate everywhere even with the broader definition that I have suggested. It is unfortunate that there are people who have felt that they were not doing what was expected of them by the discipline because a narrowly defined model of community-based research was inappropriate under the circumstances. In an attempt to address power imbalances, one must ask if they are truly addressed if the academic insists that there is a single defined model that must be used. Such an insistence will likely often lead to failure, and reinforces rather than alleviates power imbalances.

The second point reinforces the first: there is not a single way of going about community-based research — the research done under the community-based rubric is rich and varied, with different interpretations of the basic characterization outlined in sections 2 and 3. It changes and evolves over time and space. As is noted in the literature, what is at the heart of it is not a specific method, but rather a philosophy. Ferreira and Gendron (2011: 154), for instance, say of community-based participatory research that it "is an orientation to research, and not a methodology." Leonard and Haynes (2010: 289–290) write:

> In practice, 'collaboration' is multifaceted and fluctuates based on the field of research, the people involved, and their particular communities of practice. Collaboration is a philosophy and approach rather than a set of guidelines about research roles and outcomes. We recognize that the researcher's community of practice may make the process of collaboration difficult, given the practical restrictions of academic research [...] We call for a shift in the way research is approached so that collaborative consultation is itself a best practice [...]

Characterizations such as those discussed in sections 2 and 3 thus provide an overview of what might be meant by community-based research, but they should not be used to straight-jacket it — it is not a prescribed method in and of itself. I reiterate that what it means to be of practical relevance, equitably share the agenda, and generate positive action for the community cannot be restricted to those things that the academic thinks count. The ethics guidelines for the American Anthropological Association (2009) reinforce this perspective, stating as an ethical obligation the responsibility "to consult actively with the affected individuals or group(s), with the goal of establishing a working relationship that can be beneficial to all parties involved" and those of the Linguistic Society of America (2009) also reinforce it, noting that "Ideal frameworks for interaction with outside researchers vary depending on a community's particular culture and history."

What then is community-based research in linguistics? It is perhaps easier to start off with what it is not. It is not a necessary embrace of the technological preferences of documentary linguistics. It is not a mandate to develop materials for learning the language. It is not designed simply to "do some good." It does not require that all members of the team have identical or even equal responsibilities. It does not demand that there is no perceived leader. It is rather working together in ways that are appropriate in place and time, taking into account the different needs to be met and valuing the different kinds of contributions, as Leonard and Haynes (2010) point to in the quote above.

What have we learned beyond community-based research being an orientation or philosophy? From the perspective of the academic linguist, we have learned that community-based models help deepen our knowledge of language, and that collaboration with communities can bring about new kinds of research questions, as collaboration with other academics does. Community-based work is helping to transform the discipline, bringing new types of students into the academy, introducing new lines of inquiry, re-examining methodologies and what they can tell us, introducing a more overt focus on ethics, and valuing different kinds of knowledge. We have also learned that community-based research involves an investment of time and effort on the part of all involved, amidst competing demands. It can be disrupted by various forces, and the balances can be difficult to maintain. Overall, though, those academic linguists who have participated in community-based research tend to speak positively of their experiences, even in light of such challenges, finding such research personally and intellectually rewarding.

I cannot speak directly to the perspective of the community researcher. My sense from people whom I have worked with and from authors who have written from this perspective is that there are many benefits, as discussed in several of the articles in this volume. However, it is important to recall Stenzel's words — it may be difficult to know whether partners are on the same page with respect to the project and its ideals. This is likely an expected aspect of collaboration — tensions between partners arise in any kind of relationship, and choosing to remain in a relationship is perhaps some indication that something of value is present. That both the community and the academic researchers that Stenzel mentions chose to work through those moments suggests that that the research was of value for them.

We have also learned that there is much to learn about undertaking community-based research. Macaulay (2004/2012), in a reflection on her early fieldwork experiences, speaks to the need for training in the personal and psychological aspects of fieldwork, and the need to find ways to help prepare students for "real" fieldwork, through their fieldwork classes and through the development of literature on this. There are some programs that offer courses in inter-cultural collaborative fieldwork (for instance, CoLang), but by and large, this model is not addressed in linguistics courses. As Dobrin and Berson (2011: 209) point out, models are found in many other disciplines, and linguists could learn from them: "But by looking at the trajectories and outcomes of other intercultural collaborations meant to further the ideals of self-determination, conservation, and the protection of property rights, documentary linguists may be able to think in fresh ways about the challenge presented by the well-known inadequacy of good intentions to produce good outcomes." We have our experiences as academic and community researchers to draw on, but also decades of research in areas such as education, public health, and anthropology that are of value for us to study and teach as linguistics moves forward with community-based research as one valued model.

In the title of a recent article, Dobrin and Schwartz (2016: 270) pose a question: "collaboration or participant observation?" While they note that they are trying to "open up the possibilities for field linguists who, for whatever reason, may not be in a position to collaborate on this model, but who are still concerned about their social responsibilities to their host communities and the individuals who become their consultants, teachers, friends, and even kin," at the same time the title makes one question if collaboration and the ethnographic method of participant observation represent an either/or situation. Dobrin and Schwartz (2016: 270) speak to the value of participant observation

> [...] as a means for discovering what constitutes positive relations according to members of a host community, and hence gives fieldworkers a way to determine what *practices* will actually serve *best* in a given research situation, whether this ultimately leads them to pursue formal collaboration, engage in personal forms of reciprocity, conclude that a shared understanding of research goals is not really achievable, or something else as not yet unimaginable.

A good team will use participant observation, consciously or not, in order to help determine the most workable type of model, however it is that they in the end choose to work. Dobrin and Schwartz (2016: 270) write that "the theme of 'collaborative methods' is so prominent in the current literature on the ethics of linguistic field research that it has come to seem synonymous with ethical research itself," further noting that through participant observation "linguists can learn how to engage in those ways that are most meaningful to a community, in its own terms" (271). If the notion of collaboration is not regarded as monolithic, but is viewed as trying to best meet the range of responsibilities that are appropriate for the time and place, we need not ask "or" of collaboration and participant observation.

To do community-based work, it takes the R's commonly discussed in Canadian Indigenous communities, respect, relevance, responsibility, and reciprocity on the part of the participants. Successful partnerships also take some P's, some of which I mentioned earlier — patience, perseverance, persistence, and passion. More broadly, it takes acknowledging that there are different ways of understanding what it means to be community-situated, collaborative, and action-oriented. Community-based research, even considering the extended interpretation that I have given it, is likely not an appropriate approach for all. But, despite the challenges, or perhaps because of the challenges, collaborative research is, for the right people at the right time and place, stimulating as well as challenging, providing insight into language, its role, and its use that would be difficult to gain in other ways.

References

American Anthropological Association. 2009. Code of ethics of the American Anthropological Association. http://s3.amazonaws.com/rdcms-aaa/files/production/public/FileDownloads/pdfs/issues/policy-advocacy/upload/AAA-Ethics-Code-2009.pdf (accessed 20 May 2017).

Bowern, Claire and Natasha Warner. 2015. 'Lone wolves' and collaboration: A reply to Crippen & Robinson (2013). *Language Documentation and Conservation* 9. 59–85.

Centre for Community Based Research. nd. What is community-based research? http://www.communitybasedresearch.ca/Page/View/CBR_definition (accessed 20 May 2017).

Community-Based Research Canada. nd. What is community-based research? http://communityresearchcanada.ca/cbr (accessed 20 May 2017).

Community-Based Research Canada. Resources. http://communityresearchcanada.ca/resources (accessed 20 May 2017).

Crippen, James A. and Laura C. Robinson. 2013. In defense of the Lone wolf: Collaboration in language documentation. *Language Documentation and Conservation* 7. 123–135.

Czaykowska-Higgins, Ewa. 2009. Research models, community-engagement, and linguistic fieldwork: Reflections on working within Canadian Indigenous communities. *Language Documentation and Conservation* 3. 15–50.

Dauenhauer, Nora M., and Richard Dauenhauer. 1998. Technical, emotional, and ideological issues in reversing language shift: Examples from Southeast Alaska. In Lenore Grenoble and Lindsay Whaley (eds.), *Endangered languages: Current issues and future prospects*. Cambridge: Cambridge University Press. 57–99.

Dobrin, Lise M. 2005. When our values conflict with theirs: linguists and community empowerment in Melanesia. In Peter K. Austin (ed.) *Language Documentation and Description* Vol. 3, 42–52. London: SOAS.

Dobrin, Lise. 2008. From linguistic elicitation to eliciting the linguist: lessons in community empowerment. *Language* 84 (4). 300–324.

Dobrin, Lise and Josh Berson. 2011. Speakers and language documentation. In Peter K. Austin and Julia Sallabank (eds.), *The Cambridge Handbook of Endangered Languages*. Cambridge: Cambridge University Press. 187–211.

Dobrin, Lise and Saul Schwartz. 2016. Collaboration or participant observation? Rethinking models of 'linguistic social work.' *Language Documentation and Conservation* 10. 253–277.

Dolan-Reilly, Georgianna. 2013. The definition of social justice. Social Justice Solutions. http://www.socialjusticesolutions.org/2013/01/15/the-definition-of-social-justice/.

Dwyer, Arienne M. 2006. Ethics and practicalities of cooperative fieldwork and analysis. In Jost Gippert, Nikolaus P. Himmelmann and Ulrike Mosel (eds.), *Essentials of Language Documentation* (Trends in Linguistics: Studies and Monographs 178), 31–66. Berlin: Mouton de Gruyter.

Dwyer, Arienne M. 2010. Models of successful collaboration. In Lenore A. Grenoble and N. Louanna Furbee (eds.), *Language Documentation: Practice and Values*, 193–212. Amsterdam & Philadelphia: John Benjamins Publishing Co.

Essegbey, James, Brent Henderson, and Fiona McLaughlin. 2015. *Language Documentation and Endangerment in Africa*. Amsterdam & Philadelphia: John Benjamins Publishing Company.

Ferreira, Maria Pontes and Fidji Gendron. 2011. Community-based participatory research with traditional and indigenous communities of the Americas: Historical context and future directions. *The International Journal of Critical Pedagogy* 3 (3). 153–168.

Franchetto, Bruna and Keren Rice. 2014. Language documentation in the Americas. *Language Documentation and Conservation* 8. 251–261.

Gerdts, Donna. 2010. Beyond expertise: The role of the linguist in language revitalization programs. In Lenore A. Grenoble and N. Louanna Furbee. *Language documentation. Practice and Values*. Amsterdam: John Benjamins Publishing Company.

Good, Jeff. 2012. 'Community' collaborations in Africa: Experiences from Northwest Cameroon. In Stuart McGill and Peter K. Austin (eds.), *Language Documentation and Description* 11, 28–58. London: SOAS.

Grenoble, Lenore A. and Simone S. Whitecloud. 2014. Conflicting goals, ideologies and beliefs in the field. In Peter K. Austin and Julia Sallabank (eds.), *Beliefs and ideologies in language endangerment, documentation, and revitalisation. Proceedings of the British Academy* 199, 339–356. Oxford: Oxford University Press.

Holton, Gary. 2009. Relatively ethical: A comparison of linguistic research paradigms in Alaska and Indonesia. *Language Documentation and Conservation* 3 (2). 161–175.

Israel B.A., Eng E., Schulz A.J., & Parker E.A. (2005). *Methods in community-based participatory research for health*. San Francisco: Jossey-Bass Publishers.

Kroskrity, Paul. 2009. Language renewal as sites of language ideological struggle. The need for 'ideological clarification'. In Jon Reyhner and Louise Lockwood (eds.), *Indigenous Language Revitalization: Encouragement, Guidance, and Lessons Learned*, 71–83. Flagstaff, Arizona: Northern Arizona University.

Leonard, Wesley Y. and Erin Haynes. 2010. Making 'collaboration' collaborative. An examination of perspectives that frame field research. *Language Documentation and Conservation*. 4. 268–293.

Linguistic Society of America. 2009. Ethics statement. http://www.linguisticsociety.org/sites/default/files/Ethics_Statement.pdf (accessed 20 May 2017).

Linn, Mary S. 2016. Problems in defining community and language ownership in CBLR. Talk presented at the Symposium on Perspectives on language and linguistics: Community-based research (CBR). Linguistic Society of America, Washington D.C., 10 January 2016.

Macaulay, Monica. 2012. Training linguistics students for the realities of fieldwork. In Nicholas Thieberger (ed.). *The Oxford handbook of linguistic fieldwork*, 457–472 Oxford: Oxford University Press. (Originally published in Anthropological Linguistics, summer 2004, volume 46 issue 2: 194–209).

Minkler, Meredith and Nina Wallerstein. 2011. *Community based Participatory Research for Health: From Process to Outcomes*. San Francisco: Jossye-Bass.

Mithun, Marianne. 2001. Who shapes the record: the speaker and the linguist. In P. Newman and M. Ratliff. *Linguistic Fieldwork*, 34–54. Cambridge: Cambridge University Press.

Novak, Michael. 2000. Defining social justice. *First Things*. December 2000.

Office of Community-Based Research. University of Victoria. What is CBR? http://communityresearchcanada.ca/res/download.php?id=3380 (accessed 20 May 2017).

Office of Community-Based Research, University of Victoria. CBR & Partnerships. http://communityresearchcanada.ca/res/download.php?id=3382 (accessed 20 May 2017).

Penfield, Susan D., Angelina Serratos, Benjamin V. Tucker, Amelia Flores, Gilford Harper, Johnny Hill Jr., and Nora Vasquez. 2008. *International Journal of the Sociology of Language* 191. 187–202.

Pérez-Báez, Gabriela, Chris Rogers, and Jorge Emilio Rosés Labrada. 2016. *Language documentation and revitalization in Latin American contexts.* Berlin: de GruyterMouton.

Polfus, Jean L., Micheline Manseau, Deborah Simmons, Michael Neyelle, Walter Bayha, Frederick Andrew, Leon Andrew, Cornelya F. C. Klütsch, Keren Rice, and Paul Wilson. 2016. łeghágots'enetę (learning together): The importance of indigenous perspectives in the identification of biological variation. *Ecology and Society* 21 (2). 18. http:dx.doi.org/10.5751/ES-08284-210218 (accessed 21 May 2017).

Polfus, Jean, Deborah Simmons, Michael Neyelle, Walter Bayha, Frederick Andrew, Leon Andrew, Bethann Merkle, Keren Rice, and Micheline Manseau. 2017. Creative convergence: exploring biocultural diversity through art. *Ecology and Society.* https://www.ecologyandsociety.org/vol22/iss2/art4/; https://doi.org/10.5751/ES-08711-220204

Rice, Keren. 2009. Must there be two solitudes? Language activists and linguists working together. In John Reyhner and Louise Lockard (eds.), *Stabilizing Indigenous Languages: Encouragement, Guidance, and Lessons Learned*, 37–59. Flagstaff, Arizona: Northern Arizona University.

Rice, Keren. 2010. The linguist's responsibilities to the community of speakers: Community-based research. In Lenore A. Grenoble and N. Louanna Furbee (eds.), *Language documentation: Practice and values*, 25–36. Amsterdam: John Benjamins.

Rice, Keren. 2011. Documentary linguistics and community relations. *Language Documentation and Conservation* 5. 187–207.

Schensul, Stephen L., Jean J. Schenshul, Merrill Singer, Margaret Weeks, and Marie Brault. 2015. Participatory methods and community-based collaborations. H. Russell Bernard and Clarence C. Gravlee (eds.), *Handbook of methods in cultural anthropology*, 185–212. London: Rowman and Littlefield.

Stenzel, Kristine. 2014. The pleasures and pitfalls of a 'participatory' documentation project: An experience in Northwestern Amazonia. *Language Documentation and Conservation* 8. 287–306.

Vallejos, Rosa. 2014. Integrating language documentation, language preservation, and linguistic research. *Language Documentation and Conservation* 8. 38–65.

Wilkins, David. 2002. Linguistic research under aboriginal control: A personal account of fieldwork in central Australia. *Australian Journal of Linguistics*, 12 (1). 171–200.

Yamada, Raquel-Maria. 2007. Collaborative linguistic fieldwork. Practical application of the empowerment model. *Language Documentation and Conservation* 1 (2). 257–282.

Elena Benedicto
When Participatory Action Research (PAR) and (Western) Academic Institutional Policies do not align

Abstract: After the seminal work by Hale et al (1992), the linguistic profession began to question how to best approach work on endangered languages and how to interact with the respective language communities. The range of approaches identified as Participatory (Action) Research (PAR) or community-based research (CBR) began to question traditional approaches in linguistic work. This paper critically addresses the misalignments (i.e., contradictory positioning) that arise out of diverging principles and attitudes between academia and PAR approaches to research involving endangered and minority language communities. When these misalignments affect well-established power structures, the potential for conflict arises. Thus, we can use the conflict associated with these misalignments to uncover the existing power structures and imbalances, and reveal an underlying linguistic ideology prevalent in academia.

In this chapter, these misalignments are analyzed within two major areas: those that arise from within the structure of academic institutions themselves, and those that arise as a result of policies and requirements established by external funding agencies associated with academia. The ultimate goal of the paper is to make visible the existing linguistic ideologies and power structures so that we as a profession can better assess our practices in a way that recognizes and is consistent with the true partnership we engage in when doing linguistic work with a language community different than our own.

Keywords: academic power structures, linguistic ideologies, Participatory Action Research

1 Introduction

In recent times, since the publication of Hale et al. (1992), attention began to be devoted to endangered languages, especially to documenting them. After that initial push, new attention was devoted to "how" to pay attention to endangered

---

Elena Benedicto, Indigenous and Endangered Languages Lab, IELLab, Purdue University, 500 Oval Drive, West Lafayette, IN 47905, ebenedi@purdue.edu

https://doi.org/10.1515/9783110527018-003

languages and, in particular, how to relate to the communities that speak or spoke those languages. Though there is no particular consensus, a set of approaches arose that put emphasis on a more meaningful, more egalitarian relationship with the language community, among them, those that respond to some variation of Participatory (Action) Research,[1] or community-based research.

The principles of these participatory methodologies over-impose a certain type of requirements on the initiation, definition, methods, procedures and output of any research process that involves a language community and an external researcher or research team.[2] In particular, it recognizes the intrinsic right of the language community to have an active and primary role in all the stages of research. First, in the initiation stage of the research process: the community not only always has the right, of course, to initiate the type of research that it wants and needs for its own purposes and needs,[3] it also has the right to agree or not to agree to a research project initiated by an external researcher. For example, a given community may not be interested, for whatever reason, in an academic documentation process; if so, then, any external initiative should end at that point.[4]

---

[1] Participatory Action Research (PAR) was initiated, to my knowledge, within work in the social sciences (see for example the work in Christie et al, 2000). This kind of work was taken as a model to adapt to linguistic work in Benedicto et al (2007), where 3 *basic principles* are defined: (i) the self-empowerment of the language community, (ii) the existence of an egalitarian relationship between external and internal researchers, and (iii) recognition of the existence of knowledge systems of equal (and complementary) value. Viñas-de-Puig et al (2012) expands on these notions and provides further background and references on PAR in other areas, such as the medical sciences. The work by Czaykowska-Higgins (2009) and Rice (2011 and previous) on community-based research share a lot of definitional points with PAR. See the introduction to this volume as well as Rice's contribution for some discussion of concepts and definitional issues. I am adopting PAR here as part of a traditional practice in Latin America (see Rice, this volume, fn 2 citing Ferreira and Gendron, 2011, and recognizing Paulo Freire's intellectual tradition; see also Junker this volume).

[2] It is well recognized that these processes are best understood as a collaborative partnership where both parties mutually agree on the conditions underlying the relationship. As pointed out by an anonymous reviewer, an academic always has the right to accept or not accept the conditions of a collaboration and, as a result, decide not to participate in such a collaborative research.

[3] An anonymous reviewer expresses disagreement with this and states, in particular, that "communities do not have the right to initiate the type of research academics are interested in." In the opinion of this author, the right to initiate linguistic research is an inalienable linguistic right of any language community. In fact, the author has witnessed that process time and again in the context of Latin America, where a language community has established the need for such research to take place and has either conducted it through its own human resources or reached out to outside linguists when it has determined that would yield a better set up.

[4] Though this may seem obvious and straightforward, it is not uncommon to hear external academic researchers defend the, under their view, objective need to document a particular language variety for the good of humanity's knowledge. That is, putting academic knowledge above the will of the language community.

On a second stage, the community may define the goals and design of the research itself; that is, it has the right to set the goals of the research and to accept or not any goals brought in by external researchers. For example, the community may set the goal of obtaining linguistic material for an integrated summer workshop and not so much for the writing of an academic grammar. Third, the processes and internal methodologies are also to be either established or accepted/modified by the community; the community may, for example, require that a group of its youth be trained in the linguistic tasks so that they eventually may take up any documentation or linguistic tasks; and/or it may not agree, for instance, to a more traditional methodology where an external academic researcher works with a participant/informant. Finally and crucially, the language community has the right to decide on the output of the research project: which part of the language data obtained in a research project may or may not be made public (e.g., which part of the data may be confidential or private); how it can be published (the format: voice-based or written-based); who has the copyright and rights to that material (a university, an editorial house, the community itself); and the shape of the end product (e.g., what type of information should be included in a dictionary, in what order, etc...). In the end, what this highlights is that this is a process involving two parties, each with their own interests, priorities and goals, and sometimes intersecting. As with any partnership, both parties have the right to agree or not agree to a research program and ultimately an acceptable agreement must be reached by all participants for the research to proceed. This paper underlines the existence of the non-academic partner's conditions and rights on research and on the tensions that may ensue.

Whereas these conditions may mostly run on a parallel line with western-style academic ways and requirements (that is, they may not necessarily interact or enter into conflict), in some cases, academic ways and PAR ways misalign. In this paper, I address some of those misalignments and the consequences for the academic world, the language community and the academic individual (whether a member of the speaking community or not—see Mutaka's chapter in this volume for some of these issues).

In Benedicto et al (2007), PAR is identified as a methodology addressing issues of Power and Linguistic Rights; here I develop the hypothesis that it is precisely when power structures are "affected" (that is, when academic primacy is contested) that misalignment (and potentially conflict) will arise. Throughout I outline what could be identified as a system of ideologies that underlies the academic world in the hopes of initiating a conversation about how we as academics define academic work and how academia interacts in a respectful, collaborative and fruitful way with the communities we interact with and in. The data for this paper come from personal reports from colleagues, both academic and community members, and from myself, and they involve both private and public academic institutions.

I will divide potential misalignments in two groups: those that arise within an academic institution, and those that arise as a result of policies and requirements imposed by (academic) funding agencies. Though those two are to a large extent intricately related and intersect, some of the misalignments may be traced back to one or another system.[5] I will address the former in Section 2, and the latter in Section 3.

2 Misalignments arising within academic institutions

As mentioned before, by "misalignment" I refer to the situation that arises when the principles of PAR/CBR (as defined in the introduction above, in the introductory chapter of this volume, or in Rice's contribution to this volume) require a set of conditions that turn out to be at odds with current practices in academia in general and with (mostly unspoken) hierarchical systems of ideologies in place in western academia, in particular. By western academia I refer to the currently prevailing system in the US and in countries that align with the US academic system (for instance, in the way publications are used to rank universities, journals, and the perceived value of certain kinds of research). Whenever crucial differences arise or become relevant, I will make the necessary qualifications. When that clash of principles happens, we as academics need to be able to identify it, point it out to academic authorities and negotiate a more aware re-positioning of the institution according to its ethical and moral standings, as part of the necessary negotiations that lead to an agreed upon project.[6]

Under misalignments arising within the environment of academic institutions, I address the following topics, and the consequences that derive from them: the type of "product" that is considered academic or of academic quality (2.1); notions of "author" and authorship (2.2); languages of academic import

---

[5] The author recognizes other misalignments may arise due to cultural differences and personalities, etc. but the focus here is the misalignment that results from institutional policies regarding such things as outputs and practices as articulated by funding agencies (see Rice and Czaykowska-Higgins this volume).
[6] As an example of an attempt in this direction, see the Linguistic Society of America's *Resolution Recognizing the Scholarly Merit of Language Documentation* as an example of how professional organizations are working to change this system: https://www.linguisticsociety.org/resource/resolution-recognizing-scholarly-merit-language-documentation.

(2.3); notions of meaningful consent by the community (2.4); and meaningful "right of return" (2.5). I conclude (2.6) by summarizing and articulating the points treated in 2.1–2.5 into a first approach to the characterization of the system of academic ideologies.

2.1 The academic *product*

In this subsection, I address notions and conceptualizations of what can be considered an "academic product" and how it fits with the principles of PAR/CBR. At this point, it is useful to remember that PAR/CBR recognizes the right of the language community to determine the goals of the research, in particular what kind of product it wants to obtain, which tends to be one that is of relevance for and benefits the language community directly. By academic product I mean that which is recognized by academic institutions as valuable and useful for academic purposes, for example: the one that is used for evaluating promotion and tenure, for the calculation of raises, to establish and define long- mid- and short-term academic planning, to calculate what can be considered "doctoral quality work," etc.

One way of beginning to think about what properties define an academic product, in the eyes of academia, is who the public is for a particular research output, who it is addressed to, and who reads a particular "product." Let us consider, for the sake of illustrating this point, the issue of a bilingual vs a monolingual dictionary. A monolingual dictionary is that which includes definitions in the language itself, grammatical information (written in the object language) that can be used in the language-specific classroom and usage information that is culturally relevant and geared towards the needs of the language community itself. A bilingual dictionary tends to be that which crucially includes a translation to the language of the dominant group, or the language of the external researcher (which may not necessarily be that of wider use in the local environment);[7] it may also include grammatical information which is of linguistic interest (that is, of interest to the professional linguist, but not necessarily to a non-linguist community member, and usually written in the language of the translation); it may even be one where the ordering criterion or the form used as a lemma may not be culturally relevant or culturally friendly, or one where the writing system may

---

[7] For instance, that would be the case of bilingual dictionaries of indigenous languages of Latin America with translations into English, but not to Spanish the local dominant language or the language of wider communication in the area. This would mostly arise in cases when the external researcher or the associated academic institution is of Anglo-Saxon origin.

not necessarily be community-friendly or decided by consensus with community users.

In the type of experiences gathered by this author[8] a bilingual dictionary in the terms specified above tends to be considered an academic product, whereas a monolingual dictionary also as defined above tends to be considered a "community product," that is, a product whose audience is not the "relevant" one and thus not properly an academic product (though it may be considered within the category of "engagement" or "service").[9]

Let us examine this a bit further. While an academic product needs to show that the "author" shows a professional level of workmanship, that s/he is competent according to the standards of the profession, this may be evaluated independently of the format of the "product," though maybe not with the same ease. That is, the linguistic workmanship of a monolingual dictionary can be evaluated by a linguistic evaluator who, definitely, needs to have certain non-standard skills (among them, a certain knowledge of the target language or a professional ability to uncover the linguistic workmanship involved). Notice further that the two types of dictionary discussed above have both grammatical information that reveals the workmanship of the writing team, though the language in which that workmanship is manifested is different.[10] Thus, the point is not necessarily that less work or less professional work might be involved in one or the other, but that the respective intended audiences, as defined by academia and by PAR/CBR, are misaligned. If academia considers a monolingual dictionary, in the terms described above, as a non-academic product, it disregards the principles of PAR/CBR and thus enters in conflict with it. As academics aware of this point of conflict, we need to point it out and facilitate a discussion process that, hopefully, will lead to academia understanding the benefits and ethical advantages of a PAR/CBR approach.

---

8 These statements reflect the experience of those that have contributed to this work. Certainly, other experiences may exist. The point being made here is that the attitudes reported in the text do exist within academia (as part of a larger set of attitudes not contemplated here) and that their very existence is evidence of an underlying ideology.

9 For the status of "engagement" or "service" within academia, see Rice in this volume. Crucially, "engagement" or "service" activities (different from the *scholarship of engagement*) are not in the core categories to calculate academic (e.g., tenure, promotion) progress: they are a "plus" but not central (in the words of some colleagues, they are the "cherry on the cake"). An anonymous reviewer points out that the "crux is peer-review;" in fact, I would argue, the crux is who is the "peer" in peer-review: are "peers" members of the academic community only, or are "peers" members of the language community too? Who is "okayed," who is validated to be your peer?

10 There are two intersecting themes here that I will address later: authorship and language of academic communication.

Another property we may consider in determining what constitutes an academic "product" is the venue where it is published. Publication in an academic editorial house properly validates the research output since it is the channel for an overview system of peer review that sets academically recognized criteria of quality. However, internal publication by the language community, involving validation of the research output by the language community, that is, by the group who knows the language better does not qualify as appropriate validation (probably because the knowledge involved in that latter process is not considered to be the "right" kind of knowledge in the eyes of academia, something that I will come back to). The crux of this issue, then, goes back to the issue of peer review and who is considered and "validated" as an appropriate peer with the appropriate "knowledge" and authority to sanction the research.

The reason for a language community to want to publish a given linguistic material by themselves is to maintain control of the contents and the distribution, that is, to maintain ownership of the linguistic material and the final product. The language community may also want to maintain control of who has access to it; this is especially important in the case of privative or culturally sensitive material (so materials may need to be distributed only through their own school system, or through their culturally specific channels, to reach community members and not outsiders). Finally, it may also be important to the community that language material not be sold, since selling of cultural material, "selling the language" or "selling the culture," may have strong connotations of "selling out" to the dominant culture (especially given prior and even current historical and political events). Thus, while academia may be looking for a publishing venue to guarantee the (academic) quality of the product, the community may be trying to maintain control of the ownership and distribution of the materials. This is related to the fourth point of PAR/CBR mentioned in the introduction: the right of the language community to decide on the shape and conditions of the final product. Here then lies another point of misalignment between the guidelines of academia and of PAR/CBR.

Finally, a third consideration about academic "product" is what part of the research process it focuses on. In her contribution to this volume, Czaykowska-Higgins talks about the notion of "intangible outcome": in environments where PAR is practiced, the participatory "process" itself is considered a product, an intangible one that arises out of the endeavor and creates knowledge. The process by which knowledge is generated as part of a participatory practice is a product in itself, is part of how all involved are changed by it (which is one of the points of CBR as pointed out in the introductory chapter of this volume; see also Rice's chapter). URACCAN, the Nicaraguan university of the Caribbean Coast with which I have collaborated for a long time has a specific mention of PAR in its vision and mission and its defining documents, and specifically includes the process as part of one of the expected outcomes of its research projects. The emphasis on a tangible product (a product that is *written*—I will come back to this point later—in a specific format in specific *venues* and in specific *languages*) can probably be traced back to a capitalist system of production, where academia is the factory that produces items that are assigned a "value"; these products can, under such well-established conditions, be easily quantified, which is what the system can understand and process. A focus on *intangible* outcomes is very difficult to quantify for such a system and thus, very difficult to calculate, control and evaluate by that same system. That does not mean that the *process* cannot be evaluated, it only means that our current western academic system is ill-equipped to do so. This is, thus, a third point of misalignment between PAR and academia in what concerns the product: academia needs certain specifications to even be able to "see" the product—PAR is creating products (the *process*) that academia can't even "see."[11]

Wrapping up, thus, we have seen that in what concerns the nature of the *product of research*, misalignments between guiding principles of academia and PAR/CBR arise out of at least: the target audience (academic vs community); the publication mechanism (academic vs community); and acceptable parts of the research endeavor (tangible vs intangible products).

Academia wants to select its own audience (an academic audience), its own output mechanism (an academic publisher), and an "identifiable" (that is, quantifiable, tangible) product. PAR wants the same: select its own audience (the language community), its own output mechanism (self-publishing, with its own *peer* review system) and a community-relevant product (which may include an intangible product, such as the *process* itself). Though the criteria are in fact the same, the actual concrete resulting value or output is not. Up to this point when tensions have occurred out of such misalignments the prevailing value chosen has been that of academia; adopting a PAR/CBR approach means that we need to reevaluate the prioritization mechanisms.

There are two other features relevant for the *product* that need to be factored out but will be treated independently because of their wider reach: the *language* used to present the product (2.3); and the format of the product beyond the traditional publication (2.5).

---

[11] There is a point of hope for change here. As more academics work within CBR and PAR, we are seeing new and different kinds of products being "made visible" within academic settings, as the LSA's *Resolution Recognizing the Scholarly Merit of Language Documentation*, already mentioned, and this volume demonstrate. These are examples of academic scholars and community members working to adjust this misalignment, but there is still work to be done.

2.2 Matters of authorship and knowledge

Since the early times of linguistic work in western (both European and early American) academia, back in the 19TH century and well into the 20TH century, the *author* of a given research project was considered to be the person of highest status in a given academic unit leading that research project. Though in some cases the research was carried out in an individual manner many more times there was a cohort of assistants who tended to be in charge of the mechanical and not so mechanical tasks. These assistants were for the most part ignored as contributors to the work and thus unrecognized as authors.[12] The same unrecognized status was awarded to the members of the language community who provided the language data and the cultural knowledge and interpretive insight necessary to be able to decode and interpret the data appropriately, and without which the work would not be possible.

Though notions of authorship have been changing, and conceptions of multiple and diverse contributions and of team work have increased, especially in the hard sciences, work in linguistics has been slow in recognizing such contributions. To this day, the inclusion of language community collaborators as authors is rare, at most they are relegated to an acknowledgment footnote. Guidelines about authorship (e.g., those found in CITI training) still reveal a somewhat hierarchized notion of who's in and who's out of the team whose contributions will be recognized with authorship.[13]

Even nowadays, in more traditional departments in the liberal arts or humanities, single authorship is more highly valued than multiple authorship,[14] on the misguided assumption that if there are 3 authors, each has done 33% of the total work whereas a single author "clearly" has a 100% of the total work; what this misguided view does not consider is that the "total" amount of work is not the same both in quantitative terms (that is, the total amount of work invested) and, what is more interesting, in qualitative terms, (that is, in the kind and diversity of work contributed to the whole). In other words, team work (especially the teamwork of mixed teams) is not just simply the addition of the individual effort of its

---

12 This was the case, for instance, for the early dictionaries and grammars typical of the 19TH century linguistic work, both of classical languages and of emerging modern languages. The person of higher status tended to be a white male, whereas the assistants tended to be female or younger males.
13 See CITI Program at https://about.citiprogram.org/en/homepage/.
14 This probably has its origins in the tradition of the single authored book as paramount proof of worth for the tenure process, and though universities tend to revise their guidelines to indicate how collaborative work is to be evaluated, what happens behind closed doors in departmental evaluation committees is not in itself evaluated and old ways tend to prevail.

members, but also the synergies that are generated out of the collaboration. That second factor, and the effort and energy that goes into it tends to be ignored in more individualistic notions of *authorship*.

Another aspect that is worth considering here is what is being conceptualized behind the title of author. The author is supposed to be the "owner" of the main idea, the one that comes up with and develops a new idea based on a body of knowledge that precedes it and that needs to be acquired in a particular way. It thus encodes concepts of knowledge, the knowledge that has allowed that idea to be born and to be developed; knowledge that has been generated within the boundaries of a specific system, that of academia. To recognize members of the language community as authors would imply that there is knowledge behind their contribution, a kind of knowledge that, at best (that is, if it is recognized as knowledge at all), is not the kind of knowledge that western academia has generated.

Thus, accepting non-academics as (co-)authors, would imply (a) recognizing that knowledge may lie somewhere else than in academia and (b) that language community members have a kind of knowledge that is of relevance to and, thus, recognizable by academia. This, I contend, would challenge the power structures of academia, that to this day has the power to decide who holds the (relevant) knowledge and who does not (e.g., it grants degrees that "certify" precisely that). By challenging that power (to recognize what is knowledge and what is not, and who holds it or not), we are identifying another locus for misalignment and friction between the principles of academia and those of PAR/CBR: PAR/CBR recognizes that language communities hold knowledge, that that knowledge, while being different than the knowledge generated by academia, is on a par, and is of equal value to the knowledge of academia.[15] In recognizing this, academia would be forced to relinquish its current power to decide what constitutes knowledge and what does not and, more importantly, who holds that knowledge and who does not.[16]

---

15 In private conversations, not to be acknowledged publicly, traditional academics have no problem in expressing this kind of ideas: that they themselves hold the (*real*) knowledge and that, though language community members are very worthy of respect, what they have cannot be deemed knowledge on a par with their own (academic) knowledge. An anonymous reviewer, while recognizing the difference in the type of knowledge, assigns the property of "objective rationalization" to the kind of knowledge academia holds, while the community holds knowledge about "the language and language ecology." This view disregards the kind of systematic and insightful linguistic knowledge that some speakers have about their language; in such cases, the vocabulary and the framework to talk about it may be different but the quality of the knowledge itself is linguistic in nature. Ken Hale (p.c.) referred to these speakers as *natural linguists*.

16 This at the base of another related issue in academia: who is allowed to teach and under which conditions. It has been a problem for universities to work out a system to allow community members to teach language classes: though they are speakers and hold the knowledge of the

2.3 The language of academic work

Another potential locus for misalignment of priorities between academia and PAR/CBR is the choice of language used for transmission of knowledge. The language of academia, that is, the language academia chooses to present, handle, and report on research is of significance to understand what its priorities are. Of course this is an issue that intersects with that of audience that we treated in Section 2.1. English is typically the language of academic choice in western academia; this is so not only in the cases of bilingual dictionaries mentioned above but also in the cases of other academic "products" such as grammars and academic articles, and it is independent of the language that is of generalized use in the environment where the language object-of-study is spoken.[17]

In a US academic environment, a grammar written in English has a higher status than a grammar written in, say, Spanish (for a language in a Latin-American context), and the distance is even greater for a grammar written in an indigenous language. While one could argue that academia needs to be able to understand the content (let's say, to be able to evaluate the linguistic workmanship), we have already argued that such pieces of linguistic work can still be evaluated by individuals with the right skills. Of course, there is the issue of the audience, especially in the case of using an indigenous language as a vehicle of academic writing: the audience in that case is clearly the language community and we have already argued above that products addressed to such audiences are deemed, at an underlying level, irrelevant for academic purposes.

This hierarchization in the choice of language of transmission can be complex and relativized. For instance, more traditional US-based academic departments[18] have been reported to reject peer-reviewed articles written in Spanish, even though Spanish is a language of wide academic audience both inside and outside the US; in those cases, Spanish had been reportedly used to reach out to the wider community where the language described in the paper was immersed (a point to be retaken in Section 2.5).

Whereas it can be argued that cases like these can be reduced to a matter of relevance of audience (as discussed in 2.1, on the basis of a purported irrelevance of a Spanish-speaking audience), I will rather argue that this linguistic hierarchy

---

language and in many cases have developed creative methods for language teaching, they may not hold the kinds of academic degrees that would allow them to be hired by a university system.
17 See footnote 7 for this point.
18 This probably excludes practices in *foreign* language departments or in *world* languages departments (my emphasis on *foreign* and *world*—that is, the domain that "justifies," in the ideology system, the exclusion of English).

reveals a linguistic ideology system that primes English and neglects other (both immigrant and Native American, in the US-context) languages. A further indicator of this linguistic hierarchy can come from the way in which universities and programs are ranked globally (see for example the Academic Ranking of World Universities methodologies, among other notable rankings);[19] these rankings and the structures generated around them may act as silent but pervasive points of pressure for researchers to use English instead of any other language even if, at least in theory, they could use other languages.[20]

The notion of linguistic hierarchy, generated under a linguistic ideology system, may be a relativized one. While English is the highest-ranking language in US-based academic institutions and Spanish is subordinate, in other linguistic environments (e.g., Latin America), Spanish will, as the local dominant language, take that higher-ranking position over other local languages (for instance, indigenous or local languages). However, even in those cases, academic rankings may still prime English over the local dominant language (e.g., in terms of assigning value to publications).[21]

Another setting where this linguistic hierarchy, the priming of English as an academic language, is made obvious is in the conditions for acceptance of abstracts for evaluation in calls for papers. Even conferences specifically devoted to minority, endangered and indigenous languages will require abstracts, and even delivery of papers, to be in English;[22] some will accept English and another major language; some will accept presentation of the papers in the local language but will still require abstracts to be submitted in English. What this means is that an additional burden is imposed on the speakers of such languages to accommodate external academics, as opposed to external academics taking in the burden

---

19 Thanks to a reviewer for this point. Another reviewer points out that, for instance, the Nobel Prize system requires the work to be in English (either originally or in translation) to be considered.
20 In a recent presentation by a renowned African writer in Europe, he recognized that even if at some point in his career he had decided to write his fiction work exclusively in his native language (and have his work translated into English and other languages), he had "decided" to keep using English for his academic work for "survival" purposes. The irony he transmitted was not lost to the audience.
21 This is the case, for instance, in several Latin American academic systems, where a peer-reviewed publication in English is assigned more "points" than a peer-reviewed publication in Spanish.
22 At a recent SSILA (Society for the Study of Indigenous Languages of the Americas) meeting where these issues were being discussed, it was argued that the use of Spanish in presentations dealing with Latin American indigenous languages would be disruptive because it would not allow everybody to understand the presentations. This kind of reasoning clearly primes accommodating English speakers over the linguistic rights of linguists of Spanish-speaking countries: Spanish speakers need to make adjustments, English speakers do not.

of learning and becoming fluent in the minority language;[23] it also underscores the existence of a linguistic ideology that states that, at an underlying level, the minority language is not deemed to be academia-worthy.[24]

Wrapping up this subsection, then, we have seen that the misalignment that we have observed with respect to the choice of language for transmission of knowledge stems from, on the one hand, a linguistic hierarchy originating in academia out of a linguistic ideology system that primes English over other languages and, on the other hand, the right recognized in PAR/CBR approaches to have the output of research in a format that is of relevance to the language community. The primacy of the linguistic hierarchy in academia has an exclusionary effect in the language communities (who cannot access the results of the research), or an exclusionary effect on the outside researcher (if academia does not recognize work in a language other than English), and it perpetuates perceptions (that is, linguistic ideologies) of what an academic language is: which language is equipped, is "better," is "appropriate" for the transmission of knowledge (knowledge, as defined by academia itself). Adopting a PAR/CBR approach means that we take explicit steps to balance out those exclusionary effects.

2.4 (Meaningful) consent by the community: Protection of data

Academic institutions in the US have systems set up to insure that appropriate consent is given by humans providing data and that in that process of consent individuals understand what they are consenting to. These systems were initially set up to deal with individual consent and to deal with mostly biological data. Much of these systems are concerned with protecting the privacy of individuals,

---

[23] A similar argument is being made in the realm of Sign Language, where the lack of a "normalized" use of an SL in academic environments, including conferences, especially by non-Deaf academics is being pointed out.

[24] Another, more general, indicator of the existence of this linguistic ideology (regarding which language qualifies as academia-worthy) is the inability of most US-based students (both graduate and undergraduate), observed in recent years, to read relevant bibliography in a language other than English. What is worse is the attitude that if something is not in English, then that means it is not important or worth trying to find the content of, that is, a language other than English is not, by definition, transmitting academia-worth content ("... but I can't read it!" seems to imply that one is not responsible for finding out its content). This, which reveals an underlying unspoken but very active linguistic ideology, happens despite many programs requiring students to have a sensible number of hours of "another" language in their program of study.

and thus, emphasis is put into *de-identifying* data or *destroying* data, so that the individual's private identifiers disappear.

With time other issues have arisen, among them, the privacy of cultural community data. How can the privacy of communal cultural data be protected, who decides which communal cultural data needs to be protected and how can it be identified? These are all questions that are not answerable by the usual means of *de-identify* and *destroy*, since in principle we want to *preserve* that knowledge (in particular for the community), and language cannot be stripped away from the knowledge that it encodes.

There are many and very complex issues to be treated here (among them, how to define *community*),[25] that I will not be able to address. I will circumscribe myself to two issues: one is, once the community (however it is identified) has decided that some body of linguistic data is restricted or "classified," how does academia deal with it?; and the second one concerns how do we outside researchers ensure that community members fully understand the implications of how confidential data will be managed?

Academia is no stranger to dealing with confidential or classified data. In fact, most research universities in the US participate in research projects that need clearance and whose internal details, from methods to data and final results, are completely opaque to the external world. This opaqueness does not, however, prevent academia from recognizing the existence and the value of such research (for instance, for evaluation of its personnel, the researchers). However, when a language community determines that a given body of work, be it a dictionary or a compendium of plant knowledge or a compilation of oral history, constitutes classified data, that is data that is only to be seen or shared within the community (as classified data of a security project is only to be seen and shared within the security community), then academia does not recognize the existence of that work for its own academic purposes (contrary to what it does with classified research, which is recognized as research within the academic context). For instance, if a community decides that a dictionary is not to be published or distributed by an academic publisher and is not to be distributed outside the realm of the community, the academic system does not consider the existence of such a piece of research work: It does not "count" for the evaluation of its own researchers (as classified research does).[26] Given the history of aggression that

---

[25] See the introduction to this volume for a consideration of the issues around it and how the different papers in this volume raise and address the issue.

[26] This may indeed be changing as universities are beginning to extend the use of the same procedures they already have in place for (academic) evaluation of classified work into the domain of linguistic work.

many communities of endangered languages have suffered in recent past, issues of confidentiality and of data security are not irrelevant.

A potential answer to the first question posed above (once the community gives consent, how can material that is deemed confidential *a posteriori* be re-classified?), involves precisely the kind of approach that PAR/CBR facilitates: a cyclic process of consent where external researchers and the language community re-evaluate data as it is obtained in ways established through the research process may offer the chance to pre-classify or re-classify data according to criteria established by the community counterpart. In a project conducted in Central America about plants in the forest, it was decided that community members would be the ones to do the forest walks and gather information and data with the elders; a first classification of data and information would be performed at that point separating what could be shared with the outside world and what should remain within the community only. This process was repeated in other steps of the process, for instance deciding what could be included in books and materials for younger children and what for youth and for adult audiences. The crucial point here is that it is precisely the PAR/CBR approach of constant communication and collaboration with the language community that allows and facilitates this kind of strategy. It is also my experience that if such a procedure is to be explained and discussed with the university's Institutional Review Board (IRB) officials, the right formula can be found to satisfy both IRB demands and community demands.

Another option that could be brought forth is that there are archives available where confidential or classified bodies of language could be safely kept. These archives have a system of staggered protection[27] that establishes who can have access to data and what kinds of restrictions are imposed on the data. At this point, the discussion links with the second issue I want to address here, that of meaningful information. While it is true that these archives can have systems of data protection, it is also true that they cannot guarantee that level of protection. No system is absolutely secure and anything in an electronic platform can be, with more or less difficulty, accessed. Communities need to be aware of this, and given the history of (cultural and physical) aggression mentioned above, it is imperative to recognize that confidentiality cannot be insured. Ultimately, though, and more importantly, it is a question of sovereignty of a language community to decide what it shares or not. And it is up to academia to decide whether it recognizes that right or not; it is up to academia to decide whether it treats the confidentiality of anybody in the same equal way, whether it is government data or a language com-

---

[27] An example of such an Archive is the Archive of the Indigenous Languages of Latin America, AILLA, in Austin Texas. See http://www.ailla.utexas.org.

munity data, and it is up to academia to decide what status to attach to the result of confidential research, independently of the "owner" of that data.[28]

2.5 (Meaningful) right of return

In this subsection I address the general question of the "right of return," that is, how the data, results and analysis of a given language, obtained through a process of academic research, make their way back to the community where they came from. While this is also a wide-ranging topic, I will here address just a couple of illustrative issues that may shed some light into the linguistic ideologies system in academia that has been emerging out of the previous subsections. In particular, I will talk about how academia manages the relation between language data/analysis and the language community in two sample (prototypically academic) environments: the classroom and the research project. The point of this exploration is to obtain more information about potential (mis)alignments between academia and PAR/CBR and how to bridge them.

The prototypical academic classroom environment where issues related to language community arise is the field methods classroom. Field methods classes have been taught for a long time in an effort to prepare students for the trade of analyzing an unknown or little-known language and, more recently, to prepare students to collect data in a methodologically appropriate way to shed light into a particular theoretical linguistic problem under scrutiny.[29] To achieve this, the class typically works with a speaker of the chosen language, who provides language data in a typical question-answer exchange; the speaker may also meet with the students outside of class to provide further data for their final projects. In some, but not all cases, the field methods class is also used to reflect on the relation between the external linguist and the language community and on the ethical issues that arise out of that relation.

---

[28] In cases of promotion and tenure which involve research projects that contain classified data and/or results, there are mechanisms (such as letters of evaluation by personnel with clearance) that allow for meaningful evaluation of non-accessible data. I have already mentioned these potential alternatives in Section 2.1.

[29] This would correspond to a more qualitative approach to data collection in contrast to more quantitative methods typically used in experimental approaches. Note that this observation is about the *classroom* environment, not the *field* environment itself, and about the particular *techniques* used in the classroom. I fully recognize that fieldwork includes a variety of approaches that need to be articulated in a complex situation. However, the field methods *classroom* tends to be more restricted than the actual fieldwork set up and may often be used as a data gathering methodology class. See also Meyers et al. (this volume).

In terms of "right of return," the issue is what if anything is to be "returned" to the "language community."[30] In fact, there is a first question that needs to be answered: "do we need to return anything?" Though in principle this might seem an obvious question to raise, it may in fact never be posed in the first place and the issue of return may never be addressed. Even in the case that the question is posed, the answer may be "it depends on what." So, in pondering *what* can possibly be returned, there are at least two alternatives to consider. One is possibly the minimal option: to return to the speaker the data, raw and processed, obtained during class and to share the results of the research projects associated with the class in the form of a copy of the papers produced by the students. A second one is to discuss with the speaker under which format would it be useful for his or her local community to have the data.[31] In the first case there have been reports where departments have been reluctant, and have even denied access of the language speaker to research papers associated to a class, on the basis that it violates the privacy of the student that wrote it.[32] Since class papers are not publications and thus not publicly available (unless the author chooses to make them public), there is an issue here. Beyond specific "solutions" to the above situation,[33] there is the more general ethical issue of whether a language speaker has the right to

---

30 As already pointed out, the issue of how to define "community" is a complex one and for the purposes of this subsection about the field methods *classroom*, we can tentatively consider that the "community" is either the collaborating speaker or the language community where that person is embedded (which can be, for instance, a student group from a common original location, or a well-established immigrant community, to give a couple of examples).

31 For instance, in the case of a recent immigrant community, it has been useful to either have traditional stories in the form of children's story books (if there are small children growing up in the community with little support for the home language), or bilingual story books for children whose more dominant language is not the home language, or bilingual dictionaries (constructed out of the data collected) that may be useful to older adults trying to link their language to the local dominant language, just to give a few examples.

32 An anonymous reviewer suggests that this is a Family Educational Rights and Privacy Act (FERPA) issue. However, FERPA, which indeed protects the privacy of students, does not prevent the discussion in class of each other's papers and work. In fact, it is an acceptable practice to critique and discuss each other's papers in class and even pre-mark each other's papers (though the final responsibility for the grade remains with the instructor).

33 Colleagues have reported requiring students in the beginning of the semester to sign a document where they accept to share with the speaker the data they collect and the research papers with the analysis they come up with, as well as to recognize the contribution of the speaker in any future publication that may come out of their work. De-identifying the papers would not be too useful as a strategy for protecting the identity of the student-author (the original concern) since classes tend to be small and the topic of the paper identifies the author.

see what others have said about the language data[34] he or she has provided.[35] A PAR/CBR approach recognizes the linguistic rights of the speakers of the language, including the right to know what is being done with the data the speakers provide. In addition to the first "return" option presented, the second option offered above (to discuss with the speaker which possible formats would be more adequate as "return"), aligns itself more smoothly with a PAR/CBR approach in that language speaker and external researcher discuss, examine and ponder possible alternatives as equals.

The second academic environment to be discussed in relation to the "right of return" is the research project itself. As we mentioned in the introduction, a PAR/CBR approach requires the participation of the language community as an equal partner in all stages of the research project. The final stage was identified as the production of a result. The community will be invested in obtaining a product of relevance to its members. A research publication in a peer-reviewed venue is not usually a format that is of relevance to the language community. A research project, thus, needs to make provisions so that conversations to identify an appropriate "return" format in collaboration with community members are given a space within the planning of the research project, and subsequent arrangements are made to produce such products on a par with the production of academic products (such as papers, conference presentations, etc.).[36] That said, it may well

---

34 An anonymous reviewer insists on the distinction between language (information), language data and language research. Independently of the theoretical merits of such distinctions, language community members still have the right to access it all and, whereas the specific analysis (language research) may be the intellectual contribution of the researcher, the contribution of the language community in it and their ownership of language information and data still needs to be acknowledged.

35 Generally speaking, though some students may think that what they produce is outside of the speaker's interest, speakers participating in these setups tend to want to know what was discovered about their language and thus, out of plain and simple consideration, sharing it is plain good human behavior. On the other hand, some speakers have expressed the feeling that "they come, they take and we never hear back" which may be indicative of a sense of dispossession. If we know that such perceptions may exist, we may be proactive in preventing them. In some cultures, there is always a sense of engaged *quid pro quo*, of reciprocal sharing (I give you, you give me) and sharing the work may be a way of engaging in it. In a darker and, luckily, less frequent note, sharing the final work may expose errors, inconsistencies or value judgements that the student may not want revealed. Though these issues are usually spotted and dealt with earlier on, they may go undetected for a variety of reasons.

36 The works of Czaykowska-Higgins (2009 and this volume, among others) and Rice (2011 and this volume, among others) have extensively reported on how Canadian academic institutions have negotiated these kinds of approaches, including notions of "overhead" that academic institutions are used to receiving from research projects and language communities might claim as well.

be that the academic research product is of interest to the language community,[37] in which case we may face some of the issues previously discussed: the language in which the products are published, the venues where they are published, etc. It may well be that bilingual editions are needed or that the research project needs to include provisions to create translations into the language relevant to the community and to make them meaningfully accessible to the community. Again, in determining the specific parameters of all these matters, it is crucial that conversations happen between external researchers and language community members as equal partners.[38]

2.6 The underlying ideology system: a matter of power

The preceding five sections have each addressed an aspect of the kind of product that academia defines as an academic product: one that is *written* (as opposed to oral) in a *specific language* (English, as opposed to the language under research) in a specific *venue* (an academic publishing house as opposed to community means), addressed to a specific kind of *audience* (an academic audience as opposed to a language community audience), *authored* by a specific type of individual (an academic researcher not a language community member), whose specific *knowledge* is recognized as such by academia (the western researcher as opposed to community knowledge-holder).

This reveals an underlying system of ideology-based priorities, which primes things academic over things otherwise defined: what matters are the needs of the academic community, even in cases where research work could be of an equally professional nature and equally evaluated. Academia then insists on controlling the nature of what is done, how and by whom, what's acceptable and what's not, who's in and who's not, and as a way to insure the very existence and persistence of the system.

That said, one would expect that these attitudes would extend to all realms of interaction. It turns out, however, that this is not really the case. Academia does indeed negotiate its control over the research design, process and output. It does so under special conditions. These conditions arise when the funding for a particular research project, the money, comes from powerful institutions, in fact, from institutions that can be argued to be more powerful than academia: government agencies, including federal institutes, foundations and departments (of Energy, of Defense, etc.), as well as private agencies and companies. In those

---

[37] For instance, if the community is invested in developing human resources that can eventually carry out the research projects "in house."
[38] On this matter, see the chapter by Czaykowska-Higgins in this volume.

cases, academia negotiates the type of output or product (if classified/confidential then peer-reviewed publication may be obviated), the type of research agents (non-academic consultants who may not hold an academic degree but who are paid for a given expertise/knowledge, are recognized as *experts* and authors) and the type of audience (if confidential then access to the research results will be restricted to only individuals with the right clearance).[39] So, what permeates from this is that academia's attitudes with respect to controlling any and all aspects of research depends on the power status of the collaborating partner (with higher status partners academia negotiates; with lower status partners academia does not) and, in turn, the status of the collaborating partner depends on whether and how much it pays. This, in turn, poses a moral/ethical question: does academia treat partners in a different way according to their wealth?

What PAR/CBR advocates is that collaborations between language communities and academia should be on an equal-to-equal basis, that is, independent of any money involved (since, after all, research should be independent of any economic forces implicated), the terms should be agreed upon by both as equal partners and should be carried out with the same respect as granted to partners with big budgets. PAR/CBR, thus, attempts to redress the existing power imbalances as a matter of dignity, sovereignty and rights (cultural and linguistic, which are part of human rights).

One aspect that federal agencies have in recent years pushed for is the idea of the translational nature of academic research. Though this is mostly implemented in the STEM areas, one might argue that this is precisely what PAR/CBR is promoting, not in the traditional sense of developing a product of economic value, but in the sense of developing a product of intangible value, with far-reaching societal consequences. We next turn our attention to the role of funding agencies, whose standing intersects so deeply with academia.

3 Misalignments arising in interactions with funding institutions

A number of funding programs have emerged in the recent past to attend to the issue of endangered and un- and under-documented languages that was brought to light more visibly in the 1990's with the Hale et al (1992) *Language* paper. They range from national federal programs, to university/foundation collabo-

---

[39] In fact, big funding opportunities generate focus groups that discuss the needs of funding agencies and work to strategize the best way to fit into their programmatic conditions.

rations to private foundations; and the funding amounts they offer also have a wide range, from one thousand to several hundred thousand US dollars.[40] To my knowledge, none of these is linked to a language community (that is, they are all western, "outsider" entities) or has a language community advisory board. Their focus is mostly on *documentation* (i.e, acquiring data) and require the release of all data into an archive (independent of or owned by the funding agency).[41]

In this section I will examine points of misalignment between what a language community perspective like PAR/CBR upholds and how (western) funding agencies address the issue of language documentation/analysis. As a reminder, a PAR/CBR approach holds that a language community has the inherent right to maintain an active role in all the stages of a research project from conception to end-product. Though most funding agencies have some sort of statement that recognizes the existence (and, somehow, the relevance) of the language community, how much of that translates into recognizing them as equal partners is questionable at best. In National Science Foundation (NSF) documents, the term "translational" appears going back to the 2010's but it is not to be found in the most recent documents;[42] of course, the term "translational" did not refer to language communities, rather it had an applied, most directly mercantile perspective, but it had the potential to be applied in our field in interesting ways especially in producing intangible counterparts to the research performed, which could be of benefit to the language community as it would see best. The introduction of the notion of "Broader Impacts"[43] as a necessary criterion for evaluation in NSF research projects has interesting potential to be explored. The Endangered Languages Documentation Programme (ELDP) also recognizes language communities as potential beneficiaries (the last ones listed) of their documentation efforts

---

40 Some examples are, in the higher rank, the Documenting Endangered Languages (DEL), a partnership between two federal agencies, the National Science Foundation (NSF) and the National Endowment for the Humanities (NEH); the Endangered Languages Documentation Programme (ELDP) managed by SOAS at the University of London with private funding from the Arcadia foundation. On the lower end of funding, again as sample examples, we can see the Foundation for Endangered Languages, out of Britain, and the Fund for Endangered Languages, out of the USA, both private.

41 The language used in the program's description is also interesting: In the 2016 DEL Program the term *ingestion* is used (presumably, for the action of depositing language data into an archive).

42 The keyword now seems to be "transformational" in the sense of transforming the way we do research, not necessarily the way research affects society, though one could potentially see an extension in that direction.

43 Broader Impacts seeks "the potential to benefit society and contribute to the achievement of specific, desired societal outcomes," where "society" could be interpreted as including the language community.

and as participants, in as much as their participation will benefit the project, but not as active agents in the process.[44]

None of these pointers, thus, recognize the "agentivity" of an equal-to-equal relationship between the funding agency and the language community. In what remains, I will tackle three topics as a sample of what would need to be addressed to produce a more equal relationship: defining the scope of the program; a more dynamic (informed) consent process, freely agreed-upon by the language community; archiving requirements.

3.1 Defining the scope of the project

A balanced relationship between funding agencies interested in language documentation and the corresponding language community would involve a process of joint decision making about the scope and goals of the project. This would include the ability to decide if the design and implementation of any preservation and revitalization activities would be necessary or advisable. However, funding agencies typically unilaterally decide what is to be included and what not, including components that would have a direct impact on the status of the language in the community; some specifically exclude preservation and revitalization activities.[45] In fact, it seems that the more powerful the funding agency is, the less it is interested in preservation and revitalization, whereas those that specifically include those aspects are the ones with less economic power.[46]

Whereas one might argue that whoever pays has the right to decide how the money is going to be used, economic and historical power differentials may indicate that this position is not necessarily the most ethical one. In their 1992 paper, Hale et al. point out that what makes language loss different in our time is that "politically dominant languages and cultures simply overwhelm indigenous local languages and cultures placing them in a condition which can only be described as embattled" (Hale et al, 1992: 1). Those very same politically dominant cultures

---

44 Community involvement is deemed important in as much as it can improve the attitude towards the research project, and thus increase the quality of the project itself; the same is reckoned with respect to the creation of "practical language materials" (Major Documentation Project Information Pack for Applicants 2016, p. 7–8). In fact, a detailed analysis of the wording found throughout the documentation might reveal what could be interpreted as a paternalistic view of the language community, not an equal partner.
45 That is the case of the EDLP program (http://www.eldp.net/en/our+grants/grant+types/)
46 For instance, two of the agencies that explicitly include revitalization, the Endangered Language Fund (ELF) and the Foundation for Endangered Languages (FEL), are among those providing the least amount of funding (in the range of one to four thousand US dollars).

are the ones behind the funding agencies that determine that their language data are worth "saving" but their language use is not worth preserving, or at least not worth their money. It would seem that western agencies have a historical responsibility to redress and to rebalance the power differentials that were and are at the very origin of the current situation.

Another way of looking at it is that funding agencies want something, language data, primarily to serve research goals, whereas language communities have exactly what funding agencies want, language data, whose use they want to preserve. Since their goals intersect, one might argue that it is in the best interest of both, including funding agencies, to find respectful partnerships that can facilitate each other's goals.

3.2 (Informed) consent

All funding agencies require the use of ethical practices in the dealings of the researcher with the language community and, as part of that, require obtaining their consent to conduct the research. There are two issues here, however, one is the passive role of the act of granting permission (providing consent to the research that another has designed) and the character of "blanket" permission that this consent usually requires. Typically, this consent is required *a priori*, most likely in the form of a letter of agreement by some instance representative of the community. The issue is, what happens if what is then collected is deemed not shareable with outside forces? While agencies recognize different levels of a language community to stipulate restrictions on access to materials, these are extremely restricted and do not prioritize the right of the community to the final word on access. ELDP for example requires "grantees to make the materials collected and the derivatives openly available through ELAR, the Endangered Languages Archive at SOAS" and since it also requires ethical practices, it encourages its grantees to ensure that they have "addressed the implications of this requirement and have conducted the required research and negotiated the access constraint";[47] that is, there is no room for negotiating access: either the community blindly agrees to the conditions of the funding agency or there is no project. Certain leeway is, however, contemplated: a "graded access" is considered only in "exceptional cases" and "can constitute only a small amount of material and not the majority of documentary

---

47 Major Documentation Project Information Pack for Applicants 2016 (01b Application_Guidance notes for applicants_MDP_2016), p.8. Accessed on 8/22/2016 at http://www.eldp.net/en/our+grants/grant+types/

materials to be collected."⁴⁸ As pointed out, it is extremely restricted and it is *a priori* ("to be collected"). Researchers have reported on the difficulty to "convince" community members to provide such consent, and the "need" to do so, since otherwise the project will not be approved. All of this raises concerns about the potential coercive character of these consent requirements.

NSF, in its guidelines for Data Management Plans (an obligatory component of any research proposal), for the Directorate for Social, Behavioral and Economic Sciences (SBE) recognizes the need for inclusion of "provisions for appropriate protection of privacy, confidentiality, security, intellectual property, or other rights or requirements." It even states that "information the disclosure of which would constitute a clearly unwarranted invasion of personal privacy, such as information that could be used to identify a particular person" is not considered "research data" by the federal government and thus need not be retained.⁴⁹ It seems clear that audio and video recordings do identify a particular person and thus such items do not belong in the set of data that is required to be retained. However, the most recent Solicitation Program for the Documenting Endangered Languages Program (NSF 16–576, p.1) includes a revision with detailed requirements on the archiving of materials collected. The emphasis of the current Solicitation (NSF 16–576) on building computational infrastructure, on digital recording, data management and archiving, as compared to older ones (e.g., NSF 04–605, dating back to 2004), seems to ignore the proviso for the protection of personal identity in the general Data Management Plan and, more generally, the *requirement* to archive violates the right for a language community to *consent* at any and every step of the process, whether or not prior consent has been awarded.

An additional concern involves the true informed nature of consent. How do we ensure that communities understand the nature of the internet or the accessibility of an archive? Do they realize that *absolutely everybody*, no matter where on the planet, will be able to see their image and to hear their voice? That they will not be able to know who has seen and heard their voice and image? And that those same people will also potentially be able to obtain a copy and that technology is such nowadays that their image and voice can be manipulated?⁵⁰ If those

---

48 Major Documentation Project Information Pack for Applicants 2016 (01b Application_Guidance notes for applicants_MDP_2016, p.16. Accessed on 8/22/2016 at http://www.eldp.net/en/our+grants/grant+types/

49 *Data Management for NSF SBE Directorate Proposals and Awards*, p. 2–3, accessed on 8/22/2016 at http://www.nsf.gov/sbe/SBE_DataMgmtPlanPolicy.pdf

50 An anonymous reviewer questions the validity of these questions, maybe under the assumption that nowadays everybody knows the internet and its implications. However, informal conversations with elders (mostly in Europe) reveal that experience with the internet varies widely and that the true implications of shared information is not really grasped. This is also becoming

conditions, and the associated risks, are not properly understood, then *consent*, though possibly legally valid, is not really consent.

3.3 Archiving requirements

The two previous subsections interconnect at the archiving requirement. Since so much of the goals of funding agencies is to guarantee the acquisition of data (what they identify as *documentation*), it is no surprise that the requirements for archiving are so stringent. If the language community is interested in the documentation of its language and language use for its own preservation and revitalization purposes, and if it wants to have access to a given agency's funds to undertake those processes, it comes to the point where they have to relinquish all power of decision about whether to share with the outside world or not (most of the time the same world that caused their language loss to begin with). That basically amounts to blackmail:[51] if you are in dire need of our funds, you can have them if and only if you give us your data. Unfortunately, this contributes to a museistic (almost 19th century like) view of language documentation: the accumulation of data, (linguistic) objects, extricated from their natural habitat, in a repository where it is accessible to us and where we control it.

It seems then, that *documentation* is a process that serves western institutions, academia; institutions that belong to those dominant cultures that, under the view presented in Hale et al (1992) overwhelmed and embattled the languages they intend to now "save." In fact, the emphasis on archiving (the data) while forgoing the processes of preservation and revitalization of the environment for language use is reminiscent, in probably a perverse way, of the old saying "kill the indian and save the man" of the ill-fated boarding schools:[52] it seems that the current system contributes to keep what is useful to our culture (the data, the labor force of the man), but neglects, "kills," that which is "disturbing" (the indian-ness, the living culture, the environment for a living language).

---

obvious among the youth, with respect to the long term implications of sharing every single aspect of one's life. Research is ongoing about the various implications of these issues. In addition there is a significant "digital divide" across the globe, and even where digital resources are accessible there is often a culture of not employing them.

51 I recognize that this is a powerful statement that may shake our self-perception as researchers, and the conceptualization of research as a "clean," non-ideological activity. The point of this statements is to begin to uncover those power imbalances that underlie our activity as researchers and that help us become aware of issues we may not be aware of. It is a statement about the *system* not about the *individuals*, though in the end it is the individuals that sustain the system.
52 See Reyhner and Eder (2004).

These three aspects examined in this section point, again, towards an underlying ideology system that hierarchizes communities, priming the needs of western culture and subordinating the agentive role of non-western cultures, in particular, those with endangered languages. Establishing a true respectful partnership between language community and funding agencies, that would recognize the inherent rights of decision of language communities, would go a long way towards redressing power imbalances.

It is important to note that this is an analysis of the underlying *system*, not the *individuals* within that system, even though in the end it is the individuals that, collectively, sustain the system. The *power imbalances* are part of that system. In as much as we individually question the system, we become instruments in changing it.[53]

4 Final thoughts

In this paper, I have set out to examine potential loci of friction between the postulates of a PAR/CBR approach that recognizes the inherent rights of the language community to a continuous active and agentive role in the research process, and the institutionalized ways of western academia. The initial hypothesis is that such friction will arise when PAR/CBR challenges the underlying structures of power holding in western academia.

From the examination of different aspects of the way western academic institutions and funding agencies relate to language communities one can outline an underlying system of ideologies prevalent in the academic world that primes the needs of academia and western institutions over the needs and rights of non-dominant language communities. Bringing to light such a system and identifying the points of conflict with a more respectful PAR/CBR approach can pave the way for a more egalitarian mutually respectful and truly collaborative relationship between the two sides of potentially fruitful and successful partnerships.

Recapitulating, evidence for a hierarchical system of ideologies came from the priming of: the type and format of product that was deemed academic (favoring, e.g., literacy over orality, tangible publication over intangible process), English as an academic language (over not only endangered languages, but also over other larger languages such as Spanish), knowledge originating in academia (as opposed to knowledge generated within a language community), validation by academic "authorities" (as opposed to language community authorities). The behavior and

---

[53] For a critical view of the system, see also Díaz (2017).

attitudes observed in academia reveal a factor of "control" of the process and the product of research, with an interest in "accumulating" the raw material and the sourcing of the product (data, resources), under a "museistic" view of language documentation that parallels the factory model of a capitalist society.

The emphasis of documentation on *collecting* (i.e., archiving) to the exclusion of preservation, strengthening and revitalization, reveals an underlying primacy of the interests of research, of academia, over the interests and needs of the language "holders." In the same way that guidelines for the participation of human subjects in research state that the researcher cannot burden a specific population (say, a prison population) for extraction of data for the extensive benefit of another population (say, a suburban community), in the same way academia should not use a given community (the language community) for the extraction of data (language data to be archived) for the extensive benefit of a different community (the research community). This is the source for the misalignments that we have been able to observe.

Adopting a PAR/CBR approach at all levels of research (including the recognition of non-traditional "research products" and ensuring the agentive and meaningful participation of the language community at all stages of research) would go a long way towards obtaining a more ethical, less unequal research process. In doing that, documentation would, then, as Yamada (2007) stated, respond to revitalization needs.

References

Benedicto, Elena and Mayangna Yulbarangyang Balna. 2007. A model of participatory action research: the Mayangna linguists' team of Nicaragua. In *Proceedings of the XI FEL Conference on "Working Together for Endangered Languages-Research Challenges and Social Impacts"*. 29–35.

Christie, Patrick, David Bradford, Ray Garth, Bonifacio González, Mark Hostetler, Oswaldo Morales, Roberto Rigby, Bertha Simmons, Eduardo Tinkam, Gabriel Vega, Ronnie Vernooy, Noreen White. 2000. *Taking care of what we have. Participatory natural resource management on the Caribbean coast of Nicaragua*. Managua and Ottawa: Centro de Investigación y Desarrollo de la Costa Atlántica (CIDCA) and International Development Research Centre (IDRC).

CITI Program. Collaborative Institutional Training Initiative. https://about.citiprogram.org/en/homepage/. Accessed 7/1/2017.

Czaykowska-Higgins, Ewa. 2009. Research models, community engagement, and linguistic fieldwork: Reflections on working within Canadian Indigenous communities. *Language Documentation & Conservation* 3 (1). 15–50. [http://scholarspace.manoa.hawaii.edu/bitstream/handle/10125/4423/czaykowskahiggins.pdf?sequence=1]

Díaz, Esteban. 2017. Documentación desde una perspectiva crítica: Nasa Yuwe (Paez) de Colombia. Paper presented at the LED-TDR Lyon Workshop Sociolinguistics Of Endangered Languages. Profiles, Post-Vernacularity and Revitalization, Université de Lyon, 24–25 April 2017.

Endangered Languages Documentation Programme (ELDP). 2016. *Major Documentation Project Information Pack for Applicants 2016*. Accessed as <01b Application_Guidance notes for applicants_MDP_2016> at http://www.eldp.net/en/our+grants/grant+types/ on 8/22/2016

Endangered Language Fund (ELF). http://www.endangeredlanguagefund.org. Accessed 8/22/2016.

Ferreira, Maria Pontes and Fidji Gendron. 2011. Community-based participatory research with traditional and indigenous communities of the Americas: Historical context and future directions. *The International Journal of Critical Pedagogy* 3.3. 153–168.

Foundation for Endangered Languages (FEL). nd. Grants. http://www.ogmios.org. Accessed 8/22/2016.

Hale, Ken, Michael Krauss, Lucille J. Watahomigie, Akira Yamamoto, Colette Craig, Laverne Masayesva Jeanne and Nora C. England. 1992. Endangered Languages. *Language* 68 (1). 1–42.

Reyhner, Jon and Jeanne Eder. 2004. *American Indian Education. A History*. University of Oklahoma Press: Norman.

Rice, Keren. 2011. Documentary linguistics and community relations. *Language Documentation and Conservation* 5. 187–207. http://scholarspace.manoa.hawaii.edu/bitstream/10125/4498/1/rice.pdf. Accessed 7/2/2017.

Viñas de Puig, Ricard, Mayangna Yulbarangyang Balna, and Elena Benedicto. 2012. Linguistic and technical training as a community empowerment tool: The case of the Mayangna linguists' team in Nicaragua. *International Journal of Language Studies* 6 (1). 77–90.

Yamada, Racquel-Maria. 2007. Collaborative linguistic fieldwork: Practical application of the empowerment model. *Language Documentation & Conservation* 1 (2). 257–282.

Ewa Czaykowska-Higgins, Xway'Waat Deanna Daniels,
Tim Kulchyski, Andrew Paul, Brian Thom, S. Marlo Twance,
and Suzanne C. Urbanczyk

Consultation, relationship and results in community-based language research

Abstract: Community-based research (CBR) is research "...in which participants are partners and collaborators in research of mutual interest and ... usefulness to the community" (Rice 2011: 191). In this chapter, we argue that to develop mutually beneficial partnerships, a CBR project needs to ensure that consultation amongst participants is "meaningful." We illustrate this point by considering the role played by communication and meaningful consultation in establishing and carrying out a wide-ranging community-university research and language revitalization project undertaken on southern Vancouver Island in western Canada. In addition to describing our project, we distinguish between its tangible countable outputs and intangible outcomes, arguing that the latter have been more significant than the former. We show that, on our project, consulting meaningfully required 1) development and continual re-evaluation of consistent, clear, mutually-agreed-upon, and concrete lines of communication, and (re-)defining governance and management structures and protocols for the project, 2) recognizing and valuing the expertise, roles and responsibilities of all Indigenous and non-Indigenous project participants, from Elders' Advisory Committee members to coordinators of sub-projects to Elder experts, to research assistants, and 3) agreeing upon Memoranda of Understanding and Researcher Contracts that took into consideration issues of control, benefit, and ownership. In conclusion we reflect on the contributions of CBR methodology and practice to Linguistics. We suggest that developing processes of meaningful consultation is a step towards decolonizing and Indigenizing research methodologies, making them relational and accountable to the local, and transforming research relationship(s).

Ewa Czaykowska-Higgins, (all author contact c/o), Department of Linguistics, University of Victoria, Clearihue Building D341, Victoria BC Canada, eczh@uvic.ca; **Xway'Waat Deanna Daniels,** University of Victoria & Pauquachin First Nation, danielsd@uvic.ca; **Tim Kulchyski,** Cowichan Tribes, Tim.Kulchyski@cowichantribes.com; **Andrew Paul,** Tsartlip First Nation, nations@shaw.ca; **Brian Thom,** University of Victoria, bthom@uvic.ca; **S. Marlo Twance,** Penelakut First Nation, sharon.marlo@gmail.com; **Suzanne C. Urbanczyk,** urbansu@uvic.ca

https://doi.org/10.1515/9783110527018-004

Keywords: community-based language research, meaningful consultation in research, intangible research outcomes, indigenizing research methodologies

> So we gathered the Elders together ... and their question to us was "Is this meaningful consultation, or is this just a tick off of a list, or are you just putting a check mark in a box saying that you met with us to satisfy your grant requirements. [...]"
>
> (S. Marlo Twance; CURA Final Report:[1] 27–28)

> One of the Hul'q'umi'num' elders recently shared a word with us to describe the CURA project: *nuts'umot* "working as one."
>
> (Urbanczyk et al, 2006)

> [A]fter being greeted in SENĆOŦEN by a man in his twenties, one of the fluent SENĆOŦEN-speaking elders said how nice it was to hear the language spoken again.[...] According to th[is] elder [...]: "The language is revitalizing itself."
>
> (Urbanczyk et al, 2006)

---

1 The CURA Final Report is listed in the references under Czaykowska-Higgins, Daniels, Hukari, Kulchyski, Paul, Thomas-Paige and Urbanczyk 2011.

---

* Without the support and direction of the Elders who have contributed to the CURA Project discussed in this chapter, and without their dedication to revitalizing the Hul'q'umi'num' and SENĆOŦEN languages, the CURA Project would not have been possible. **Huy ch q'u. HÍSWḴE.** We acknowledge and raise our hands to the members of the Elders Advisory Committees: Lou Claxton, late Manny Cooper, late Ivan Morris, Florence James, Sally Norris, Ruby Peter; the Elders who participated on the CURA Steering Committee: Mabel Mitchell, late Pete Seymour, and Philomena Pagaduan; and to the Elder Researchers and Research Associates: late Dr. Earl Claxton Sr., Belinda Claxton, late Willie Seymour, late Rose Henry, Irvine Jimmie, Dr. Arvid Charlie, Myra Charlie, Wayne Charlie, Albie Charlie, Violet Charlie, late Henry Edward, Roy Edwards, Violet George, Melvin Good, late Irene Harris, Ray Harris, Alice Jimmy, Bernard Joe, late Abraham Joe, Gus Joe, Mary Ellen Joe, Veronica Kauwell, late Rennie Louie, Sr., Janet Moore, late Ed Seymour, late Angus Smith, Auggie Sylvester, Laura Sylvester, and late Abner Thorne. We also acknowledge the partner organizations and their leaders: the Hul'qumi'num Treaty Group and Al Anderson, the Saanich Native Heritage Society and John Elliott Sr., First Peoples' Heritage Language and Culture Council, First Peoples' Cultural Foundation and Tracey Herbert, and then Chair of Linguistics at the University of Victoria, Leslie Saxon. We also acknowledge those who served as Steering Committee members over the years: Deanna Daniels, Charlotte Elliott, Joe Elliott, John Elliott Sr., Linda Elliott, Audrey Henry, Tom Hukari, Tamara Knott, Mabel Mitchell, late Pete Seymour, Brian Thom, Suzanne Urbanczyk, Ewa Czaykowska; and coordinators, Al Gerow, Tim Kulchyski, Lou-ann Neel, Andy Paul, Marlo Paige (Twance). Finally, thank you to all the other participants — Research Associates, trainees, students, technicians, administrative staff, multimedia advisors, technicians, and colleagues who contributed in multiple and crucial ways to this project. This research has been supported by the Social Sciences Research Council of Canada (833-2003-1031).

1 Introduction

Central to definitions of community-based research are notions of collaboration and partnership between participants. Rice (2011: 191), for instance, refers to CBR as research "[...] in which participants are partners and collaborators in research of mutual interest and of usefulness to the community." Community-based language research (CBLR), or CBR practice focused on language, specifically includes in its definition the statement that "[t]his kind of research involves a collaborative relationship, a partnership, between researchers and (members of) the community within which the research takes place." (Czaykowska-Higgins 2009a: 24). In a community-based language project, collaboration and partnership often involve learners, speakers, other stakeholders, Elders, insider and outsider linguists "working together at every stage of the research process" (Strand et al. 2003: 10) and thus sharing in the creation of knowledge.

There are many different components to building and maintaining partnerships and collaborative research relationships. In this chapter, we characterize and discuss one foundational component that, drawing on the words of Elders with whom we worked on a multi-year linguistics and language revitalization project, we refer to as *meaningful consultation*. By outlining possible ways of practicing and understanding meaningful consultation in a research relationship, our chapter is intended to contribute 1) towards the defining of community-based practice in linguistics, and 2) to a broader conversation about how community-based vision and research methodology may be shaping the field of linguistics.

Our discussion grows out of, and is situated in, the context of a community-university collaborative project that took place on Coast Salish[2] territory on Vancouver Island (British Columbia, Canada) between 2002 and 2010. The chapter therefore begins by setting out and locating ourselves within that context, and then focuses on defining and characterizing meaningful consultation as it arose in that context. We illustrate that, on our project, consulting meaningfully required 1) development and continual re-evaluation of consistent, clear, mutually-agreed-upon, and concrete lines of communication, and (re-) defining governance and management structures and protocols for the project, 2) recognizing

---

[2] In this article, we use the term 'Coast Salish' to refer to the Hul'q'umi'num' and SENĆOŦEN speaking communities living at the southern end of Vancouver Island. The term can also be used more generally to refer to a subset of languages from the Salish language family. For a list of other languages in British Columbia that are considered to be Coast Salish, see the First Peoples' Language Map of British Columbia (http://maps.fpcc.ca/language_index?filter0=Coast+Salish).

and valuing the expertise, roles and responsibilities of all Indigenous and non-Indigenous project participants, from Elders' Advisory Committee members to coordinators of sub-projects to Elder experts, to research assistants, and 3) agreeing upon Memoranda of Understanding and Researcher Contracts that took into consideration issues of control, benefit, and ownership.

The collaborative project discussed here was in many ways unusual in terms of its scope and size and in terms of its outcomes of consultation and process. However, for that reason, it is an interesting illustration of possible ways in which CBR can contribute to research practice in linguistics. Therefore, in the final sections of the chapter, we reflect on the contributions of CBR methodology and practice to the discipline. We take it as given that consultation and the form(s) it takes are always and necessarily dependent on their context and are based in relationships. Nevertheless, the process of consultation, no matter how it is carried out, is central to any collaborative research project; as such, we suggest, consultation can be understood as an actual, essential, significant, intangible outcome and result of a project. Understanding consultation in this way is a step towards what Indigenous thinkers have called decolonizing and indigenizing research methodologies, making them relational and accountable to the local (Smith 1999; Battiste and Henderson 2000; Kovach 2009; Weber-Pillwax 2001). It is thus part of a process of re-defining and transforming relationship(s) in research in ways that are congruent with principles of reciprocity, respect, relevance, responsibility, and relational accountability (e.g., Kirkness and Barnhardt 2001; Wilson 2008).

2 Prologue: Contexts

Maori scholar Graham Smith has said that within Indigenous research a prologue "encompasses essential information for the reader to make sense of the story to follow" (quoted in Kovach 2009: 3). A prologue asks the reader to acknowledge the teller, context, place, history, and intellectual antecedents. As Rice (2011: 201) notes, community-based research or collaboration "does not force a particular way of working [...] beyond the consultation that is determined to be necessary by those involved." However, as Rice also notes, in problematizing notions of collaborations, scholars such as Dobrin (2008), Holton, (2009) and others (e.g., Crippen and Robinson 2013; Dobrin and Berson 2011; Good 2012; Lüpke 2009; Stebbins 2012; Shulist 2013), have argued that collaboration and thus consultation are contextual and culturally-determined (see also contributions to this volume, such as those of Rice and Pérez-Báez). Since this chapter has grown out of a project that all the co-authors participated in, both the project and its local, historical and intellectual contexts have informed the understanding of collaboration and meaningful consultation discussed here.

2.1 The CURA Project

The project, whose official title was *Language Revitalization in Vancouver Island Salish Communities: A Multimedia Approach* (aka the *Coast Salish Language Revitalization CURA Project*, or CURA Project), focused on two Coast Salish languages of Southern Vancouver Island, SENĆOŦEN and Hul'q'umi'num'. SENĆOŦEN is the heritage language of four First Nations communities of approximately 3000 WSÁNEĆ people. At the time of the project, it was spoken fluently by approximately 20 Elders, with about 4% of the population being semi-fluent, and 5% of the population learning the language in schools (*Report on the Status of B.C. First Nations Languages; Amrhein et al.* 2010). Six Hul'q'umi'num'-speaking First Nations, with a population of approximately 6200, are partners in the Hul'qumi'num Treaty Group (HTG), a coalition founded in 1993 to negotiate a treaty with the province of B.C. and with the Government of Canada. According to the 2010 *Status Report*, about 120 people spoke Hul'q'umi'num' at the time of the CURA Project, with 5% being semi-fluent, and 17% reported to be learners.

The CURA Project was initiated in 2001–2002: STOLĆEŁ John Elliott, Sr., a SENĆOŦEN language teacher, language champion, and Chair of the Saanich Native Heritage Society (SNHS), representing four historically SENĆOŦEN-speaking First Nations, approached the University of Victoria, through contact with Salishanist Ewa Czaykowska-Higgins, about initiating a collaborative project that could provide support and funding for the SENĆOŦEN-speaking community's language initiatives. At around the same time, the Hul'qumi'num Treaty Group, with a long-standing relationship with Salishanist Tom Hukari, hired Salishanist Suzanne Urbanczyk to prepare a *Strategic Plan for Hul'q'umi'num' Language Revitalization* (Urbanczyk 2002). And, also around the same time, STOLĆEŁ John Elliott and Peter Brand, both teachers at the ŁÁU,WELNEW Tribal School, began working with First Peoples' Cultural Foundation on a prototype of *FirstVoices. com*, the Aboriginal language archiving site. The CURA Project arose out of these already established relationships, common goals and aspirations. It began with the forming of an alliance between the Saanich Native Heritage Society, the Hul'qumi'num Treaty Group, First Peoples' Cultural Foundation (FPCF) and its sister organization the BC Crown Corporation First Peoples' Heritage, Language and Culture Council (FPHLCC; now known as First Peoples' Cultural Council), and the University of Victoria (UVIC; Linguistics). After consultation in community and between alliance members, the partners applied in 2002 to the Social Sciences and Humanities Research Council of Canada's recently instituted Community-University Research Alliance (CURA) grant program for a development grant; in 2003 we applied for a full grant and received $977,000 for five years of funding. The project started 1 January 2004; with a one-year extension it ended on 31 December 2009, with wrap-up continuing well into 2011. Its purpose was 1) to contribute towards rebuilding living language in Hul'qumi'num Treaty Group and Saanich Native Heritage Society communities; 2) to produce research and materials, and build capacity in research, culture and protocol relevant to language revitalization, useful to communities, in the communities and in the university; 3) to establish solid partnerships between the Coast Salish communities and the University of Victoria; 4) to learn more about how the partners could work together, respecting culture and protocol; 5) to enable conditions that would allow revitalization to continue after the project. Over its lifespan, the CURA Project supported and was associated with 10 Hul'q'umi'num' and 9 SENĆOŦEN language documentation and revitalization projects, as well as projects on governance and intellectual property, and projects on theoretical linguistic questions and on research methodology.

The co-authors of this chapter were all actively involved in the governance and/or management of the CURA Project, particularly in its last few years. Ewa Czaykowska-Higgins was Principal Investigator and Director in 2002–2004, 2007–2010, Co-Investigator 2005–2007, as well as a participant in several SENĆOŦEN projects, and UVIC Facilitator for the SENĆOŦEN projects. Xway'Waat Deanna Daniels, who is of Hul'q'umi'num' ancestry, was Chair of the CURA Steering Committee, and, as then Manager of Language Programs for First Peoples' Heritage, Language and Culture Council, was also a FPHLCC representative on the CURA Steering Committee. Tim Kulchyski, a Cowichan Tribes member and employee of the Hul'qumi'num Treaty Group, was the Coordinator for the Hul'q'umi'num' documentation and revitalization projects, and an active participant in several of the Hul'q'umi'num' projects. Andrew Paul, a member of the Tsartlip First Nation, was Coordinator for the SENĆOŦEN language documentation and revitalization projects and a participant in one SENĆOŦEN documentation project. Brian Thom was, until 2010 a senior advisor and negotiator for the Hul'qumi'num Treaty Group, who had received a community mandate to prioritize language revitalization work as part of the overall reconciliation work on treaty negotiations. He participated on the CURA as a founding contributor, advisor to the project, and a Facilitator for the Hul'q'umi'num' projects. S. Marlo (Paige) Twance, a Penelakut First Nation member, was the Coordinator for the CURA Project as a whole, a Master's student at the University of Victoria, and the lead in one Hul'q'umi'num' documentation project. And Suzanne Urbanczyk was Principal Investigator and Director 2005–2007, Co-Investigator both before and after that period, and participant in several key Hul'q'umi'num' and SENĆOŦEN documentation and revitalization projects.

2.2 Local, national, international contexts

> Our language has a feeling by itself that speaks to your soul, that tells of ancient understanding [...] that's what our children are missing. We need a plan of how to get their heads back to SENĆOŦEN [...] but we don't have that much time.
> (ȻOSINIYE Linda Elliott, SENĆOŦEN language teacher 2003)

> That Cowichan part of our language is tied to our culture. I usually hear our people saying "our culture is tied to our language." That's how I hear it, from the old people. And without language you have no culture. That's how they say it.
> (Hul'q'umínum' Elder; quoted in *HTG Strategic Language Plan*, Urbanczyk 2002)

The Canadian province of British Columbia has approximately 34 of the 60 or so Aboriginal languages spoken in Canada, and thus has considerable linguistic diversity.[3] The history of Indigenous languages in British Columbia specifically and in Canada more generally is a history of colonization and assimilation, partly through residential schools and educational systems. However, it is also a history of strong and increasingly active and passionate movements to stop language loss. Both the SENĆOŦEN and the Hul'q'umi'num' communities have been working for many years to maintain community control over their languages, and to make their languages fully alive again; the CURA Project was intended to contribute to this process.

The movements associated with language reclamation in Canada are closely tied to the fight for recognition of Aboriginal identity, rights, land title, and empowerment. The *Royal Commission on Aboriginal Peoples* (1996), for instance, noted the connection between Aboriginal languages and what it called a "distinctive world view, rooted in the stories of ancestors and the environment." The *RCAP* added that Aboriginal languages are a "tangible emblem of group identity" that can provide "the individual a sense of security and continuity with the past [...] maintenance of the language and group identity has both a social-emotional and a spiritual purpose" (quoted in *Truth and Reconciliation Commission* 2015b: 152). More recently, and partly informed by the findings of

---

[3] In the Canadian context, the term "Aboriginal" refers to Inuit, Métis and First Nations peoples and languages. "Indigenous" is a broader term, encompassing the term "Aboriginal."

RCAP, the *Truth and Reconciliation Commission of Canada* (*Truth and Reconciliation Commission*), whose purpose has been to explore the history and effects of residential schools on Aboriginal peoples in Canada, has linked reconciliation — "establishing a mutually respectful relationship between Aboriginal and non-Aboriginal peoples in [Canada]" (*What We Have Learned, Truth and Reconciliation Commission* 2015a: 113) — to speaking and understanding an Aboriginal language. Sabrina Williams, an intergenerational survivor from British Columbia expressed that link:

> I didn't realize until taking this language class how much we have lost —all the things that are attached to language: it's family connections, it's oral history, it's traditions, it's ways of being, it's ways of knowing, it's medicine, it's song, it's dance, it's memory. It's everything, including the land. [...] And unless we inspire our kids to love our culture, to love our language [...] our languages are continually going to be eroded over time. So, that is daunting. Yeah. **So, to me that's part of what reconciliation looks like.**
> (Truth and Reconciliation Commission 2015b: 157)

In Canada, as in countries like the USA, Australia, and New Zealand, with similar colonial histories, language reclamation movements are closely tied to the development of Indigenous scholarship about Indigenous knowledge(s), ways of knowing, empowerment, governance, history, and, in an academic context, the ethics of research and research methodologies. The *Royal Commission on Aboriginal Peoples*, Volume 5, Appendix E, for instance, discusses principles of Aboriginal research, including the value of Aboriginal knowledge, the importance of undertaking collaborative research, of ensuring access to research results, of ensuring community benefit, and implementation of *RCAP* guidelines in research contracts and agreements.[4] The work of Indigenous scholars reflects the intellectual climate of Indigenous research within which the CURA Project took shape:

> [Indigenous peoples] want their communities and their knowledge and heritage to be respected and accorded the same rights, in their own terms and cultural contexts, accorded others in the area of intellectual and cultural property. They want a relationship that is beneficial to all.
> (Battiste and Henderson 2000: 132)

In the same vein, V. Kirkness and R. Barnhardt discuss initiatives within higher education that are transforming the "landscape of higher education for First

---

4 Appendix E of Volume 5 Renewal: A Twenty-Year Commitment can be found at <http://www.collectionscanada.gc.ca/webarchives/20071124125036/http://www.ainc-inac.gc.ca/ch/rcap/sg/ska5e_e.html#Appendix%20E:%20Ethical%20Guidelines%20for%20Research>. Accessed 12 February 2016.

Nations/American Indian people", laying out principles they call the Four R's: that universities need to Respect Indigenous people, produce work or education that is Relevant to Indigenous worldviews, that offers Reciprocity in relationships, and that ensures that Indigenous people have Responsibility for their own lives (Kirkness and Barnhardt 2001: 1). Writing from a Maori perspective, G. Smith (2000: 214) calls for the need for Indigenous peoples to "develop theoretical understandings and practices that arise out of our own Indigenous knowledge." And L. T. Smith (1999: 2) "[...] identifies research as a significant site of struggle between the interests and ways of knowing of the West and the interests and ways of resisting of the Other."

Within the field of linguistics as well, since the early 1990s there has been considerable discussion about what a "responsible linguistics" should be in a time when many languages are endangered. Hale et al's (1992) influential piece calls for a linguistics that includes the possibility of collaborative models of working with language communities (Watahomigie and Yamamoto 1992: 11), includes consideration of issues of self-respect and community empowerment (Craig 1992: 23), implies intellectual, scholarly and political responsibilities to a language and its speakers (England 1992: 32), and acknowledges the agency of speakers in decisions concerning the languages they speak. As Hale (2001: 76) wrote, "[t]he scientific investigation of a given language cannot be understood in isolation. [...] Linguists are inevitably responsible to the larger human community which its results could affect."

The CURA Project's conception was in response to and was deeply influenced by these aspects of its local, national, international and intellectual contexts. It was also influenced and guided by its specific Coast Salish context, and thus by Coast Salish protocols and understanding of respect, as well as by academic protocols and expectations. As a result, the partners began their work together by laying out, in the funding application, a set of guiding "Principles of Respect" for the project:

Principles of Respect
- **Equality:** SENĆOŦEN and Hul'q'umi'num' have equal (not necessarily identical) status and respect within the structure of the grant.
- **Control:** The communities should exercise control over information related to their knowledge and heritage.
- **Management:** The research should be managed and evaluated jointly by the communities and other partners.
- **Benefit:** The communities should benefit from training and employment opportunities generated by the research.
- **Governance:** The communities should have direct input into developing and defining research practices and projects related to them.

– **Ownership/sharing**: Sensitive information should not be made public; the communities will share royalties that might be generated, will have access to and copies of all the material produced; communities' cultural rights to and ownership of the results will be safeguarded.

These Principles of Respect were based on principles discussed in the *Royal Commission on Aboriginal Peoples* (1996) and laid out in the Canadian *Tri-Council Policy Statement on Ethical Conduct for Research Involving Humans* (Canadian Institutes of Health Research, Natural Sciences and Engineering Research Council of Canada, Social Sciences and Humanities Research Council of Canada, 1998). As a team, we felt from the beginning that it was necessary to foreground the goals, needs, leadership, roles, and rights of the Indigenous partners on the CURA Project as one step towards unsettling the privilege that historically has resided in Euro-American academic institutions and, by extension, with academic participants involved in research related to Indigenous peoples and communities. The following section illustrates ways in which these principles were put into effect or influenced the Project.

3 Methodologies and meaningful consultation

The Principles of Respect laid out above provided a framework for the CURA Project. Implementation of these principles was not always straightforward, however. In fact, we spent the whole period of tenure of the project working on trying to get it "right." There were several points in the life of the project that involved false starts, when large shifts in conceptualization and implementation needed to, and did, occur. There were periods of misunderstanding and even of conflict. For all of us co-authors, there were moments when participating in the CURA Project was, simply put, very hard. Nevertheless, what made it ultimately possible for the project to succeed to the extent that it did was that, as mentioned above, we had already built relationships prior to the project starting, and had further built on these prior relationships through a process of consultation that allowed us to continue to consult with each other, however we could, to make sure that project participants felt listened to and heard by others in the partnership.

The Final Report of the CURA Project (Czaykowska-Higgins et al 2011; referred to throughout the paper as CURA Final Report CFR), lays out in some detail what we as a team consider we learned on the Project. In the next subsection we summarize briefly some of the key points related to consultation described in that report. Section 3.2 provides examples of how we tried to put meaningful consultation into practice.

3.1 Relationship, trust, consultation, collaboration

> It seems to be the same thing, the same principle used in all human conditions. [...] You have to have a rapport. You have to know those people. They have to know who you are. They have to know how you operate [...]
>
> (Andy Paul; CFR: 26)

> [...] it takes time to develop a relationship with communities, and it's a hit and miss. If you don't get that relationship, then, you know, in a community-based format, it's not going to work.
>
> (Deanna Daniels; CFR: 26)

From the perspective of those of us working on the CURA Project, a central component of community-based research is relationship. Building relationship requires consultation, it leads to trust, trust leads to consultation that is meaningful, meaningful consultation leads to further development of relationship, and this circle of building and reinforcing relationship through consultation leads to fruitful collaboration.

Building relationship through consultation takes time — taking into consideration academic time frames and the pace of community partners. It requires patience, good will, and honesty to get a relationship started and to let it develop.

> Make sure your heart's in the right place and your intentions are good, expect a steep learning curve, and be truthful and honest. It is not about the researcher, it is about the community and its ideas. I think a lot of researchers are still trying to understand that [...] Community-based research is the people letting you participate in their life, because it is their life that you're taking from.
>
> (S. Marlo Twance; CFR: 28)

In the context of the history of colonization and of language loss, an additional need for building a relationship is a safe space in which to consult and work together. Doing language revitalization work, or working with language in communities where using one's language was grounds for punishment "[...] can get muddy really fast, and really painful really fast [...] The ground you walk on is unpredictable with this kind of work, and you have to have a lot of compassion, especially with a community-based project." (S. Marlo Twance; CFR: 28).

Building relationship and consultation also require finding out who to talk to in a community and how to consult appropriately:

> Don't come to the community and think that you know. You've got to go in and along with that language group, those language people, find out where things are at. And if you don't have the depth or the sincerity to see that through, you might as well not bother.
>
> (Andy Paul; CFR: 28)

At the most basic level, for the academic members of a research project this means asking and finding out, if one doesn't know already, who the stakeholders are, who the decision makers are, what the protocols are, what the expectations are for the results of a project and for how to work together. For the community participants in a project the same kinds of questions arise; universities have very specific ways of conducting themselves and very specific expectations, none of which are obvious to those who are not used to them. Consultation and relationship thus allow for the development of infrastructure locally, in response to local needs and vision and ways of working, but in combination with (and sometimes in opposition to) the ways of academic institutions.

In addition, consultation and relationship allow for and encourage training and building capacity for *all* partners in a community-based project. In a traditionally Euro-American university setting, most research projects have historically been conducted under the control of a university-based researcher, according to the expectations of the academic process (see, also, Benedicto, this volume). However, community-based research aims to contribute to democratization of knowledge, social action and social change, and thus to shift power differentials in a research situation (Czaykowska-Higgins 2009a: 25). Consequently, as our colleague Tom Hukari pointed out, "[...] in a community-based project, the university really has to bend over backwards to realize it's a community project" (CFR: 30). In this statement, "university" refers to both university-associated researchers and to the academic institutions themselves. In fact, any academic institution that is a partner in a community-based project needs to take responsibility to build capacity within the university setting to adequately support community-based research. It needs to commit to the idea that there is going to be change and innovation in process and in outcomes (Tim Kulchyski, CFR: 29). In the following section we point out three ways in which the university as an institution did try to change.

Most important, though, within the Canadian context at least, is that the cornerstone of a project like the *Coast Salish CURA*, which involved Indigenous languages and language revitalization research and activities, needs to be consultation with, guidance from, and the valuing of the expertise of, community

Elders. Elders in this Canadian context are considered to be the keepers of language and cultural knowledge, of world view, of showing "how things are tied together" (Tim Kulchyski, CFR: 27): Elders are the "connection [...] to the old world [...] the way it used to be" but they are also "the future" since it is they who are able to instil the language into the new speakers (Deanna Daniels, CFR: 25). Having such a pivotal role in communities means that Elders are the "most important and most valuable piece" to the language: "No Elder, no language. No language, no project" (Andy Paul, CFR: 27). In our project, the Elders were not only the keepers of language, but they were also our guides: they asked the hard questions, they kept us honest, they kept us accountable, they made sure the project stayed on track and was guided by and further developed the principles of respect with which we started.

The elements of *meaningful consultation*, then, as we have briefly outlined them here include: relationship, trust, patience, good will, honesty, taking time, having compassion, thinking locally and academically, taking responsibility for and being open to change, learning to learn, learning who to take guidance from, valuing the expertise of language community members and especially of Elders, and working according to principles of respect.

3.2 The practice of meaningful consultation

On the *Coast Salish Language Revitalization CURA Project* there were three areas of the partnership that proved to be critical sites for working towards meaningful consultation. The first of these involved working out appropriate structures for consultation, including decision-making, governing, and managing the project. The second involved consciously thinking about the expertise of project participants and about shifting roles in research. And the third involved thinking about and agreeing upon questions of ownership, benefit and control over project outcomes and outputs.

3.2.1 Structures for consultation

Over the course of the CURA Project, trying to allow for consistent, clear, and mutually agreed upon lines of communication between all the different partners and participants in this wide-ranging project meant that there was continuous development, (re-)evaluation and re-development of consultation structures. Ultimately we ended up distinguishing two types of consultative structures, those involving governance and those involving management of the CURA Project and of its various sub-projects.

Governance of the project was provided by 1) two Elders' Advisory Boards (one representing HTG and one representing SNHS), each consisting of three Elders appointed by the community partners, and 2) by a Steering Committee. In the original conception of the Steering Committee, agreed to by all partners, it consisted of three co-Directors (one representing the University of Victoria partner, one representing First Peoples' Heritage, Language and Culture Council and one representing First Peoples' Cultural Foundation) plus one representative each from the Hul'qum'inum Treaty Group and Saanich Native Heritage Society. Within months of beginning to operationalize the project, it became clear that the committee structure was not sufficiently representative of all the partners, despite best intentions at the outset: having a level with three co-Directors proved to be too hierarchical, so that the structure did not allow for straightforward decision-making and did not give equal voice to the language communities. Not only was this not in keeping with the Principles of Respect with which we had started the Project, but it also meant, not surprisingly, that decisions about and work plans for projects kept stalling. In 2005, therefore, re-structuring of the committee took place to ensure equality and appropriate respect at the table, to give the representatives of the language communities ultimate approval for sub-projects, and to distribute the balance of decision-making to better include the people highly engaged at the community level, while recognizing the continued need for representation and input from institutional partners on the Steering Committee. The final shape of the Steering Committee included two SNHS members and two HTG members chosen by the HTG and SNHS partners, one FPHLCC member, one FPCF member, and two UVIC members (including the Principal Investigator/Director of the project); a Chair was elected from amongst the Steering Committee representatives, and decisions were made by consensus (where possible).[5] The flexibility that all partners showed in working together to modify the structure contributed to building trust, and led to other important changes in administrative procedures and power shifts on the Project.

The Elders' Advisory Boards provided direction, guidance and vision for the CURA Project and for individual sub-projects. Although these Boards were "advisory" in nature (recognizing that "advisory" is often a euphemism for continuing disempowered colonial relationships where Advisory Boards in natural

---

[5] The original conception of the Steering Committee was put together for the funding application in 2002–2003. The major re-structuring took place in 2005 under the direction of Suzanne Urbanczyk, Director/PI 2005–2007, Deanna Daniels, FPHLCC representative and then Steering Committee Chair, and Lou-Ann Neel, the Project Coordinator at the time. The project had been running for approximately 18 months at that point.

resource management, for instance, do not have actual decision-making power (Mulrennan and Scott 2005)), the actual mandates that came from the Elders participating in the Boards were treated with dignity and respect in ways that continually and powerfully shaped the decisions taken — from issues of funding to accountability to what the actual subjects and methodologies of research would be. The Steering Committee provided leadership in business and research issues, put into practice and maintained the Project vision and the guidance and mandates provided by the Elders' Advisory Boards, tried to ensure community needs were met and respected, worked on knowledge mobilization, and tried to ensure university and granting agency requirements were met. The Steering Committee met monthly, varying locations of the meetings so that traveling to meetings was distributed equally amongst the representatives.

Project management was needed to translate the vision and guidance of the Elders and the decisions of the Steering Committee into practical reality. The Project management structure included a Director (who was also the Principal Investigator of the CURA Project) and a Project Coordinator who oversaw the functioning and administration of the whole project, and two Community Coordinators (one for HTG, one for SNHS) who oversaw the specific community projects. In the last couple of years of the Project we also added two Facilitators, one for each community: the Facilitators were academics who met regularly with their corresponding Community Coordinators. The Community Coordinators and Facilitators served together as the bridges or conduits between university and community, and did the important work of translating and mediating between the two.

Because the Project was so wide-ranging and involved so many different sub-projects and participants, so many different needs and expectations, and therefore many administrative challenges, at around the same time as the re-structuring of the Steering Committee took place, the then Project Coordinator initiated the establishment of a CURA Binder/Guide which set forth all the governance, management, and administrative policies and procedures needed to allow for consistent functioning of the Project. It also laid out the roles and responsibilities of team members and the terms of reference for the various committees and projects. This Binder/Guide was continuously added to and up-dated. One useful addition was a Lines of Communication diagram and explanation that reflected the ways that communication was taking place on the Project. The Lines of Communication diagram ensured consistency in communication, and it also allowed us to be clear about who was communicating to whom and for what purpose at any given time: since many of us had different roles on the project, being aware of "which hat" we were wearing at any one time was particularly important for decision-making.

Clearly the structures for consultation on the Project were complex, but what is significant is that they were appropriate to that Project, they strove to achieve equal representation in decision making, they strove to reflect and respect the vision and guidance of Elders and of community members and to support sub-projects that were relevant to the community partners, and they strove for transparency in decision-making processes and in reporting. In addition, the processes of working together with flexibility and openness to change, and especially the processes of re-thinking the initial governance structure, proved to be highly significant for facilitating the Project's continuation. Finally, it is important to recognize that the University of Victoria tried to find ways to accommodate the inclusive decision-making framework, which included community members, for key financial and strategic decisions that we have described here. This was one way in which the university took responsibility for change.

3.2.2 Recognizing and valuing expertise

> It is time for Indigenous peoples and Indigenous research to break free from the hegemony of the dominant system, into a place where we are deciding our own research agendas.
> (Wilson 2008: 17)

As mentioned above, one of the goals of community-based research methodology is democratization of knowledge. Democratization of knowledge is one possible result of meaningful consultation. In the context of the CURA Project, knowledge democratization included recognizing, valuing and foregrounding Coast Salish as well as non-Coast Salish knowledge, ways of knowing and of creating knowledge. It also included recognizing and valuing appropriately all knowledge holders and creators, thus shifting power and control in the research process.

In our Project we did this in two ways: First, the CURA Steering Committee decided early on in the Project to use CURA funds as much as possible to build capacity within the two language communities for language maintenance and revitalization work, and to do this by hiring and training as many community members as possible (by the time the Project was over, more than 90 community members had been funded as participants or researchers). Second, decisions were made (which were sometimes deliberate and sometimes emergent from particular contexts) to change research roles and responsibilities in as many areas of the project as possible. In particular, in a typical linguistic research scenario the academic linguist is the expert who poses research questions, sets the research agenda, and is often thought of as a disinterested observer and recorder of facts, while the language community members "provide the data."[6] In our Project we worked on shifting to a mode of research in which language speakers and community members were recognized as experts, provided the intellectual vision and content and guided the shape of research, in addition to transcribing and translating stories and other language material, working on pedagogical materials, and so on. The linguists on the relevant sub-projects also served in the capacity of recorders, organizers, maintainers of databases, facilitators, and assistants in the research process, rather than always being the research agenda setters. For the academics involved in the project, these role "reversals" were unsettling, requiring the un-learning of ways of being researchers that had been instilled in graduate school. Being unsettled is often freeing in unexpected ways, however: On the CURA Project, it made it possible for different ways of thinking about goals and outcomes and their value to come to the forefront. It helped to strengthen the sense of partnership and team on the Project. In addition, the role "reversals" that occurred on the Project made a substantive difference in how the projects were carried out and in their material outcomes (see, for example, Dwyer 2010; Rice 2011).

In this team-based approach projects were initiated in various ways (Rice, this volume).[7] Some involved speakers/community members and academic partners collaborating on the initial work plans and execution of projects. Others involved speakers and community members initiating and setting projects in motion, with linguists brought in after the initial stages in order to support the research. And still others involved a combination of approaches.

The Snuw'uylh project, for instance, was requested by Elders from HTG, but it also fit in with the academic work of the CURA Coordinator, who was a Masters student in Education while also working on the CURA (Thomas-Paige 2009). The term "snuw'uylh" refers to traditional teachings and values from a Hul'q'umi'num' perspective. The project interviewed and recorded Hul'q'umi'num' Elders talking about traditional teachings in Hul'q'umi'num'. The interview questions and the scope of the project were developed in partnership between the Elders and the researcher; the Elders guided the project, approving all content and outcomes. The Elders' goal was to find a way to teach younger generations the philosophy of their ancestors, and through the teachings to assist younger people to find a more

---

[6] This paragraph is based on Czaykowska-Higgins (2009b).
[7] See, for instance, Gerdts (2010), Linn, Berardo, and Yamamoto (1998), Yamada (2007) for discussion of roles in research, and Leonard and Haynes (2010) for discussion of empowerment and initiating a project.

positive way of living, to help them reclaim their identities and to find success in modern times. In this project, the academic was led by the vision and content provided by the Elders; the academic work in turn was the means through which the Elders shared their Coast Salish perspective and knowledge.

Another example of a project initiated and requested by Elders was the SENĆOŦEN Philosophy of Living Project. By organizing the categories of documentation and the ways in which they were documented according to the SENĆOŦEN Philosophy of Living, the project encompassed and documented language for community members and university researchers in a culturally relevant way. The project included training SENĆOŦEN speakers in vocabulary and forms of address needed for speaking in the Big House and in public. It included work towards a SENĆOŦEN dictionary, production of culturally relevant word lists and related audio material, and development of documentation for future use at the tribal school. Additionally, project members developed a method of recording with which they were comfortable, and which they called the "3Rs Documentation Method: Review, Revise, Record." Using the Philosophy of Living to shape documentation was based on the inspiration of the two Elders who were working on documentation, partly in response to the insistence of a third Elder that the project needed to find principles of organization for the documentation. The work grew out of one particular Elder's years of dedication and commitment to the language. The project team included in addition a Community Research Assistant, and a volunteer Research Assistant from UVIC. It was facilitated by the coordinator for SENĆOŦEN projects who was a hub and sounding board, and was supported and guided by the SNHS representatives on the CURA Steering Committee, and by one of the CURA linguists. In this project, as in the HTG Snuw'uylh project, the Elders were the experts and the leaders; as a result the project brought SENĆOŦEN community ways into a university setting, and made the university more familiar to the participating community members.

A third project envisioned and initiated by an Elder was the *SENĆOŦEN SḰÁL ŁTE-SENĆOŦEN Teaching Grammar*. In this project, an Elder led a team consisting of himself as lead researcher, a linguist, and a community Trainee/Research Assistant. The Elder envisioned the *Teaching Grammar* as consisting of 9 units, one for each month of the school year, and as involving thinking in SENĆOŦEN from the first day of classes. The work routine established was collaborative, with the Elder and his assistant working 5 mornings a week on such aspects of the grammar as sentence patterns, vocabulary, and cultural context, and the linguist working 2 mornings a week preparing draft chapters and working with the Elder to appropriately describe the patterns. After drafts of each chapter were prepared, they were reviewed by other Elders, and were recorded.

Kovach (2009: 36) discusses what she calls an increasingly common approach to research within the Indigenous landscape as one in which a non-Indigenous principal researcher works with a junior Indigenous researcher on a project whose research design includes Indigenous methods within a methodology that has credibility in the Western research community. She says,

> On my less cynical days, I believe that this approach is an attempt to recognize the history of Western research within Indigenous communities and make reparations. Yet it is nevertheless problematic. Indigenous methods do not flow from Western philosophy; they flow from tribal epistemologies. If tribal knowledges are not referenced as a legitimate knowledge system guiding the Indigenous methods and protocols within the research process, there is a congruency problem.

Although the CURA Project did resemble the "common approach" critiqued by Kovach, in that it had a relatively traditional Western academic structure (at the time the project started that structure likely made it possible for the partnership to access funding), nevertheless, the impetus for the CURA Project came from the SENĆOŦEN and Hul'q'umi'num' communities and was in response and in relation to activities already led by and taking place in those communities. For the academic linguists, this meant that the experience of participating in the Project shifted their understanding of results, outcomes and what constitutes knowledge. The academics' experience thus also contributed in small but clear ways to (re-)defining institutional understanding of results and outcomes — thus, subsequent to the CURA Project's conclusion, the university took some responsibility for change by giving a measure of consideration in tenure-and-promotion processes to the kind of collaborative work that the academic participants in the CURA Project participated in (though this has been hard-fought). Moreover, the act of shifting researcher roles so that Elders and other community knowledge holders were lead researchers on projects created space(s) for Coast Salish knowledges. In this sense, the CURA Project tried to "[...] shift the power of the researcher in controlling the research process and outcome. Methodologically, this mean[t] gathering knowledge that allows for voice and representational involvement in interpreting findings [...]" (Kovach 2009: 82). Consequently, research results and processes were not simply academically acceptable, but, significantly, they were also relevant, meaningful to, and respectful of, the HTG and SNHS communities and their knowledge.

3.2.3 Ownership, benefit and control

A third area of the CURA Project which allowed the CURA members to work towards meaningful consultation involved the development of structures for encouraging responsibility to the community partners and reciprocity in research process and results. In particular a Memorandum of Understanding signed by the community and university partners, and accompanying Researcher Contracts, were developed, through collaboration between HTG and UVIC, to allow for community control, benefit, ownership and protection of intangible cultural property (see http://www.hulquminum.bc.ca/pubs/UVic_HTG_MoU_signed.pdf). The MoU and contracts were later adapted by SNHS and formed the basis for an agreement between SNHS and UVIC.

A report prepared for the Department of Canadian Heritage (Thom 2006) presents the development of the HTG-UVIC MoU as a case study in respecting and protecting Aboriginal intangible property. The report defines Aboriginal intangible property as "traditional, indigenous knowledge held within aboriginal communities as their intellectual property" (p. 1). It points out that, as consultation with HTG Elders and leaders made clear, communities need protection of the customary laws and protocols that are related to their cultural knowledge[8] (including language), while at the same time needing documentation of this knowledge to support their rights and their traditions. The questions that arise, then, are how to protect the intellectual property from exploitation or misappropriation by outsiders, how to protect sacred and/or privately- or collectively-owned songs, or stories, or performances, etc., and how to ensure that non-community members do not profit from collective community traditions.

To address these questions, in addition to defining Aboriginal intangible property, the MoU's and Researcher Contracts spell out ways to protect this property through defining researcher responsibilities in documentation and publication, through establishing disposition of research, ownership, consent, confidentiality and royalties, considering the university's intellectual property rights, and providing a means for dispute resolution. Most importantly for purposes of this chapter, they set "out a process for the communities and the researchers to work together to make informed decisions about prioritizing and approving research questions put forward" (Thom 2006: 5). This process crucially relies on "listening to the community and Elders' concerns", on "good systems of communication", with "clear terms of reference" and depends on established and establishing good long term relationships. In other words, on the CURA Project, the MoU's and Researcher Contracts were tools that contributed to creating space and establishing processes for meaningful consultation. They were also tools that caused the university to change and bend a bit as an institution by having to consider new formal mechanisms for protecting ownership and research results, and

---

8 For additional reflection on ancestral knowledge in Coast Salish territories, see Thom (2017).

by creating a new default to the University IP policy that better respected the positions of the communities rather than simply privileging university researchers. As such, these tools were a creative means of empowering Indigenous governance and self-determination, in spite of the limitations of conventional intellectual property rights and the default policies of the academic institution involved in the Project.

In this section, then, we have laid out some of the factors that contribute to consulting meaningfully on a community-based language research project. As mentioned at the beginning of this section, there were moments when participating in the CURA Project was, simply put, very hard. Attempting to put into practice meaningful consultation opened up spaces for all of us to re-think the way decision-making power and privilege are distributed and ultimately to re-shape the long-term outcomes of the Project. This was particularly important in relation to academic researchers, as we worked consciously to reposition the power and privilege that is easily — and indeed often inherently — associated with academic institutions. It also forced us to grapple with differences in the ways in which power and privilege are experienced by academic researchers and community researchers, and about difficulties specific to being a researcher within one's own community. Re-thinking power and privilege in turn challenged us to change structures of accountability, and pressed us to consider when and whether academic questions, priorities, or desired long-term outcomes were the same as community ones. As we discovered, they often were not: For example, producing an article about community-based language research methodology and how such methodology fits with and/or affects academic research practice would be a typical academic output, and it is also potentially a useful contribution to research practice and to a discipline. However, producing such an article as part of a project like the *Coast Salish CURA Project* is not necessarily a priority for a community that is working towards making its language fully alive again. Such an article may well affect the research practice of academic researchers who subsequently read it, and consequently might change how they view their role as allies in a language revitalization process, and might therefore be a useful contribution to the ultimate success of a community-university language revitalization partnership. Nevertheless, for a community working towards language revitalization, more immediate priorities could be development and assessment of documentation, resources and processes that contribute directly to language learning and the valuing of language in the community. Therefore, writing an academic article might be an excellent step to take, but in a community-based project it might be a more valuable output after other goals and priorities have been met. It appears to us that in grappling with these kinds of challenges, we were working towards relationships of co-existence — on both personal and institutional levels.

We hope our experiences as Indigenous and non-Indigenous participants on the Project offer potential stepping-stones for the great challenges of unsettling and decolonization.

3.3 Practicing in a Coast Salish way: Relationality and process

> [T]he shared aspect of an Indigenous ontology and epistemology is relationality (relationships do not merely shape reality, they *are* reality). The shared aspect of an Indigenous axiology and methodology is accountability to relationships.
>
> (Wilson 2008: 7)

> The shared aspects of relationality and relational accountability can be put into practice through choice of research topic, methods of data collection, form of analysis and presentation of information.
>
> (Wilson 2008: 7)

When we look back on the CURA Project what becomes clear is that all the way through the Project the Elders and Steering Committee community partner representatives were trying to steer the Project to a practice in research that reflected and incorporated Coast Salish ways and knowledge.

The centre of Coast Salish practice was and is relationality. Indigenous scholars have argued that in Indigenous research, key aspects of a healthy relationship must include "Respect, Relevance, Responsibility and Reciprocity" (e.g., Kirkness and Barnhardt 2010). It was in the process of maintaining and building relationships and being accountable to those relationships in the CURA Project that we consulted each other, and that we therefore attempted to work towards reciprocity, to respect, be responsible to, and work towards producing outputs and outcomes relevant to the Coast Salish partners whose languages were the focus of this collaborative research undertaking. Whether consciously or not, in the course of the CURA Project our collective steps were being steered towards Indigenizing the *Coast Salish Language Revitalization CURA* research process and results.

Within this context, the results of the Project can be divided into two broad categories, which we defined in the CURA Midterm (Urbanczyk et al, 2006) and Final Report (Czaykowska-Higgins et al, 2011) as *tangible outputs* and *intangible outcomes*.[9] Tangible outputs are "countable, quantifiable, material and deliverable"

---

9 The communities had final approval for both CURA Reports, ensuring that they represented their thoughts, words, and statements.

(CFR: 21). On the CURA Project they include the Snuw'uylh Master's Thesis, *SENĆOTEN SḰÁL ŁTE-SENĆOTEN Teaching Grammar*, the Philosophy of Living CDs, the MoU's and Researcher Contracts, and other "deliverables" including databases, articles, reports, conference presentations, workshops, and on-line language lessons. The "deliverables" also included five Hul'q'umi'num' DVDs (two with accompanying booklets documenting the use of Hul'q'umi'num' language related to Big House Speaking, Naming, and Cedar and Weaving), and an illustrated, bilingual Hul'q'umi'num'-English guide to culturally important species found in a local National Park Reserve.

Intangible outcomes are not easily countable or quantifiable, but we would argue that in a Project such as the *Coast Salish CURA*, the intangible outcomes were particularly significant: as we have tried to suggest above, they included building capacity for conducting research and language revitalization in the partner communities and amongst the university participants. For instance, leaders in the WSÁNEĆ community have spoken about how the Project contributed to building capacity and to creating momentum towards the strong and very successful language revitalization movement taking place in the WSÁNEĆ community. One outcome of this language revitalization movement is a partnership with Indigenous Education and Linguistics at the University of Victoria that has led to the delivery of post-secondary language education programs in the community. In the Hul'q'umi'num' communities, DVDs and the accompanying texts have been integrated into the core materials being used by the current generation of language teachers. People involved with the bighouse have received sacred teachings from the DVDs in the language from knowledge holders who have now passed on. It is hard to overstate how important this is — and yet how such a product made for the private, sacred ceremonies of the Coast Salish peoples could not circulate widely in academic contexts. There is also a great deal of interest in Hul'q'umi'num' and SENĆOTEN language courses, and new language projects both in partnership with academic institutions and funded by First Peoples' Cultural Council. As far as the University of Victoria is concerned, the CURA Project's presence on campus was related to the hiring of Lil'wat scholar and educator, Dr. Lorna Wanosts'a7 Williams as Canada Research Chair in Indigenous Knowledge and Learning; amongst many other accomplishments, Dr. Williams developed and offered a Linguistics course in Community-Based Initiatives in Language Revitalization, and led the development of undergraduate and graduate academic programs in Indigenous Language Revitalization at UVIC, all of which have inspired and educated many students and faculty members and have contributed to Indigenous knowledges and learning at the university. In the Midterm Report for the CURA Project, Urbanczyk et al (2006) wrote that "[l]anguage revitalization activities can be thought of as local events with global effects; like ripples in a pond, the effect of a few key actions or decisions can radiate out, to touch many people." Although the CURA Project did not conduct formal surveys to quantify its impact, it is clear that the capacity-building the CURA Project contributed to has touched many people in different places and spaces.

Other intangible outcomes illustrated here include democratizing knowledge and its production, shifting research roles, striving for collaboration and meaningful consultation. The most significant of the intangible outcomes, however, was process, and specifically the process of meaningful consultation through which the Project was being steered towards relational accountability. In this sense, the process of consultation itself can be thought of as a key result of the Project. In this sense, too, the community-based research philosophy and methodology that shaped the CURA Project is like other qualitative research methodologies, including Indigenous methodologies, for which process as well as content are significant (see Kovach 2009: 25).

4 Shaping linguistic research: Transformation?

> Indigenous communities demand a decolonizing outcome from research.
> (Kovach 2009: 86)

> Local knowledge is a *process* — a process of negotiating dominant discourses and engaging in an ongoing construction of relevant knowledge in the context of our history and social practice.
> (Canagarajah 2005: 13)

In this chapter we have illustrated one community-based language research project's experience and results, focusing on the concept of meaningful consultation as one of the key components of the research process. We have also suggested that meaningful consultation in the context of our project can be understood as one of the avenues through which the Project was guided by Coast Salish practices and values; these contributed to the structure and focus of the Project and its various sub-projects, methods of research, roles and responsibilities in the Project structure, and thus contributed to steering the Project towards relational accountability.

We are not arguing in this chapter that all community-based projects should follow the practices and expectations of the CURA Project exemplified here. That would in fact be counter to the notion of relational accountability that we have discussed. If language documentation and revitalization research projects are indeed going to be accountable to relationships, then, like the *Coast Salish CURA Project*, they must take the local context into account. In some contexts, relationships are not and cannot be of the kind illustrated by our Project and therefore the practice that was adopted in the CURA Project cannot be appropriate (see, for instance, Shulist 2013; Dobrin 2008). As Canagarajah (2005: 13) suggests, "[c]elebrating local knowledge refers to adopting a practice."

However, the introduction of community-based methodologies into language documentation research and thus into the field of linguistics provides an opportunity for re-thinking how linguistic research can be carried out. It provides an opportunity for pushing boundaries, for re-imagining and opening spaces (see Stebbins 2012), for building bridges between people and institutions and practices. It creates the possibility for different ways of thinking and knowing to inform and instruct how research is carried out, rather than to see difference as an impediment or a problem. It requires self-criticism and self-reflection: learning in relationship to each other, knowing as a process of "self-in-relation" (Graveline 1998: 52). It allows positive social relations to be integrated into research practices, which Dobrin and Schwartz (2016) argue is one of the motivations for the increasing emphasis on collaboration in discussions of linguistic fieldwork.

Ultimately introducing community-based and collaborative practice into the toolbox of linguistic methodologies opens up the possibility for transforming research in linguistics. As we have suggested here, in the *Coast Salish CURA Project*, the community-based research methodology was informed and transformed by Coast Salish knowledge and practice. Kovach argues, "[...] decolonizing theory and methods that work in tandem with tribal epistemologies shape-shift the traditional social relations of research. Such methods act to give power back to the participant and the participant's community" (Kovach 2009: 82). Such methods, when practiced in a project like the CURA Project, which involved Indigenous and non-Indigenous participants, researchers, organizations, epistemologies and ontologies, can be, and in our case were, unsettling, very powerful and therefore potentially decolonizing in intent (see Regan 2010 on "unsettling").

If community-based research as a methodology does open the possibility of shifting traditional social relations in research and of creating space for Indigenous and other perspectives then it provides the possibility of outcomes that are congruent with decolonization and Indigenization of linguistic research methodologies and thus of shaping the discipline of linguistics. And, as Smith (1999: 140) says in speaking of decolonization in relation to Indigenous research, "[n]egotiating and transforming institutional practices and research frameworks is as significant as the carrying out of actual research programmes."

References

Amrhein, Hannah, Suzanne Gessner, Tracey Herbert, Xway'Waat (Deanna Daniels), Megan Lappi, Doug Hamilton-Evans, and Alex Wadsworth. 2010. *Report on the status of BC First Nations languages. First Peoples' Heritage, Language and Culture Council*. Brentwood Bay, BC. http://www.fpcc.ca/files/PDF/2010-report-on-the-status-of-bc-first-nations-languages.pdf. (Accessed 15 March 2016).

Battiste, Marie and James (Sa'ke'j) Youngblood Henderson. 2000. *Protecting Indigenous knowledge and heritage: A global challenge*. Saskatoon: Purich Publishing Ltd.

Canadian Institutes of Health Research, Natural Sciences and Engineering Research Council of Canada, Social Sciences and Humanities Research Council of Canada. 1998. *Tri-Council policy statement: Ethical conduct for research involving humans*. (with 2000, 2002, 2005 amendments). http://www.pre.ethics.gc.ca/archives/tcps-eptc/docs/TCPS%20October%202005_E.pdf (accessed 20 May 2017).

Canagarajah, A. Suresh. 2005. Reconstructing local knowledge, reconfiguring language studies. In A. S. Canagarajah (ed.), *Reclaiming the local in language policy and practice*, 3–24. New York: Routledge.

Craig, Colette. 1992. A constitutional response to language endangerment: The case of Nicaragua. *Language* 68: 17–24.

Crippen, James and Laura Robinson. 2013. In defense of the lone wolf: Collaboration in language documentation. *Language Documentation & Conservation* 7. 123–135.

Czaykowska-Higgins, Ewa. 2009a. Changing fieldwork roles in community-based language research. Paper presented at the 1st International Conference on Language Documentation and Conservation, University of Hawaii, Honolulu, Hawaii. https://scholarspace.manoa.hawaii.edu/handle/10125/4998 (Accessed 20 May 2017).

Czaykowska-Higgins, Ewa. 2009b. Research models, community-engagement, and linguistic fieldwork: Reflections on working within Canadian Indigenous communities. *Language Documentation & Conservation* 3 (1). 15–50.

Czaykowska-Higgins, Ewa, Deanna Daniels, Thomas Hukari, Tim Kulchyski, Andrew Paul, Marlo Thomas-Paige, and Suzanne Urbanczyk. 2011. *The Coast Salish language revitalization CURA Project: Language revitalization in Vancouver Island Salish communities. A report on a community-based language research project*. University of Victoria, Victoria, BC. http://web.uvic.ca/~slrpcura/Coast_Salish_CURA_Report.pdf. (Accessed 15 March 2016).

Dobrin, Lise. 2008. From linguistic elicitation to eliciting the linguist: Lessons in community empowerment. *Language* 84 (2). 300–324.

Dobrin, Lise and Josh Berson. 2011. Speakers and language documentation. In Peter K. Austin and Julia Sallabank (eds.), *The Cambridge Handbook of Endangered Languages*, 187–211. Cambridge: Cambridge University Press.

Dobrin, Lise and Saul Schwartz. 2016. Participant observation in linguistic fieldwork. *Language Documentation & Conservation* 10. 253–277.

Dwyer, Arienne M. 2010. Models of successful collaboration. In Lenore A. Grenoble and N. Louanna Furbee (eds.), *Language documentation: Practice and values*, 193–212. Amsterdam: John Benjamins Publishing Co.

England, Nora. 1992. Doing Mayan linguistics in Guatemala. *Language* 68: 29–35.

Gerdts, Donna B. 2010. Beyond expertise: The role of the linguist in language revitalization programs. In Lenore A. Grenoble and N. Louanna Furbee (eds.), *Language Documentation: Practice and Values*, 173–192. Amsterdam: John Benjamins Publishing Co.

Good, Jeff. 2012. 'Community' collaboration in Africa: Experiences from Northwest Cameroon. In Peter Austin and Stuart McGill (eds.), *Language Documentation and Description* 11, 28–58.

Graveline, Jean. 1998. *Circle works: Transforming Eurocentric consciousness*. Halifax: Fernwood Publishing.

Hale, Ken, Michael Krauss, Lucille Watahomigie, Akira Yamamoto, Colette Craig, Jeanne LaVerne and Nora England. 1992. Endangered languages. *Language* 68. 1–42.

Hale, Kenneth. 2001. Ulwa (Southern Sumu): The beginnings of a language research project. In Paul Newman and Martha Ratliff (eds.), *Linguistic Fieldwork*, 71–101. Cambridge: Cambridge University Press.

Holton, Gary 2009. Relatively ethical: A comparison of linguistic research paradigms in Alaska and Indonesia. *Language Documentation & Conservation* 3 (2). 161–175.

Kirkness, Verna. J. and Ray Barnhardt. 2001. First Nations and higher education: The four R's: respect, relevance, reciprocity, responsibility. In Ruth Hayge and Julia Pan (eds.), *Knowledge across cultures: A contribution to dialogue among civilizations*. Hong Kong: Comparative Education Research Centre, The University of Hong Kong.

Kovach, Margaret. 2009. *Indigenous methodologies: Characteristics, Conversations, and Contexts*. Toronto: University of Toronto Press.

Leonard, Wesley and Erin Haynes. 2010. Making "collaboration" collaborative: An examination of perspectives that frame field research. *Language Documentation & Conservation* 4. 268–293.

Linn, Mary, M. Berardo and Akira Yamamoto. 1998. Creating language teams in Oklahoma Native American communities. *International Journal of the Sociology of Language* 132. 61–78.

Lüpke, Friederike. 2009. At the margin – African endangered languages in the context of global endangerment discourses. *African Research and Documentation* 109. 15–41.

Mulrennan, Monica and Colin Scott. 2005. Co-management – An attainable partnership? Two cases from James Bay Northern Quebec and Torres Strait, Northern Queensland. *Anthropologica*. 47 (2). 197–214.

Regan, Paulette. 2010. *Unsettling the settler within: Indian residential schools, truth telling, and reconciliation in Canada*. Vancouver & Toronto: UBC Press.

Rice, Keren. 2011. Documentary linguistics and community relations. *Language Documentation and Conservation* 5. 187–207.

Royal Commission on Aboriginal Peoples. 1996. *Highlights from the Report on the Royal Commission on Aboriginal Peoples: People to people, nation to nation*. http://www.aadnc-aandc.gc.ca/eng/1100100014597/1100100014637. (Accessed 15 February 2016).

Shulist, Sarah. 2013. Collaborating on language: Contrasting the theory and practice of collaboration in Linguistics and Anthropology. *Collaborative Anthropologies* 6. 1–29.

Smith, Graham H. 2000. Protecting and respecting Indigenous knowledge. In Marie Battiste (ed.), *Reclaiming Indigenous Voice and Vision*, 209–224. Vancouver: UBC Press.

Smith, Linda Tuhiwai. 1999. *Decolonizing methodologies: Research and Indigenous Peoples*. London: Zed Books.

Stebbins, Tonya. 2012. On being a linguist and doing linguistics: Negotiating ideology through performativity. *Language Documentation & Conservation* 6. 292–317.

Strand, Kerry, Sam Marullo, Nicholas Cutforth, Randy Stoecker, and Patrick Donohue. 2003. *Community-based research and higher education: Principles and practices*. San Franciso, California: Jossey-Bass.

Thom, Brian. 2006. Respecting and protecting Aboriginal intangible property: Copyright and contracts in research relationships with Aboriginal communities. Department of Canadian

Heritage, Copyright Policy Branch, Ottawa, Ont. http://web.uvic.ca/~bthom1/Media/pdfs/intangibleprop/Thom_2006_Protecting_ICPs_CaseStudy_3.pdf. (Accessed 1 March 2016).
Thom, Brian. 2017. Entanglements in Coast Salish ancestral territories. In Françoise Dussart and Sylvie Poirier (eds.), *Entangled territorialities: Negotiating Indigenous lands in Australia and Canada*, 174–202. Toronto: University of Toronto Press.
Thomas-Paige, Marlo. 2009. *In the voices of the Sul-hween/elders, on the Snuw'uyulh teachings of respect: Their greatest concerns regarding Snuw'uyulh today in the Coast Salish Hul'qumi'num Treaty Group territory*. Victoria, BC: University of Victoria MA thesis.
Truth and Reconciliation Commission. 2015a. *What we have learned: Principles of truth and reconciliation*. www.trc.ca. (accessed 12 February 2016).
Truth and Reconciliation Commission. 2015b. *Honouring the truth, reconciling for the future: Summary of the Final Report of the Truth and Reconciliation Commission of Canada*. www.trc.ca. (accessed 12 February 2016).
Urbanczyk, Suzanne C. 2002. Strategic plan for revitalizing the Hulʼqʼumiʼnumʻ language. Report prepared for the Hul'qumi'num Treaty Group. Ladysmith, BC. http://www.hulquminum.bc.ca/our_work/projects (accessed 20 May 2017).
Urbanczyk, Suzanne C., Deanna Daniels, Tim Kulchyski, Marlo Paige, Andy Paul, and Ewa Czaykowska-Higgins. 2006. *Language revitalization in Vancouver Island Salish Communities: A multimedia approach—CURA midterm report*. University of Victoria, Victoria, BC manuscript. Submitted to Social Sciences and Humanities Research Council of Canada, October 2006.
Watahomigie, Lucille J. and Akira Y. Yamamoto. 1992. Local reactions to perceived language decline. *Language* 68. 10–17.
Weber-Pillwax, C. 2001. What is Indigenous research? *Canadian Journal of Native Education* 23 (2). 166–174.
Wilson, Shawn. 2008. *Research is ceremony: Indigenous research methods*. Halifax/Winnipeg: Fernwood Publishing.
Yamada, Racquel-Maria. 2007. Collaborative linguistic fieldwork: Practical application of the empowerment model. *Language Documentation & Conservation* 1 (2). 257–282.

Colleen M. Fitzgerald
Creating sustainable models of language documentation and revitalization

Abstract: In the years since the alarm was raised by linguists (Hale et al. 1992) regarding the survival of many of the world's estimated 7,000 languages, many programs have developed to support language maintenance and revitalization. These programs have been situated in both academic and tribal/grassroots institutions. After at least three decades of such programs, it is clear that many of these programs do not survive. In this paper, I outline the essential properties of successful and sustainable approaches, in part drawing from my own work at the University of Texas at Arlington's Native American Languages Lab. In analyzing the components of a sustainable model, I focus on collaborations primarily in the United States, in Texas and Oklahoma. This case study thus presents one exemplar of how community-based research operates in a larger regional context. This makes the case that long-term capacity building and training is essential.

---

* This material is based upon work supported by, and conducted while serving at the National Science Foundation. Any opinions, findings, and conclusions expressed in this material are those of the author, and do not necessarily reflect the views of the National Science Foundation. I would like to acknowledge the many colleagues, partners and funding sources without whose support this paper would not be possible. For the Oklahoma Breath of Life workshop activities, thanks to Co-Director Mary Linn and the National Science Foundation for grant BCS-1065068. My thanks to Jim Parrish and Teri Billie of the Choctaw Language Program and to Candessa Tehee and Roy Boney, Jr. of the Cherokee Language Program, as well as David Ludlow, Freeman Jesse, Rae Queton who worked with our graduate field methods students. The Cherokee ethnobotany project was possible thanks to participation by David Crawler and John Ross of the Cherokee Language Program and UT Arlington Sustainability Committee Grant. For the CoLang 2014 and related activities, my thanks to the National Science Foundation for grant BCS-1263939, "2014 Institute on Collaborative Language Research (CoLang/InField)" and to Jonelle and Beryl Battise, and to the Alabama-Coushatta Tribe of Texas for their hospitality and support of our CoLang field methods class working with the Alabama language. My thanks also go to the many colleagues and students who have been part of these projects, especially Mary Linn, Joshua Hinson, Brad Montgomery-Anderson, Dylan Herrick, Racquel Sapien, Tracy Hirata-Eds, Daryl Baldwin, Marcellino Berardo, Jack Martin, Candessa Tehee, Roy Boney, Jr., and students Lori McLain Pierce, Samantha Cornelius, Joshua Jensen, Dan Amy, Kimberly Johnson, Libby Tatz, Vicki Caña, Devin Hornick, Stephen Self, Nathaniel Eversole, Vitaly Voinov, Nick Williams, Eric Katz, Juliet Morgan, Nicole Umayam, Loren Hov, Adrienne Tsikewa, and Abby Denemark.

Colleen M. Fitzgerald, Department of Linguistics and TESOL, The University of Texas at Arlington, Box 19559 — 132 Hammond Hall, Arlington, TX 76019-0559 USA, cmfitz@uta.edu

https://doi.org/10.1515/9783110527018-005

Training is best realized as dynamic, and with rich, multilateral mentoring networks. These collaborations establish an intellectual infrastructure that is a resource for the region, with multiple experts in tribal and academic contexts on a variety of topics. It is this human infrastructure that is the lynchpin of a sustainable model.

Keywords: training, sustainability, American Southwest, revitalization

1 Introduction

Training plays an increasingly important role in many community-based approaches to indigenous language documentation and revitalization. A good description of what falls under this umbrella comes from Genetti and Siemens (2013: 61):

> This term [training] is used broadly to cover a diverse array of activities, from one-on-one instruction to short workshops, small classes, intensive institutes, and formal degree programs. In its simplest conception the term 'training' refers to the transfer of skills and knowledge from one person to another [...] The transferred skills range from orthography development to filmmaking to linguistic analysis, and so on.

Recent work supports the effectiveness of training as a response to language endangerment and revitalization (for example, McCarty et al. 2001; Dobrin 2008; Jukes 2011; Fitzgerald and Linn 2013; Genetti and Siemens 2013; Fitzgerald and Hinson 2016). This is especially true as large-scale training venues like the Institute on Collaborative Language Research (CoLang) assume an increasingly important role in national and international contexts.

Training offers an interesting lens for viewing what it means for language projects to be community-centered, community-based, grassroots-driven or some combination of the three. An excellent, early example of community-centered projects where training and intellectual interchange serve as the cornerstone comes from the indigenous language collaborations between tribal organizations and academics in Oklahoma. Descriptions of these collaborative projects appear in the 1990s as part of the then-emerging literature on language endangerment (i.e., Hale et al. 1992) and they motivate the importance of training as a response to language endangerment (i.e., Watahomigie and Yamamoto 1987, 1992). Current projects in Oklahoma and neighboring regions are characterized by ongoing activities that vary considerably in terms of what we might consider explicitly community-driven, but training continues to play an integral role. As I will show here, because projects often involve overlapping participants, different training events build on and reinforce each other and maintain continuity.

Because language activities are offered with some regularity, this cultivates a deeper knowledge among all involved.

In this chapter, I will focus on collaborative work done in conjunction with UT Arlington's Native American Languages Lab and with our partners. These projects thus serve as a training-oriented case study, which I use to make several key claims about models of community-based language research. From this case study, I make the following claims. First, work in the Oklahoma region shows itself as a sustainable model that has endured over a relatively long time period as far as language revitalization is concerned. Second, that this sustainability is possible when training includes certain fundamental properties (outlined further below) and when training is characterizable in terms that I describe as involving multilayered, dynamic, decentered in authority and complex. This creates intellectual infrastructure that acts as a resource in the region because there are multiple experts who support both their own program and those of other programs. I further argue that where there are sustainable, effective models of endangered language research, these models thrive because they critically blur the distinction between revitalization and documentation. Finally, despite not being explicitly community-driven (at least in its current incarnation), I demonstrate that this case study exemplifies one instantiation of a community-based language research model.

These various projects occur in the southeastern United States, generally focused on Oklahoma, but extend into Texas (at or near the site of my home institution in the greater Dallas-Fort Worth metroplex) and, to a lesser extent, to neighboring southeastern states like Louisiana. Having been involved in this context for about eight years, it is a good time to reflect on the growth and development in my students, my collaborators, and the range of stakeholders who participate in various projects – myself included. There are pools of experts, both indigenous and academic, that we all draw on as resources. Stepping back at this point also offers an opportunity to contemplate how a richly-networked area with existing intellectual infrastructure can morph into an even more developed context for language revitalization, language documentation, and training, facilitating for the many parties involved the development of new strengths and the improvement of existing skills. This type of long-term capacity building, where no one person is the cornerstone, but rather, training is the cornerstone, offers a model of potentially sustainable language revitalization at a grassroots level and in academic-tribal collaborations, and in creating experts who are both community and academic.

Turning to how this chapter is organized, I start with a brief background on Oklahoma and the larger southeastern United States, and then turn to a quick summary of the beginning of three decades of a renaissance of language documentation and revitalization in Oklahoma. I then talk about recent and ongoing collaborative language documentation and revitalization projects where I have been involved. Going from specifics to generalizable, I present a model of the key elements of sustainable language documentation and revitalization projects before concluding the paper.

2 Oklahoma languages

Oklahoma and the greater American southeast serve as an example of a language area created by and showing the effects of forced removal. In the early 19th Century, expansion by Euro-Americans into the south and westward had major implications for indigenous populations in those regions. The most significant implication came through federal policy. The Indian Removal Act of 1830 serves as a tragic legacy from Andrew Jackson's presidency, as the federal law removing Native Americans from their homelands to the west of the Mississippi River. The forced removal (Trail of Tears) moved Southeast tribes into what was then called Indian Territory, but is now the state of Oklahoma, disrupting these Indian nations from their aboriginal homelands. As a result, affected tribes, the Cherokee, Choctaw, Chickasaw, Seminole and Muscogee, have one or more eastern and western bands because not everyone went on this march to Indian Territory. Due to this and a host of other forced marches to Indian Territory, the state of Oklahoma is now home to 39 federally or state recognized tribes, most of which represent communities where related bands have also been able to remain in their indigenous homelands. Another consequence is the interaction in revitalization projects and training between communities representing languages from different families.

To understand the Oklahoma linguistic context, the essential background actually requires looking at collaborative work in Arizona that preceded it and laid the foundation for subsequent approaches to documentation and revitalization in Oklahoma. The model for Oklahoma was in large part developed first in Arizona, as linguist Akira Yamamoto partnered with the Hualapai tribe. Yamamoto was active in both places (but in Arizona first) and transferred some approaches from Arizona to Oklahoma. From 1973–1975 in Arizona, Yamamoto was part of a Hualapai language-education collaboration developed with tribal members Jane Honga and Lucille Watahomigie. As the Hualapai created a bilingual education program, the need for a regional resource for the community to create credentialed bilingual teachers became clear. Watahomigie, who was the sole certified teacher, became the program's director. In 1978, the inaugural Yuman Language

Institute made its debut. In the years that followed, the institute grew to include members of other languages and eventually became the American Indian Language Development Institute (AILDI), now housed at the University of Arizona. The Hualapai academic-tribal partnership lays out the principles underlying their efforts:

> What the Hualapai program encourages is COLLABORATIVE research. This entails that no one person does the work for any other person or group; rather, members of a collaborative team do the work with other team members. In the domain of research, the principles of the collaborative model go beyond any specific research project. The goal of collaborative research is not only to engage in a team project but also, and perhaps more importantly, to provide opportunities for local people to become researchers themselves. As Watahomigie and Yamamoto state (1987: 79), "It is vitally important that anthropologists and anthropological linguists undertake the responsibility of training native researchers and work with them to develop collaborative language and cultural revitalization and/or maintenance programs." Watahomigie and Yamamoto (1992: 12)

The training-oriented, collaborative, community-based research model made its way to Oklahoma, where communities approached Yamamoto, who was on the faculty at the University of Kansas in Lawrence. Tribal interest in Akira Yamamoto's collaborative work in Arizona was initiated by first the Euchee language community, and later the Loyal Shawnee tribe (Linn et al. 1998). These early efforts began a tradition of partnering with Oklahoma tribes and successfully connecting graduate students with indigenous language communities. In addition, the interest led to the creation in 1992 of Oklahoma Native American Language Development Institute (ONALDI), as an intensive language institute patterned after Yamamoto's experiences with AILDI, with the same kinds of goals: training bilingual teachers, developing pedagogical materials and increasing linguistic knowledge of the indigenous languages. ONALDI morphed into a new organization in 1996, the Oklahoma Native Language Association (ONLA), a grassroots organization led by community members. ONLA structured training workshops with a shorter duration in answer to what community members desired, since shorter workshops are more manageable with people's schedules and other demands.

ONLA holds annual workshops[1] offering training and support for indigenous language teachers and advocates and has served as the cornerstone of regional language work, bringing together language teachers and learners,

---

[1] The annual October meetings have lost some momentum since government shutdown in 2013, when the absence of travel funds meant many tribes were unable to travel and the ONLA meeting was cancelled.

policy makers, academics and more. Over the course of the following decade, there was a renaissance of Oklahoma indigenous languages, driven in large part by indigenous community members, but also drawing on strong collaborations with and contributions by academic partners such as Akira Yamamoto, and his graduate students: Mary Linn, Marcellino Berardo, Lizette Peter, Tracy Hirata-Edds, and Brad Montgomery-Anderson. Included in this renaissance are the emergence or growth in individual tribal language programs, and the beginning of a Native American Languages collection in 2002 at the University of Oklahoma (via Sam Noble Museum), with Mary Linn brought on as the founding curator for this community-based language archive (Linn 2014). Another important development was several faculty hires in Oklahoma as Linn, Berardo and Montgomery-Anderson all held faculty positions in Oklahoma during the first part of the decade.

Soon after the establishment of OU's Native American Languages Collection, some of the most current comprehensive statistics for Oklahoma languages were collected by Linn (2004), Table 1[2] below. As might be expected, the linguistic situation is much starker now in 2016. The numbers of speakers in 2004 show how dramatically threatened these languages were, with 16 of the languages at that time having no fluent first language speakers within the state. Linn et al. (2002) notes that of Oklahoma languages, only Kickapoo (at that time) was being learned by children in the home, giving an early sense of the negative trajectory of these speaker numbers.

Considering the current vitality of Oklahoma languages in 2016, a few languages are "robust" (as far as Native American languages go), and those would currently be Cherokee, Choctaw, Kickapoo and Creek (Seminole/Mvskoke). Kickapoo likely has the youngest speakers. Roughly half of Oklahoma's languages are sleeping languages, some recently so, others at least a generation back, and the remaining languages are fragile or very fragile in terms of having only elderly speakers and speakers in very, very small numbers.

---

[2] Some additional clarification or comments for this chart: Pawnee includes South Band and Skiri dialects, and Wichita is including Wichita, Keechi, Waco and Tawakonie dialects/languages; those with speakers of the language in other states include Arapaho, Cheyenne, Potawatomi, Fox (Meskwaki), Cherokee, Seneca-Cayuga, Ponca, Choctaw and Seminole. Seneca-Cayuga, Sac and Fox, and Alabama-Quassarte represent linguistically distinct, but federally consolidated tribes or bands. Natchez and Euchee are not federally recognized, but are linguistically distinct entities; both are linguistic isolates. Finally, federally recognized tribal towns are grouped under Creek if historically, Creek or related dialects were spoken there.

3 Oklahoma language reclamation and revitalization in the new millennium

The Native American Languages Lab (NALL) focuses on indigenous languages currently located in the Southwest United States, with an eye to serving communities and their language needs, including onsite technology or linguistic training, database construction and development, and support for grant development. We play a role in supporting training and related teaching and service activity, and involving students in community-based language research projects.

Table 1: Total population c. 1993 and number of speakers for Oklahoma languages (Linn 2004)

Languages by Family	# Speakers	Languages by Family	# Speakers
Algonquian		**Kiowa-Tanoan**	
Absentee Shawnee (2,000)	200	Kiowa (9,050 in 1986)	300
Arapaho (3,000)	100	**Muskogean**	
Cheyenne (4,762)	100	Choctaw	4,000
Citizen Band Potawatomi (18,000)	n/a	Chickasaw	1,000
		Creek	6,000
Delaware (Lenape)	0	Seminole	(w/Creek)
Eastern Shawnee (1,550)	0 (?)	Alabama-Quassarte (800)	0
Kickapoo (1,800)	1,500	Hitchiti (?)	0
Loyal Shawnee (8,000)	14	**Natchez**	
Miami (6,000)	0	Natchez	0
Ottawa (367)	0	**Penutian**	
Peoria (2,000)	0	Modoc (200 in early 1990s)	0
Sac and Fox (2,200)	20	**Siouan**	
Athapaskan		Iowa (366)	0
Plains Apache (924)	3	Kaw (1,678)	0
Fort Sill Apache (103)	0(?)	Osage (11,000)	5
Caddoan		Otoe-Missouria (1,550)	1(?)
Caddo (3,371)	25	Ponca (2,360)	24
Pawnee (2,500)	7	Quapaw (1,927)	0
Wichita (1,764)	0–5	**Tonkawan**	
Iroquoian		Tonkawa (186)	0
Cherokee (122,000)	9,000	**Uto-Aztecan**	
Keetoowah Band Cherokee (7,450)	(w/Cherokee)	Comanche (8,500)	100
Wyandotte (3,617)	0	**Uchean**	
Seneca-Cayuga (2,460)	0	Euchee (Yuchi) (2,500)	10

Service-learning (Bringle and Hatcher 1995; Fitzgerald 2007a, 2009, 2010) helps to meet community language needs and to give students valuable experiences acquiring and using skills in putting their theoretical and technical skills to practice in a meaningful way. Through the NALL, I lead and organize (and co-lead and co-organize) language workshops primarily in Oklahoma and Texas. This ranges from the creation of specific trainings upon request for a language program, support of grant applications, or other collaborations with partners in tribes and universities, bringing the energy and efforts of my students as a resource for these efforts. NALL activities also include advocacy, outreach, and public engagement in support of Native American languages and communities. With help from my partners in tribes and at other universities, we mentor and train students in both the linguistic side of the work and in how to work with communities. This work is done in conjunction with many collaborators at both tribes and universities, and I will draw from two primary examples to show how, in the context of community-based language research, there is considerable range in how that is realized with the community collaborations and roles surfacing in different, sometimes more diffuse ways, such as in planning, determining themes, and so on.

Here I turn to a period of time where I have been involved in the region in a variety of ways, covering six years from 2009 to 2015. These years include several major grant-funded workshops with a focus on training in language documentation and revitalization, the Oklahoma Breath of Life Workshop (abbreviated OKBOL) and CoLang 2014 (cf. CoLang website). In addition, I started a new revitalization-driven collaboration with the Chickasaw Language Revitalization Program. Because some of these projects are covered in more detail elsewhere (Fitzgerald and Linn 2013; Fitzgerald and Hinson 2013, 2015, and 2016), I focus on two other examples, the first is our "talking dictionary" workshops, and the second is the Cherokee-UT Arlington sustainability project, both projects where I have been a key agent in the activities, where service-learning has provided the conceptual underpinnings for involving my students, and where established workshops or recurring venues have been productive in fostering projects.

3.1 Dictionary software as a tool for relationship-building

A great example of how these different components intersect comes from examining the different roles played by training in Fieldworks Language Explorer (FLEx), a software tool which integrates lexicography and interlinearization of texts.[3]

---

[3] Special thanks to the following for all their work on UTA FLEx projects: Nathan Eversole, Joshua Jensen, and Vitaly Voinov.

FLEx became the cornerstone of a collaborative National Science Foundation grant submission for the 2012 Oklahoma Breath of Life Workshop, which Mary Linn and I co-directed. Part of the innovations we introduced was using databasing both as a method to teach linguistics and to generate new linguistic research on a given language. The UT Arlington team bore primary responsibility for the FLEx component of OKBOL. Between 2010 and 2014, UT Arlington conducted FLEx trainings at 17 different workshops or workshop venues in 4 different states. This includes the 2012 and 2014 Oklahoma Breath of Life Workshops (OKBOL) and the 2014 Institute on Collaborative Language Research (CoLang 2014). For the most part, the participants in these workshops were indigenous community members, many involved in their own community's language program. We frequently billed these as "Talking Dictionary Workshops" and integrated training on how to add audio or photographs, how to use semantic fields to categorize vocabulary for lesson plans, and what exported forms as PDFs or as webpages look like for FLEx projects. How were we able to generate such interest and such capacity for doing this? And what were the more intangible results from this approach?

The key to having the capacity to do this much training revolves around five elements. First, there needed to be a core group of ready students who knew how to use FLEx on at least a basic level. In addition to doing some open training workshops, I also integrated it as a required tool in our graduate field methods sequence. Second, the UTA team created pre-made language-specific "starter kits," which included creating individualized FLEx shells for as many of the Oklahoma languages as might be represented at the 2012 workshop. The idea behind this was that the hardest part of using FLEx might well be to start a project, so if our team started the project for each of the attending languages, participants could focus their energies on learning the software, learning the linguistics, and learning the structure of their language. Over the course of the OKBOL grant, the UTA team created shells for 30 languages total (26 Oklahoma languages plus 4 other Native American languages).

A third important element was that we piloted training repeatedly to test accessibility and clarity and to determine how best to support participants. In 2011, an early training in preparation for the OKBOL workshop focused on Chickasaw, Choctaw and Sauk language program participants learning FLEx. Software installation took over a large portion of the start of the session. One participant asked for screen shots of what we were doing because taking notes was not effective, both because of the participant being a visual learner, but also because screenshots show what is going on in a way that words cannot, especially for software training. From this, we moved from preparing software installation instructions onsite to doing much of that preparation prior to a workshop and eventually, to creating a mobile laptop lab where everything was pre-installed.

The other major development was the creation of a FLEx handbook with screenshots, an index and reader-friendly instructions, as well as contact information for our UTA team for follow up questions.

Fourth, we made sure to have floaters, people with some knowledge of the software who roamed the room and answered individual questions. Software training is most effective when people have a computer where they can use the software as it is being taught, and it is least effective when participants have individual questions that slow down the training. In teaching FLEx, many times the questions were straightforward and often related to navigation issues. This also promoted a collaborative approach. Although one person leads the training, floaters help with pacing since they see when multiple people are struggling or when the instructor is moving too fast. As people chime in with some direction or guidance to the instructor, it becomes clear that this is support, that everyone is trying to help out, and that all roles are useful in the endeavor. Fifth, wherever possible, students led the training, which had numerous benefits. Students learned to teach community members by doing it, usually with a smaller audience. Community members became familiar with students. This created relationships that could be further built on in future workshops.

In considering the more intangible results, the workshops were something that people were interested in and we benefitted from doing them as much as the participants appreciated attending. A great example of how these elements intertwined to build relationships comes in our relationship with the Choctaw Language Program in Oklahoma. For the academic year starting fall 2011, I was slated to co-teach a one-year sequence in field methods. I hoped to work with Choctaw speakers and reached out to their language program, went up and visited, and we talked about parameters and what our class might do to give back as a thank you. I asked the language program if they would suggest speakers in the Dallas area. This created an opportunity to start a relationship with the Choctaw program, and they sent two attendees to a FLEx training a few months later in December 2011. After the academic year wrapped up, they requested an onsite training as part of the Choctaw teacher in-service days prior to their school year starting, which we did in Durant in August 2012. One of our field methods graduate students, Lori McLain Pierce, was interested in continuing to work with Choctaw, and we were able to work with the language program to get her set up and to shepherd her through the Choctaw Nation's IRB process for her approval to do research. To facilitate Lori being better known with the Choctaw teachers who hold community classes, we did a FLEx training at the ONLA meeting in October 2012, which gave people a face to go with a name. And about a year later, our Cherokee language consultant for the field methods class that started in the fall 2013 semester came from David Ludlow, one of the Choctaw language consultants, reaching out to his contacts at the Urban Inter-Tribal Center. Mr. Ludlow is well-known and respected among the Dallas-Fort Worth community members, and that has opened up opportunities for doing language-related events for the local Native American community.

The FLEx workshops also built relationships across different academic institutions. Other contributors to these workshops included Mary Linn and several generations of grad students from the University of Oklahoma, Brad Montgomery-Anderson at Northeastern State University, and Jack Martin at the College of William and Mary, and institutional hosts for different sessions included ONLA, the American Indian Language Development Institute (AILDI) at the University of Arizona, Choctaw Language Program and the Chickasaw Language Revitalization Program.

3.2 The Cherokee-UTA collaboration

While the previous example focused on how we used one tool, FLEx software, as a way of facilitating training and fostering relationships, this example focuses on how we have drawn on existing relationships to strengthen them and to develop new partnerships. Northeastern State University, in the heart of Cherokee country, hosts an annual Symposium on the American Indian where ONLA and Akira Yamamoto regularly hosted an indigenous language documentation and revitalization seminar. As I became involved in this annual event, I became familiar to many of the Cherokee language program staff and instructors in Tahlequah, such as Durbin Feeling, Ed Fields as well as the newer generation of NSU and other Cherokee instructors like Ryan Mackey and Wyman Kirk.

UT Arlington's field methods courses have meshed well by coordinating with tribal language programs and by drawing on the general concepts of service-learning and giving back to the community. Building on earlier success partnering with the Choctaw language program, I reached out to the Cherokee Language Program's then-manager, Candessa Tehee about whether there might be interest in doing something like that with their program for the field methods sequence scheduled to start in fall 2013. I was also able to secure a small internal Faculty Fellowship on Sustainability in the Curriculum from UT Arlington on "Traditional Ecological Knowledge, Sustainability and Indigenous Language Documentation." The Cherokee Nation's Department of Natural Resources has been active as environmental stewards and in preserving traditional and ecological knowledge in the community in various ways, such as basket making exhibits at the Cherokee Heritage Center, the dissemination of heirloom seeds through

CN's Seed Bank, and the publication of Cherokee-language books (and their English translations) on traditional plants and their uses.

Field methods courses typically include the elicitation of grammatical information, more recent language documentation projects seek to include cultural and other traditional knowledge, including Traditional Ecological Knowledge (TEK). Documenting biological knowledge is underutilized in linguistic fieldwork, but recent attention has highlighted the importance of training in this area. This knowledge reflects how indigenous cultures interact with their ecosystems, as well as being a vital part of daily life and ritual referenced in various speech genres (song, autobiography, folk tales, proverbs, etc.). In addition, with the rapid climate change occurring worldwide, there is an urgency in documenting TEK while this is possible (see Velásquez Runk and Carpio Opua this volume for discussion of documentation along these lines).

Adding a unit on "Traditional Ecological Knowledge, Sustainability and Indigenous Language Documentation" to the field methods course facilitated a collaboration with the indigenous language experts of the Cherokee Nation, and with experts at the nearby Botanical Research Institute of Texas. The creation of this curriculum unit served several functions, including training budding linguists how to document language and indigenous knowledge, contributing a service project (the video documentation) and fostering ties between UT Arlington, the Cherokee Language Program and BRIT. The final goal was to create a set of videos documenting Cherokee language and ecological knowledge, with subtitles in both Cherokee and English.

While the field methods course kicked off in fall 2013, we were unable to go to Tahlequah until April 2014, when we filmed speakers and began our initial local contacts through the new manager of the Cherokee Language Program, Roy Boney, Jr. The timing of this was too close to the end of the semester for much more to be done than the filming, but over the next year, we were able to process the videos and deepen the relationships between UT Arlington, Cherokee Nation and BRIT thanks in large part to strong interest by two students, Samantha Cornelius and Vicki Caña, and strong working relationships with David Crawler and John Ross from the Cherokee language program. Thanks to the Sustainability funds, and the need to work on the transcription and translation of the videos, the UT Arlington team made an additional visit to Tahlequah and the Cherokee team made two trips to visit us at UT Arlington, Language Work in Tahlequah. During CoLang 2014 (the intervening summer), Roy Boney and Candessa Tehee taught a workshop on "Using Technology for Language Documentation and Revitalization in Digital Domains," where they shared the Cherokee Nation's activities with a wider national and international audience.

During the summer and into the fall, several undergraduate research assistants worked on inputting the transcriptions and translations into ELAN. Samantha and Vicki each continued working on this and other Cherokee projects during the following year in coursework, and each was able to secure local departmental research grants to assist with that work. We also gave a collaborative presentation on the project in Hawai'i with both teams (Fitzgerald et al. 2015) at the conference.

By integrating coursework and community in this way, the field methods course has fostered student interest in Native American languages and it has provided a model for how to collaborate respectfully with Native communities. The video project itself ended up being much more labor intensive than originally envisioned, and the videos are in the final stages of processing. University students provided the labor on this project, but the videos will be disseminated by the Cherokee language program, probably through the Cherokee Nation's YouTube channel. While containing traditional knowledge, the videos also have usefulness as pronunciation tools and are being used as part of an investigation into prosody by Samantha, who has since decided to work on Cherokee for her dissertation project. This development has been received with considerable excitement by the Cherokee Language program staff, who have a good relationship with Samantha and are interested in her work because it will lead to a better understanding of Cherokee phonology and pronunciation, which could be utilized in language revitalization.

Samantha's familiarity with Cherokee was a key factor in selecting her as a mentor for Richard Zane Smith at the 2014 Oklahoma Breath of Life. In that workshop, three people attended for the Wyandot language, two who were having their first experience with the language, and the third, Richard, who had a more advanced level of exposure, having been involved in learning his language and teaching it for quite some time. Wyandot, also known as Huron (cf. Mithun 1985) is a Northern Iroquoian language which had fluent first language speakers up until the early 1960s in Oklahoma (Kopris 2001). The language has excellent text documentation collected in 1910–11 (cf. Barbeau 1960). Samantha served as the linguistic partner for Richard in the level two (more advanced) track of the 2014 Oklahoma Breath of Life, thus drawing on what she had learned about the Cherokee language, as well as how the Cherokee speakers trained her to work with Native language community members.

This approach to field methods integrates students like Samantha into productive and respectful collaborations that have long-term viability for sustaining language activity in the region. Participation in the existing grassroots revitalization workshops in Tahlequah at the local university made me a familiar face to the Cherokee program. The participation of Cherokee presenters at CoLang and at the documentation conference highlights what they are doing and brings new voices to larger venues. A focus on products like videos in the language creates a multi-use item that supports community goals on revitalization and preservation of traditional knowledge and provides authentic materials for the linguistic analysis of Cherokee connected speech. The willingness of communities to collaborate strengthens the region as a whole by contributing to examples of productive collaborations and to the training of our students. The willingness of students to be part of revitalization workshops or field methods courses means that the students are also integral to the endeavors, and that they benefit from learning how to do this work, while down the line, other communities benefit from the efforts of these students and community members as the skills are deployed to other workshops or revitalization and documentation projects.

4 Sustainable models of endangered language research

With its roots in forced removal and Indian wars, Oklahoma's borders contain a dramatic number of tribes and distinct languages and even language families, and as Table 1 showed, a fragility in terms of speakers. Strong tribal grassroots desires to support Native languages fostered early collaborations with academics like Akira Yamamoto and his students. As one generation retires and new generations emerge, the region's many languages and language programs stay active in language revitalization and continue different kinds of collaborations and partnerships with academics in the region.

From this case study, with its focus on more recent activity, we see that language documentation and revitalization activities here are characterized by training playing a fundamental role. In fact, positive relationships between tribal language activists and teachers with linguist-academics is one of the elements which has made the Oklahoma language research model sustainable; the relationships and the experiences and skills of all the people involved constitute a renewable resource. But more than that, there are interwoven, mutually supportive relationships between those of us involved in the region, and these relationships are dynamic, changing, and complex.

The dynamic relationships that characterize the community-based language work in Oklahoma in the last few decades are not unidirectional relationships, centered on linguists (academics) training community members. Rather, these are mutually enriching relationships where the "community" is recognized as trainers as much as the "academics," along the lines of Fitzgerald and Hinson (2013).

Both groups are involved in training and mentoring students and language learners, regardless of institutional affiliation. The networks of these relationships are multilayered and mutually reinforcing, which provides sustainability in language revitalization and documentation activities over the long-haul, and shows how effective and sustainable models critically blur the distinction between revitalization and documentation. By necessity, I would argue, language documentation in Native American communities of the U.S. (and Canada) cannot be separated from language revitalization. Integrating both components into materials creation for indigenous language classes, such as documenting traditional knowledge, as in our Cherokee project, where language analysis can also be done – these multi-use approaches mean that documentation is at its best when it is easily mobilized for revitalization purposes. Further, in our region, the emerging leaders in language programs are doing graduate work in linguistics and revitalization, like Joshua Hinson whose doctorate is in progress, or completing doctorates, like Candessa Tehee. This creates a further blurring of roles because the categories of community member and academic are not as distinct for this generation of indigenous scholars.

Stepping back, it is possible to examine some of the shared properties of successful and sustainable models of endangered language research. AILDI, started in Arizona as grassroots linguistic training for Yuman languages, has been one such enduring model. AILDI can be characterized in terms of three key macro properties: community situated, collaborative and action-oriented. These are characteristics that define community-based research, and I would argue they are essential for sustainable models of community-based endangered language research.

In Table 2, I outline what I would argue are the key and essential properties that underlie sustainable models of community-based language research, drawing from our Oklahoma efforts and projects. Most are extracted directly from the projects in Section 3 above, but six of the properties were not directly addressed: leadership development, portable skills (i.e., not bound to language work), activism, outreach, recognition that language is more than language, and institutional stability.

These properties are more abstract and in fact, not directly taught or trained. Leadership development, I would argue, is an outgrowth of the long-term activity in the region. At some point, people retire or pass on, and for activities to continue, someone must pick up their responsibilities and keep them going. In the region, there are also many opportunities to bring language to the public, whether by the Texas premiere of the Navajo version of *Star Wars*, or by the developing signage in indigenous languages, or by sharing on social media for Native language fairs and contests.

Table 2: Essential properties of sustainable models of community-based language research

Space where indigenous expertise and knowledge is valued
Respect for expertise in all its forms
Intellectual resources (including but not limited to linguists)
Knowledge transfer
Intergenerational interactions
Fostering collaborations of all types
Productivity (product creation and dissemination)
Reciprocity
Indigenous drive (grassroots energy, communities taking charge of their own language)
Multivalent, reciprocal and multilayered mentoring networks
Democratizing training
Learning outside the classroom
Service learning/ethical underpinnings
Commitment to grassroots and (international) sharing expertise
Leadership development
Portable skills that are not bound to language work
Activism
Outreach
Recognition that language is more than language (either implicit or explicit)
Institutional stability

These are not language-specific characteristics, and because they are transferrable into other activities, I would argue they help in the sustainability of language research by enabling participants from all backgrounds to develop in ways that are valuable in other disciplines and workplaces. Language work is sustained when there is always a person willing to take it on, to support a learner or a teacher from another community, or to host a workshop. Skills independent of language have value in many domains, whether that skill be issue advocacy, grant-writing, technology, working with elders, or building ethical and respectful collaborations.

Not all language revitalization contexts are scalable, an important point to keep in mind, especially as communities seek to set goals for their language programs. For example, the well-known Hawaiian and Māori examples serve as incredible revival stories to communities seeking to energize their indigenous languages. However, implementing these revival models would be challenging in the context of a place like Oklahoma, where so many languages and communities co-exist. Extrapolating from these kinds of language revitalization contexts, as I have done in this chapter, offers another perspective on how to create a sustainable, scalable community-based language research for language documentation and revitalization.

References

Barbeau, C. Marius. 1960. Huron-Wyandot traditional narratives. Translations and Native texts. *National Museum of Canada Bulletin 165*. Ottawa.
Bringle, Robert B., and Julie A. Hatcher. 1995. A service learning curriculum for faculty. Michigan Journal of Community Service Learning, 2.112–122.
CoLang 2014 website http://www.uta.edu/faculty/cmfitz/swnal/projects/CoLang/ (Retrieved February 5, 2016)
Dobrin, Lise. M. 2008. From linguistic elicitation to eliciting the linguist: Lessons in community empowerment from Melanesia. *Language* 84 (2). 300–324.
Fitzgerald, Colleen M. 2007a. Indigenous languages and Spanish in the U.S.: How can/do linguists serve communities? *Southwest Journal of Linguistics* 26. 1–14.
Fitzgerald, Colleen M. 2007b. Developing language partnerships with the Tohono O'odham Nation. Working together for endangered languages: Research challenges and social Impacts. Maya Khemlani David, Nicholas Ostler, and Caesar Dealwis (eds), *FEL Proceedings XI*, 39–46. Bath, England: The Foundation for Endangered Languages.
Fitzgerald, Colleen. 2009. Language and community: Using service-learning to reconfigure the multicultural classroom. *Language and Education* 23 (3). 217–231.
Fitzgerald, Colleen. 2010. Developing a service-learning curriculum for linguistics. *Language and Linguistics Compass* 4 (4). 204–218.
Fitzgerald, Colleen M. and Joshua D. Hinson. 2013. 'Ilittibatoksali 'We work together': Perspectives on our Chickasaw tribal-academic collaboration. In Mary Jane Norris, Erik Anonby, Marie-Odile Junker, Nicholas Ostler and Donna Patrick (eds.), *FEL Proceedings XVII (Ottawa, 2013) FEL XVII: Endangered Languages Beyond Boundaries: Community Connections, Collaborative Approaches, and Cross-Disciplinary Research*, 53–60. Bath, England: The Foundation for Endangered Languages.
Fitzgerald, Colleen and Joshua Hinson. 2015. Using listening workshops to integrate phonology into language revitalization: Learner training in Chickasaw pronunciation. Paper presented at the *4th International Conference on Language Documentation and Conservation*, University of Hawai'i, Honolulu, Hawai'i, 26 February–1 March 2015.
Fitzgerald, Colleen M. and Joshua D. Hinson. 2016. Collecting texts in endangered languages: The Chickasaw narrative bootcamp. *Language Documentation and Conservation* 10. 528-548. http://hdl.handle.net/10125/24717 (accessed 20 May 2017)
Fitzgerald, Colleen M. and Mary S. Linn. 2013. Training communities, training graduate students: The 2012 Oklahoma Breath of Life Workshop. *Language Documentation and Conservation*. 7. 252-73. http://hdl.handle.net/10125/4596 (accessed 1 May 2017)
Fitzgerald, Colleen M., Roy Boney, Jr., Samantha Cornelius, Vicki Caña, David Crawler and John Ross. 2015. Designing pedagogy from Cherokee language and ecological documentation. Paper presented at the *4th International Conference on Language Documentation and Conservation*, University of Hawai'i, Honolulu, Hawai'I, 26 February–1 March 2015. http://hdl.handle.net/10125/25347 (accessed 5 April 2016)
Genetti, Carol and Rebecca Siemens. 2013. Training as empowering social action: An ethical response to language endangerment. In Elena Mihas, Bernard Perley, Gabriel Rei-Doval and Kathleen Wheatley (eds.), *Responses to language endangerment. In honor of Mickey Noonan. New directions in language documentation and language revitalization*, 59–77. Amsterdam: John Benjamins.

Hale, Kenneth L., Colette Craig, Nora England, Laverne Masayesva Jeanne, Michael Krauss, Lucille Watahomigie, and Akira Yamamoto. 1992. Endangered languages. *Language* 68 (1). 1–42.

Jukes, Anthony. 2011. Researcher training and capacity development in language documentation. In Peter K. Austin and Julia Sallabank (eds.), *The Cambridge handbook of endangered languages*, 423–446. Cambridge: Cambridge University Press.

Kopris, Craig. 2001. *A grammar and dictionary of Wyandot*. Buffalo, NY: SUNY dissertation.

Linn, Mary. 2004. Oklahoma's Native Languages. Ms., Sam Noble Museum of Oklahoma Museum, University of Oklahoma. http://samnoblemuseum.ou.edu/wp-content/uploads/2014/12/ok-spkrs-w-notes.pdf (Retrieved October 10, 2011)

Linn, Mary S. 2014. Living archives: A community-based language archive model. In *Language Documentation and Description, Special Issue on Language Documentation and Archiving*, 12. 53–67. http://www.elpublishing.org/PID/137 (Retrieved February 6, 2016)

Linn, Mary, Marcellino Berardo, and Akira Y. Yamamoto. 1998. Creating language teams in Oklahoma Native American communities. *International Journal of the Sociology of Language*, 132 (1). 61–78.

Linn, Mary S., Tessie Naranjo, Sheilah Nicholas, Inee Slaughter, Akira Yamamoto, and Ofelia Zepeda. 2002. Awakening the languages. Challenges of enduring language programs: Field reports from 15 programs from Arizona, New Mexico and Oklahoma. In Barbara Burnaby and Jon Reyhner (eds.), *Proceedings of the Annual Conference on Stabilizing Indigenous Languages (7th, Toronto, Ontario, Canada, May 11–14, 2000)*, 105–126. Flagstaff, AZ: Northern Arizona University.

McCarty, Teresa, Lucille J. Watahomigie, Akira Y. Yamamoto, and Ofelia Zepeda. 2001. Indigenous educators as change agents: Case studies of two language institutes. In Leanne Hinton and Ken Hale (eds.), *The green book of language revitalization in practice*, 371–383. Boston: Brill.

Mithun, Marianne. 1985. Untangling the Huron and the Iroquois. *International Journal of American Linguistics* 51 (4). 504–507.

Watahomigie, Lucille J. and Akira Yamamoto. 1987. Linguistics in action: The Hualapai bilingual/bicultural education program. In Donald D. Stull and Jean J. Schensul (eds.), *Collaborative research and social change: Applied anthropology in action*, 77–98. Boulder, CO: Westview Press.

Watahomigie, Lucille. J. and Akira Y. Yamamoto. 1992. Local reactions to language decline. *Language*, 68 (1). 10–17.

Gabriela Pérez Báez
Slowly, slowly said the jaguar: Collaborations as a goal of linguistic field research over time

Abstract: Linguistic research has become increasingly collaborative (Benedicto et al. 2007; Czaykowska-Higgins 2009; Rice 2006 and 2011; Grenoble and Furbee (eds.) 2010; *inter alia*). However, collaborations have become almost a condition for research endeavors (cf. Dwyer 2010 which considers that non-collaborative linguistic research is unethical). This chapter is motivated by what the author sees as insufficient discussion about the process involved in building a collaboration, the time that such a process might take, and the factors that might enable it, including time. This process is illustrated through a case study of the author's interaction with speakers of Isthmus Zapotec (Otomanguean) from La Ventosa, Oaxaca, Mexico. In this case, the collaboration was only possible when (a) the author had sufficient knowledge about the language to be able to earn the respect and acceptance of highly knowledgeable community members of social prominence, and about the sociolinguistic landscape to be able to identify viable opportunities for collaboration, (b) a critical number of community members became committed to the collaboration and (c) the author was in a position to secure the necessary funding to respond to the collaborators' expectations in the long-term. In this case, the linguistic research began as linguist-focused research (Czaykowska-Higgins 2009) and evolved into a collaborative-based research over a period of more than ten years. The intention of this chapter is to advocate for allowing researchers the time that collaborations need to crystalize and to consider collaborations as a goal of linguistic research rather than a condition for it.

Keywords: language documentation, collaborative research, endangered languages, Zapotec languages, research ethics

1 Introduction

Language documentation has become increasingly collaborative over the last decade. Some works, however, present collaborations almost as a condition for field research. This paper is motivated by what I consider to be insufficient

Gabriela Pérez Báez, Department of Anthropology, National Museum of Natural History, MRC 112, Smithsonian Institution, 10th and Constitution Avenue NW, Washington, DC 20560, perezbaezg@si.edu

https://doi.org/10.1515/9783110527018-006

discussion about the conditions needed in order to develop collaborations of value to all involved. The focus is on whether a researcher might have sufficient knowledge about a language, has had the time to develop a strong enough rapport with members of the relevant community and assemble the necessary resources in order to effectively contribute towards a meaningful collaboration by the time s/he is to engage in one.

This paper begins with an analysis in Section 2 of some of the most influential works in the emerging subfield of community based-research (CBR) to extract the core messages dictating the principles by which linguistic research is to be conducted. In later sections, I contrast these principles with the experience acquired through my interaction with speakers of Diidxazá (Isthmus Zapotec, Otomanguean) from La Ventosa, Oaxaca, Mexico. In Section 3 I explain the origins of research into Diidxazá as linguist-focused and show its evolution towards CBR over a period of six years. Section 4 describes the conditions that were necessary for effective CBR to be possible. The case study is described in detail to explain in Section 5 that a forced collaboration in the early stages of the research would have been unlikely to yield results as favorable as those that have emerged over time. In fact, had an early – and forced – collaboration been dissatisfactory to the community members involved, future work on the Diidxazá language could have been at risk. As such, I advocate for allowing researchers the time to develop such collaborations and considering collaborations as a goal of linguistic research rather than a condition for it even if this process involves linguist-focused research in the early stages.

2 Rationale

Language documentation has become an important means for linguists to respond to the call for action issued in Hale et al. (1992) in support of the world's endangered linguistic diversity. As a result, there has been a need to develop best practices in terms of methods of documentation and as it pertains to the ethics that ought to guide linguists in their interaction with the speakers of the languages they intend to document. The resulting literature generally addresses ethical shortcomings in research termed linguist-led and linguist-focused (Czaykowska-Higgins 2009) and lone ranger linguistics (Dwyer 2010; see also Crippen and Robinson 2013 in support of this method and subsequent discussion in Bowern and Warner 2015 and Robinson and Crippen 2015) in which the researcher is considered to be the sole agent and beneficiary of the research.

The alternatives proposed in a now ample body of work (Cameron 1992; Benedicto, Dolores and McLean 2002; Benedicto et al. 2007; Crippen and Robinson 2013; Czaykowska-Higgins 2009; Dobrin 2008; Dwyer 2006; England 2002; Gerdts 1998; Grenoble and Furbee (eds.) 2010; Grinevald 1998; Hale 2001; Rice 2006 and 2011; Yamada 2007 *inter alia*), promote models of CBR that converge in a common goal: to foster linguistic field research that is driven equally by all parties involved and that benefits them all. These works often cite as the motivation for their proposals the realization that disparities exist in the ability of participants to determine the direction of the research. These disparities are often attributed to distinctions between community-internal and community-external linguists, academics and non-academics, and linguists and providers of language data. The imbalances in question are described as favoring the academically trained community-external linguist over most other participants, notably the speakers of the language in question.

Many of the proponents of CBR are contributors to this volume. As such, rather than summarizing the position of some of the aforementioned works, it will be more efficient to delve right into a particular issue that arises from the strong move to promote CBR: that CBR has come to be presented in certain works as a condition for research endeavors. Consider Dwyer (2010: 54) which states that "Lone ranger linguistics [is] considered of "marginal ethicality" " and Gerdts (2010: 191) which suggests that "The linguist will have to compromise long-range scholarly goals to meet the community's immediate needs." More to the point of this paper, there seems to be a discrepancy between the number of works that propose CBR in one form or another, and the attention given to a discussion about the conditions that are necessary in order for effective CBR to be possible. Without sufficient consideration of what CBR entails, and with linguist-led research discouraged to the point of questioning its ethicality, early stage research is compromised in a number of ways and so are the prospects of developing successful CBR-based projects.

The impetus to contribute this chapter to the volume comes from my own experience as a linguist working since 2003 to document and analyze aspects of Diidxazá. The research was linguist-led and linguist-focused at the outset. In fact, it remained so for several years, slowly morphing into CBR in 2012 and becoming what I would consider to be an effective CBR project only in 2014. In the section that follows I describe the various stages of my interaction with a group of speakers of Diidxazá and highlight the factors that enabled CBR. This case study shows that linguist-focused research is necessary and may very well be the only appropriate model of research under certain circumstances. It suggests that both the researcher and the members of a language community need time in order to become effective collaborators in the CBR sense.

3 A case study in the research and documentation of Diidxazá

Diidxazá is considered to be a Central Zapotec language (Kaufman 1993–2007 ms) belonging to the Zapotecan branch of the Otomanguean stock of Mesoamerican languages.[1] In most regions where Zapotec languages are spoken, closely related varieties exhibit significant dialectal differences which can hamper communication between geographically and genetically close varieties. Dialectal diversity throughout the Isthmus of Tehuantepec in the southern Mexican state of Oaxaca is mostly concentrated on features such as the phonological status of the back vowels [u] and [o] and tonal patterns which do not hamper communication. As such, it is considered that Diidxazá is spoken in 22 municipalities of the Isthmus of Tehuantepec (Marcial Cerqueda 2014 ms). Diidxazá is reportedly spoken by over 100,000 (INALI 2008) speakers, making it one of the indigenous languages with the largest community of speakers in Mexico. As Marcial Cerqueda (2014 ms) explains, however, there is a clear and rapid shift towards Spanish in the region. In the largest towns, Diidxazá has been minoritized with speakers of Diidxazá amounting to only 40% of the population in Juchitán de Zaragoza and 23% in Tehuantepec, formerly a center of the Isthmus Zapotec indigenous culture. Further, out of the 22 municipalities, only in Santa María Xadani are children learning the language as their L1. As such Diidxazá is considered to be undergoing a process of slow to accelerated shift (*extinción lenta, extinción acelerada* as per Marcial Cerqueda 2014 ms) and is categorized as vulnerable by the Catalogue of Endangered Languages.[2]

Diidxazá has been documented in one form or another for close to a century, with published works dating back to the mid-1950s. Notably, three vocabularies have been published on the language (Pickett 1959, 2007[3], Jimenez Girón 1979, and Jiménez Jiménez and Marcial Cerqueda 2000). However, no extensive, analytical and synthetic lexicographic work has been published on the language and yet, Diidxazá is of particular interest to diachronic studies of Zapotecan (Zapotec and Chatino) languages because it has preserved pre- and post-stress vowels, which have been lost in numerous other varieties of Zapotec. As such, the Project for the Documentation of the Languages of Mesoamerica (PDLMA) directed by Terrence Kaufman and John Justeson who were later joined by Roberto Zavala Maldonado

---

[1] Diidxazá is the self-designated denomination for the language which is also referred to in the literature as Isthmus Zapotec, Juchitán Zapotec and *Juchiteco*. The Instituto Nacional de Lenguas Indígenas lists the language under the name of *zapoteco de la planicie costera* (INALI 2008).
[2] http://www.endangeredlanguages.com/lang/1061 accessed on January 15, 2016.
[3] http://www.mexico.sil.org/resources/archives/35335 accessed on January 20, 2016.

took on the task of documenting the Diidxazá lexicon extensively along with similar documentation of numerous other Mesoamerican languages. Their objective was to rigorously document the lexicon in strategically selected languages to inform the reconstruction of proto-languages of various Mesoamerican families.

The documentation of the Diidxazá lexicon within the PDLMA was initiated by Terrence Kaufman who worked with a speaker from the community of La Ventosa, Javier López Cartas. Both worked together in 1995 and 1996 outside the community and within a research center set up in designated locations in the south of Mexico. Researchers and speakers of the languages being documented would gather together there for a number of weeks of intensive documentation work in the summer. The PDLMA expanded and held a similar research effort during most summers until 2010. During that time, the documentation of the Diidxazá lexicon was carried out by Marilyn Feke in 2000, and by me, from 2003 after my first year in a doctoral program in linguistics, and from then onwards. It is this research which is the focus of the following subsections.

3.1 Linguist-focused research

To make explicit what was suggested above, the research carried out under the auspices of the PDLMA was linguist-focused. The documentation was highly technical, with rigorous documentation of phonological, phonotactic and lexical features, as well as semantic, syntactic, morphological and semantic categorization, inflection, derivation and examples. Certainly, there was always the intention to publish the documentation in a manner that would reach the language communities and with this in mind, the documentation was trilingual with Spanish and English. However, the work was driven by a clear linguistic research agenda based on intensive work that required, for instance, that the speakers of the documented languages leave their communities (as did the researchers, of course) for several weeks at a time. The documentation could not capitalize on the many benefits that come with fieldwork based in the language community but the PDLMA was willing to forego this for the purposes of increasing efficiency in the documentation. More importantly, the research center approach allowed for researchers to exchange views on the analysis of the language and become familiarized with numerous other languages, both within their language family of interest and outside. Workshops were held once or twice a week for researchers to present analyses on any number of features of their languages of interest. As a result, over a period of up to nine weeks each summer for a total of at least three summers, researchers devoted their full attention to rigorous linguistic analysis thereby increasing their scholarly knowledge by leaps and bounds.

Between 2003 and 2010, I participated in five research seasons with the PDLMA, focused entirely on the documentation of the lexicon of Diidxazá. In 2003, I worked with Mr. Rosalino Gallegos Luis from the municipality of Santa María Xadani and in the following years I worked with Mrs. Rosaura López Cartas from the town of La Ventosa, the sister of Mr. López Cartas who had previously worked with Kaufman. During this time, the lexical database grew to include some 12,000 lexical entries – a rather large number of entries considering that Zapotec languages do not rely on lexicalization as much as other Mesoamerican languages. The Diidxazá lexical database included two modules with nouns, verbs and modifiers, and modules on plant and animal related terms, grammatical words, numerals, toponyms, sound symbolism, ethnomedicine and proper names and nicknames. All entries included rigorous stress marking, morpheme boundaries and the orthographic representation of tone – a unique feature being that lexical documentation of Zapotecan languages outside the PDLMA has generally omitted tone marking.

Now, there is one very important benefit that, as a researcher, I derived from working in this setting. The intensive PDLMA format allowed me to develop a great deal of knowledge about Diidxazá and related languages in a relatively short period of time. I developed an in-depth understanding of the tonal system and of the stress patterns that are entirely dependent on the lexical roots, and the inflectional and derivational processes in which they can participate. Of course, developing this knowledge was my duty as a linguist, but the quick process of acquisition of knowledge of Diidxazá and of related languages was critical as I began interacting with an increasing number of members of the Diidxazá-speaking community. My knowledge of the language has been at the core of my ability to engage in effective CBR as I explain in the following sections.

3.2 Emergence of a collaboration

The Diidxazá research within the PDLMA continued with Mrs. López Cartas in the summers of 2004, 2007, 2008 and 2010. In 2009, however, I found the opportunity to expand beyond the lexical documentation through the Spatial Language and Cognition in Mesoamerica (MesoSpace) project.[4] This research involved experimental tasks in addition to elicitation work, all to be carried out in La Ventosa itself. In this context, Mrs. López Cartas took on the role of research assistant during the three weeks of fieldwork involved. Mrs. Reyna López López, a young woman who had been trained by the PDLMA as a transcriber for a large survey

---

4 NSF Award No. BCS-0723694, PI Jürgen Bohnemeyer, University at Buffalo.

of Zapotecan (Zapotec and Chatino) languages, joined the research team as an expert transcriber. A young relative of hers also contributed to the project as a transcriber. The collaboration remained limited to research-driven tasks which were so specific as to make it difficult to identify applications for use of the data in the community. Bowern and Warner (2015) consider relationships of this kind – where the researcher hires community members as research assistants – to constitute a type of collaborative research. Based on my knowledge of and experience with Mexican societies (I was born and raised in Mexico), this was not a comfortable arrangement as it still implied a hierarchy based on one person having access to funds to pay community members. This, in my view, was not an arrangement where all involved were equals and I did not consider it CBR yet. However, the three weeks of field research in La Ventosa allowed for interaction with the broader community. In particular, it provided the opportunity for me to reveal to speakers the technical knowledge I had acquired by then about Diidxazá. And the relationship with Mrs. López Cartas and Mrs. López López grew stronger which was later crucial for the development of a more equal collaboration.

3.3 Increased participation

During the PDLMA's 2010 season, I worked on verification of entries, including 1000 plant-related entries of which over 300 were plant names. It became evident that while the phonology and other structural aspects of the lexicography were accurate, the plant descriptions were not adequate. Specifically, while the documentation was often rich in botanical and cultural details about the plants, it was not sufficient to ensure that the species corresponding to Diidxazá plant names could be accurately identified by a user of the lexical database. It was evident that an interdisciplinary documentation effort involving the collection of botanical specimens in addition to language and knowledge documentation would be the only way to ensure that the documentation would be comprehensive and accurate. I discussed this with Mrs. López Cartas and Mrs. López López and with their interest and support, I designed a pilot research project.[5]

The project was carried out in April 2012 over a period of 10 days of collection of herbarium samples and language and knowledge documentation in addition to preparation time. The nature of the project required significant interaction with the local authorities to ensure the issuance of a permit to collect botanical

---

5 Funded by an award from the Small Grants program of the Smithsonian's National Museum of Natural History, PI Gabriela Pérez Báez.

samples in the La Ventosa territory. It also required that I meet knowledge bearers and work with some of them as guides and providers of data. The collaboration with Mrs. López Cartas and Mrs. López López grew significantly. They were both critical in advising me as to how to navigate my interaction with the authorities. In addition, their roles as research assistants and transcribers grew in terms of the responsibilities they entailed and that my collaborators were interested and willing to take on. Further, the team grew to include two knowledge bearers, Mrs. Velma Orozco Trujillo who had been my hostess in 2009, and Mr. Fernando Sánchez López, as well as a young high school student assistant.

The project resulted in a collection of 104 herbarium samples and associated photographs and audio. By the end of the project, discussion began as to how to utilize the documentation for community benefit. The products of the documentation effort, and notably the photography, lent themselves to the production of printed materials. I was able to work with collaborators from La Ventosa and Juchitán de Zaragoza to figure out what kind of materials might make sense. At the same time, I was able to engage a multimedia design student, Lic. Mayra Fernández Jacinto from the Universidad Popular Autónoma del Estado de Puebla who happened to be of Northern Sierra Zapotec origin, to work with us on the design of the materials. The final selection of the type of materials to produce was a combination of input from community collaborators, Lic. Fernández Jacinto and myself. Lic. Fernández Jacinto then designed a suite of prototypes including a bingo-style game and a memory game as well as a prototype for a multimedia interface for an eventual large scale collection of ethnobotanical materials. I was able to show the proposals to my collaborators and Lic. Fernández Jacinto was able to carry out community consultations on site in La Ventosa leading to final designs. As these materials were being designed and produced, I began to work on the conceptualization of a full blown ethnobotany project which set the stage for the emergence of a project that could finally be considered to constitute CBR. I describe below the consultation process that defined this larger project.

4 The emergence of community-based research

In July 2013, I visited La Ventosa and presented to my collaborators the idea of a one-year ethnobotanical project. This coincided with the opening of a cultural center named Bacusa Gui that had just been built in La Ventosa. A member of the local government with whom I interacted during the pilot project informed me of the creation of the center and asked me to introduce myself to its directorial committee as he felt that my interest in and technical knowledge of Diidxazá could make a contribution to the center. The evolution of the ethnobotanical project as well as what ensued from the interaction with the cultural center were quite revealing about the factors that may have a bearing on the outcomes of CBR.

I followed up with the Comité Cultural María Chéu responsible for the Centro Cultural Bacusa Gui and set up a meeting for Haley de Korne, then a Smithsonian Fellow doing doctoral research on education in an endangered language setting in the Diidxazá-speaking region, and me to meet with the three members of the committee. In preparation for the meeting, Ms. de Korne and I discussed the approach we would take during the meeting and informally discussed some of the recommendations that are stated in the literature aimed at researchers looking to work at or with an endangered language community. The discussion centered around what I describe as the recommendation that the researcher ought to take a passive stance. Consider the following recommendation: "Linguists shouldn't march in. They really need to be able to be quiet, sit and listen and be able to gain the knowledge of the people, and understand them first." (Leonard and Haynes 2010: 287). My knowledge of Mexican societies and cultures and my experience interacting with La Ventosa members told me that this approach was not appropriate but we agreed to take it. As we began the meeting we stated that we were there to listen and learn. Sure enough, our interlocutors replied with some surprise that in fact, they were hoping for ideas and suggestions from us. It was clear to me at that point, that there was an expectation that as specialists in our particular disciplines, we ought to put forward our expertise in a proactive way. So we switched gears, I took on a leading role and was reassured that if my research was to make an impact beyond my academic interests, a proactive stance, leadership and direction on my part was not only appropriate but in fact expected of me.

In what follows, details on the evolution of the relationship with the center and its committee members will be interspersed as appropriate. In the meantime, let us return to the ethnobotanical research project. Adequate documentation of the flora of a particular locality requires botanical collection on a weekly basis over the course of a year. I proposed the creation of a 1-year project that would involve botanists who would provide training and supervision, and a photographer to ensure that the visual documentation would be of the highest quality. In addition, the team would involve a specialist in educational linguistics, Ms. de Korne. The community collaborators would be trained to carry out weekly plant collection and data input. The botanists would take turns to visit La Ventosa on a monthly basis. The photographer would also visit once a month to coincide with the botanists' visits. Since my travel involved costly international travel, I would manage the project from afar, joining the field research every three months on average and carrying out language and knowledge documentation. The project was accepted by the team and began in late September 2013.⁶ Following the opportunity for collaboration with the Comité Cultural María Chéu, it was decided that the team would work out of the Centro Cultural Bacusa Gui, openly and in view of anybody present in the center. That gave the project a great deal of visibility. Critically, children were attracted to the work and approached the team with eagerness to learn about the plants and their Diidxazá names. Light bulb moment! Children who mostly had only passive knowledge of Diidxazá were overly enthusiastic about language learning as a means to gain access to knowledge about plants and this in turn informed the team of the potential for revitalization that the ethnobotany project had. The trouble was that funding was available for the basic research only.

Fortunately, the bingo and memory games commissioned following the pilot project in 2012 were ready by the time the one-year project would begin and could be presented as a means to return the preliminary research to the community. 1,000 game sets were printed and delivered in September 2013 for distribution in La Ventosa and other Diidxazá-speaking towns free of charge.⁷ We organized an event open to the public intended to present the project to the community broadly and began to distribute the game sets there. Over the course of the next year, and in tandem with the one-year research project, the distribution of the games was largely carried out by members of the project team. The games reached 6 libraries, 8 cultural centers, 23 education institutions (preschool to high school), and over 800 individual households across the 22 municipalities where Diidxazá is spoken.⁸ The emerging long-term project and the distribution of the games helped in the organic coalescence of a team of collaborators interested in language and knowledge documentation with an emerging vision of applied uses of linguistic research for revitalization. This was entirely fortuitous, but it allowed everyone in the team, including myself, to envision the potential impact of the ethnobotany project beyond the basic research and sowed the seed for community leadership and CBR.

4.1 Retention of research results

The emerging vision seemed ideal for a proposal to the recently issued call for submissions to the 2013 Smithsonian Grand Challenges. For this grant, projects needed to "advance research and [...] broaden access, revitalize education,

---

6 Funding was made available through a research allocation from the Recovering Voices initiative of the Smithsonian's National Museum of Natural History.
7 The printing was funded by the Recovering Voices initiative of the Smithsonian's National Museum of Natural History.
8 Data gathered and provided by team member Haley de Korne.

strengthen collections-based research or utilize collections in novel ways."[9] The proposal built "on ongoing lexico-botanical documentation [...] and acknowledges the extraordinary interest of the community in this line of research, to develop a model for local retention of research results through community stewardship. It proposes community consultations meant to produce a program of short- and long-term initiatives through dissemination of botanical research results." The grant was awarded and formal community consultations were built around each of my field research trips in Spring, Summer and Fall 2014 as well as Spring 2015.[10] All team collaborators participated in these consultations in addition to various other community members including authorities and members of the Comité Cultural María Chéu.

The strategy for retention – rather than return – of research results evolved over the course of the ethnobotanical research project, but from the start, it centered on two notions articulated by team collaborators: the hope that the momentum generated by the research would outlive the research project and that the research would reach as many people as possible, and especially the children of La Ventosa, for the benefit of ecological conservation and language revitalization. This evolved into the development of children workshops that would capitalize on the skills and knowledge of our team members by presenting a variety of activities to teach Diidxazá and ecological knowledge. The workshops began loosely in early 2014 and were initially designed and organized by the community-external researchers in the team.[11] The workshops offered art and play-based activities intended to introduce basic conversational Diidxazá to the children as well as exposing them to plant diversity and ecological conservation. By the third workshop in July 2014, though, the workshops were designed by the La Ventosa collaborators, notably Mrs. López López in consultation with Ms. de Korne and with contributions from a second doctoral student Kate Riestenberg, both of whom were trained in educational linguistics and second-language acquisition and were able to provide pedagogy to culturally-based curricula.

By the time this paper was written, a dozen workshops, including summer camps, had been provided to children ages 5 to 15 with an attendance between

---

[9] As stated in the Smithsonian internal call for proposals circulated via internal email on June 3, 2013.

[10] Smithsonian Consortium for World Cultures grant entitled *Documentation and Revitalization of the Language and Traditional Ecological knowledge of the Isthmus Zapotec Community*, PI Gabriela Pérez Báez.

[11] The workshops were initially funded by the Grand Challenges grant and upon its closing, by additional funds from the Recovering Voices initiative of the Smithsonian's National Museum of Natural History.

30 and 60 children at any one time. The workshops which initially were sporadic quickly became regularized into monthly offerings. A portfolio of 12 monthly workshops has now been developed to guide the team, and the team builds upon it to enhance and adapt to emerging circumstances. The team grew by two additional community members including one of the members from the Comité Cultural María Chéu and a young woman who is a second-language speaker of Diidxazá. By the time this paper was written, however, the team had already submitted a successful grant funded regionally and two additional proposals for national funding to continue on.

In terms of dissemination of the research results, from the beginning of the Grand Challenges grant, we began to consider the feasibility of a variety of products. Knowing the limitations of printed matter as a means to disseminate information on a collection that grew to include 1,361 herbarium samples, over 5,000 photographs, 200 audio files, and a database with over 1,000 lexical entries including over 250 plant names, the grant provided funding for the creation of a website that would present the entire collection. An online platform was selected building partially on the proposal for a CD-based multimedia format that Lic. Fernández Jacinto presented as part of her own community consultations. It became evident, rather quickly, that the increased access to the internet through cibercafés and in a growing number of homes would provide infinitely better options for the presentation and update of the data. For instance, the online interface would be directly fed from the Smithsonian's EMu collections management platform via a content management system. The collection was launched live in June 2016 through a pilot website of the National Ethnobotanical Herbarium Online at https://neho.si.edu/. The data can be searched both by Zapotec taxonomic concepts and by botanical ones and is displayed in Diidxazá in addition to Spanish and English.

In addition, and in consideration of the still existing limitations of access online and a prevalent appreciation for printed matter, the team decided to create a set of fact cards with a selection of the most relevant plants from the collection, for use primarily in education settings. The fact cards idea emerged also following an initial proposal for a printed graphic display of plant data by Lic. Fernández Jacinto and the suggestion from Smithsonian Botanist Vicki Funk that if creating a herbarium in La Ventosa was not feasible or efficient due to cost, maintenance needs and climactic challenges, perhaps a reproduction of digitized herbarium samples could be an alternative. In April 2015, I worked with the team to curate a selection of 54 plant names for which full color fact cards would be created. In summer, and once enough herbarium samples had been identified, mounted, accessioned to the Smithsonian collections, and digitized, I worked on the production of full color, 8.5" x 14" double-sided laminated fact card sets. I was able to capitalize on this effort to produce a revised version of the bingo-type game with improved, professional photography and to include all the same cultural data from the fact cards as well. To respond to the fact that literacy in Diidxazá is markedly limited among speakers of the language, I also produced a literacy workbook, the first of its kind. These materials were delivered to the team in 2015 and have been distributed throughout the Diidxazá-speaking region at no charge.

5 Discussion

In Section 4, I summarized the process by which linguist-focused research successfully evolved into CBR in La Ventosa. This evolution was only possible when the following conditions were met:
1. Having sufficient knowledge of Diidxazá to be able to earn the respect and acceptance of highly knowledgeable community members of social prominence;
2. Having built trust and demonstrated a commitment to the revitalization of Diidxazá;
3. Having sufficient sociolinguistic and cultural knowledge as to be able to identify opportunities for collaboration and navigate political conflict; and
4. Being in a position to manage a large project and assemble the resources needed to sustain the collaboration long-term.

Allow me to explain. Had I attempted to engage in CBR at the outset, in the early stages of my training as a linguist, I would not have had enough knowledge about the language to be entrusted with a language project or to be sought out as an expert who could make a valuable contribution to the Diidxazá-speaking community. In fact, Mr. Gallegos Luis with whom I worked during my first season with the PDLMA in 2003, had high expectations with regards to the knowledge of Diidxazá that anyone assigned to work with him ought to have. Since he was exposed to Terrence Kaufman's knowledge – monumental by any standards after some 50 years of documentation and analysis of Mesoamerican languages – working with a newbie such as myself was difficult for Mr. Gallegos Luis to tolerate. In fact, this was a motivating factor for seeking a more tolerant collaborator for my second summer with the PDLMA. Contrast this with my experience being approached in Summer 2013 by a member of the government of La Ventosa who felt that my knowledge of Diidxazá and my commitment to its preservation could make a valuable contribution to the work of the Centro Cultural Bacusa Gui. Over the last three years, I have been able to work closely with members of the Diidxazá intellectual community, writers, historians, teachers of the language. Had I not had enough to offer about the language that was not already common knowledge among Diidxazá intellectuals, I would have had little to nothing to contribute to their work. However linguist-focused the work in the context of the PDLMA might have been, it provided me with the foundation necessary to become an asset to the Diidxazá-speaking community.

The success of the CBR that materialized around the ethnobotany project was built upon years of building trust and a track record of commitment to Diidxazá revitalization. While in the early years with the PDLMA my work was with one speaker only, working with Mrs. López Cartas intensively for weeks at a time over a number of years allowed for a strong bond to emerge and for trust building. Having gained her trust, Mrs. López Cartas was happy to introduce me to the La Ventosa community including the authorities. In turn, the interactions with different governments in the context of the MesoSpace research in 2009 and the ethnobotany pilot project in 2012 and with a couple more collaborators each time, allowed me to build a track record of reliability as a collaborator and leader.

These interactions in turn taught me much about the sociolinguistic profile of La Ventosa and of the Diidxazá language community, the local culture and social norms, and the political complexities. The critical role of cultural knowledge as a requirement in any type of CBR has not been downplayed in the literature. Guérin and Lacrampe (2010) state that learning (about) the language was a factor enabling collaboration. Dobrin (2008) describes various cases where a lack of understanding of the community leads to unproductive, unsuccessful and even problematic interactions. Dwyer (2010: 198) recognizes the "steep learning curve" associated with acquiring adequate cultural knowledge. All the while, however, Dwyer (2010: 191) which considers lone ranger linguistics to be of marginal ethicality does not discuss how a researcher is to engage with a community prior to having acquired enough cultural knowledge in order to develop CBR. Crippen and Robinson (2013) take on precisely this issue and present two damaging experiences by graduate students who attempted to establish collaborations while still at the foot of the steep cultural learning curve.

Navigating the socio-cultural and political particulars of La Ventosa and the larger Diidxazá-speaking region was a complex, sensitive matter. Municipal and agency (a unit that has certain autonomy but is subordinate to municipal entities) authorities including their cabinets change every three years, which brings about instability to varying degrees. A controversial election in late 2013 led to a dispute in La Ventosa which resulted in the occupation of the Centro Cultural Bacusa Gui building by what became an alternate government in opposition to the one occupying the official government offices. The impact of this greatly affected the project, as children stopped visiting the center, most activities ceased in the center, and the ethnobotany project eventually had to move to the home of one of the team members. The workshops have migrated from one location to another ever since as they could no longer be held at the center. Any move on our part as a team, and on my part as principal investigator, could have easily been interpreted as favoring one political group over the other. I do not think I would have been able to navigate such a difficult situation in earlier years.

The CBR that emerged from the ethnobotany project happened after I had worked on Diidxazá for 10 years and had been interacting with frequency and with enough community members for 4 years. Also, by then, I had been employed by the prestigious Smithsonian Institution for over 3 years which gave me credibility. I would like to think that over these many years, I may have acquired enough knowledge and maturity to face the types of challenges mentioned in the previous paragraph, and perhaps more importantly, to face the responsibility that comes from being the lead person in the large and often growing collaborative and interdisciplinary ethnobotany project that evolved into a revitalization project. Consider the demands: as PI it was my responsibility to manage funds, to discuss wages with every member of the team individually, to work out logistics, to manage a work team with five local collaborators at the outset and two more who joined for the workshops, two accomplished botanists, one photographer and two doctoral students. While some of the content for the educational materials was curated in collaboration with the local experts, the content development, design and production was under my entire responsibility. So was the production of the project website. And I assumed the responsibility that if any of our team collaborators had an accident while on a collection hike, I would have had to step forward and respond. Consider the level of experience of most of the scholars contributing to the literature on collaborative field linguistics. Of the works that are cited in this chapter, most are written by some of the most seasoned researchers with established lines of research and long-standing community relations: Benedicto et al. (2007), Dwyer (2010), Cameron (1992), Czaykowska-Higgins (2009), Dobrin (2008), Grenoble and Furbee (eds. 2010), Rice (2006, 2011). However, these works provide little to no background as to how these highly experienced researchers got CBR up and running and what came before CBR actually materialized.

One more point needs to be made related to research leadership, namely whether the linguist has the right to direct the research within the ideal proposed of shared research direction. The La Ventosa team members were very clearly interested and willing to take on leadership roles with respect to the workshops and the distribution of printed materials, but not in other aspects of our collaboration. Further, with regards to the workshops, there remains an expectation that I ought to be involved not only as a consultant, but also in a leadership position. As such, the expectation that I will continue to serve as a leader in the CBR remains even after many consultations in which I explicitly have proposed other arrangements. The team members' interest in the workshops only emerged as a result of their participation in the research project. The "need" for workshops could not have been known had the linguist-focused ethnobotanical research project not taken place. Contrast this with the directive that "The linguist will have to compromise long-range scholarly goals to meet the community's immediate needs" from Gerdts (2010: 191). CBR in La Ventosa was made possible following project ideas that were motivated by linguist-focused research.

Often, the collaborations described in the literature are based on substantial pre-existing infrastructure and funding, and capitalize on a pre-existing long-term interaction with the relevant community. Benedicto et al. (2007) describe work that involves the Regional University URACCAN which included an Institute of Linguistics offering professionalization courses for teachers, and a bachelor's degree in Bilingual Intercultural Education. A state-run bilingual school system was already in existence. Funding was available from URACCAN, Purdue University, the European Union and the National Science Foundation. Dwyer (2010) describes a collaboration with the Kickapoo Nation School, an institution with a 20-year history, and a collaboration on the documentation of Ega spoken in Ivory Coast based on long term relations between the Université de Cocody (Ivory Coast), University of Uyo (Nigeria) and the University of Bielefeld (Germany), with oversight by the Ministry of Education. Leonard and Haynes (2010) is based on a collaboration with highly experienced, committed community researchers and language advocates Daryl and Karen Baldwin. These examples are to mention but a few cases where the ideal CBR is grounded on a significant infrastructure of community relations and resources which take time to assemble.

In this regard, the present volume fills a gap in the CBR literature in that several of its chapters provide detailed explanations as to how CBR develop and how long it took. For example, Akumbu (this volume) describes work initiated by the Summer Institute of Linguistics (SIL) Cameroon in 1998 which was later taken over by the Cameroon Association for Bible Translation and Literacy (CABTAL) in 2004. The work which has included orthography development and literacy classes seems to have built upon the author's own linguistics research and technical knowledge of Babanki (Akumbu holds a Master's and a PhD in Linguistics) and documentation, notably the Babanki-English lexicon (Akumbu 2008) which he initiated in 2002 and revised in 2006. Akumbu joined CABTAL that same year. This CBR case built on a collaboration that had the expertise of a native speaker and linguist of Babanki, and grew over a period of 8 years before the first literacy classes became available in 2006 in Babanki villages.

CBR described in Bischoff, Fountain and Vincent (this volume) seems to have built upon documentation that began in the 1920s, and critically, on the involvement of Coeur d'Alene member Lawrence Nicodemus in the development of an orthography and pedagogical materials in the 1970s. In fact, the chapter states that much of the work was carried out by community members until the involvement in the 21ST century of community-external linguists including two of the co-authors of the chapter. As such, this is a case of CBR which dates back about a decade and a half, but which builds upon documentation that began decades earlier, and critically, builds upon active work by community members for over 30 years before the community-external researchers became involved in what is described as CBR in the chapter in question.

The collaboration described in Czaykowska-Higgins et al. (this volume) was built around a partnership between six established organizations of which five were community-based organizations. This is one more case that builds upon existing involvement of community members prior to the development of CBR. Of special value in this chapter are the quotes about CBR from collaborators with one quote in particular alluding precisely to time as a critical factor for successful CBR: "[...] it takes time to develop a relationship with communities [...]" (Deanna Daniels CFR: 26 via Czaykowska-Higgins et al. this volume).

In the case of the ethnobotany project in La Ventosa, a great deal of resources were necessary to make the project and the ensuing collaboration happen and be sustained. An initial pilot project and associated grant writing was required and over a year's worth of planning afterwards was necessary prior to the implementation of the basic research project. This was possible thanks to the availability of research support from the Recovering Voices initiative at the Smithsonian's National Museum of Natural History. In addition, a large institutional grant had to be secured in order to support the retention of research module which is what propelled the collaboration and revitalization work forward. An internal collaboration between the Anthropology, Botany and IT departments at the National Museum of Natural History and an interinstitutional collaboration between this museum, the National Museum of the American Indian and the Center for Folklife and Cultural Heritage was necessary in securing this grant. Additional collaborations were necessary with the National Herbarium (MEXU) in Mexico, the Jardín Etnobotánico de Oaxaca, Servicios Integrales a Pueblos Indígenas BENI ICHI IN A.C. and the Sociedad para el Estudio de los Recursos Bióticos de Oaxaca in order to manage the collection of herbarium samples, facilitate the identification of species, etc. In total, over 40 individuals in Mexico and the United States comprise the list of those who contributed to the project in one way or another and in addition to the large team of project researchers.[12] The conditions that have enabled the ongoing collaboration had to be cultivated over time – a not insignificant amount of time.

---

[12] In La Ventosa: Sr. Pedro Castillo de la Cruz, Sra. Rosaura López Cartas, Ing. José López de la Cruz, Lic. Rogelio López López, Sr. Víctor López López, Sr. Francisco López Montero, Sr. Hageo

6 Conclusion

This chapter has argued that the literature advocating for CBR does not sufficiently address the conditions needed for a researcher to carry out effective CBR. This is significant given the forceful recommendations to follow the CBR model on grounds that not doing so is close to unethical. Numerous contributions to the present volume go into great detail about the phases of development of CBR in a variety of contexts, and in doing so fill an important gap in the literature. The present paper provides an additional context within which to consider the contributions to the present volume. This chapter describes the CBR between the author and members of the Diidxazá language community which developed over a period of about a decade. For comparison purposes and in order to gather additional empirical data, this chapter makes reference to other chapters in this volume where CBR timelines are mentioned.

This chapter is not a critique of CBR. Quite on the contrary. It attempts to fill a void in our knowledge about the factors that enable CBR, with the hope that we will all be better informed and equipped to develop CBR effectively. This chapter does advocate for giving researchers the time to develop the necessary relationships and resources to engage in CBR if and when the conditions allow for it. I have provided a case study in support of considering time, relationships and resources as critical conditions of CBR and of advocating for CBR as a goal of linguistic field research rather than a condition for it.

References

Akumbu, Pius W. 2008. *Kejom (Babanki) – English lexicon*. Ga'a Kejom Development Committee. Bamenda: AGWECAMS.
Benedicto, Elena, Demetrio Antolín, Modesta Dolores, M. Cristina Feliciano, Gloria Fendly, Tomasa Gómez, Baudillo Miguel, and Elizabeth Salomón. 2007. A model of participatory

---

Montero, Sr. Pedro Rasgado, Citlali Toledo Burke, Diana Lenia Toledo Rasgado, Dr. Manuel Ríos, Sr. René Valdivieso Rasgado, and numerous La Ventosa families who granted us access to their gardens. In the National Museum of Natural History Botany department: Warren Wagner, Sylvia Orli, Melinda Peters, Chris Tuccinardi, Ingrid Lin, Carol Kelloff, Sabrina Crane, Linda Welzenbach, Dr. Larry Dorr, and the members of the plant mounting volunteer unit; In Informatics: Tom Hollowell, John Keltner, Lauren Greenstein, Dennis Hasch, the Technical Review Board; In Smithsonian OCIO: Edward Monk. In addition, Rebecca Bartlett, Sean Heavy, Ha Pham, Dr. Jonathan Amith, Dr. Alejandro de Ávila, Mtro. Víctor Cata, Lic. Mayra Fernández Jacinto, Dr. David Gernandt, Lic. Mario Lugos, Ing. Adelfo Martínez, Dra. Silvia Hortensia Salas Morales.

action research: The Mayangna linguists' team of Nicaragua. In Maya Khemlani David, Nicholas Ostler and Caesar Dealwis (eds.), *Proceedings of the XI FEL Conference on 'Working together for endangered languages - research Cchallenges and social impacts'*, 29–35. Kuala Lumpur, Malaysia: SKET, University of Malaya and Foundation for Endangered Languages.

Benedicto, Elena, Modesta Dolores and Melba McLean. 2002. Fieldwork as a participatory research activity: The Mayangna linguistic teams. In Julie Larson and Mary Paster (eds.), *Proceedings of the Twenty-Eighth Annual Meeting of the Berkeley Linguistics Society: General session and parasession on field linguistics (2002)*, 375–386. Berkeley, CA: University of California at Berkeley.

Bowern, Claire and Natasha Warner. 2015. 'Lone wolves' and collaboration: A reply to Crippen & Robinson (2013). *Language Documentation & Conservation* 9. 59–85.

Cameron, Deborah. 1992. "Respect, please!": Investigating race, power and language. In Deborah Cameron, Elizabeth Frazer, Penelope Harvey, M.B.H. Rampton, and Kay Richardson (eds.), *Researching language: Issues of power and method*, 113–130. New York: Routledge.

Crippen, James A. and Laura C. Robinson. 2013. In defense of the Lone wolf: Collaboration in language documentation. *Language Documentation & Conservation* 7. 123–135.

Czaykowska-Higgins, Ewa. 2009. Research models, community engagement, and linguistic fieldwork: Reflections on working within Canadian Indigenous communities. *Language Documentation & Conservation* 3 (1). 15–50.

Dobrin, Lise. 2008. From linguistic elicitation to eliciting the linguist: Lessons in community empowerment from Melanesia. *Language* 84 (2). 300–324.

Dwyer, Arienne M. 2006. Ethics and practicalities of cooperative fieldwork and analysis. In Jost Gippert, Nikolaus P. Himmelmann, and Ulrike Mosel (eds.), *Essentials of language documentation*, 31–66. New York: Mouton de Gruyter.

Dwyer, Arienne M. 2010. Models of successful collaboration. In Lenore A. Grenoble and N. Louanna Furbee (eds.), *Language documentation: Practice and values*, 193–212. Amsterdam: John Benjamins Publishing Co.

Gerdts, Donna B. 1998. Beyond expertise: The role of the linguist in language revitalization programs. In Nicholas Ostler (ed.), *Endangered languages: What role for the specialist? Proceedings of Second Foundation for Endangered Languages Conference*, 13–22. Bath, England: Foundation for Endangered Languages.

Gerdts, Donna B. 2010. Beyond expertise: The role of the linguist in language revitalization programs. In Grenoble, Leonore A. and N. Louanna Furbee (eds.). 2010. *Language documentation: practice and values*, 173–192. Amsterdam: John Benjamins Publishing Co.

Grenoble, Leonore A. and N. Louanna Furbee (eds.). 2010. *Language documentation: Practice and values*. Amsterdam: John Benjamins Publishing Co.

Grinevald, Colette. 1998. Language endangerment in South America: A programmatic approach. In Lenore A. Grenoble and Lindsay J. Whaley (eds.), *Endangered languages: Current issues and future prospects*, 124–159. Cambridge: Cambridge University Press.

Guérin, Valérie and Sébastian Lacrampe. 2010. Trust me, I am a linguist! Building partnerships in the field. *Language Documentation & Conservation* 4. 22–33.

Hale, Ken, Michael Krauss, Lucille J. Watahomigie, Akira Y. Yamamoto, Colette Craig, LaVerne Masayesva Jeanne and Nora C. England. 1992. Endangered languages. *Language*, 68 (1). 1–42.

Hale, Kenneth. 2001. Ulwa (Southern Sumu): The beginnings of a language research project. In Paul Newman and Martha Ratliff (eds.), *Linguistic Fieldwork*, 71–101. Cambridge: Cambridge University Press.

Holton, Gary. 2009. Relatively ethical: A comparison of linguistic research paradigms in Alaska and Indonesia. *Language Documentation & Conservation* 3 (2). 161–175.

INALI (Instituto Nacional de Lenguas Indígenas). 2008. *Catálogo de las lenguas indígenas nacionales: variantes lingüísticas de México con sus autodenominaciones y referencias geoestadísticas*. Diario Oficial de la Federación, 14 de marzo de 2008 (Sección 1: 31–78, Sección 2: 1–96, Sección 3: 1–112). http://www.inali.gob.mx/pdf/CLINcompleto.pdf (accessed 26 January 2014).

Jiménez Girón, Eustaquio. 1979. *Guía gráfico-fonémica para la escritura y lectura del zapoteco. Pa sicca rica Diidxazá xti Guidxiguie'. Cómo se escribe el zapoteco de Juchitán*. Juchitán, Oaxaca: Editorial Vitoria Yan.

Jiménez Jiménez, Enedino and Vicente Marcial Cerqueda. 2000. *Neza diidxa': ni gacané binnihuaniisi gu'nda', gucaa ne güi' diidxazá (Vocabulario zapoteco: auxiliar del modelo pedagógico de diálogo cultural y alfabetización)*. Juchitán, Oaxaca: Centro de Investigación y Desarrollo Binnizá.

Kaufman, Terrence. 1993, revised in 1994, 2000, 2001, 2002, 2003, 2004, 2006 and 2007. Proto-Zapotec(an) reconstructions. University of Pittsburgh manuscript.

Leonard, Wesley Y. and Erin Haynes. 2010. Making "collaboration" collaborative: An examination of perspectives that frame linguistic field research. *Language Documentation & Conservation* 4. 268–293.

Marcial Cerqueda, Vicente. 2014. *Plan de acción para el impulso de la lengua zapoteca en el Programa de Gobierno Municipal 2014–2016*. Manuscript.

Pérez Báez, Gabriela. 2016. Addressing the gap between community beliefs and priorities and researchers' language maintenance interests. In Gabriela Pérez Báez, Chris Rogers and Jorge Emilio Rosés Labrada (eds.), *Language documentation & revitalization in Latin American contexts*, 165–194. Berlin: de Gruyter Mouton.

Pickett, Velma (compiler). 1959. *Vocabulario Zapoteco del Istmo*, 1st edn. México, D.F.: Instituto Lingüístico de Verano. http://www.mexico.sil.org/resources/archives/35335 (accessed January 20, 2016).

Pickett, Velma (compiler). 2007. *Vocabulario Zapoteco del Istmo*, 5th edn. México, D.F.: Instituto Lingüístico de Verano.

Rice, Keren. 2006. Ethical issues in linguistic fieldwork: An overview. *Journal of Academic Ethics* 4 (1–4). 123–155.

Rice, Keren. 2011. Documentary linguistics and community relations. *Language Documentation & Conservation* 5. 187–207.

Robinson, Laura and James Crippen. 2015. Collaboration: A reply to Bowern and Warner's reply. *Language Documentation & Conservation* 9. 86–88.

Yamada, Racquel-Maria. 2007. Collaborative linguistic fieldwork: Practical application of the empowerment model. *Language Documentation and Conservation* 1 (2): 257–282.

Bertney Langley, Linda Langley, Jack B. Martin, and Stephanie Hasselbacher

The Koasati Language Project: A collaborative, community-based language documentation and revitalization model

Abstract: This chapter describes the Coushatta Tribe of Louisiana's Koasati Language Project from its inception through the establishment of academic collaborations to the language documentation and revitalization efforts active at the time of writing. Koasati had been well researched from a scholarly point of view when Bertney and Linda Langley began their work on the Koasati Language Project, yet they found that state-of-the-art linguistic methods of the twentieth century, though thorough and rigorous, had a narrow and distant university-based audience. The resulting products and publications could not, therefore, meet the needs of the Coushatta Tribe as they embarked on their community-driven research and language revitalization project. This chapter explores how participants in the Koasati Language Project identified gaps in the previous linguistic work on Koasati—including the lack of well-documented everyday conversation, leisure reading materials, and teaching resources—and developed culturally appropriate methodologies to fill those gaps and community-specific means of disseminating their work. This suite of collaborative approaches has resulted in a wider variety of linguistic data than previously recorded, scholarly publications, and broad community investment and ownership that will help ensure the future vitality of the Koasati Language Project.

Keywords: Coushatta, Koasati, language documentation, language revitalization, community-driven research

---

Bertney Langley, Coushatta Heritage Department, P.O. Box 10, Elton LA 70532 USA, blangley@coushattatribela.org
Linda Langley, McNeese State University and Coushatta Heritage Department, P.O. Box 10, Elton LA 70532 USA, llangley@coushattatribela.org
Jack B. Martin, College of William and Mary, Department of English Language and Literature, P.O. Box 8795, Williamsburg, Virginia 23187-8795 USA, jbmart@wm.edu
Stephanie Hasselbacher, College of William & Mary, P.O. Box 8795 Williamsburg, VA 23187-8795, srhasselbacher@email.wm.edu

https://doi.org/10.1515/9783110527018-007

1 Introduction

Linguists, anthropologists, and other social scientists have shown interest in recent years in exploring and critiquing models of the working relationships arising between communities and academic researchers (see e.g., Czaykowska-Higgins 2009; Rice 2011; Crippen and Robinson 2013 ; Stenzel 2014; Bowern and Warner 2015). In what might be called traditional, university-driven research, language documentation is planned and conducted by academics who are typically outsiders to the community under study. In its extreme form, a "lone wolf" researcher will visit a community, identify speakers to work with, decide on a research agenda, apply for funding, and publish (or not publish) the results. An alternative to a university-driven research model is a community-driven one in which the community either conducts the study or is involved to varying degrees in setting the research agenda.

The question we will address in this paper is how adopting a community-driven approach to language documentation affects the type and quality of research that is done. We will address this question by drawing on recent attempts by the Coushatta Tribe of Louisiana to document the Koasati language.[1] Our experience suggests that community-driven research has dramatic impact in the following areas:
- the types of documentation projects chosen and their sequence;
- the methods used;
- the types of data collected;
- the number of speakers participating and their roles in the work; and
- the extent to which materials produced are embraced by the community.

2 Setting, previous research, community response

2.1 Setting

Koasati is a Muskogean language spoken by some 200 of the approximately 900 members of the Coushatta Tribe of Louisiana, and by a smaller number of individuals in the Alabama-Coushatta Tribe of Texas. A few speakers were born as late

---

[1] When the tribe received federal re-recognition in 1973 they chose the English spelling of their name, and thus are officially called "the Coushatta Tribe of Louisiana." Koasati (CKU) is the language of the Coushatta people. See Hasselbacher (2015b) for an ethnography of the Coushatta language revitalization project.

as 1985, but most of those who use the language on a daily basis were born before 1960. There is a perception in the community that the most fluent and knowledgeable speakers are passing on.

Indigenous language shift to English is often attributed to colonial oppression, lack of political power, forced removals, "English-only" boarding schools, and other historical factors. Due to the tribe's unique history of diplomacy and movement from their ancestral lands to avoid conflict, Coushatta individuals avoided most of these events, and significant shift to English was not widely observed until the 1980s.

2.2 Previous research

From an academic perspective, Koasati had been relatively well documented in the twentieth century compared to many other Native North American languages.[2] The earliest known record of the Koasati language is a word list recorded by Albert S. Gatschet in 1885 (Gatschet 1885). John Swanton (n.d.a, n.d.b, n.d.c) later collected a more extensive vocabulary list and series of texts. The manuscript originals are held by the National Anthropological Archives. Archival materials also include Mary Haas's field notes from her visits with speaker Jackson Langley in the 1930s (Haas 1934), Lyda Taylor's brief ethnographic manuscript (Taylor 1937), and a 1963 collection of seven-inch reels with recordings of speaker Bel Abbey (Fischer 1963). Gene Burnham, working with the Summer Institute of Linguistics, produced some descriptive work and language learning pamphlets in the 1970s (Burnham 1979). More recently, Geoffrey Kimball produced an important reference grammar (Kimball 1991), dictionary (Kimball 1994), and text collection (Kimball 2010). Other publications have focused primarily on specific grammatical topics: morphological differences between men's and women's speech (Haas 1944; Kimball 1987, 1990; Saville-Troike 1988; Hasselbacher 2013); use of the dual number in narrative speech (Kimball 1993); and switch reference (Rising 1992).

Viewing this body of research, academics and linguists might conclude that Koasati is more than minimally documented: indeed, the suite of reference grammar, dictionary, and texts is often touted as the gold standard of language documentation. The fieldwork necessary to complete these materials was done at a time when the Tribe itself was not concerned with language revitalization or documentation. In the 1970s, leaders of the Tribe were active in gaining state

---

[2] In the nineteenth century, Koasati was spoken in western Louisiana, in eastern Texas, and by one tribal town within the larger Muscogee (Creek) Nation of present Oklahoma. The population in Oklahoma had shifted to Muskogee and English by the mid-twentieth century.

and federal recognition and in ensuring that their children had adequate schooling and opportunities for jobs. Thirty years later, however, everyone was acutely aware that the language was disappearing. In 2006, the Tribe very much wanted to revitalize its language, to make use of previous research, and to fill gaps in documentation. From this perspective, previous research was often seen as inadequate. The main difficulties were: a) accessibility; b) audience; c) orthography; d) methods; e) cultural sensitivity; and, f) copyright.[3]

Linguistic documentation is only useful for community-based preservation and revitalization efforts if it is accessible to community members, in every sense of the word. In 2006, no one in the Coushatta Tribe knew what researchers had visited the Tribe, what materials were held in archives, and how copies of materials could be obtained. Gatschet's and Swanton's materials had been archived at the National Anthropological Archives. Mary Haas had held onto her field notes until her death, when they were sent to the American Philosophical Society. It was fairly easy to obtain Geoffrey Kimball's published works, but he had never archived the primary materials (his field notes, recordings, etc.). Since online searches rarely turn up virtual copies of actual documents, viewing and gathering archival holdings often requires extensive travel, reproduction and scanning costs, a high degree of computer literacy, and the ability to network with academics, archivists, and librarians.

When previous field notes, recordings, and other primary materials on Koasati were acquired in 2007, it became obvious that the audience for these works was fairly narrow. Researchers tended to have a set of specific interests (verb paradigms, kinship terms, traditional stories, etc.). Researchers had produced almost no learning materials and had not documented everyday conversation. In short, what academics had gathered in the twentieth century was designed for an academic audience and thus out of step with what the community needed in 2007.

Orthography also presented a significant roadblock for many Coushatta community members. Swanton's handwriting is notoriously difficult to read. The phonemic system that Mary Haas used in the 1930s was for an academic audience: she never taught members of the community how to use it. She used <ł> for the voiceless lateral fricative, <c> for the postalveolar affricate, and a middle dot after a vowel for a long vowel (e.g., <a·>). Geoffrey Kimball later modified that system, using <ł> for the voiceless lateral fricative and a colon after a vowel for a long vowel (e.g., <a:>). Two sample entries from his 1994 dictionary appear below.

---

[3] Coauthor Martin would like to add that his own research in the 1990s is subject to these same criticisms. The point here is to openly examine practices prevalent in the twentieth century to measure their successes and limitations.

łibítlin V2AIII *vn* łibítka *an* łibítli 1 to cave in (one place or time). 2 to be crushed in (one place or time) *pl* łibíhlin.
łibó:lin V3A *vn* łibo:hilká *an* łibó:ka to be squashed (PL SUBJ) *sg* łibóskan.

As much sense as these entries might make to a linguist, community members struggled with them. They couldn't read the special characters, they tended to interpret the colons as syllable breaks, and the extensive abbreviations and distance between the headword and the definition created barriers to finding the information they sought. Once again, assumptions about the audience had led to specific decisions about orthography and format that impeded community use.

Of the different researchers who had visited it was only the missionary Gene Burnham who spent time developing a community orthography and distributing children's books using it.[4] His system used <th> for the lateral fricative, <ch> for the postalveolar affricate, double vowels for long vowels, and underlining for nasal vowels. Although use of digraphs made words longer, the system was much easier for community members to read.

Methods that were standard in the twentieth century also led to difficulties in the community. In keeping with the practices of the time, John Swanton, Mary Haas, and Geoffrey Kimball had each found a single, knowledgeable speaker to work with, and then proceeded to describe the language largely on the basis of that individual's speech. When publications resulted, they were presented to the outside world as though they were a description of the entire speech community. In one famous example, Haas (1944) reported that Koasati had a distinction between men's and women's speech and that women's speech was on the decline. That conclusion appears to have been based on a statement by Jackson Langley, her main consultant: it represented his observation about language use rather than a description of use in the community. Four decades later, Kimball called that conclusion into question, suggesting that the "men's" speech ending was instead a mark of social prominence and noting that it was actually the "women's" speech form that took over (Kimball 1987, 1990). Whether Haas or Kimball was correct, the problem is that Haas's original statement was not based on a survey of the community and merely repeated her consultant's observation. Now twenty-five years after Kimball's work, it is difficult for the community to

---

4 To ensure community collaboration and ownership of his work, Burnham formed the non-profit organization "Coushatta Bible Translation Committee, Inc." with community members. This organization was officially chartered with the Louisiana Secretary of State on the 12th anniversary of the tribe's federal re-recognition (June 27, 1985). Then Tribal Chairman Ernest Sickey and Cultural Committee Chairman Bertney Langley served as the first corporate officers.
https://coraweb.sos.la.gov/CommercialSearch/CommercialSearchDetails_Print.aspx?CharterID=297330_93C42.

evaluate historical data or to choose between conflicting findings of respected linguists. When a form of speech is unknown or no longer in modern use, there is endless speculation as to whether the academic made a mistake, whether the speaker knew an older language, and/or whether they had miscommunicated. Additionally, Coushatta community members often have a different suite of methodological standards and values than academics, including concerns about the linguistic and cultural competency of the academic and proof of engagement with a sufficiently broad sample of linguistically authoritative speakers, which further complicates their evaluation of previous linguistic literature.

One point affecting the reception of previous scholarship in the community relates to issues of cultural sensitivity. The community views their traditions and language with great pride, yet the reference materials that have been published seem to present their traditions as curiosities. Kimball's 1994 dictionary, for example, included his collection of personal names and nicknames of those living and deceased (which struck many as odd in a reference work). Some community members felt there was an overrepresentation of terms for sex. Kimball also decided to include forms from Indian Territory collected by Gatschet in the 1800s, but the community in Louisiana didn't recognize many of those forms. In a recent text collection (Kimball 2010), the author voiced his own opinion as to the comparative fluency of his sources in the community. He also felt it appropriate to note that a respected former chief "is remembered as having an extraordinarily high sex drive" (p. 4). All of these problems signaled to the community that the work is about them and not for them. These problems could have been avoided if the community had been actively involved in the project or if they had at least understood what researchers were doing and had been given a chance to review the work.

Finally, we feel it is important to raise issues pertaining to copyright and language documentation. The only published[5] dictionary of Koasati (Kimball 1994) was funded by the National Science Foundation. The copyright is held by the University of Nebraska Press. In 2006, the Coushatta community wanted to change the spelling to that used in the community, to make corrections in the dictionary, to delete information that was offensive, and make derivative works (an audio dictionary, an app, a children's dictionary, etc.). The author was not willing to share his notes, files, or recordings, however. This meant that the Tribe had to embark on its own dictionary project and to repeat much work that had already been done. Securing funding for language documentation is even more

---

5 Community member Douglas John produced an 80-page handwritten dictionary that included 690 words and phrases (John, 1930). This work was preserved by the local DAR chapter, but never widely distributed in the community.

difficult, however, when the academic community believes a language has been adequately described.⁶

Please note that these concerns do not negate the value of previous linguistic work. Many participants in the current language project recognize elders such as Jackson Langley (who worked with Swanton and Haas) and Bel Abbey (who worked with Kimball) as respected language authorities. Koasati speakers and learners use Kimball's dictionary to refresh their memories or to settle disagreements about words. The earlier literature, however, does not provide practical tools for teaching, learning, and leisure reading. The existing literature on Koasati needed to be re-situated and reformatted in the context of a consensus-based process, which the Coushatta Heritage Department and Koasati Language Committee began to do in the early years of their work. Previous academic work on Koasati had been reviewed for publication according to the standards and formats of scholars (with peer review by other academics): In 2006, the participants in the Koasati language project wished to focus on the standards and formats required by Coushatta language activists, teachers, and learners (which entailed peer review by the community and a shift in audience toward the community).

3 A community-driven language documentation project

3.1 Project inception

The Coushatta Tribe of Louisiana had never conceptualized or implemented a language documentation or revitalization project prior to 2006. Although most of the community was aware of at least some of the previous linguistic research described above, most people were not accustomed to reading or writing Koasati in any format on a regular basis. Although inter-generational Koasati transmission had declined dramatically in the previous decade, the majority of tribal members were not aware of actions that could be taken to reverse this trend. Many of the tribal elders who were native Koasati speakers, even those who had helped with previous linguistic research, stated that they

---

6 To our knowledge, funding agencies generally do not ask applicants about copyright. We feel strongly that dictionaries, at least, should be copyrighted or licensed in such a way as to allow the community to modify the work and to create derivatives.

had not fully understood the research as it was being done, and therefore were not accustomed to being active partners in documenting or revitalizing their language.

In 2006 the University of Arizona's American Indian Language Development Institute (AILDI) began a new NSF-funded training program on Documenting Endangered Languages (DEL). The RFP requested research teams comprised of a native speaker and a university-based scholar, with a goal of developing community-academic partnerships for future DEL grant applications. The Coushatta Tribal Council supported an AILDI application from Bertney and Linda Langley,[7] approved key documentation planning decisions,[8] and also sponsored a presentation to the community upon the Langley's return from AILDI which was attended by over 300 tribal members (Langley and Langley 2009). Based in part on the overwhelming support of the tribal community, the Coushatta Tribal Council formed a partnership with McNeese State University to apply to NSF for Documenting Endangered Languages funding. In May 2007 they received an award (NSF award #0804096) to record, transcribe, and translate Koasati conversations. Linda and Bertney Langley served as principal investigators on this project.

3.1.1 Major project activities

From the initial program discussions, the Coushatta Council made it clear that the Koasati Language Project would be entirely developed, managed and maintained by the tribal community. Through a series of open community meetings, they solicited a large group of volunteers to serve on the Koasati Language Committee, which serves as the steering committee, advisory board, and decision-making body for all project components and products. Another foundational component of developing the project was an initial meeting between the Tribal Council and all university researchers to clarify desired research procedures and protocol, including requirements that tribal members be provided with informed consent release forms and that the tribe maintain intellectual property rights on all

---

[7] The Langleys are a husband-wife team comprised of a native Koasati speaker with experience in tribal governance and an academic anthropologist who has lived in the tribal community for twenty-five years.

[8] **Alíílamo** (thanks) are due to Akira Yamamoto, who first suggested working with Dr. Jack Martin, Susan Penfield, Phil Cash Cash, D. Terence Langendoen, and other AILDI faculty. For countless hours of hard work and dedication to the tribe, the Tribal Council extends special thanks to Dr. Martin and his students at William and Mary, McNeese State University faculty, and members of the Koasati Language Committee.

materials produced. A key step in ensuring community participation and support for the project was visiting with individual tribal elders and families to listen to ideas and concerns before beginning project activities.

In order to fulfill the terms of the grant and begin documenting Koasati conversation, the community first had to develop a writing system. The project team consequently held a community workshop in June 2007. As Hasselbacher (2015b) has described, there was a great deal of excitement about developing a standard way to write the language. Language Committee member Claudine Hasting was recorded as follows:

> Anap, honaathiikaap "Kowassaati naathiihilka inchaahila" kahhan stachayokpaahoosit. Inchaalih chabannaap staatilitik chasankot, kaanon ontakkotot ommo, kantik, hasaikaahoosin chikkiilillaho inchaalit. Mootohon, "Inchaahilas" kahhok stiisan stachayokpaahoosit.

> Me, I was really happy when they said they are going to write the Coushatta language. I would try to write it but I never could. I probably didn't do it good, but I have a lot written down. And then, when they said we would write it [as part of the official language project], I was so happy.

Over the course of just two days, the community discussed and voted on the spelling of each sound in the language. We were later surprised to find that the spelling that was approved was virtually identical to what Gene Burnham had developed in the 1970s, with <th> for the lateral fricative, <ch> for the postalveolar affricate, and <aa>, <ii>, etc. for long vowels (Figure 1).

In a concerted effort to make the new spelling more visible, tribal members worked in small groups to develop popular products such as t-shirts with Koasati slogans, bumper stickers, posters, and a Koasati coloring book. Subsequent workshops led to a monthly newsletter with writings in Koasati, children's books, lessons for a sixth-grade language course, and a topical dictionary. These materials were all produced in a way that was felt to be culturally appropriate: meetings were held at the tribal Fire Department and open to the entire tribal community, everything written down was projected overhead for discussion, and people volunteered their time and took turns cooking. The regular schedule of community workshops helped to generate and maintain community support and visibility for the project. Summer camps for children generated additional interest.

One bilingual community member, Loretta Williams, took a special interest in learning to transcribe and translate. She was motivated in part by a desire to leave a record for her children. She subsequently spent the next several years using Fieldworks Language Explorer and ELAN to transcribe and translate the audio and video recordings the project collected, including a number of

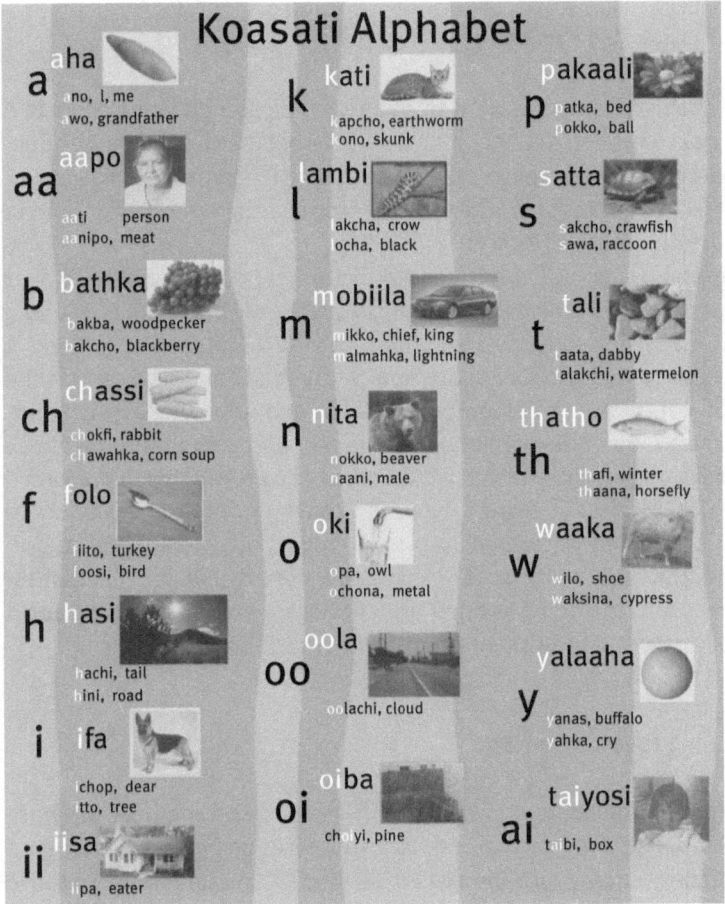

Figure 1: The Koasati alphabet. Poster by Heather Williams. Reproduced by permission from the Coushatta Heritage Department

interviews relating to language attitudes recorded by Stephanie Hasselbacher for her PhD thesis (Hasselbacher 2015a and 2015b).[9]

During the course of the funded research, it became clear that Koasati had a system of grammatical tone that had largely escaped previous researchers. The contrast was evident in pairs like the following (with the community spelling first followed by phonetic spelling in brackets):

---

[9] These recordings and associated ELAN files have been deposited with the Endangered Languages Archive (http://elar.soas.ac.uk/deposit/0075).

Chokoolil. [tʃokòːlí-l] 'I'm getting seated.'
Chokkoolil. [tʃokkǒːli-l] 'I am seated.'

The first word above refers to an event in progress. The second word refers to a state resulting from an event, and is signaled by different tone and (often) by doubling of the onset of the penultimate syllable of the verb stem. In 2012 we applied for NSF funding to study this and other outstanding issues in phonetics[10] and to produce an audio dictionary of Koasati.

The first printed version of a new Koasati dictionary, with an audio CD, was distributed to each tribal family by the Tribal Council in August 2008. In keeping with project protocol, all publication copyrights belong to the Coushatta Tribe of Louisiana. Self-publishing the dictionary and pedagogical materials serves the dual purpose of maintaining community ownership and providing a quick turnaround of requested materials. Language Committee and community members who worked with previous linguists stated that they had seen errors in published materials but felt powerless to correct them; they have since become very active partners in correcting and tracking changes in publication drafts. Three subsequent editions of the "talking dictionary" have now been developed and distributed to the community, including another print version, a smart-phone app and a web-based version (www.koasatiheritage.org and http://koasati.wm.edu).[11]

3.1.2 Transitioning to revitalization

By 2012, the grant to document conversation had ended and the tribe began to place greater emphasis on language revitalization. The active involvement of the tribal community throughout the project facilitated this transition, because documentation had consistently been undertaken with revitalization in mind. For example, tribal members participating in documentation workshops also

---

10 See Gordon, Martin, and Langley (2015) for a discussion of phonetic structures in Koasati. The community welcomed and enjoyed participating in this phonetic research (the study was funded by National Science Foundation grant #1065334). Some elders viewed it as a way to double-check their spelling of common speech occurrences such as vowel lengthening, nasalization, and final consonant clusters.

11 A reviewer raises the question of compensation for linguists working with communities. If a linguist is not paid by the tribe and is not allowed to publish through an academic press, then how is this model sustainable? We are choosing to self-publish for now so that the community can see the work that is being done and can offer feedback. With time, the community may be comfortable with publishing in a more permanent format. The academics were also welcome to publish articles on specific topics (e.g., phonetics). The community in fact enjoyed hearing about these research projects and learning that their language had tone.

worked with researchers and students to produce teaching posters, smartphone apps, games, song booklets, children's videos and other pedagogical materials. Although community members initially expressed great interest in digital teaching resources, printed materials such as a children's picture dictionary, phrase book, and conversation book are the most widely and frequently used pedagogical resources (Coushatta Tribe of Louisiana 2010, 2011, 2013, 2015).[12]

Documentation is in many ways easier than revitalization: Linguists have well-developed techniques for making recordings, transcribing them, and analyzing them. Starting an immersion school, finding long-term resources, training teachers, and developing a curriculum are much more difficult projects financially and politically. The community had many meetings during this time to discuss options for teaching children in an immersion environment. In 2015 Heather Williams became the first tribal member to graduate with both a degree in Early Childhood Education and an Immersion Teaching Certificate, and she immediately set about getting Tribal Council approval for partial-immersion teaching of 3–5 year-olds in the tribal head start program. Ms. Williams is now the school's director, and team-teaches immersion classes with an Elder speaker who is a long-time language advocate and active member of the Koasati Language Committee. Initial observations indicate that students are actively engaged in the learning process, the immersion classroom is lively and fun, and students are speaking Koasati both at school and in their home environment.[13]

There was also considerable community interest in producing teaching materials for older children and adults. Developing pedagogical materials was not as straightforward as might be imagined based on the existing research on Koasati, however. For example, the community had access to a full reference grammar (Kimball 1991), but that work was addressed to linguists and is largely an attempt to isolate and identify the affixes in the language: it is not really possible to use that work to create a sentence someone would want to say. We consequently had

---

[12] A community-driven project such as this one often requires a balancing act between the goals of researchers and community members (see Czakowska-Higgins et al. this volume; Rice this volume). This is particularly evident when working to develop digital pedagogical media such as video games and language apps. Although significant benefits can be gained from utilizing technology in support of language learning, accompanying challenges can consume excessive time and resources (e.g., hardware and software purchases, maintenance of assets, data storage, and training.) See Little et.al. (2015) for a discussion of balancing digital and traditional Indigenous language teaching and learning methods within a collaborative community-university program as well as Miyashita et al. (this volume).
[13] The community is working with researchers to develop an evaluation strategy for language revitalization. Current plans include both written and on-line surveys of changes in language use and ideology.

to do a great deal of research on the language as we conducted other sorts of documentation.

Because coauthor Martin lives in Virginia, much fieldwork had been confined to visits during the summer or spring breaks. In 2014, however, Martin offered a course for five undergraduates at William and Mary who met via webcam with Koasati speakers in the Coushatta Heritage Department. For one academic semester the group worked together, producing a set of classroom activities, a draft of a teaching grammar, and a book of conversations. The constructed conversations were especially useful. Each week one member of the staff would be asked to write a conversation between two individuals (perhaps in a funny situation). The linguistics students would then go over that conversation with speakers to find out where each word came from and how the sentence was built up. The students subsequently visited the Tribe and assisted in using a website called Memrise to produce electronic flashcards with audio for the conversations.[14]

From its inception, the Koasati Language Committee has promoted the use of spoken language in natural settings. Project activities have incorporated a mixture of informal social activities, such as community gatherings and meetings of basket-weavers, with naturally-occurring Koasati, and summer camps where Koasati is taught to tribal youth. A variety of teaching methods are utilized depending on the preferences of the teacher(s) and learner(s). Modified master-apprentice situations are popular, involving small groups of learners and mentors for situations like the Tribal Princess contest (which now requires spoken Koasati from each contestant). In one case, three generations of tribal members worked together to record and teach songs (a semi-fluent speaker recorded his mother singing an old gospel favorite, another fluent speaker transcribed the song and gave it to her daughter, who used both the recording and the written lyrics to teach the song to a tribal teenager).

Full-immersion Koasati classes at McNeese University for community high school students were taught in June 2016; this was the first time that Koasati had been taught anywhere for college credit. Students were evaluated using a rubric based on the European common framework for spoken and written language. Initial assessment indicated that all of the students increased at least one level in proficiency.[15]

---

14 Koasati Conversations and Koasati for Kids, located at www.memrise.com. Koasati 101 was added in January 2016 to accompany the immersion class.
15 We developed the Koasati evaluation rubric after examining the most commonly used Proficiency Assessments, including the U.S., Canadian, and European measures (American Council on the Teaching of Foreign Languages, *Association Canadien des Professeurs d'Immersion*, and the European Common Framework). We found that the Canadian (ACPI) spoken and written language referentials could most readily be modified to include features specific to Koasati in the

4 Comparing university-driven research to community-driven research

The Koasati Language Project is a community-driven research project that in many ways serves to balance previous university-driven research.[16] As our own project has unfolded, it has led to numerous discussions about previous researchers, their methods, and about academic research in general. Here we highlight a few of the differences that begin to emerge when research is conceived of, initiated by, and conducted by community members.

We note first that community-driven research is by its nature political. In order to be successful, community-driven research must meet the needs of the community or run the risk of losing support. Many of the traditional goals of language documentation (a full dictionary, reference grammar, etc.) are projects that require years of concentrated effort to complete. When a community itself embarks on a long-term project, it is better politically to have a constant flow of products that will justify the work. In the case of the Koasati Language Project, we did this by first publishing a topical dictionary and then a small dictionary. This was then followed by a larger dictionary with audio. The community could see that we were making progress and was then willing to volunteer their time.

Managing a community-driven project can also have an effect on the methods used. When most linguists are doing lexicography, for example, they work one-on-one with speakers. The speaker may not see what the linguist writes, and the community may not have access to those notes until years later. When our group conducted lexicography, however, it was in a classroom at the Fire Department. The whole community was invited and lunch was provided. The spelling of

---

analysis. ACPI referentials also had the advantage of linking directly to the European Common Framework. The authors also examined language assessments that have been used in Indigenous programs throughout the U.S., such as the Salish (http://www.interiorsalish.com/languageassessment.html) and Northwest Tribal (http://pages.uoregon.edu/nwili/language-proficiency-benchmarks) programs. The Coushatta Tribe is very appreciative to Dr. Michelle Haj-Broussard of the University of Louisiana-Lafayette for her assistance in developing this evaluation rubric, and for her ongoing support of Koasati language revitalization efforts.

16 We make a distinction here between research that is primarily based in a language community, and research which is entirely driven by the language community. In the latter model, the community decides what research is needed and seeks out specific researchers to provide expertise. Although there are other models of collaboration, in this case the Coushatta community deliberately sought more control over the research because of past experiences (see Czaykowska-Higgins et al. this volume; Rice this volume; and Junker this volume).

words, their definitions, and example sentences were projected to the group on a screen, and there was interesting and lively discussion.[17]

A community-driven research project may collect data that is quantitatively and qualitatively different from a university-driven project. We believe that participants in a community-driven project are more likely to understand the products that will result from the research. This may make them more generous with their time and knowledge (the elders we worked with spent hours and hours volunteering their time). It might also mean that they refrain from discussing some topics because they don't wish it to appear in print. This is, in fact, the result we want. In the Koasati Language Project, we were surprised when work on constructed conversations suddenly yielded many new insights into how specific grammatical forms were used. Kimball (1991: 190–193), for example, notes two suffixes -*laho* and -*laha* that he calls "irrealis; future". Kimball offered examples of each suffix, but the difference between them was not clear to us until Kathy Poncho wrote the following dialogue about a teacher speaking to a classroom of children:

(Teacher)	**Himaayap hompahil*laha*, hompankon.**
	Today we're going to play a game.
(Students)	**Naason hompahil*laha*?**
	What are we going to play?
(Teacher)	**Hompahil*laha*, Choskani, Choskani, Saalakla.**
	We're going to play Duck, Duck, Goose.

It was examples like this that helped us understand that -*laha* is used for more immediate and more definite futures. Linguists and anthropologists are fond of collecting traditional narratives, but those are often told in the remote past and not particularly good sources of linguistic data. It takes conversational data (even constructed conversational data) to understand many features of grammar.

Our Koasati Language Project was fortunate to have the generous participation of dozens of Elder speakers, young adults, and even children. This broad participation was possible because it was a community project operation within community norms. The tradition in this community is for people to come together, visit, and share a meal. That's how our project was conducted. Of course, the type of participation also differed. In university-driven linguistic research, an academic generally poses questions, and a community member passively gives translations or judgments. In the Koasati Language Project, community members were being trained to conduct interviews, to edit sound files, to teach lessons, to

---

[17] Our initial assumption was that we would document more variation in a group setting. We are now less certain of this, as some, particularly younger speakers deliberately stayed quiet when the form they used differed from others. This was true even when we had addressed language variation and had encouraged speakers to share their own way of speaking.

publish newsletters and books, and to use software to transcribe and translate interviews. The project thus created expertise that will undoubtedly lead to future projects.

One of the most important consequences of the community-driven approach taken is that the community embraces and takes responsibility for every product that emerges. Two elders on the Language Committee, Dan and Janice Sylestine, have spent countless hours going over every definition in our dictionary and checking again to make sure the changes are made. Heather Williams spent weeks on a children's book, checking first with her mother, and then with the committee. This tendency is so pervasive that Hasselbacher (2015b) invents a term "iterative authorship" to describe it. It is a process that differs from traditional peer review, but that succeeds in this context.

There is little doubt that the traditional Lone Wolf model can produce a great deal of research on a language. In the case of Koasati, however, that research created a rift between the community and academics. In order to repair that, we deliberately shifted very heavily toward community goals and away from academic research interests, but even in that context we were able to carry out considerable research on lexicography, on grammatical tone, and on grammar.

The evident appeal and success of the community-driven approach raises possibilities for additional academic research in projects such as this, such as the local factors that work for, or against, a program's success (Dobrin 2008: 303); the contrast between Western and indigenous knowledge systems in program content and evaluation (Grenoble and Whitecloud 2014: 3); and generational shifts in language usage and ideology (Hasselbacher 2015b; Nevins 2004: 284).

5 Conclusion

In February 2009, the Coushatta Tribe produced its first indigenous-language newsletter, named *Kowassaati Aathiihilka* (Koasati News). A stack of newsletters was left on the counter of the Coushatta Café, a popular lunch spot for tribal members and employees. When Loretta Williams, the official transcriber for the Koasati language project, went to the café, she would be asked to read the newsletter out loud, to demonstrate that the text did in fact encode Koasati. "Is it really," one man asked, "written in Indian?"

Seven years later, written Koasati is widely available in the community, though Elder speakers still prefer to hear rather than read Koasati. The majority of tribal members are aware of language learning resources, are comfortable using at least some of these resources, and perceive opportunities to become involved in what is still widely known as "the language project". The initial atmosphere of hesitancy evidenced by the reaction to the first newsletter has shifted dramatically with tribal members involved in projects such as writing Koasati poems and slogans, and plans for the new tribal convenience store including all-Koasati interior signage.[18] The community attitude is best summarized in a slogan developed for the 2012 Koasati Language camp tee-shirt: *"Kosnap, Kowassaatok om: Konnaathiihilką Ahitchaachilkaap, Komaati Ahichaachilkalaho"* (We are Koasati: If We Protect our Language, We will Protect our People).

References

Bowern, Claire, and Natasha Warner. 2015. 'Lone wolves' and collaboration: A reply to Crippen & Robinson (2013). *Language Documentation & Conservation* 9. 59–85. http://hdl.handle.net/10125/24634 (accessed 20 May 2017).

Burnham, Gene. 1979. *Naas Mathaali & Naas Onapa*. Elton, LA: Coushatta Tribe of Louisiana.

Coushatta Tribe of Louisiana. 2013. *Koasati dictionary*. Elton, LA: Coushatta Heritage Publications in Language and Culture.

Coushatta Tribe of Louisiana. 2015. *Koasati conversations*. Elton, LA: Coushatta Heritage Publications in Language and Culture.

Coushatta Tribe of Louisiana. 2010. *Stahooba Naathiihilka (Koasati picture dictionary)*. Compiled by Heather Williams. Elton, LA: Coushatta Heritage Publications in Language and Culture.

Coushatta Tribe of Louisiana. 2011. *Ittooyat Naathiihilkas (Koasati phrase book)*. Elton, LA: Coushatta Heritage Publications in Language and Culture.

Crippen, James A. and Laura C. Robinson. 2013. In defense of the lone wolf: Collaboration in language documentation. *Language Documentation & Conservation* 7. 123–135. http://hdl.handle.net/10125/4577 (accessed 20 May 2017).

Czaykowska-Higgins, Ewa. 2009. Research models, community engagement, and linguistic fieldwork: Reflections on working within Canadian Indigenous communities. *Language Documentation & Conservation* 3 (1). 15–50. http://hdl.handle.net/10125/4423 (accessed 20 May 2017).

Dobrin, Lise M. 2008. From linguistic elicitation to eliciting the linguist: Lessons in community empowerment from Melanesia. *Language* 84 (2). 300–324.

Fischer, John L. 1963. Koasati, Bel Abbey, 1963 [sound recording]. John L and Ann K. Fischer Fischer Sound Recordings, 1961–1976. National Anthropological Archives.

Gatschet, Albert S. 1885. Koassati vocabulary. National Anthropological Archives MS 902.

Gordon, Matthew, Jack B. Martin, and Linda Langley. 2015. Some phonetic structures of Koasati. *International Journal of American Linguistics* 81 (1): 83–118.

---

18 The Tribal Council member overseeing the project worked closely with Language Committee members to make this happen. His decision to use only Koasati signage was unanimously supported by the entire Council.

Grenoble, Lenore and Simone S. Whitecloud. 2014. Conflicting goals, ideologies and beliefs in the field. In Peter K. Austin and Julia Sallabank (eds.), *Endangered languages. Beliefs and ideologies in language endangerment, documentation and revitalization*, 337–354. London: British Academy.

Haas, Mary. 1934. Alibamu-Koasati and Creek vocabulary and texts. Field notes. American Philosophical Society, Philadelphia, PA.

Haas, Mary. 1944. Men's and women's speech in Koasati. *Language* 20. 142–149.

Hasselbacher, Stephanie. 2013. 'Easy, little bit slow, and soft': Ethnohistorical evidence for changes in Koasati gender deixis since the 1930s. Paper presented at the American Society for Ethnohistory Annual Meeting, New Orleans, Louisiana.

Hasselbacher, Stephanie. 2015a. Koasati and 'all the olden talk': Ideologies of linguistic conservatism and the mediation of linguistic authority. *Native South* 8.

Hasselbacher, Stephanie. 2015b. '*Written in Indian': Creating legitimized literacy and authorized speakership in Koasati*. Williamsburg, VA: The College of William and Mary dissertation.

John, Douglas. 1930. Dictionary: Coushatta Indian Tribe language. Lafayette, LA: Galvez Chapter of the National Society of Daughters of the American Revolution, American Indians Committee.

Kimball, Geoffrey. 1987. Men's and women's speech in Koasati: A reappraisal. *International Journal of American Linguistics* 53 (1): 30–38.

Kimball, Geoffrey. 1989. Peregrine Falcon and Great Horned Owl: Ego and shadow in a Koasati tale. *Southwest Journal of Linguistics* 9 (1): 45–74

Kimball, Geoffrey. 1990. A further note on Koasati 'men's' speech. *International Journal of American Linguistics* 56 (1): 158–162.

Kimball, Geoffrey. 1991. *Koasati grammar*. Lincoln, NE: University of Nebraska Press.

Kimball, Geoffrey. 1993. Two hunters, two wives, two fogs and two clawed witches: The use of the dual in a Koasati narrative. *International Journal of American Linguistics* 59 (4): 473.

Kimball, Geoffrey. 1994. *Koasati dictionary*. Lincoln, NE: University of Nebraska Press.

Kimball, Geoffrey. 2010. *Koasati traditional narratives: Kowassâa:Ti Incokfa:Lihilkâa*. Lincoln, NE: University of Nebraska Press.

Langley, Bertney and Linda Langley. 2009. Kowassaaton Ilhaalos: Let us hear Koasati: Developing and implementing the Koasati language project, In Candace K. Galla, Stacey Oberly, G. L. Romero, Maine Sam, and Ofelia Zepeda (eds.), *American Indian Language Development Institute: Thirty year tradition of speaking from our heart*. Tucson, AZ: American Indian Language Development Institute, 20–26.

Little, Carol Rose, Travis Wysote, Elise McClay, and Jessica Coon. 2015. Language research and revitalization through a community-university partnership: The Mi'gmaq research partnership. *Language Documentation & Conservation* 9. 292–306. http://nflrc.hawaii.edu/ldchttp://hdl.handle.net/10125/24644 (accessed 21 May 2017).

Nevins, Eleanor M. 2004. Learning to listen: Confronting two meanings of language loss in the contemporary White Mountain Apache speech community. *Journal of Linguistic Anthropology* 14 (2). 269–288.

Rice, Keren. 2011. Documentary linguistics and community relations. *Language Documentation & Conservation* 5. 187–207. http://hdl.handle.net/10125/4498 (accessed 21 May 2017).

Rising, David P. 1992. *Switch reference in Koasati discourse*. Summer Institute of Linguistics and the University of Texas at Arlington Publications in Linguistics, Publication 109. Dallas; Arlington: Summer Institute of Linguistics; University of Texas at Arlington.

Saville-Troike, Muriel. 1988. A note on men's and women's speech in Koasati. *International Journal of American Linguistics* 54 (2): 241–242.
Stenzel, Kristine. 2014. The pleasures and pitfalls of a 'participatory' documentation project: An experience in Northwestern Amazonia. *Language Documentation & Conservation* 8. 287–306. http://hdl.handle.net/10125/24608 (accessed 20 May 2017).
Swanton, John R. n.d.a "First series" of Koasati texts 1912–1920. NAA MS 4154.
Swanton, John R. n.d.b "Second series" of Koasati texts 1912–1920. NAA MS 1818.
Swanton, John R. n.d.c ". NAA MS 4154.
Taylor, Lyda Averill. 1937. *A Comparative Study of Southeastern Cultures*. New Haven: Yale University MA thesis.

Ardis Eschenberg and Alice Saunsoci
Full collaboration of native speaker and linguist, working together for language revitalization

Abstract: This chapter describes the roles and the patterns formed by a native language speaker of Umóⁿhoⁿ (Omaha) and a linguist over sixteen years of working together. Their work is explored within the framework of Community Based Research (CBR), which provides for linguistic work that is "for, with and by community members" (Czaykowska-Higgins 2009: 15). This framework corrects a power imbalance in traditional models of the linguist-speaker relationship, reframing it from expert-consultant to that of equal collaborators. In addition, the authors explore their collaboration from the Umóⁿhoⁿ (non-western) lens, examining how Umóⁿhoⁿ cultural values guided, underscored and led to success in their collaboration. While not all linguists conducting fieldwork do so for an extended time, each forms a relationship with those they document. From the outset, this relationship should be considered not only in terms of western values and ethics, but also in terms of how it will be perceived by and benefit the native language speakers and community (Czaykowska-Higgins 2009; Dobrin 2008). When the linguist is an outsider, this perception is based on cultural values and roles within a community being extended to the work of the outsider and may not be those expected or intended by the outsider. The successful collaboration of a linguist and native speaker presented in this paper was based on traditional cultural values and attests to the validity of utilizing CBR in the field situation to guide work successfully.

Keywords: extended fieldwork, cultural values, collaboration, relationship, community-based research, native language speaker

---

Ardis Eschenberg, Hale Alakaʻi, 121D, Windward Community College, 45-720 Keaʻahala Rd., Kaneohe, HI 96744, ardise@hawaii.edu
Alice Saunsoci, Nebraska Indian Community College, c/o Ardis Eschenberg, Hale Alakaʻi, 121D, Windward Community College, 45-720 Keaʻahala Rd., Kaneohe, HI 96744, ardise@hawaii.edu

https://doi.org/10.1515/9783110527018-008

1 Introduction

Ardis Toiⁿgthehe Eschenberg and Alice Moⁿshiⁿhoⁿthi Saunsoci collaborated on Umoⁿhoⁿ (Omaha) language documentation and revitalization for sixteen years. Their relationship, built on a shared devotion to language and a deep foundation of caring, began when they both started teaching at the Umoⁿhoⁿ Nation Public School. Over ten years they worked together there, at the Umoⁿhoⁿ Alcohol Program and at Nebraska Indian Community College, where Dr. Eschenberg became Academic Dean and Mrs. Saunsoci became Director of the Umoⁿhoⁿ Language Program. Mrs. Saunsoci adopted Ardis, giving her the name of her own adopted mother, Toiⁿgthehe.

Moⁿshiⁿhoⁿthi, an enrolled member of the Omaha Tribe of Nebraska, spoke only Umoⁿhoⁿ until the age of nine. She was a proud member of the Thatada clan and lived by the original Umoⁿhoⁿ traditions as a Pipe Carrier, Sundancer, and Champion Women's Traditional Dancer. She was mother of six drums and was dedicated to her family and community. She taught the Umoⁿhoⁿ language for sixteen years. She held an Associate of Arts in Human Services from Nebraska Indian Community College, where she also served as a board member. She worked actively with related tribes through the Dhegiha Language Preservation Society.

Ardis first came to the Umoⁿhoⁿ Nation to conduct fieldwork for her dissertation, *The article system of Umoⁿhoⁿ* (2005). She met Alice on the first day she began volunteering at the Culture Center of the Umoⁿhoⁿ Nation Public School. Originally planning to volunteer for three months, Ardis stayed for ten years, largely due to her relationship with Alice and commitment to language preservation. She moved to Hawaii in 2010 but the two continued to work together over the phone and through infrequent but treasured meetings until Moⁿshiⁿhoⁿthi passed in 2015. Their work culminated in the book, *500+ verbs in Umoⁿhoⁿ* (2016). Their collaboration also resulted in a two-year program of Omaha language coursework at the Tribal College, documentation of speakers from each clan and across many families in this tribe, one dissertation describing syntactico-pragmatic parameters of the article system of Omaha, and an increase in language awareness for their community.

Through language work, they formed a deep interpersonal relationship and tie that endured distance and upheld a common humanistic interest. This was done through the recognition of the skills, knowledge, and strengths each possessed, defining individual roles to promote maximum effectiveness, and creating patterns in their teaching, documentation, and presentation, which were repeated and refined. This chapter describes the roles and the patterns they formed in their work together, as well as obstacles they encountered and how they negotiated these obstacles. Their work is considered in the framework of community-based research (CBR), which provides for linguistic work that is "for, with and by community members" (Czaykowska-Higgins 2009: 15). This framework corrects a power imbalance in traditional models of linguist-speaker relationship, reframing it from expert-consultant to that of equal collaborators. It is conceived primarily by and for western linguists to frame their practice, in response both to linguist experience and community demands (e.g. Czaykowska-Higgins 2009: 28). In the final section of this chapter, the authors explore their collaboration from the Umoⁿhoⁿ (non-western) lens, examining how Umoⁿhoⁿ cultural values guided, underscored and led to success in their collaboration, which also supports CBR. This work is dedicated to Alice Moⁿshiⁿhoⁿthi Saunsoci, as an effort to inspire other such collaborations and life work.

2 Collaboration in the classroom

From the beginning, Alice and Ardis enjoyed teaching together. Over the course of their ten years of work, they developed mutually supportive roles in the classroom that recognized and underscored their individual strengths. A native speaker, Alice possessed not only fluent speech, but also cultural understanding of Umoⁿhoⁿ students. Due to this, she was always the primary language instructor. She ran the classroom and their lessons, graded all oral assessments, and provided for the scope and sequence of cultural topics and lessons.

Ardis, a linguist who possessed teaching experience at the college level, had strengths in linguistic analysis, language pedagogy, and expectations of college instruction. She created the syllabi, homework assignments, handouts, and other written materials for the class. Ardis graded written assignments, kept attendance, and turned in grades and paperwork. Working with Alice, she developed scope and sequence for the curriculum based on major patterns in Umoⁿhoⁿ (e.g. verb conjugations, noun phrase structure, sentence structure etc.), and documented lessons.

Czaykowska-Higgins notes that a goal of CBR is often to train community members in academic research practices and subjects (Czaykowska-Higgins 2009: 42). In this collaboration, mutually defined roles existed, but each also learned the other's role. Ardis learned Umoⁿhoⁿ and took a greater role in teaching if Alice did not feel well. Alice learned grammatical patterns, how to build lessons around these, and how to assess students' acquisition. For example, when she produced a verb that they had not documented, Alice would often start to recite the person forms and write them down before Ardis even asked. They would then giggle at each other, knowing they had reversed roles. This collaboration emphasized the 4 R's underlying collaborative, community based research – respect, responsibility, relationships, and reciprocity (Rice 2004, this volume). The authors respected each other's strengths and knowledge, which was shared reciprocally. Both took responsibility for their roles and centered their teaching on their relationship.

A regular pattern in classroom teaching aided lesson planning, focused on their strengths, and provided predictability for students. In a typical class, the first and last 15 minutes were allotted for questions in English, usually about the lesson or cultural topics. The bulk of class was conducted in Umo^{n}ho^n immersion. Students were instructed to only speak Umo^{n}ho^n and to act it out or remain silent rather than using English. To accomplish this, the instructors modeled appropriate responses (both verbal and non-verbal), repeated information, acted out content, used non-verbal cues, and limited the language to that of the immediate context. This led to student success in an immersion environment despite very limited fluency. Encouragement, positive reinforcement, and respect for all were tenets of this immersion. This set the stage for respectful relationships with students as per Rice (2004) and led to student interest in further language and linguistic training. Five students committed to immersion language training in a two year program. Several others also took a language documentation class offered by the authors. This multiplied language research and teaching by the community, as promoted by CBR.

The immersion lessons themselves were highly structured, providing repetitive themes for students. Each day would begin with a short rote prayer. Then, students would be asked about the weather and about how they felt. Students also learned to introduce themselves in a culturally appropriate way, which enabled them to introduce themselves at community events and with elders. Beginning with only one phrase, each of these grew by one new phrase per week until students could participate well in small talk and introductions. These introductory activities were used every day for four semesters, giving students a solid foundation in basic conversation and also giving predictability to a class in a subject that was at once native and foreign to them, as the majority of students were not speakers. These topics also created larger community coherence and collaboration as these themes were also taught at other community education centers such as the public schools, Headstart, and the Alcohol Program.

After these introductory activities, immersion continued through hands-on language application. Initial activities were primarily commands and responses, using the methodology of Total Physical Response (Asher 2009). However, due to the importance of the verb in Umo^{n}ho^n grammar, the order of commands introduced was based primarily on verb conjugation type, rather than the sequences recommended in Asher (2009). These command-response drills were then usually followed by an activity, which explored a limited set of the verbs in the given pattern. For example, the verb "to draw" might be used with students drawing animals or another semantic set at the board. This might be followed by the verb "to erase," which conjugates similarly. Depending on the scope of the lesson, students would either have to do the action commanded, command the next student, answer a question with using the first person singular form (i.e. "I drew the buffalo"), ask the next student a question using the second person, say what others students had done using the third person, or say what we all did using the first person plural form. Thus, the same lesson could be used with increasing scope, and the patterns were reinforced and expanded with new verbs. Activities could be simple games (e.g. musical chairs, go fish), everyday activities (e.g. cooking, eating, folding clothes, drawing), or complex games used to test acquired patterns (e.g. monopoly, a Valentine's game requiring verbs for buying, eating, and going, a definite article game). Games could be either existing games, such as card or board games, re-created in Umo^{n}ho^n, or games made by the instructors to reinforce concepts.

This focus on verb conjugation patterns and teaching through immersion activities, coupled with structured, repeated components in each class, not only promoted student acquisition but also empowered Alice as a Speech Community Linguist (Yamada 2007) to become empowered to build lesson plans relying on grammatical concepts. She mastered the pattern of how to teach the conjugation, which allowed her to introduce and reinforce new verbs. It also made it so that patterns were acquired without the need to resort to technical linguistic jargon. The terms often developed when the students or Alice referred to a pattern in discussion after a lesson. For example, naming a verb class "bth verbs" resulted from Alice's comment that "I bth this and I bth that with all these verbs." Yamada (2007) promotes using accessible terms.

3 Collaboration outside the classroom

3.1 Documentation

Documentation of lessons was a primary need in creating a two year Umo^{n}ho^n curriculum. The native speaker and linguist met before and after each class to develop, review and refine lessons together, as well as document verbs. While the linguist primarily performed the written, as well as audio and video, recording of the language, the speaker was also well trained in the orthography and wrote down words and phrases, documenting the language. As noted above, several additional students were further trained in documentation. They continue to impact the community today when the authors no longer teach the language. Alice's son, Frank Thugana Saunsoci, trained by the authors, continues what Alice founded, teaching Umo^{n}ho^n at the tribal college and documenting elders. Alice's daughters, Alison Genewi^n Saunsoci and Renee Sho^{n}ge Xube Wi^n Sans Souci, and her son, Andre Paso^n No^{n}zhi^n Saunsoci, all work in capacities that include language revitalization, carrying on their mother's tradition. Several other former students are now active in language and cultural practices and revitalization as well.

Roles formed for teaching and lesson documentation carried over into the realm of speaker documentation. The linguist Ardis often wrote grant proposals to fund efforts. The speaker Alice identified appropriate speakers based on cultural knowledge, role in the tribe, and other factors, such as availability and fluency. Ardis created appropriate paperwork, such as check requests, informed consent forms, etc., and set up recording equipment and disseminated materials. Alice ensured that speakers understood the paperwork and gave input on who could have copies of the recordings and for what purposes it might be used. Ardis recorded while Alice conducted the interview or spoke with the speaker, which allowed recordings to be completely in Umo^{n}ho^n and speakers to interact with a community person they knew.

Again, clearly defined roles based on strengths, knowledge and training allowed linguist and native speaker to function together well as a team. Both would help one another as needed. The relationship was reciprocal and respectful with each taking responsibility for their part. The knowledge and role of both were validated and formed a greater whole. While the native speaker did not necessarily learn the linguist's role, other community members were trained, as recommended by Yamada (2007). Alice's decision-making in whom to interview and guiding of the topics and conversation exemplified research by, with, and for the community (Czaykowska-Higgins 2009).

3.2 Presentations

This team of native speaker and linguist also frequently presented together. The synergy developed in teaching and documentation created a foundation here as well. For linguistics conferences Ardis would write an abstract with input from Alice. As linguist, she would also complete any necessary paperwork and create handouts and powerpoints. At the conference Alice would introduce them as a team, and Ardis would introduce the topic they were presenting, noting linguistic and pedagogical concepts. Often they would do hands-on enactments of lessons, where, similarly to in the classroom, Alice led and Ardis served as model student. Other times Alice provided examples of grammatical usage, context, and cultural underpinnings. As with teaching, these presentations were enjoyed by both linguist and native speaker because each was able to excel in their role. Roles were not exchanged but the native speaker presented in primarily academic linguistic conferences successfully with positive feedback. This empowered the native speaker and exemplified research done with, by and for the community, modeling it for the larger academic community (Czaykowska-Higgins 2009).

3.3 Publications

Both linguist and native speaker were aware of the need to document the language through written form. However, their sixteen years resulted in fewer publications than might have been desired. The linguist's dissertation (Eschenberg 2005) and a chapter in a proceedings for a conference was published (Eschenberg 2004). A curriculum with many associated materials was created and published via the tribal college website, but when the website was revamped, this curriculum disappeared. As it was archived at the college and paper copies existed, this curriculum continues to be used. The largest body of work that was created through this partnership was the documentation of verb conjugation patterns and meaning over their sixteen years of collaboration (Eschenberg and Saunsoci 2016).

While the publications resulting from this partnership were few, each one represents a significant collaboration between native speaker and author. They document language in a way that is informed both by cultural practitioner and by theoretical linguist. Their verb book embodies this synergy, creating a work that is valid for both tribal members learning the language and also linguists, as promoted by CBR (Czaykowska-Higgins 2009).

4 Obstacles and concerns

While their relationship and life work were a huge source of fulfillment to both authors, they also experienced barriers and setbacks to their work. Potential obstacles to a full collaboration between linguist and native speaker include difficulties of cross-cultural communication, possible limitations, taboos, and ties created by adoption or "fictive kinship," as well as concerns for native peoples entering into a close working relationship with an outsider, differing motivations and goals for linguists and community members, privacy concerns for tribal members in documentation, and implications on career pathways and mobility for linguists who choose to work as a part of a community (Czaykowska-Higgins 2009; Dobrin 2008; Yamada 2007).

While both authors spoke English fluently and communicated primarily through this means, their backgrounds and worldviews were substantially different. Ardis was raised in downstate New York and attended college in New Orleans, St. Petersburg (Russia), and Buffalo. Alice was raised in the capital of the Omaha Nation in Macy, Nebraska. At the age of nine, she attended boarding school in Pipe Stone, Minnesota. Later, she attended college in Macy, Nebraska. As mentioned in the introduction, Alice practiced her traditional ways strongly and with pride. Ardis was largely unaware of Umo^{n}ho^n ways prior to fieldwork. Thus, differences in understanding of how the world operated – from the making of a grilled cheese sandwich to the animacy of rocks – could not be taken for granted. However, Alice adopted Ardis as a daughter and showed her the kindness, support, and understanding one would show their own child. Ardis worked hard to learn from mistakes and tried not to impose her cultural values and understanding on their language work in the tribal setting. This kindness, love, and mutual respect allowed them to grow through differences, underscoring the value of relationship promoted by Rice (2004) and others (see especially Rice, Czaykowska-Higgins et al., Langely et al., and Velásquez Runk and Carpio Opua this volume).

Within an indigenous community, one's role in society, including with whom they socialize and in which manner, are often prescribed to a greater extent than in western society. Thus, ties created by adoption or "fictive kinship" can impact the work of a linguist. There may be individuals and/or families who do not or must not socialize with you, based on their kinship via your adoption. For example, Umo^{n}ho^n mother-in-laws do not traditionally talk to son-in-laws. While Alice definitely helped Ardis to navigate the social system of the tribe, to be respectful and to know her relationships to relatives, taboo relationships did not affect their work to a large extent. However, Ardis was definitely exposed more to those who were closer to her adopted mother. This can impact documentation as other speakers can be overlooked. Ardis and Alice specifically planned recordings and actively selected members from a variety of clans to overcome potential selection bias.

Similarly, when a native person enters into a close working relationship with an outsider, this can have both positive and negative impacts (Czaykowska-Higgins 2009; Dobrin 2008). The outsider can validate their knowledge and help them grow skills. They may also be there a short time and not respect the relationship appropriately, treating it as a casual relationship. Ardis and Alice worked to have a balanced relationship, recognizing each other's strengths and skills. Their long association attests to their respect for and reciprocity and responsibility to their relationship.

Linguists and community members often have differing motivations and goals for language documentation (e.g. Czaykowska-Higgins 2009:42, 44, this volume; Dwyer 2010: 209; Gerdts 1998). For example, while linguists need to publish and present about the languages they study, tribal peoples may desire privacy for certain knowledge or language, viewing it as sacred. Federal grant providers also may look unfavorably upon applications which do not guarantee that all documentation be made publicly available, contrary to community desires (see Benedicto and Velásquez Runk and Carpio Opua this volume for discussion along these lines). Ardis and Alice had to learn to walk this path together and attempted to do so with extreme transparency that could occur due to their respect, reciprocity, and relationship (Rice 2004). For example, conversations occurred when a certain sentence or form was useful for Ardis' dissertation. If it was part of a larger work that a speaker did not want shared with the general public, the speaker was asked whether just the sentence or form could be used. Sometimes, Alice thought of other examples that might be used to prevent infringing on private materials, but still support a presentation or publication. At each point, the validity of the language primarily as a means of communication and cultural expression of the tribe, rather than scientific subject, was underscored. While certain verbs were not included in their verb book because they were considered taboo, this loss was considered small compared to the larger body that could then be published without controversy or regret.

Just as fieldwork decisions can affect grant funding, these decisions also impact linguistic career trajectories. Few tribes have positions available for resident linguists. Opportunities for mentoring by senior linguists to promote career growth are also less likely to be available in a given community. Generally, for the linguist to remain in the community over a period of years, rather than a summer or sabbatical, they must be independently wealthy or find a role that exists in the community. Due mainly to this, Ardis accepted a role in academic administration at the tribal college, which allowed her to also teach in the classroom with Alice. This provided a means for her to continue her work on the reservation. However, the responsibilities of chief academic officer also took much of her time away from language work. Ultimately, this foundational position in her career also caused her to pursue further career moves in academic administration, rather than linguistics.

5 Cultural values

Collins (1998) found that linguists and native speakers often have different views on language and its analysis, which is supported by Rice (2004).[1] Similarly, the nature of collaboration and good "field" relations may be conflicting. Dobrin (2008) found that the underlying values placed on language and language activities may be very different for linguists and speech communities. Ardis and Alice consciously relied on Umo^{n}ho^n traditional values to guide their work and decision-making. Their relationship was based on these values. That is, the authors were not guided by CBR when they worked together but, upon analysis, their methods conformed well to CBR. This attests to the validity of applying CBR in similar situations. The traditional Umo^{n}ho^n values underlying their work are explored below.

5.1 Éwithe wó^{n}githe 'we are all related'

Commonly, Umo^{n}ho^n prayers are ended in *éwithe wó^{n}githe* 'we are all related.' This recognizes the importance of relationship and kinship, which is the basis for Umo^{n}ho^n tribal organization, the *huthuga*. The *huthuga*, or tribal circle, placed each clan in the tribe in a specific place in relationship to other clans and the four directions. Each clan had specific roles, functions and names associated with it. When Alice adopted Ardis and gave her a name, she gave her a place in the circle in relation to her. Others then knew how to relate to her. Her role was a direct function of Alice's role. Alice was known as a keeper of language and tradition. This facilitated their work, their personal relationship and community understanding of this relationship.

This value of and role built upon relationship also shaped their work both in whom they worked with and how they collaborated. As noted above, Alice actively looked at the representation of different clans in documentation to ensure breadth, using her cultural value of relationship to evaluate her documentation work. Ardis, in her role and relationship as a daughter, was respectful and solicitous of Alice. She worked to provide the documentation and support that allowed Alice to concentrate in her role as source and instructor of language. This relationship appropriately placed elder as central and respected. Ardis did not act as source or teach the language without Alice. Alice continued in her role as elder and source after Ardis moved. Each had

---

[1] See Langley et al. and Florey this volume for similar discussion.

responsibilities to the other based on their relationship; these continued over time and separation. They were a team in a specific, culturally appropriate and recognized way.

5.2 *Washkó^n* 'be strong, try your best'

In encountering difficulty, Umo^{n}ho^n are encouraged to *washko^n-a/ga!* 'be strong!', to do their best. This value was underscored in the work of Alice and Ardis. Both struggled to maintain employment that would allow for their language work. They worked hard to share and document the language despite financial insecurity, remote location, and other difficulties. In teaching, they overcame a lack of curriculum, support materials, and teacher training in Umo^{n}ho^n.

They also maintained this philosophy personally, recognizing that the other was consistently trying her hardest and giving each other the benefit of the doubt. For example, when Ardis made a cultural misstep, Alice displayed understanding and patience, explaining what happened. This kindness was a result of their relationship (mother-daughter) and also a result of an understanding that each was trying her best.

In the classroom, this value was consistently emphasized to students. They were expected to respond and try their hardest in an Umo^{n}ho^n language only environment. As long as they were trying, they were praised and encouraged. This created a classroom space where all participated because they responded in the culturally appropriate way to a cultural expectation. Students tried their hardest for teachers who tried their hardest.

5.3 *Úshko^n údo^n* 'have good ways, be kind'

Kindness, forgiveness, and benevolence also are integral to the Umo^{n}ho^n concept of *úshko^n údo^n* 'to have good ways, to be kind.' This concept of goodness includes cultural values such as *wa'éthe* 'pity' and *thahó^n* 'thanks.' Umo^{n}ho^n are encouraged to be humble, to pity those who have less or do wrong, and to be thankful for what they have. When Ardis made errors, Alice showed pity (kindness), not shame or harshness.

Related to the values of thankfulness and kindness, is that of generosity. When one is blessed with good circumstances, she should share or *wagáthe* 'give away' and *ithíshi* 'feed' others. The following sentence illustrates this value of generosity: *Ithákizhno^n go^n Umo^{n}ho^n niashi^{n}ga íwabthishi tami^{n}k^{h}e.* 'Because I'm thankful, I'm going to feed the people.' Such people with good ways are respected: *Nú-akʰa wanóⁿdehide wathá'etha, éwoⁿgoⁿ ébthizhuba*. 'He's concerned with people (helpful), pities people, therefore I respect him.' These cultural values of kindness, thankfulness, pity, and generosity were also foundational to the relationship and work of Alice and Ardis. Food was an integral part of teaching. Students regularly cooked and ate together. Coffee was almost always present in case company visited. Grants were written so that speakers could be compensated well for their sharing of language. These activities embodied generosity of their program.

Knowledge, like food, was also to be shared. Alice did not hoard her language skills but shared them throughout the community. Ardis also worked to share knowledge about the language and how to document. This generosity was the foundation for their work in the classroom. They shared as instructors and expected students to share also.

Generosity was a basis for Ardis and Alice's relationship as well. Each shared their knowledge with the other, which allowed them to work together with understanding of their mutual roles. Alice described their relationship in the following sentence: *Gáshi wathítoⁿ zhuóⁿkigthai-ki nóⁿde oⁿthóⁿkisa*. 'Having worked together a long time, we're comfortable with each other.'

Their model of collaboration tied to native values of knowledge sharing and relationship, allowed them to work together comfortably, with an understanding of the other person, their role, and their values. It gave strength and comfort.

6 Further implications and conclusion

While not all linguists conducting fieldwork will do so for an extended time, each will form a relationship with those they document. From the outset, this relationship should be considered not only in terms of western values and ethics, but also in terms of how it will be perceived by and benefit the native language speakers and community (Czaykowska-Higgins 2009; Dobrin 2008). When the linguist is an outsider, this perception is based on cultural values and roles within a community being extended to the work of the outsider. These perceptions may not be those expected or intended by the outsider. This paper presented a successful collaboration of a linguist and native speaker, which was based on traditional cultural values and attested to the validity of using Rice's 4 R's (this volume) and CBR in the field situation to guide work successfully.

References

Asher, James J. 2009 [1996]. *Learning another language through action*, 7th ed. Los Gatos: Sky Oaks Productions, Inc.
Collins, James. 1998. Our ideologies and theirs. In Bambi B. Schieffelin, Kathryn A. Woolard, and Paul V. Kroskrity (eds.), *Language ideologies. Practice and theory*, 256–270. New York: Oxford University Press. (also in *Pragmatics* 2–3. 405–415).
Czaykowska-Higgins, Ewa. 2009. Research models, community engagement, and linguistic fieldwork: Reflections on working within Canadian Indigenous communities. *Language Documentation & Conservation* 3 (1). 15–50.
Dobrin, Lise. 2008. From linguistic elicitation to eliciting the linguist: Lessons in community empowerment from Melanesia. *Language* 84 (2). 300–324.
Dwyer, Arienne. 2010. Models of Successful Collaboration. In N. Louanna Furbee and Lenore A. Grenoble, (eds.), 193–212. *Language Documentation: Practice and Values*. Amsterdam: Benjamins: Postprint.
Eschenberg, Ardis. 2004. The operator projection, Omaha and diachronic syntax in RRG. In Brian Nolan (ed.), *Proceedings of the 2004 Role and Reference Grammar Conference*, 72–91. Dublin: Institute of Technology Blanchardstown.
Eschenberg, Ardis. 2005. *The article system of Umo^{n}ho^n*. Ann Arbor: UMI.
Eschenberg, Ardis, and Saunsoci, Alice. 2016. *500+ Verbs in Umo^{n}ho^n*. Createspace Independent Publishing Platform.
Gerdts, Donna. 1998. Beyond expertise: The role of the linguist in language revitalization programs. In Nicholas Ostler (ed), 13–22. *Endangered languages: What role for the specialist?* Proceedings of Second Foundation for Endangered Languages Conference. Bath, England: Foundation for Endangered Language.
Rice, Keren. 2004. Ethical issues in linguistic fieldwork: An overview. http://www.chass.utoronto.ca/lingfieldwork/pdf/2.pdf (accessed 11 August 2015).
Yamada, Racquel-Maria. 2007. Collaborative linguistic fieldwork: Practical application of the empowerment model. *Language Documentation & Conservation* 1 (2). 257–282.

Marie-Odile Junker
Participatory action research for Indigenous linguistics in the digital age

Abstract: In this paper, I reflect on my journey as a linguist exploring new methodologies when working with speakers of endangered languages in the era of digital technologies. I show that adopting a participatory action research framework can lead to unexpected positive developments. I also show how information technologies have allowed us to reach and engage a large community of speakers. Asking questions like "how do I make my intervention as a linguist in a language community support the maintenance of this language and empower its speakers?" led to the creation of several collaborative websites for Cree and Innu languages (see below), to an Algonquian Linguistic Atlas (www.atlas-ling.ca) and to our current collaborative project entitled: A digital infrastructure for Algonquian Languages: Dictionaries and Linguistic Atlas. This project now includes eleven participating dictionary teams and many communities of speakers sustaining each other.

Keywords: Participatory action research, information technology, websites, databases, dictionaries, linguistic atlas, indigenous languages, Canada, Algonquian, Cree, Innu

1 Participatory action research in linguistics

Life journeys are often guided by a question and end up being more about the path taken than the answer found. As a new graduate in Linguistics, I joined an interdisciplinary group exploring Participatory Action Research (henceforth PAR) (Manoukian 1990; Smith 1999; Morris and Muzychka 2002; Chevalier and Buckles 2013a), in my post-doc year in 1992 at Carleton University.

---

* I am grateful to the many individuals, community language activists, and kindred-spirits across disciplines who have made my Participatory Action Research journey possible. The list of names would be too long to include here, but can be found on the Credits sections of the various websites cited. Writing of this paper was partially funded by the Social Sciences and Humanity Research Council of Canada (SSHRC) grants # 35-2014-1199, 611-2016-0077 and 890-2013-0022. Thanks to Claire Owen for proofreading my non-native English and to two anonymous reviewers for their valuable comments.

Marie-Odile Junker, School of Linguistics and Language Studies, Carleton University, Ottawa, Ontario, Canada K1S 5B6, marieodile.junker@carleton.ca

https://doi.org/10.1515/9783110527018-009

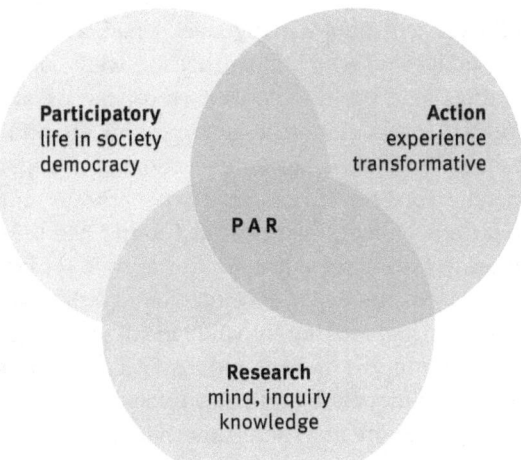

Figure 1: Participatory action research (from Chevalier and Buckles, 2013b: 2).

PAR seeks to understand the world by trying to change it, collaboratively (see Fig. 1 below). PAR was very new to me, and some of its key ideas seemed the opposite of what I had been taught: the focus was on the research process, and this process was more important than the goal. The research "subjects" were partners and could define the topic(s) of research. This paradigm challenged how I had learned to set goals, define results, and publish them. It questioned scientific neutrality and impartiality. I was the only linguist; all the others were psychologists, medical doctors, anthropologists, or international development experts. They were considering mental health patients, Indigenous people, or illiterate women in the Congo as valid research partners, capable of formulating and answering valid research questions that would positively impact their lives. I quickly learned that Linguistics had not been on the PAR agenda and vice-versa[1].

This led me to formulate the following question for myself and my field: "How do I make my intervention as a linguist in a language community support the maintenance of this language and empower its speakers?" I did not know how, I just started paying attention. At the time I was working on noble

---

[1] See Junker (2002) and Czaykowska-Higgins (2009, this volume). Like Benedicto (this volume), I do not make a strong distinction between PAR and CBR, except perhaps that PAR's focus on action goes a little bit further in calling you to the Gandhian stance: "Be the change that you wish to see in the world." This "activist" dimension challenges the culture, practices, power and role of Academia itself, as seen clearly in Benedicto's paper. It can also challenge the governing cultures of partner organizations.

theoretical questions like quantification in natural language. I had ventured outside most commonly-known languages on which most theories were based, and was curious to see if our findings held up in lesser-known or lesser-documented languages. I started listening to my elicitation sessions, paying attention to what the speakers were really saying, those little hesitations, comments, sighs, and moments of waning or waxing interest. I started sharing my hypotheses, and getting the speakers' insights. I started commenting on what I found beautiful in the language, and paid attention to how a speaker felt after a work session with me. I focused more on the quality of the experience for them (which was not always successful, of course) and started looking for what speakers thought would be useful to them and their community.[2] I had entered the PAR framework and was practising it.[3] After I became an associate professor, I decided I would follow my heart and not worry about promotion anymore. This changed my life.

2 A journey into information and communication technologies

2.1 The eastcree.org website and research with East Cree communities

By the mid-1990s, the Crees in Quebec, who had obtained their own school board,[4] had made Cree the official language of instruction from kindergarten to grade three. There was a great need for teaching resources in the Cree language,

---

[2] One of my first attempts included publishing a linguistic paper in Cree, co-written with my East Cree language consultant. I am grateful to John Nichols, editor of the *Papers of the Algonquian Conference* for being open to the idea, despite the technical challenges of the syllabics at the time. See Blacksmith and Junker (2001). Louise Blacksmith's name appears first on the Cree version, mine on the English version. The exercise of writing linguistic description in Cree in such a non-traditional genre for Cree, gave us very interesting insights into the language itself and forced us to be simple and clear in English. It was also the start of developing grammatical terminology in Cree for the teachers. See Benedicto (this volume) on the hegemony of English as an academic language.
[3] As a PAR practitioner, I have chosen to write this chapter as a personal narrative, so that it could be read by the Indigenous language speakers I work with. For that I am using a genre that can easily be translated into Cree, Innu or Atikamekw, known as *tipâchimuwin*.
[4] The *James Bay And Northern Quebec Agreement* (in French: *La Convention de la Baie James et du Nord québécois*), signed in November 1975, provided for the establishment of the *Cree School Board* and the *Cree Board of Health and Social Services of James Bay* serving Cree communities in Quebec.

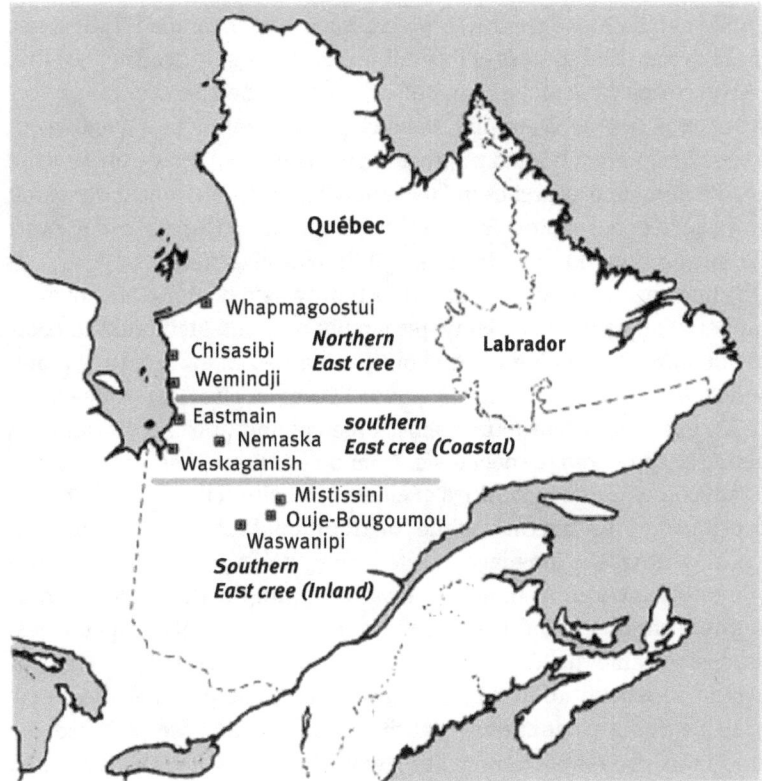

Figure 2: Map of Cree communities in Quebec, Canada

with the challenge of serving nine different communities separated by hundreds of kilometers (Fig. 2).

One of these needs was for an East Cree grammar, which I started working on, guided by the PAR framework, trying to co-write it with Cree speakers in a way that would be accessible. Information technology and the internet were quickly developing, and although internet connections were slow and unreliable, the Canadian government had made it a priority to network the North. I bet on them keeping their promises, and launched in 2000 the eastcree.org website with Louise Blacksmith, a Cree speaker with whom I was working. Our goal was to offer an online grammar and other language resources needed for the Cree teachers and students. The idea (new at the time) was that the grammar could be interactive, contain oral material and be modified as we discovered more. The Cree Programs department of the School Board joined us right away as official partner, and we went on developing online resources together ever since. In 2004, we launched an online dictionary (Junker et al. 2004–present).[5] We graduated from simple HTML pages to web database design. The success of the online dictionary surprised us. The first year, about 5000 words were looked up, but we soon reached an average of over 1000 words per week (> 55,000 annually), which is remarkable for a language of 12,000 speakers. Despite the limited number of speakers who know how to write the language, the number of searches in Cree is very high. It is facilitated by search engines that we developed to allow for various orthographies (Junker and Stewart 2008), taking into account our targeted users' abilities and difficulties.

One of the most beautiful aspects of PAR is that you do not know in advance what will happen. You go from academic researcher to group facilitator, to coordinator, and you end up teaching things you just learned a few months before, as needed – not what you learned during your PhD years. The Oral stories database is such an example. I had toured most Cree communities in the summer of 2002, meeting with language specialists, from one of these discussions arose the concern that copies of old recordings of elders left behind by anthropologists would be lost. It had struck me that, while the traditional mode of transmission was mainly oral, writing the language and teaching the writing system was the primary focus of instruction. At that time I was grappling with the question of how information technology could be of service to predominantly oral cultures. From our discussion came the idea that stories had to be available to teachers in a way that would support traditional oral transmission, and perhaps allow new developments like doing comparative oral literature. For that we digitized the recordings and I ran a series of sound editing workshops in which we developed Cree-based categories to tag the stories. We developed a searchable database[6] where the stories could be listened to and downloaded. Those sound editing and database entry workshops were held in several Cree communities and included participants such as Cree curriculum developers, language consultants, high school drop-outs and radio station employees eager to learn about digital technology. Elders walked in, asking to be recorded and featured in the database. Other academics who had older recordings volunteered their material to be added. The database grew to include over 500 stories (Junker and Luchian 2007). Finally the editorial management was fully transferred to Cree Programs in 2008.

Other eastcree.org developments follow a similar pattern of bringing together people with converging interests: the terminology forum was developed to host

---

5 The online dictionary has had many editorial team members over the years. We reference it as (Junker et al. 2012), date of the last major revisions. It site also includes the Cree thematic dictionaries (Visitor et al. 2013) and has integrated links to grammatical resources (Junker 2000-present).
6 See: stories.eastcree.org

the results of terminology workshops, where both health professionals and Cree consultants from the Cree education and health organisations were brought together to develop medical terminology in Cree (Junker et al. 2005, 2016). The educational resource catalogue is a tool for inventory, distribution and information about Cree books, that also provides reading in Cree on the web via the book descriptions.[7] Interfaces in Cree help promote standard orthography and surfing the web in a Cree environment.

Challenges have been many: the initial difficulty of having syllabic characters on the web (Harvey 2004; Jancewicz and Junker 2011), continuing software and browser updates, internet access, and recently the challenge of app development with its constant industry-driven updates, have forced us to always look for new solutions and collaborations. Capacity building in the Indigenous communities has been essential, not only for language description and documentation, but also for technology, including training the IT support staff serving the Cree communities. The politics of language within Cree institutions, where the Cree language can be both at the heart of healing and sometimes a festering wound of shame and self-hatred, has not made the work easy. What has worked, though, is to gather people of good will and find a common vision or common interests, sometimes across institutional boundaries, in order to create the community of speakers and language lovers that moves things forward.

2.2 Innu language documentation

The eastcree.org website experience attracted requests from other language groups. In 2004, I started working on an online pan-Innu dictionary in a Community-University Research Alliance grant[8] that soon led to other projects. In 2009, Innus from Institut Tshakapesh joined the Crees for an online language lessons development workshop I was holding at Carleton University (Junker and Torkornoo 2012). This led to the development of a series of Integrated Web Tools for the Innu language (Junker et al. 2016). The Innus went further than the Crees in populating their oral stories database with new material: audio and video.[9] They also asked us to help develop a catalogue of language resources and train

---

7 See: catalogue.eastcree.org
8 CURA grants are large 5-year grants of the Social Sciences and Humanities Research Council of Canada. This particular one (2005–2010, PI Marguerite MacKenzie) encompassed Innu communities in both Quebec and Labrador (www.innu-aimun.ca).
9 See: histoires.tshakapesh.ca

their staff to help them manage their sales.[10] Again, my role was to facilitate the various projects and fill in where resources or skills were not available in the Innu communities. Not only was the governance structure of the Innus quite different, but the people in charge of language had very different backgrounds and training.[11] So we had to adapt and be resourceful. Again, the PAR framework helped figure out what was needed and when; as well as what was no longer needed. For example, we developed standard instructions for video documentation that was taking place in the communities. We sent our project technician to meet and visit the technicians serving the schools. In March 2017 we completed a training in video editing so that the entire documentation, editing and publishing process is now in the hands of our partner, the Institut Tshakapesh. We remain available for support. In the community of Ekuanitshit we recently guided the creation of a language lab tailored to using the resources we had developed. None of this had been planned in advance; the need arose and we responded. But what started to happen was a synergy between various language groups having similar needs to maintain their language.

2.3 The Algonquian Linguistic Atlas

The first sign of this convergence of needs and goals happened in 2004 when the Linguistic Atlas was born. In 2002, I had created a simple *Cree Conversation* CD and manual (Junker et al. 2002), with some Cree students who I had hired for the summer to work on a long-term database project for East Cree Verb Paradigms. I wanted those young people to see something concrete come out of their summer job – the Verb Paradigms did indeed take us another 12 years! (See Junker and MacKenzie, 2015a–b). Soon I got requests from other groups to adapt the CD to their language. I shared all my material with them in exchange for them returning their new sound files to me and letting me share them on an interactive map.[12]

---

10 See: catalogue.tshakapesh.ca

11 Unlike the Cree from James Bay, the Innu do not have their own School Board. The Institut Tshakapesh is a cultural organisation that groups most Innu bands and aims to serve all Innus in Quebec. The colonial language they speak is French, while the Innu in Labrador tend to speak English. Thanks to the collaborative structure established across provinces through the CURA project for the dictionary, web resources are now developed in collaboration with the Labrador Innus whenever possible.

12 I would like to credit here two Cree women, whose names I don't remember, who drove me back to the airport after a language conference in Prince Albert in 2004 where I had been invited to speak about the eastcree.org website and offer a workshop on language and technology. We were talking about conversation recordings we had made at the conference and a map I had

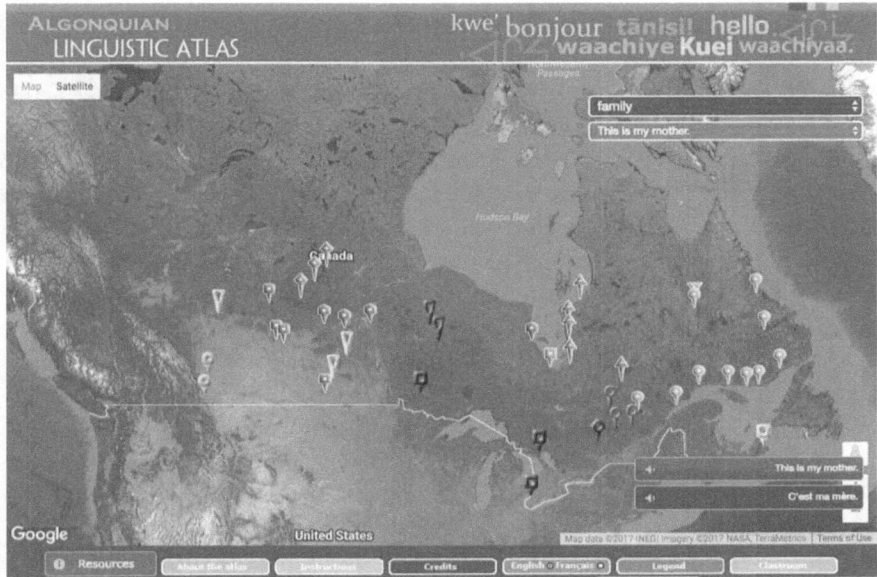

Figure 3: The Algonquian Linguistic Atlas (from www.atlas-ling.ca: Junker, ed. 2005–2018)

In 2005, Google Maps came out and the technology was there for us to develop an interactive Atlas (Junker and Stewart 2011). Because it was based on a conversation CD, and because its most important goal was to bring together linguistic groups that had been artificially divided by colonial history, the Linguistic Atlas was developed more from a language-activist's than a dialectologist's perspective. It contains words, phrases, sentences, short stories and songs. Equivalent phrases are not based on etymologies, but on pragmatic situations. It fosters language preservation and transmission, and connects groups facing similar challenges to preserving and maintaining their language. At the end of 2016 the Atlas featured 47 languages and dialects, 52 speakers and over 19,000 sound files (Fig. 3). Unforeseeably, many urban Indigenous people and some of Indigenous descent use it to reconnect with their roots.[13]

---

shown of the language family to which they were unaware they belonged. Suddenly the idea of "map+sound" flashed in my head, as a tool for connecting, healing the broken links between distant relatives separated by colonial provincial divisions.

[13] A Cree mother recently reported to us that her son, attending school down south, downloaded the Cree conversation app on his phone to play phrases from his community before going to sleep in order to lift his spirits.

2.4 Algonquian online dictionaries and web resources

The Atlas also had the effect of bringing together academics and language activists involved in making dictionaries. In recent years, a team of Algonquianists has come together to develop a common digital infrastructure for Algonquian dictionaries that would allow for sustainable maintenance of those minority language resources in the digital economy. The collaborative research model builds on PAR insights and on information and communication technologies to document Indigenous languages of the Algonquian family and to offer online resources for the communities in question.[14]

This group effort allows for transfer of expertise, shared open-source technological and resource development, and shared pedagogical and documentation approaches. Long-term capacity building is happening between academics and communities of speakers. The connections fostered are among academics; between academics and Indigenous organisations, communities and individuals; and importantly, among Indigenous people themselves. To give a few examples of such collaborative community-to-community spin-offs: Innus are adapting a collection of East Cree books to Innu, and Atikamekws are developing read-along books together with Innus. Forays into medical terminology development for Labrador Innu (MacKenzie et al., 2014) inform similar terminology development for the whole Cree continuum. A recurring challenge for Indigenous language resource development is lack of continuity due to financial and institutional instability. Our working together allows us to bridge some gaps by "piggy-backing" on each other until the tide turns again. Also, the outreach of information technology can be very powerful, and some of our Indigenous partners have done a great job using Facebook pages and community radio networks to promote language work.[15]

As more commonalities emerge, problems can be solved more quickly and our successes can inspire and empower each other. Each group and each participant tends to bring their own strength to the collaboration. I find it remarkable that people are so willing to share their knowledge, successes and even mistakes in a transparent and non-competitive way – beyond the good-natured rivalries and pitches about our respective institutions, we are not in competition with each other, but in a shared race to tackle common challenges such as language endangerment, education, and cultural survival.

---

14 See: resources.atlas-ling.ca
15 See for example the Institut Tshakapesh Facebook page entitled: Innu-Aimun.

3 Conclusion

Participatory Action Research (PAR) and Information and Communication Technologies (ICT) are a perfect match. The process-oriented, consultative, collective nature of PAR and the availability, diversity-enhancing and outreach qualities of ICT, especially towards youth, are meant to work together. It is because of ICT that our work has reached so many more people, across and outside the ivory tower of academia. It is because of PAR that I keep asking if – and ensuring that – the technological and linguistic tools we are developing are really enhancing the well-being of our communities of speakers.

My journey into PAR has made me extremely grateful to have been part of something unfolding that seems much greater than myself. I have learned so much from my Indigenous and academic partners, encountered amazing people, surfed on the cusp of a technological revolution, and ridden a wave of change where many things are truly intangible, but deeply rewarding.

References

Blacksmith, Louise and Marie-Odile Junker. 2001. ᐁᐱᒡᐊᔭᒥᐦᑖᒡ, ᐛᔮᐁᐧ ᐁᐊᔨᒥᐦᑯᒡᐁᐧᐦᐊᓂᐦ ᐃᐦᑐᐊᐁᐊᔨᐊᓇᐧᐅᐌᐧᐃᒡᑎᐦᐧₓ (Oviation, Coreference and Relational verb forms in East Cree.) In John Nichols (ed.), *Actes du trente-deuxième Congrès des Algonquinistes / Papers of the 32nd Algonquian Conference*, 264–268. Winnipeg: University of Manitoba.
Chevalier, Jacques M. and Daniel J. Buckles. 2013a. *Participatory action research: theory and methods for engaged inquiry*. New York: Routledge.
Chevalier, Jacques M. and Daniel J. Buckles. 2013b. *Handbook for Participatory Action Research, Monitoring and Evaluation*. Ottawa: SAS2 Dialogue.
Czaykowska-Higgins, Ewa. 2009. Research Models, Community Engagement, and Linguistic Fieldwork: Reflections on Working within Canadian Indigenous Communities. *Language Documentation and Conservation* 3 (1). 15–50.
Harvey, Christopher. 2004. Unicode as a Standard Framework for Syllabics and Other Special Characters. In H.Christoph Wolfart (ed.), *Papers of the 35th Algonquian Conference*, 125–136. Winnipeg: University of Manitoba.
Jancewicz, Bill and Marie-Odile Junker. 2011. Cree syllabic fonts: development, compatibility and usage in the digital world. In Karl S. Hele and J. Randolph Valentine (eds.) *Papers of the 40th Algonquian Conference*, pp. 118–132. Albany, NY: SUNY Press. (Conference held in October, 2008).
Junker, Marie-Odile. 2002. Participatory Action Research in Linguistics: What Does it Mean? / La recherche participaction en linguistique: Enjeux et significations. Presented at: Session on Ethics of Archiving Languages and Fieldwork, organized by the Aboriginal Language Committee, *Canadian Linguistics Association Annual Congress*, University of Toronto.
Junker, Marie-Odile (ed). 2009–2018. *Algonquian Linguistic Atlas*. (formerly: *Cree-Innu Linguistic Atlas*: 2005–2008) https://www.atlas-ling.ca/ (accessed 21 May 2017).

Junker, Marie-Odile (ed.) 2000–2018. *Eastcree.org*. https://www.eastcree.org/ (accessed 21 May 2017).

Junker, Marie-Odile., Louise Blacksmith, Marguerite MacKenzie, Luci Salt and Annie Whiskeychan. (2002). *Cree conversation Manual/ Manuel de conversation crie*. Edited by Marie-Odile. Junker. Available from https://www.atlas-ling.ca/ and https://www.eastcree.org/pdf/CreeConvManualCol.pdf/

Junker, Marie-Odile (ed.). (2002). *Cree conversation crie – iinuu iyiyuu ayimitaau*. [CD ROM]. Chisasibi, QC: Cree School Board

Junker, Marie-Odile., Yvette Mollen, Hélène St-Onge and Delasie Torkornoo. (2016). Integrated Web tools for Innu language maintenance. In MacCauley, M., M. Noodin and J. R. Valentine (eds.) *Papers of the 44st Algonquian Conference*, pp. 192–210. Albany, NY: SUNY Press. (Conference held in October, 2012).

Junker, Marie-Odile and Delasie Torkornoo. (2012). Online Language Games for Endangered Languages: jeux.tshakapesh.ca, www.eastcree.org/lessons. *Proceedings of EDULEARN 12: International Conference on Education and New Learning Technologies*. Barcelona, Spain. pp: 6662–6673.

Junker, Marie-Odile and Terry Stewart. (2011). A Linguistic Atlas for Endangered Languages: www.atlas-ling.ca. *Proceedings of EDULEARN 11: International Conference on Education and New Learning Technologies*. Barcelona, Spain. pp: 3366–3377.

Junker, Marie-Odile and Terry Stewart. (2008). Building Search Engines for Algonquian Languages. In Karl S. Hele and Regna Darnell (eds*). Papers of the 39th Algonquian Conference*. London: University of Western Ontario Press, 378–411. Updated version available from http://www.marieodilejunker.ca/pdf/JunkerStewart2008-PAC39.pdf

Junker, Marie-Odile and Radu Luchian (2007). Developing web databases for Aboriginal language preservation. In *Literary and Linguistic Computing* 22(2), 187– 206. Originally published online on December 8, 2006 doi:10.1093/llc/fql049

Junker, Marie-Odile and Marguerite MacKenzie (2015a). *East Cree (Southern Dialect) Verb Conjugation* (4th ed.). Available at: https://southern.verbs.eastcree.org

Junker, Marie-Odile. and MacKenzie, M. (2015b). *East Cree (Northern Dialect) Verb Conjugation* (4th ed.). Available at: https://northern.verbs.eastcree.org

Junker, Marie-Odile, MacKenzie, M., Salt, L., Duff, A., Salt, R., Blacksmith, A., Weistche, P., and Diamond, P. (eds.). (2012). *Dictionnaire du cri de l'Est de la Baie James sur la toile: français-cri et cri-français (dialectes du Sud et du Nord)* (3rd ed.). Retrieved from https://dictionnaire.eastcree.org

Junker, Marie-Odile, MacKenzie, M., Salt, L., Salt, R., Blacksmith, A., Weistche, P., and Diamond, P. (eds.). (2012). *The Eastern James Bay Cree Dictionary on the Web: English-Cree and Cree-English (Northern and Southern dialects)* (3rd ed.). Retrieved from https://dictionary.eastcree.org

Junker, Marie-Odile (ed.). (2003–2016) *East Cree Terminology Forum* https://terminology.eastcree.org . Coedited with Mimie Neacappo since 2015.

MacKenzie, Marguerite, Dawson, E. Goodfellow-Baikie, R. and Hasler, L.A. (eds.). (2014) *Innu Medical Glossary*. Sheshatshiu, Labrador: Mamu Tshishkutamashutau - Innu Education Inc. 245 p. Also available as app at: http://www.innu-aimun.ca/english/download-the-apps/

Manoukian, Violetta. (1990). *Participatory development: paradigm shift in theory and practice*. (Master's thesis). Carleton University, Ottawa, Ontario.

Morris, Marika and Martha Muzychka, (2002). Participatory research and action: A guide to becoming a researcher for social change. Ottawa: CRIAW-ICREF.
Smith, Linda Tuhiwa. (1999). *Decolonizing methodologies: Research and indigenous peoples*. New York, NY: Zed Books.
Visitor, Linda, Marie-Odile Junker and Mimie Neacappo. (Eds). (2013). *Eastern James Bay Cree Thematic Dictionary (Northern Dialect)*. Chisasibi, QC: Cree School Board.
Visitor, Linda, Marie-Odile Junker and Mimie Neacappo. (Eds). (2013). *Eastern James Bay Cree Thematic Dictionary (Southern Dialect)*. Chisasibi, QC: Cree School Board.

Mizuki Miyashita, Jackelyn Van Buren, Rebecca Goff,
S. Megan Lunak, Annabelle Chatsis, and Scott Schupbach

Implementing collaborative research in Blackfoot language instruction

Abstract: Depending on the researcher's unique field situation, there are many ways that community-based research (CBR) is realized (Rice 2006, this volume). Regardless, there are characteristics that all CBR projects have in common, and detailed case studies are useful for researchers who aspire to implement CBR in their own work and for community members who are involved in language activities. This chapter presents a case study of a collaborative project with linguists and Blackfoot

---

* First and foremost, we would like to show great appreciation for the late Darrell R. Kipp for supporting and encouraging us in our collaboration. We regret that we are not able to show him this article, but we hope to continue finding the meaning of collaborative work, keeping his valuable words in our minds. We also thank Dr. Donald G. Frantz for assisting us with Blackfoot orthography and structure; Chuck Harris for accommodating the project support and space at the Social Science Research Lab at The University of Montana; Brandon Goff for providing us with countless hours of technological assistance in kind; former student members, Jeremy Lee, Sara Schroeder, and Shiho Yamamoto for creating such wonderful artwork; our student voice actors from the Cuts Wood School, *Aakaikakatosaaki* (Treyace Wellman), *Naatosikkanasoyaki* (Summer Kennerly), *Katoyissaakii* (Justine Mombery), *Ponokanna* (Trae Kennerly), and *Makoyiistakiaakii* (Leissa Wolf Mountain Woman); and students in the Elementary Blackfoot course (NAS 141) at The University of Montana for participating in the first public test-runs of our animated video. We would also like to thank the audience at the 3rd International Conference on Language Documentation and Conservation (ICLDC) where we presented an early version of this paper. Also, we would like to acknowledge Kevin McMinigal, the cartographer in the Department of Geography at the University of Montana. We also thank Shannon Bischoff and Carmen Jany for their encouragements as co-editors of the volume, Marie-Odile Junker for valuable comments, and anonymous readers for their comments and feedback. All errors are our own.

Mizuki Miyashita, University of Montana, Linguistics Program, Social Science Building, 32 Campus Dr., Missoula, MT 59812, mizuki.miyashita@umontana.edu
Jackelyn Van Buren, MSC03 2130, Linguistics, 1 University of New Mexico, Albuquerque, NM 87131, jackelynvb@unm.edu
Rebecca Goff, Native Teaching Aids, 35773 Airport Road, St Ignatius, MT 59865, becky@nativeteachingaids.com
Megan Lunak, Blackfeet Nation, 302 Badger Creek, Valier, MT 59486, meganlunak@gmail.com
Annabelle Chatsis: University of Lethbridge, 4401 University Dr. W., Lethbridge AB. TIK 3M4, annabelle.chatsis@uleth.ca
S. Scott Schupbach, Independent Scholar, ssschupbach@gmail.com

https://doi.org/10.1515/9783110527018-010

language teachers: the creation of an animated film used as a language instruction supplement. It describes our experience of community relationship building, a process which is an important part of CBR. It also lays out how the language material was developed, as well as its application and limitations, a process which is not usually reported in mainstream academic linguistic research. Building an ongoing partnership that continues beyond the project's completion is essential if a community's goals include creating pedagogical materials to which linguists may contribute. As a result, a relationship-building collaborative project is not "merely" community service but holds the same priority as linguistic research, and should be considered as such for linguists aiming to conduct research under a CBR model.

Keywords: Blackfoot, teaching material, collaboration, community, animated video

1 Introduction

This paper presents a case study of a collaborative project with linguists and Blackfoot language teachers. Community-based research (CBR) between linguists and language communities is increasing as a research model due to greater awareness of the importance of meeting local communities' needs. CBR emphasizes conducting "research *on, for* and *with*" community members (Cameron et al. 1992: also see Rice this volume). Research based on a collaborative methodological framework is, in most cases, best equipped to meet the unique needs of both the community and the researcher (Yamada 2007; Czaykowska-Higgins et al. and Langley et al. this volume).

The literature from the past two decades presents a growing number of discussions and reports of community-based research (e.g., Brooks 2013; Dobrin 2008; Holton 2009; Rice 2011; Wilkins 1992; Yamada 2007; Stebbins 2012; also, Junker and Bischoff et. al. in this volume). Thus, examples exist of field experiences in which scholars acknowledge the importance of CBR research. However, not all researchers describe the examples explicitly. Furthermore, common CBR practices, such as the creation of pedagogical materials, have traditionally been considered community service rather than research contribution, and so the process of relationship building that naturally develops from such work tends to be absent from linguistic publications (cf. Yamada 2011; Velásquez Runk and Carpio Opua this volume). Consequently, actual details of the work involved, how such relationships are built, and the limitations are rarely described, although these are real and important stages for members collaborating together. To complicate matters, there are many different ways that CBR is realized, depending on the researcher's unique field situation (Rice 2006, this volume).

Detailed case studies are useful for researchers who want to implement CBR in their own work and for community members who are involved in language activities. In this chapter, we present our account of a mutually beneficial collaborative project between linguists and Blackfoot community members. This project exemplifies an important stage in CBR: relationship building. First, we describe who was involved and what the members' needs were at the time of the project. Second, we outline step-by-step the animation video project that developed through collaboration between linguists at the University of Montana and Blackfoot language instructors in the Blackfoot community. Finally, as part of the discussion, we suggest that if a community's goals include creating pedagogical materials to which linguists may contribute, then it is important to build an ongoing partnership that continues after the project is completed. Thinking together about the materials' application and how these materials can be used is an example of such an ongoing partnership. We claim that a relationship-building collaborative project is not "merely" linguists' community service but holds the same priority as linguistic research such as elicitation or language documentation. Stabilizing the reciprocal relationship is vital so that the community members gain something from collaborating with linguists. Simultaneously, this chapter sheds a light on the process of theorizing CBR as it exemplifies that CBR may not be a standalone project.

2 Blackfoot background

Blackfoot is an Algonquian language spoken in southern Alberta and northwestern Montana. The reported speaker population estimate is 3,200 in Alberta (Statistics Canada 2011) and 50 in Montana (Darrell Kipp p.c. 2011). Almost all children, if not all, learn English as their first language at home as most parents are also monolingual English speakers. Though public schools offer "language and culture" courses on the Blackfeet reservation (US), the content tends to be limited to nouns (e.g., colors and animals).[1] There are descriptive grammars (Uhlenbeck 1938; Taylor 1969; Frantz 2009) and a dictionary (Frantz and Russel 1995), of which users are usually linguists. Some community-based language-culture documentation and revitalization activities are conducted by the Piegan Institute.[2]

---

[1] Public schools in Browning, Montana started to offer language immersion courses in 2015 (Hall 2015). Also, public schools on the reserves in Canada seem to be striving to improve language education strategies, according to a former member of the Kainai Board of Education.
[2] See Kipp (2000) for more information about the Piegan Institute.

Figure 1: Map of Blackfoot-speaking bands. © Kevin McManigal

2.1 Brief history of the ongoing collaborative relationship

The relationship between linguists at the University of Montana and the Piegan Institute can be traced back to the initial encounter between the linguist, Miyashita, a faculty member in the Linguistics Program at The University of Montana, and the former director of the Piegan Institute in 2005, the late Darrell Kipp (Kipp et al. 2015). From the first meeting, mutually beneficial collaboration among linguists and language teachers was the main priority.

A number of small projects conducted in collaboration since then contributed to building a relationship between Miyashita and the language teachers. As shown in Table 1, the projects previously undertaken involved both linguists and language teachers at various levels. The first two projects involved recording lullabies and conversations in Blackfoot, both of which were funded by small grants: APS Phillips Funds and Jacobs Research Funds, respectively (e.g., Miyashita and Crow Shoe 2009; Miyashita 2011). Two more projects focused on the development of

Table 1: Documentation and language material activities prior to the animation project

	Linguists	Community members	Activities
2007	Miyashita	Ms. Crow Shoe (Piegan Institute)	Lullaby recording
2008	Miyashita	Ms. Many Bears (Piegan Institute)	Conversation recording
2007–09	MA students	none	Vocabulary list on web
2009	Miyashita	Annabelle Chatsis	Course materials
2010–11	MA students	Annabelle Chatsis (UM)	Picture book "Ponoka ki Sisttsi"

teaching materials, mainly due to the additional participation among MA linguistics students interested in endangered languages. The students worked as volunteers with supplemental tuition support from Campus Corps which was available at that time through the Office of Civic Engagement at the University of Montana (UM). Van Buren and Goff were Linguistics MA students (2010–2012) during this time and both self-taught Blackfoot grammar. Schupbach was also an MA student (2011–2013) and had attended the Blackfoot class in his third semester. Annabelle Chatsis is a native speaker and served as an adjunct Blackfoot instructor at the university (2009–2015). Miyashita had supported Chatsis' course material development at the initial stage, including syllabus making, identifying objectives and learning outcomes, and creating an assessment and examination system (Miyashita and Chatsis 2013). The Department of Native American Studies provided additional compensation to Miyashita for the first semester (Spring 2009), and the extra tasks counted as one teaching load for another semester (Fall 2010). Her involvement after the first two semesters were considered service activities. Chatsis was also Miyashita's language consultant for her Blackfoot research, assisting in transcribing and translating connected speech in Blackfoot. Chatsis' time was compensated from institutional small grants and a Humanities Montana fellowship.

This chapter describes the animated video project, created in 2011–2012. We focus on this project because it involved extended collaboration among linguists and community members compared to the previous projects. It should be emphasized, though, that the relationship among the linguists and Blackfoot teachers had already been established through these earlier projects.

The animated video project team described here also consisted of linguists and Blackfoot teachers. In addition to collaborating members previously described (i.e., Miyashita, Chatsis, Van Buren, Goff, and Schupbach), Megan Lunak, a teacher at the Cuts Wood School, and her students also assisted. Lunak is a second language learner of Blackfoot.

This particular project had no funding. Only the MA students had support: Goff and Van Buren were able to utilize Campus Corps, though participation was voluntary, and Schupbach was partially supported by a research assistantship

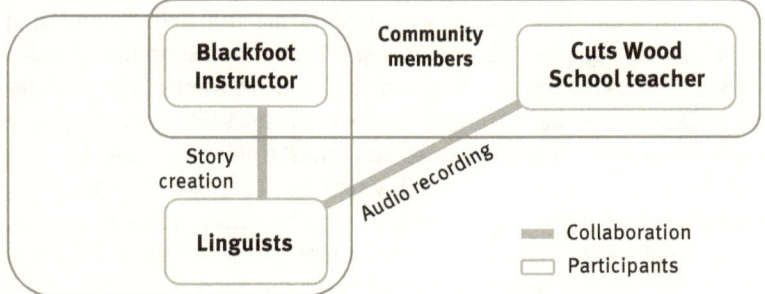

Figure 2: Project's team organization

from the small internal grant given to Miyashita in 2012–2013. In sum, there were three major groups involved in the collaborative activities. The constituency of participating groups and the collaboration relationships are illustrated in Figure 2. In addition, the student members actively volunteered in the Blackfoot language class. Van Buren assisted Chatsis in transferring her teaching materials into PowerPoint files for class instruction, Goff recorded Chatsis' class activities when requested, and Schupbach created materials for in-class activities. These activities helped strengthen the personal relationship with Chatsis and helped them gain an understanding of the materials useful for the Blackfoot language classroom setting.

3 Animated video project

As mentioned, the animated video project started as a continuation of an earlier project in 2010–11, the picture book *Ponoka ki Sisttsi* 'Elk and Little Bird', which consists of four scenes for each animal: color description, activity of walking or flying, eating, and sleeping.[3] Phrases are in the imperfective aspect, and therefore there is a conceptual discrepancy between the phrase when denoting ongoing motion and the fixed, unmoving image in the picture book.[4] That is, it is conceptually difficult to perceive ongoing action when faced with a still image. An animated image, on the other hand, provides a visual aid which is capable of more accurately representing differences of use of grammatical aspect, a distinction important in the language. The initial animated version of *Ponoka ki Sisttsi* included imperfective aspect and third person singular morphology marked on four different verb roots (Schroeder

---
[3] http://www.umt.edu/blg/projects1/picturebooks.php
[4] A verb with the durative affix *á-* often is translated as progressive in English glosses (see Frantz 2009). We refer to this aspect as imperfective following the analysis presented by Dunham (2007).

et al. 2011; Van Buren et al. 2012). Chatsis, who used the material in class, preferred using the book and the animated version as a set. The improved animated video project described in this chapter was designed to include movements and scenes incorporating additional linguistic features. In the following sections, we describe the process of developing the animated video and how the video was used.

The stages of the project occurred roughly in the following order with some overlap between stages: story development, image creation, voice recording, image-animating, showing to the class, and follow-up activities. Each stage involved varying degrees of collaboration among team members, described in the following sections.

3.1 Story development

We were aware that the storyline for the video could be traditional or developed by a native speaker. However, the MA students developed the story for two main reasons. One is that a traditional story is often tied to a specific season for retelling, and we aimed for a very short story that is free from the traditional constraint. The other is that the linguists preferred to have conscious control of length and linguistic features to be covered in the story. Under Miyashita's supervision, Van Buren and Goff wrote a short story for the video in Blackfoot using the *Blackfoot Grammar* (Frantz 2009) and *Blackfoot Dictionary of Stems Roots, and Affixes* (Frantz and Russell 1995) and consulted Chatsis as well as Dr. Donald Frantz, an expert on Blackfoot linguistics, on matters of grammar and cultural appropriateness. The story is titled *O'towaawahkao'pa Ponoka* 'A Walk with Elk (lit. We all walk with Elk)'. In this story, *ponoká* 'elk' is walking through the forest and sees three different kinds of animals: *sisttsi* 'little bird', *ksísskstakiiksi* '(two) beavers' and *káánaisskiinaa* 'mouse'. The elk is a guide or narrator for the reader by reporting what he sees and wonders aloud about what the other animals are doing. The animals do not notice the elk, but they tell the audience who they are and what they will do. As each animal performs an action, the elk describes what the animals are doing.

There are five significant components to the story development. First, we included animals that are culturally respectful and natural to the Blackfoot community (e.g., beavers, mice, crows, elk, bears, owls, etc.). During the process of making the story, Van Buren and Goff had a series of meetings with Chatsis. These consultations shaped how the story was written in that only culturally appropriate characters and themes were used. For example, they were informed that *sipisttoo* 'owl' was a messenger of dark news, usually death, and *kiaayo* 'bear' was a taboo word for members of a certain society (Wissler and Duvall 1908; Wissler 1913). Second, we included educational information about the animals. For example, the little bird flies south in winter, the beavers build a home from wood in a large body of water, and the mouse swims when necessary. This information has the added potential benefit of initiating further discussions in the language which could also involve components of natural science useful for classroom settings when used in grade school. Third, we embedded several important linguistic features into the dialogue, such as verbs inflected for first, second, and third person in both singular and plural, and verbal affixes denoting imperfective and future expressions. We also received consultation from Dr. Frantz regarding Blackfoot morphosyntactic structure and Chatsis for discourse norms. Following their suggestions, we included the phrase *Óki níkso'koaawa* 'Hello my relatives' which is used as a greeting in the beginning of stories and used the expression *po'kiiyook!* 'Come with me! (lit. 'Follow me!')' as an equivalent of English 'Let's go' in this type of narrative context. Fourth, we created a narratological framework in which the target phrases occur repetitively. Because the elk is a narrator, every time he sees an animal, he repeats the same phrase *aikiiwaatsiksi* 'what is he doing?' The expression of *nitaanikko* ... 'my name is ...' occurs four times when every animal introduces himself; and the future and imperfective expressions are repeated as each animal explains what he will do and subsequently the elk reports what the animal is doing. In sum, the phrases explicitly used in the story consist of sixteen verb stems, six nouns, and three discourse markers, which we believe were not intimidating to new learners. The final developmental component was to develop scenes that allow for more advanced expressions to be orally added using the image or scenes provided by the video. Such advanced linguistic features include future tense, perfective aspect, obviation, and inverse constructions (Frantz 2009). Obviation is a grammatical way to distinguish between multiple third-person participants in the discourse; the inverse construction is a grammatical structure that indicates grammatical relation of participants without a change in the location of person markers. In other words, having multiple characters can create a situation where the obviative and inverse, common structures in Algonquian languages, are used. Additionally, other inflected words could easily be taught depending on how an instructor breaks down the video.[5]

3.2 Artwork design, voice recording, and animating images

Prior to this animation project, the animals and backgrounds were made by former student members using colored and patterned papers. They had created

---

[5] We also discuss manipulation of video playing depending on the instructor's teaching plan (see 4.2).

an elk, little bird, mouse, and beaver, but only used the elk and little bird.[6] Van Buren and Goff incorporated the unused characters and backgrounds into the second project by scanning them into Photoshop and creating the scenes for each conversation in Flash.

For voice recording, Miyashita contacted Lunak at Cuts Wood School to inquire about the possibility of students' participation as voice actors, as she had previously shown interest. Prior to the recording session, copies of images in sequence and Blackfoot scripts were prepared and sent to Lunak electronically. She examined the level of the complexity involved in each character's lines, and selected five students to voice-act the characters. During the preparation correspondence, an important agreement was made between linguists and Lunak: students would practice the lines before the recording, but they would pronounce the scripts in the current version of the language, New Blackfoot.[7] The students from Cut Wood School at the time of this project were mainly learning New Blackfoot because the fluent speakers assisting them were speakers of this dialect. We decided to use New Blackfoot to motivate the students, encourage them to feel comfortable speaking, and increase more opportunities to use the language and not to change their grammar to the form that is no longer used and which could hinder efforts for language revitalization. Although the linguists who created the dialogue consulted descriptive grammars, many current speakers use different forms that have undergone language change. For example, Old Blackfoot words and phrases, such as *niita'pái'siksikimi* 'coffee', *nomohto'too* 'I arrive (from somewhere)', and *áíkiiwaatsiksi* 'What is she doing?', are reduced to *niita'psiksikimi, nitohto'too,* and *aikiiwaats* (or even *aikiiwa*), respectively.[8] Example New Blackfoot phrases used in the project are *aikiiwaats* instead of *aikiiwaatsiksi* 'what is s/he doing?' and *ksisskstaki* 'beaver' pronounced as *tsistaki*.[9]

The recording was conducted at the Cuts Wood School on April 11th, 2012. Miyashita and Goff traveled to Browning, located on the Blackfeet Reservation

---

[6] Sara Schroeder, a former BLG member (2009–2011) designed several animals and backgrounds.
[7] New Blackfoot is a variant of Blackfoot mainly spoken by younger generations (60s and possibly some 70s) and Old Blackfoot is spoken by elderly speakers (80s and up). There is no extensive and formal documentation, but we notice that there are quite a few variants of this dialect. Similar traits, though, tend to be consonant substitutions, word contraction, allomorphic simplification, and morpheme reduction. See Miyashita and Chatsis (2013, 2015) for examples.
[8] The form *nitohto'too* does not represent phonological reduction but does represent morphological reduction. The source affix has variations of *omoht-* (after a person prefix), *iiht-* (word initially) and *oht-* (elsewhere) (Frantz 2009). The use of the *oht-* form after a person prefix *nit-* (first person) indicates a type of morphological reduction.
[9] The third person singular nonaffirmative suffix *-waatsiksi* is reduced to *-waats* (Frantz 2009).

in northwestern Montana, to conduct a recording session at the Cuts Wood School. Students first rehearsed their phrases with Lunak and then recorded lines separately. Each voice actor pronounced their parts three or four times. Throughout the session, students were enthusiastic about taking part in this process. After the recording sessions, Goff listened to the recordings at UM and selected the best take from each line of the voice actors. The best takes were then segmented into separate files to be used in the image-animating process.

Goff animated the images, which involved several steps. First, she manipulated the scanned images using Photoshop. In this process, she digitally dissected each animal character into body parts to make animal images walk and talk, and separated some parts from the background images to make the clouds move and the sun shine. Second, these images were exported into Flash Animation Studio, a program used at the time by animators to create movies out of drawings. Third, audio files for each character were uploaded to the program. The animated images were mapped to the duration of the audio files in both movement of body and mouth. An example snapshot from the scene where the mouse is swimming is shown in Figure 3.

Thus, creation of the animated video involved all participants shown in Figure 2 earlier.

Figure 3: Snapshot from the video "O'towaawahkao'pa Ponoka"

4 Application: A key to building a trusting relationship

Teaching materials are most beneficial when effectively used in the classroom. After the creation of the video, linguists showed the completed product to Chatsis and Lunak separately. Both teachers approved of the product, and intended to use the video in their classes in the fall. The teachers informed the linguists that they had shown the video to the class. Through such informal discussions, we became aware that collaborative follow-up activities are an important part of the project because linguists can guide teachers to take advantage of presenting different linguistic features available through the materials. If teachers are given materials but no guidance on their linguistic application, the materials may not be as useful.

4.1 Blackfoot at the University of Montana

In this section, we describe the activities that followed the creation of the animated video project. The video was first implemented in the Blackfoot course at the University of Montana, which is taught as a series of two semesters. Enrolled students typically come from various backgrounds, ranging from Blackfoot heritage language learners to non-Blackfoot Native American students, in addition to non-Native American students (Miyashita and Chatsis 2013). During the period of the follow-up activities, less than 25% of the class was Native American with the majority being descendants of Blackfoot speaking bands. Others were descendants of neighboring tribes, such as Cree.[10] For students of Blackfoot ancestry, the heritage language may only have been partially acquired or not at all in the home. Heritage learners of Blackfoot included students with varying degrees of proficiency, as well as parents who wanted to teach their own children Blackfoot but needed support in the form of language materials and explicit instruction.

Being the only instructor of Blackfoot in the university, Chatsis had flexibility in designing her course. She welcomed the opportunity to utilize the video in which she was also involved. In fall semester 2012 Chatsis introduced the animated video *O'towaawahkao'pa Ponoka* to the students by showing it once in class, and reported to linguist members that her students had shown interest and given compliments on the project.[11] However, we realized that the video had more to

---

[10] The semesters before and after the period included Native American students from Flathead Salish, Ojibwe, Navajo, and Crow communities.
[11] Chatsis had also shown the video version of the first picture book, *Ponoka ki Sisttsi* as well as the video described here. However, this chapter focuses only on the second video.

offer than just viewing it. In order to test different lesson plans, linguist members offered Chatsis an opportunity to conduct a trial lesson plan using the video.

Schupbach took the lead in assisting Chatsis. It was an obvious selection because he was also attending the language class, and Chatsis knew that he understood the grammar she had covered in class. In addition, Schupbach was able to bring various ideas from his experience and training as a UM instructor for English as an Academic Second Language (EASL) courses. During the meeting between Chatsis and Schupbach, they recognized that the Blackfoot class tended primarily to be lectures consisting of explaining phrases and their translations with an emphasis on repetition and memorization. They identified class enhancement ideas to include more personal-interactive learning methods (e.g., students producing the language via questions and answers (Ellis 1999)) and to adopt additional structured/detailed lesson plans.

Later in the same semester, Chatsis showed the movie to the class and spent time reviewing the phrases used in the movie. Schupbach designed a lesson plan to explore some of the video's potential instructional uses. The lesson plan included naming and counting objects not overtly mentioned in the text, describing the objects (e.g., their size, color, location), and activities that would facilitate student participation and conversation. The colors and objects identified were not a part of the video's main plot, but these were words and phrases the students had been introduced to in earlier classes, which made for good review. Additionally, there were objects in scenes new to the students that Chatsis introduced by pointing out and discussing in Blackfoot. Also, she was able to introduce questions like *áyaaksikííwaatsiksi ponokáwa?* 'What is Ponoká about to do?' by pausing a video and making students guess what the character's action might be. This allowed for use of the future tense. As opposed to the lecture style that had been the main teaching method, the inclusion of question-answer exchanges made the course content more communication-oriented. This led to a long-term change in the course with more varied lesson plans that included interactive games, such as scavenger hunts created by Chatsis.

4.2 Cuts Wood School

The application of the video material also took place in the other constituency, Cuts Wood School. The Cuts Wood School was established in 1995 by the Piegan Institute, which was founded in 1987 and runs several community-based projects that aim to increase the number of fluent Blackfoot speakers and promote Native cultural awareness (Kipp 2000, 2007). Though the school started as a total immersion program, with internal structural changes due to various circumstances, the two instructors at the time of the collaboration project were non-native second language learners. There were two classes led by the two teachers, K-3 and 4-8 with approximately 24 students. Lunak taught the 4th -8th grade class, and as described earlier, the students from her class participated in the project as voice actors.

Lunak used the video right away in her class. The teachers at the Cuts Wood School had freedom to develop the curriculum. That is, teachers were able to use their own assessment systems to improve the students' performance without giving them grades. Lunak spontaneously incorporated the video into her class by using the video to introduce new words to her students, and by playing it many times, as her focus in teaching was repetition. She made a comprehension sheet in English to check whether students were learning the new words in order to share the results with the linguist video creators. Most students felt that the new words were somewhat easy to pick up after watching the video.

Following the initial implementation of the video, Miyashita and Lunak had several informal discussions. According to Lunak, the students showed a distinct ability to remember the words from the video and reportedly did not have to translate into English first in order to comprehend the words and use them in sentences. She also mentioned that they would use the words innovatively (i.e., in sentences not from the video). After viewing the DVD and reading and hearing the word pronounced, students were able to identify that same word on a worksheet. In addition, it was exciting for the students to hear their own voices and voices of classmates with the animated characters.

In the course of several informal message exchanges, several key points were raised. First, before the video lessons, students were already successfully naming objects and learning stories and commonly used phrases such as *oki, niistó nitáanikko...* 'hello my name is...', *tsá niitá'piiwa* 'how are you (lit: how is it)', and *istópit* 'sit down'. However, they had not often been challenged to produce novel phrases inflecting verb roots. In addition, language teaching materials tended to be noun-based because their development was influenced by and adopted from well-taught languages like English, which is typologically distinct from Blackfoot, a mostly verb-based language (like other Algonquian languages). Thus, Lunak's classroom enhancement idea was to include more verb-oriented lessons. Furthermore, verb-based lessons are effective for language learning as they create situations for effective and realistic communication (Holm et al. 2003).

In October 2012, Miyashita and Goff travelled to Cuts Wood School to assist Lunak with the use of the video in her class. We suggested that her students watch the movie several times and try two activities. The first activity consisted of a role-play reading exercise: each student reads the role of one of the animals and replicates the voice as a voice actor. The role-playing component was something Lunak already practiced as students tend to engage more in activities that are fun. However, performance level varied in the exercise the linguists introduced because it involved reading the Blackfoot script. Reading is not necessarily the focus at Cuts Wood School, and students who use written materials (e.g., a dictionary) on their own performed better than those who do not. Whether an exercise includes a reading component should take such factors into account.

The second suggested activity involved a gesture game. In this game, one student makes a gesture and another person (either a teacher or student) asks a question to the rest of the class: for example, they ask *áíkiiwats* 'what is he/she doing?', one of the repeated phrases in the story. Depending on the student's gesture, the answer might be *áíhpiyiwa* 'she is dancing', *áókska'siwa* 'she is running', *áótsimma* 'she is swimming', *áyo'kaawa* 'she is sleeping', etc. Verb practice is the focus. If an answering student is not sure about her answer, then she can ask the gesturing student *kitáíhpiyihpa* 'are you dancing?'. Then, the answer could be *aa, nitáíhpiyi* 'yes, I am dancing' if correct, and *saa nimáátaihpiyihp* 'no, I am not dancing' if incorrect. The purpose of the different prompts is to elicit different person/number suffixes in the student responses. If no one is successful, students can ask the gesturing student the question, *kitáíkiihpa* 'what are you doing?'. Then the answer may be given in first person singular. Students successfully navigated the game and especially enjoyed when humorous gestures were given. One obstacle was the ease in falling back to noun-oriented activities. For example, one student started gesturing an animal. In this case, students can be guided back to the verb-oriented activities by asking the student gesturing an animal, *kitáíkiihpa* 'what are you doing?'.

5 Discussion

5.1 Relationship-building and benefits

As mentioned earlier, the animated video project was not the beginning of the relationship-building between linguists and community members. This project, however, was the first collaborative project that involved extensive exchanges from the development stage through the usage of the material. In other words, this project exemplified the "*by* the community" aspect of CBR. In addition, it became apparent that a pedagogical material creation project should include follow-up collaboration, and it is important to maintain a relationship between linguists and community members. If the produced materials are not used, then the project is not going to be *for* the community. Thus, both the development and the application ought to be part of the collaborative process.

It is also important that all members benefit from the process, otherwise the project is not *with* the community. Our experience provided everyone involved with an awareness of the interdisciplinary nature of each stage of the project and the realization that a team with a diverse and complementary skillset is a significant component of collaboration. The project resulted in multiple outcomes for linguists, language teachers, and Native students. Schupbach conducted research on Blackfoot demonstratives with Chatsis being his language consultant, and completed an MA thesis (Schupbach 2013). Participating in elicitation sessions as a language consultant led Chatsis to consciously think about Blackfoot linguistic structure; her awareness and observation resulted in co-authored articles (Chatsis et al. 2013; Miyashita and Chatsis 2015). Chatsis and Lunak co-authored a conference presentation with linguist authors at the 3rd ICLDC conference in 2013. Needless to say, linguists benefit from working together with speakers and community members in their research. Teachers, on the other hand, became more aware of their language's linguistic structure and variation within the language. Consequently, Chatsis came to reach out for more action-oriented course activities such as skits, role-playing, and games. Lunak also felt students were more engaged when her classes included fun elements like role-playing. One of the voice actors, now a college student, actively participates in language documentation activities led by community organizations such as the Piegan Institute and Blackfeet Community College. In addition, we would like to note that this project encouraged Goff to further contribute to community needs by establishing Native Teaching Aids eight months after her graduation. Native Teaching Aids creates digital and physical materials for indigenous language teachers and learners.[12] So far, she has worked with ten nations across five states (Montana, Washington, Hawaii, Alaska and Alberta). Additionally, Goff returned to Cuts Wood School and offered a video editing workshop to students and is currently collaborating with the Piegan Institute and will be accepting three alumnae of Cuts Wood School as apprentices in linguistics studies, graphic design, and web development. She continues to aim to build bridges between researchers and language educators/learners in order to make materials in the language more easily accessible to community members. For example, materials are customized and created in collaboration with members of the community. Thus the project exemplifies how collaboration between specialists and native speakers provides mutual benefits to both linguists and language communities.

5.2 Limitations

There are also limitations to the described collaboration in terms of its size and continuation. The size of the project was small, mainly for two reasons. First,

---

[12] www.nativeteachingaids.com

there was no funding except Campus Corps for the graduate students and the faculty linguist's small internal grant. Second, because the actual video creators were Master's students, the project had to be small enough to be finished before their graduation; the MA program in linguistics is a two-year program. Continuation of established partnerships is probably the most significant challenge to such projects. It is extremely difficult to maintain stable long-term relationships with members of such collaboration for a variety of reasons. After graduation graduation, students leave, new students must be trained with respect to the language, ethics, community's historical backgrounds, etc. Also in our case, there were changes in the community teachers' circumstances after the project. Chatsis took a new job in Canada not involving language teaching. Lunak is no longer an instructor at the school. With the passing of the late Darrell Kipp in November 2013, the school is now renamed Cuts Wood Academy and its internal structure has changed. In addition, the Campus Corps program which was housed under the Office of Civic Engagement at the university was terminated the year after the project was completed. When circumstances change, therefore, continuation and future collaborative opportunities are at risk. Continuous relationships must involve not only the engagement of the interested members but also the stability of the members' situations that support their engagement. In order to carry out further projects, a collaborative relationship might have to be rebuilt from the beginning involving new members. Therefore, CBR is a dynamic and ongoing process that adapts to changing circumstances.

6 Conclusion

The definition of CBR proposed by Czaykowska-Higgins (2009: 24) is "Research that is **on** a language, and that is conducted **for**, **with**, and **by** the language-speaking community within which the research takes place and which it affects." She also adds that "[t]his kind of research involves a collaborative relationship, a partnership, between researchers and (members of) the community within which the research takes place." Our collaborative project described in this chapter, including its development, application and limitations, is not an example of mainstream academic linguistic research. However, it lays out an instance of a relationship-building process which is a part of CBR. Also, we believe that CBR related activities should be on-going, considering several previously conducted projects contributed to the development of our partnership. As we have shown, though continuation of partnerships and relationships are necessary for CBR projects, many lives were involved and various personal and institutional settings changed during our projects, presenting challenges to maintaining the relationships, partnerships, and the projects begun. We believe that our case study contributes to theorization of CBR and suggests that a CBR project may not necessarily be a single or isolated project. We hope that our project description and discussion here will provide others with an example of what a CBR project might encompass and that it will guide others when conducting CBR when necessary and appropriate.

References

Brooks, Joseph. 2013. When repatriation is not 'giving back': evidence from a meeting with the Hua of Papua New Guinea. *Paper presented at the 3rd International Conference on Language Documentation and Conservation*. University of Hawai'i, 28 February – 3 March.

Cameron, Deborah, Elizabeth Frazer, Penelope Harvey, M.B.H. Rampton, and Kay Richardson. 1992. *Researching language: Issues of power and method*. New York: Routledge.

Chatsis, Annabelle, Mizuki Miyashita and Deborah Cole. 2013. A documentary ethnography of a Blackfoot language course: Patterns of variationism and standard in the organization of diversity. In Shannon Bischoff, Deborah Cole, Amy Fountain, and Mizuki Miyashita (eds.), *The persistence of language: Constructing and confronting the past and present in the voices of Jane H. Hill*. Amsterdam and Philadelphia: John Benjamins.

Czaykowska-Higgins, Ewa. 2009. Research models, community engagement, and linguistic fieldwork: Reflections on working within Canadian indigenous communities. *Language Documentation & Conservation* 3 (1). 15–50.

Dobrin, Lise M. 2008. From linguistic elicitation to eliciting the linguist: Lessons in community empowerment from Melanesia. *Language* 84 (2). 300–324.

Dunham, Joel. 2007. The 'durative' in Blackfoot: Understanding imperfectivity. In Amy Rose Deal (ed.), *Proceedings of SULA 4: Semantics of Under-Represented Languages in the Americas, University of Massachusetts Occasional Papers in Linguistics* 35, 49–64. Amherst: University of Massachusetts Graduate Linguistics Student Association.

Ellis, Rod (ed). 1999. *Learning a second language through interaction, Studies in Bilingualism* Vol. 17. Amsterdam and Philadelphia: John Benjamins.

Frantz, Donald G. 2009. *Blackfoot grammar*. 2nd edn. Toronto: University of Toronto Press.

Frantz, Donald. G. and Norma Jean Russell. 1995. *Blackfoot dictionary of stems, roots, and affixes*. Toronto: University of Toronto Press.

Hall, Miriam. 2015. Browning First To Use Native Language Immersion Funds. *Montana Public Radio*. Dec, 14. http://mtpr.org/post/browning-first-use-native-language-immersion-funds. Accessed 25 March 2017.

Holm, Wayne, Irene Silentman and Laura Wallace. 2003. Situational Navajo: A School-Based, Verb-Cantered Way of Teaching Navajo. In Jon Reyhner, Octaviana Trujillo, Roberto Luis Carrasco and Louise Lockard (eds.), *Nurturing Native languages*, 25–52. Flagstaff, AZ: Northern Arizona University.

Holton, Gary. 2009. Relatively ethical: A comparison of linguistic research paradigms in Alaska and Indonesia. *Language Documentation & Conservation* 3 (2). 161–175.

Kipp, Darrell. 2000. *Encouragement, guidance, insights, and lessons learned for Native language activists developing their own tribal language program*. Ardin Hills, MN: Grotto Foundation.

Kipp, Darrell. 2007. Swimming in Words. *Cultural Survival Quarterly* 31 (2). 36–43.
Kipp, Darren, Jesse DesRosier and Mizuki Miyashita. 2015. Memoir and Insights of Darrell R. Kipp. In Jon Reynher, Joseph Martin, Louise Lockard and Willard Sakiestewa Gilbert (eds.), *Honoring our elders: Culturally appropriate methods for teaching Indigenous students*, 1–14. Flagstaff, AZ: Northern Arizona University.
Miyashita, Mizuki. 2011. Five Blackfoot Lullabies. *Proceedings of The American Philosophical Society* 155 (3). 276–293.
Miyashita, Mizuki and Annabelle Chatsis. 2013. Collaborative development of Blackfoot language courses. *Language Documentation & Conservation* 7. 302–330.
Miyashita, Mizuki and Annabelle Chatsis. 2015. Respecting dialectal variations in a Blackfoot language class. In Jon Reynher, Joseph Martin, Louise Lockard and Willard Sakiestewa Gilbert (eds.), *Honoring our elders: Culturally appropriate methods for teaching Indigenous students*, 109–116. Flagstaff, AZ: Northern Arizona University.
Miyashita, Mizuki and Shirlee Crow Shoe. 2009. Blackfoot Lullabies and Language Revitalization. In Jon Reyhner and Louise Lockard (eds.), *Indigenous Language Revitalization: Encouragement, Guidance & Lessons Learned*. 183–116. Flagstaff, AZ: Northern Arizona University.
Rice, Keren. 2006. Ethical issues in linguistic fieldwork: An overview. *Journal of Academic Ethics* 4. 123–155.
Rice, Keren. 2011. Documentary linguistics and community relations. *Language Documentation & Conservation* 5. 187–207.
Schupbach, S. Scott. 2013. *The Blackfoot demonstrative system: Function, form, and meaning*. Missoula, MT: University of Montana thesis.
Schroeder, Sara, Jeremy Lee, Shiho Yamamoto, Rebecca Yares, Jackelyn Van Buren, Annabelle Chatsis and Mizuki Miyashita. 2011. Creation and application of animated digital picture book for teaching Blackfoot. Paper presented at 7th Annual Conference on Endangered Languages and Cultures of Native America, University of Utah, 22–23 April.
Statistics Canada. 2011. 2011 Census of Population.
Stebbins, Tonya N. 2012. On being a linguist and doing linguistics: Negotiating ideology through performativity. *Language Documentation and Conservation* 6. 292–317.
Taylor, Allan. R. 1969. *A Grammar of Blackfoot*. Berkely: University of California Berkeley dissertation.
Uhlenbeck, Christianus Cornelius. 1938. *A concise Blackfoot grammar*. Verhandelingen der Koninklike Akademie van Wetenschappen. Afdeeling Letterkunde, Nieuwe Reeks, Deal 41.
Van Buren, Jackelyn, Rebecca Yares, S. Scott Schupbach, Annabelle Chatsis and Mizuki Miyashita. 2012. Teaching an endangered language with animation. *Paper presented at 8th Conference on Endangered Languages and Cultures of Native America*, University of Utah, 23–24 March.
Wilkins, David. 1992. Linguistic research under aboriginal control: A personal account of fieldwork in central Australia. *Australian Journal of Linguistics* 12 (1). 171–200.
Wissler, Clark and David Charles Duvall. 1908. *Mythology of the Blackfoot Indians Vol. 2*. New York: Anthropological Papers of the American Museum of Natural History.
Wissler, Clark. 1913. Societies and dance associations of the Blackfoot Indians. In *Anthropological papers of the American Museum of Natural History Volume 11*, 359–460. New York: Anthropological Papers of the American Museum of Natural History.
Yamada, Raquel-María. 2007. Collaborative linguistic fieldwork: Practical application of the empowerment model. *Language Documentation and Conservation* 1 (2). 257–282.
Yamada, Raquel- María. 2011. Integrating documentation and formal teaching of Kari'nja: Documentary materials as pedagogical materials. *Language Documentation & Conservation* 5. 1–30.

Shannon Bischoff, Amy Fountain, and Audra Vincent
100 years of analyzing Coeur d'Alene with the community

Abstract: We present a case study involving the development of the Coeur d'Alene Online Language Resource Center (COLRC). The COLRC provides a suite of digital Coeur d'Alene/Snchitsu'umshtsn language resources including a bilingual searchable dictionary, audio recordings, and hundreds of pages of unpublished legacy materials documenting Snchitsu'umshtsn/Coeur d'Alene language and culture. Additionally, the COLRC provides access to resources representing 100 years of collaborative work recording Coeur d'Alene language and culture. The paper reports on the digital resources created, their origin, and development from the perspective of three participants who worked on the project. The project as described serves as a case study in the development of digital resources in the spirit of community-based research while illustrating the value of legacy materials that reflect earlier collaborations that should not be forgotten. Finally, the paper argues that community-based research, in addition to functioning as a methodology, practice, or philosophy, can also serve as a tool to reflect on earlier relationships among community members and academic scholars in order to better understand the complex relationships that have come before in such endeavors.

Keywords: Coeur d'Alene, Snchitsu'umshtsn, digital resources, legacy materials, online dictionary

---

Shannon Bischoff, Purdue University Fort Wayne, Department of English & Linguistics, 2101 E. Coliseum Blvd., Fort Wayne, IN 46805-1499 USA, bischofs@ipfw.edu
Amy Fountain, Department of Linguistics, P.O. Box 210025, The University of Arizona, Tucson AZ 85721USA, avf@email.arizona.edu
Audra Vincent, Director, Language Center, P.O. Box 408, 810 'A' St., Plummer, ID 83851 USA, avincent@cdatribe-nsn.gov

https://doi.org/10.1515/9783110527018-011

1 Introduction

In this brief discussion we[1] describe a century of collaboration between what we will refer to as *academic scholars* (e.g. those affiliated with academic institutions in their endeavors) and *indigenous community scholars* of the Coeur d'Alene Tribe (e.g., those indigenous scholars that come from the community), throughout the 20th century and into the 21st. We claim that this work, in large part, was done in the spirit, and at times to the letter, of the definition of community-based research (CBR) as articulated by Rice (this volume). Our discussion excludes the various collaborative efforts between indigenous community members and non-indigenous community members, such as those between various Catholic priests and community members in the early part of the 20th century (e.g. the *Teepees* project of the late 1930s and early 1940s as discussed by Brinkman 2003: 49–50). It also excludes collaborations between academic scholars who became part of the community at some level in the later part of the century in the development of the official language program (Brinkman 2003: 56–81). The collaborations developed between academic scholars and indigenous community scholars described here were often community focused, to varying degrees, and they had unanticipated consequences for the types and nature of collaborations that followed. These collaborations thus serve to illustrate the importance and value of academic-community collaboration for future generations. Further, they demonstrate that CBR can also serve as a lens through which to revisit and better understand a complicated past.

Relationships, and thus collaborations, are complex, as is history, and what is presented here is limited by constraints on space, access to a clear articulation of the intentions of all those discussed, and the challenges faced when reconstructing the past.[2] That said, we will make the claim that from an academic perspective the work of indigenous community scholars Dorthy[3] Nicodemus, Julia

---

[1] 'We' are two academic scholars who are not community members (Bischoff, Fountain) and an academic scholar trained in linguistics who is also an indigenous community scholar (Vincent). Vincent is the Program Manager of the Coeur d'Alene Tribe's Language Programs. Support for the project described included funding from the National Science Foundation through the Documenting Endangered Language Program (BCS-1160394 & BCS-1160627).
[2] For an illuminating discussion of the lives of those who participated in the collaborations discussed here, see Brinkman (2003), Wickwire (1993), and Faulk (1997, 1999).
[3] Brinkman (2003) informs us that although Reichard (1938, 1947) spelled her name Dorothy, on her tomb the spelling was Dorthy. We use Dorthy here.

Antelope Nicodemus, Lawrence Nicodemus, Tom Miyal,[4] and academic scholar Gladys Reichard in the early 20th century, described below, can be understood as a form of CBR, and that this work in particular has led to much collaborative research in the spirit, and emerging definitions, of CBR (see esp. Rice and others this volume). Further, we conclude that this history suggests that there might be a middle ground between what Czaykowska-Higgins (2009) refers to as a linguist-focused model of language research and what she refers to as community-based language research (here referred to as CBR). We also suggest that CBR may emerge out of a linguist-focused model, or what appears on the surface to be linguist-focused, and lead to a more CBR centered approach similar to what is described in Pérez Báez (this volume) and Rice (this volume).

In the following sections, each of which has been developed primarily by one of the three co-authors of this paper, we begin by presenting a brief sketch of select collaborations and the resulting linguistic and cultural resources developed in the 20th century, framed within contemporary models of CBR. Next, we focus on how these resources are shaping contemporary collaborations and being shaped by 21st century technology. Section 4 describes how the resources discussed have shaped the experience of one community member who is a trained linguist and the Director of the Coeur d'Alene Language Programs, and how these resources are being used by the Coeur d'Alene community today. In section 5 we provide some concluding remarks.

2 20th century Coeur d'Alene collaborations

Perhaps the most influential published and unpublished works recording the Coeur d'Alene language and culture of the 20th century involved a small, closely-linked group of individuals.[5] From the community, a small number of families played a key role in the documentation of the language and culture in the early

---

[4] Tom Miyel (aka *Taamiyel*, Tom Yell) is a *Coeur d'Alene* version/pronunciation of his baptismal name, Damien, aka Octave Damien Basil (Raymond Brinkman pc).

[5] This section was primarily developed by co-author Bischoff, an academic scholar who has worked extensively with the 20th century materials described here. We use the term *collaboration* in its daily usage sense to mean *a joint effort to accomplish a task or project*. It is not exactly clear how each individual felt about what they were doing. However, Reichard's (1947) and Brinkman's (2003) accounts of these collaborations suggests that there were shared goals. Lawrence Nicodemus' travels to Columbia University in the late 1930s to continue work with Reichard and his lifetime of dedication to documenting, preserving, and revitalizing the language and culture also support this interpretation of the relationship among those working together at this time.

part of the century and also in the community centered revitalization efforts at the close of the century. The Nicodemus and Antelope families were central to these efforts. Specifically, Kwaruutus⁶ Nicodemus, Dorthy Nicodemus, Lawrence Nicodemus, Julia Antelope Nicodemus, Susan Antelope, Maurice Antelope, and Morris Antelope are known to have played important roles in the work.⁷ During the first half of the 20th Century, Gladys Reichard, an anthropologist and former student of Franz Boas, was the most prominent academic scholar working in the community. James Teit,⁸ a "store clerk, ethnographer, author and political activist" (Wickwire 2016) who worked as an interpreter for Franz Boas, also contributed early works. Towards the end of the century it was students of Anthony Mattina, primarily Ivy Doak and Raymond Brinkman, who continued to work with these resources while building new relationships and partnerships with community members. It is also important to note Gary Palmer who worked closely with the Tribe and Lawrence Nicodemus for many years within a CBR framework.

Kwaruutus Nicodemus, "chief informant among the Coeur d'Alene" (Teit 1930: 122), and James Teit collaborated in the recording of cultural and linguistic data as early as 1904 (Teit 1930; Reichard 1947). This collaboration resulted in the publication of texts referred to as "myths" (Teit 1917) and an ethnographic sketch recording what is described as pre-contact culture of the Coeur d'Alene (Teit 1930). Teit and Nicodemus' collaboration was built upon in the late 1920s, after both had passed, when Gladys Reichard arrived in Coeur d'Alene country. Working with, and building on, the materials that Kwaruutus Nicodemus and James Teit had compiled, Reichard formed a partnership with Kwaruutus Nicodemus' widow, Dorthy Nicodemus.⁹ She also worked closely with Julia Antelope Nicodemus, daughter-in-law of Dorthy, and Julia's son Lawrence. Julia Antelope Nicodemus learned to write the language and working with Reichard

---

Further, what we know of Teit and how he worked with and advocated for indigenous communities suggests the same (see Wickwire 1993).

6 Teit (1930) spells the name Qwarótus; however, we use the traditional spelling of the Tribe here acknowledging that the Tribal community often spells the name with an initial lower case.

7 It is important to note that there have been a number of community members and families who have actively worked towards the documentation and revitalization of the Coeur d'Alene language and culture, and that issues of economy do not allow us to discuss them all here.

8 Teit's work and life may also support the argument that there is perhaps a middle ground between linguist-focused research and community-based research (Czaykowska-Higgins 2009). Teit conducted a good deal of linguist-focused research but he also served as translator, assistant, and advocate for the Interior Tribes of British Columbia as well as the Indian Rights Association in their political efforts in the early 1900s (Wickwire 2016).

9 Brinkman (2003) notes that it is not clear how the partnership between Dorthy Nicodemus and Gladys Reichard came about.

recorded the verbal art of Dorthy in the form of narratives, analyzing the language and culture. Julia also contributed her own versions of a small number of the texts, which she transcribed and translated as well. Reichard (1947: 2) notes the following regarding the importance of Julia's contributions to the project: "Without Julia's thorough understanding of the task and her valuable advice as to ways to going about it my results both linguistic and mythological would have been much more scanty."

At this time Reichard also formed a collaborative partnership with Tom Miyal who contributed to the narratives she was collecting. Julia's son, Lawrence Nicodemus, was also involved in the recording and organizing of the narratives in the summers of 1927 and 1929 during Reichard's visits. In 1935 Lawrence, at the encouragement of his mother Julia, traveled to New York City to work with Reichard in the analysis of the texts recorded in those two summers of 1927 and 1929 and to study at Columbia University through the assistance of Reichard (Reichard 1947; Brinkman 2003). The result was a grammar (Reichard 1938), stem list (Reichard 1939), and English translations of the texts (Reichard 1947).

We believe the documentation and resulting works produced by this group reflect what Himmelman (2006) describes as *language documentation*, based on the state of the language and the language community at the time, available technological resources, and the various uses of this "record of language" over the years by academics and community members.[10] The goal of the documentation, we believe, was "not a short-term record for a specific purpose or interest group, but a record for generations and user groups whose identity [was and] is still unknown and [who have or] who may want to explore questions not yet raised at the time when the language documentation was compiled" (2).

The bibliographies of most, if not all, of the works carried out on the Coeur d'Alene language and culture, for both research and community goals, after the 1940s (e.g. Reichard 1958–61; Sloat 1966; Nicodemus 1975a, 1975b; Nicodemus

---

10 While Himmelmann (2006) acknowledges the Boasian tradition in which this work was begun, we believe that Reichard focused on the *primary data* available, had an *explicit concern for accountability* as illustrated in the various published outcomes, demonstrated a concern and attempt to ensure *long-term storage and preservation of primary data* through deposits of work in archives, and worked with limited, but *interdisciplinary* teams as demonstrated by the work conducted with Adele Froelich and the various community members participating in the documentation. We also believe that there was a strong *close cooperation with, and direct involvement of, the speech community* which we define as those that worked directly with her on the project (see Brinkman 2003, Reichard 1938 and Reichard and Froelich 1947 for detailed discussion). However, we acknowledge this is subject to interpretation, and the realities of the period put comparison of today's documentation standards as described by Himmelmann at some remove.

et al 2000a, 2000b; Doak 1997; Brinkman 2003; Frey 2005) show that these works have been inspired, influenced, and/or informed by the materials resulting from the above collaborations (see Faulk 1999 for discussion of the quality and importance of this work in Salishan and Coeur d'Alene studies).[11]

Upon Lawrence's return from New York, with a set of greater linguistic skills and a meta-awareness of Coeur d'Alene grammar, Father Byrne of the Catholic Church was inspired to work with him to reinvigorate what was already then a language in great decline (Brinkman 2003). This was perhaps Lawrence's first encounter with attempts to use his knowledge of Coeur d'Alene and linguistics for direct maintenance and revitalization purposes. As Brinkman describes, Lawrence Nicodemus would go on to work on the documentation, preservation, and revitalization of Coeur d'Alene throughout his life, and thus the 20th century (Lawrence Nicodemus passed in 2004). Working with Joseph Bitar in the 1970s Nicodemus helped develop the orthography used by the Tribe today (Brinkman 2003; Doak and Montler 2000). In addition, he developed numerous pedagogical resources, which included the first Coeur d'Alene/English and English/Coeur d'Alene dictionaries. He also instructed classes at the Coeur d'Alene Tribal school as well as co-instructed high school and college level courses in the language (Brinkman 2003; Nicodemus 1973; Palmer and Nicodemus 1982, 1985; Palmer et al. 1987; Nicodemus et al 2000a, 2000b).

Raymond Brinkman, former Director of the Tribal Language Programs, who worked closely with Lawrence Nicodemus and the various materials generated by his mother Julia Antelope Nicodemus, grandmother Dorthy Nicodemus, Tom Miyal, and Gladys Reichard, notes that the "group worked as a team and were aware that they were documenting the language and culture for future generations" (p.c).[12] The records show that Julia Antelope Nicodemus and Gladys Reichard worked very closely together (see Reichard 1939, Reichard 1947; Brinkman 2003). The record also shows that Julia encouraged her son to go to Columbia University, where he eventually studied with Reichard on the language. Upon his return Lawrence became one of the most important community members in the advocating for, and implementing of, revitalization efforts: Importantly, using

---

11 For a full list of Coeur d'Alene publications see Bischoff et al (in press — an earlier but incomplete version is available at the following link http://linguistics.ubc.ca/files/2014/03/Bischoff-etal-final.pdf).

12 It is perhaps important to note that Brinkman, while the Director of the Language Programs, was an outsider and his views may not reflect the views of the community or other linguists who worked extensively in the community and with the resources mentioned. That said, he worked within the community for over 20 years and worked very closely and personally with Lawrence Nicodemus.

skills he learned from Reichard and his work on the original documentation project.

In short, the work begun by Kwa̱ruutus Nicodemus and James Teit at the dawn of the 20th Century, directly or indirectly lead to the collaborative relationship between Dorthy Nicodemus, Julia Antelope Nicodemus, Lawrence Nicodemus, and Gladys Reichard. We believe that whatever the nature of these collaborations may have been, they played a profound role in the future collaborations of those that worked with Coeur d'Alene throughout the 20th century, and as we will demonstrate below, continue to play a major role in collaborations between academic scholars and community scholars today. In particular the collaboration between Gladys Reichard and Julia Antelope Nicodemus made it possible for Lawrence Nicodemus to play a primary role in various collaborations documenting and revitalizing the language into the early 21st century. This record suggests to us that while it may have been the case that Reichard[13] initiated the documentation of Coeur d'Alene in the spirit of what Crippen and Robinson (2013) describe as "lone wolf" research or what Czaykowska-Higgins (2009) describes as a "linguist-focused model" of research, that the work evolved quite early on to something closer to CBR. This is demonstrated through the relationship between Gladys Reichard and Julia Antelope Nicodemus. Further, the work begun by this team, through Lawrence Nicodemus and the body of data and resources he collected and developed, has continued to conform with the basic tenets of CBR as defined by Rice (2009, 2010, 2011) and Czaykowska-Higgins (2009, this volume), but is perhaps most closely aligned with Rice (this volume). That is, we view the work described below regarding contemporary projects as an extension of this work, not as something new.

---

13 Reichard is a complex figure and while one of the key concepts of CBR, *social justice* (Rice this volume), may not have been a part of her lexicon, her conduct in various communities with which she worked suggests it was a guiding principle in her work. This is illustrated in the development of the Hogan School on the Navajo Reservation where Reichard and community members worked to develop writing and literacy practices in Navajo, and the community members began a Navajo language newspaper (see Faulk 1999 chapter 19 for discussion). Reichard's conduct at the Hogan School is reminiscent of her work with Julia Antelope Nicodemus and Lawrence Nicodemus a few years earlier. We caution that the image we are painting of Reichard does not detract from the collaborative relationships we are discussing. We believe Reichard's collaborators, especially Julia and Lawrence were equal agents in the production of linguistic resources, but were also empowered to be their own agents of language maintenance and revitalization via their own resolve to acquire academic linguistic skills and use them for their community-focused goals. Reichard, and/or the collaborative partnership she had with Julia and Lawrence Nicodemus, we believe, was at least a catalyst for the community-based research Lawrence undertook.

Table 1: Significant Nicodemus/Antelope 20th Century Collaborations

Years	Participants	Products
1904–1909	Kwaruutus Nicodemus and James Teat	Teit 1917, 1930
1927, 1929, 1935	Dorthy Nicodemus, Julia Antelope Nicodemus, Lawrence Nicodemus, Tom Miyal and Gladys Reichard	Reichard 1938, 1939, 1947, 1958–61
1964	Lawrence Nicodemus and Clarence Sloat	Sloat 1966
1973–1975	Lawrence Nicodemus	Nicodemus 1973, 1975a, 1975b
1982–1985	Lawrence Nicodemus and Gary B. Palmer	Palmer and Nicodemus 1982, 1985
2000	Lawrence Nicodemus, Wanda Matt, Reva Hess, Gary Sobbing, Jill Maria Wagner and Dianne Allen	Nicodemus et al 2000a, b

The claim that Lawrence's work is a continuation of CBR is exemplified at various stages in Lawrence's life, but especially in his work with the development of the Tribal orthography (1970s); pedagogical resources developed with Gary Palmer (1980s) and later with Wanda Matt, Reva Hess, Gary Sobbing, Jill Maria Wagner, and Dianne Allen (2000s); and the development of the Tribal Language Program (1990s). We believe that viewing the work described above, and the construction of the historical past itself, through the lens of CBR (as explored by Rice this volume) provides a fuller, more complex understanding of historical relationships between communities, community members, and anthropologists and linguists than would be possible otherwise. This, we believe, makes CBR more than just a research methodology, but also a tool to conceptualize the past and the present or, as Rice (this volume) suggests an orientation or philosophy – an orientation or philosophy that lends itself to reconceptualizing the past. We also believe that the work discussed here helps to motivate the consideration of a third alternative to the binary distinction proposed by Czaykowska-Higgins (2009), in the spirit perhaps of Pérez Báez (this volume) allowing us to consider the moment, or moments, when research begun as linguist-focused becomes community-based; or when research is *at once* linguist-focused *and* community-based. This distinction may be at the heart of the recent debate between Crippen and Robinson (2013) and Bowern and Warner (2015) in that it rests firmly on notions about what constitutes collaboration and the nature of the relationships in collaborative work as well as what counts as meaningful outcomes. That is, we believe CBR may not be one end of a binary approach, but rather part of a continuum that can be at once a practice, a tool for re-assessing past relationships and practices, and an orientation or philosophy to research. We explore a more recent set of outcomes from the Coeur d'Alene works developed in the 20th century in the next section.

3 21st century Coeur d'Alene collaborations and the influence of technologies

At the beginning of the 21st century, much work was being undertaken by members of the Coeur d'Alene Community, and by scholars of Coeur d'Alene, to advance the collaboration begun in previous years.[14] This included the development of significant resources for the teaching of the Coeur d'Alene language by Nicodemus and others (Nicodemus 1973, 1975a, 1975b; Nicodemus et al 2000a, 2000b), the advancement of theoretical work on Coeur d'Alene grammar by academic scholars including Ivy Doak (e.g. Doak 1992, 1997; Doak and Mattina 1997; Doak and Montler 2000), Shannon Bischoff (2001, 2007, 2011a, 2011b), Audra Vincent (2014), and the beginning of an effort to render the products of earlier collaborations more readily accessible to both scholars and community members.

By 2010, co-author Bischoff and Musa Yasin Fort, an undergraduate student at University of Puerto Rico Mayagüez, conceived and completed a pilot project to digitize and begin to repatriate the materials produced by the collaborations described in Section 2, so that they would again be available to the Coeur d'Alene community. Bischoff and Yasin Fort's work was begun after it had become clear that many of the products of previous collaborations had become inaccessible to the community, and that some were in danger of permanent loss. At the onset of that project, Bischoff reached out to the then Director of Language Programs at the Coeur d'Alene Tribe to identify the goals and needs within the community. Objectives identified by the Director included the development of a searchable online English/Coeur d'Alene dictionary, and the development of digital access to the heritage materials created by the researchers described above. These goals overlapped with academic interests in the emerging field of digital language archiving, and the project was undertaken to serve both community and scholarly needs. It should be noted that these actions and this project were greatly inspired by the work of Junker described in this volume.[15]

---

[14] This section was primarily developed by co-author Fountain, an academic scholar who has worked primarily on the technologies described in this section.
[15] In 2005 Bischoff attended a talk by Junker at the Workshop on the Structure of Constituency in Languages of the Americas at the University of Toronto. The talk presented work described

Table 2: Primary language resources in the CAOLR (Bischoff and Fountain 2013)

Resource	Original Source
Coeur d'Alene/English root dictionary (searchable)	Lyon and Greene-Wood 2007
Coeur d'Alene /English stem list (searchable)	Reichard 1939
Coeur d'Alene /English affix list (searchable)	Reichard 1938
Field notes (typed, handwritten, 1,200 pages, 48 narratives, available as pdf and png)	Reichard et al, unpublished
Published English translations of narratives	Reichard with Froelich 1947
Guide to conversions between orthographic conventions (Reichard's, Salishan, Coeur d'Alene community orthography)	Various
Links to other web-accessible public works	Doak 1997, Doak and Montler 2006, Reichard 1938, Reichard with Froelich 1947, Teit 1917

Bischoff and Yasin Fort developed and released the Coeur d'Alene Archive and Online Language Resources (CAOLR)[16] in an attempt to meet both the goals of the Tribal Language Programs and their own academic goals. In one summer they managed to digitize more than 1,200 pages of original field notes produced by Reichard and the Nicodemus group, collect and secure copyright permissions to incorporate and/or link to earlier scholarly work, and various other previously published but now hard-to-find resources on the language, as listed in the table below. All of these materials had been gathered in the CAOLR, and shared with the Coeur d'Alene Language Programs, by the summer of 2009. Remarkably, this work had been done with no external funding, by two enthusiastic volunteers (Bischoff and Yasin Fort) who were relatively new to web development and language archiving, and who had no special training in these areas.

One of the most innovative features of the CAOLR was the set of options users had to view the previously unpublished field notes digitized by Bischoff and Yasin Fort. In addition to full-screen displays of pdf or image (png) files, users could select a split- screen view, illustrated in figure 1 below, showing the evolution of each set of hand- written field notes to typed manuscript versions. Both the top

---

in Junker (this volume) which planted the seed for the project described, which in turn was the inspiration in great part for this volume.
16 The original CAOLR remains available at http://lasrv01.ipfw.edu/crd_archive/start1.html. It has since been redesigned and re-implemented as the Coeur d'Alene Online Language Resource Center (COLRC).

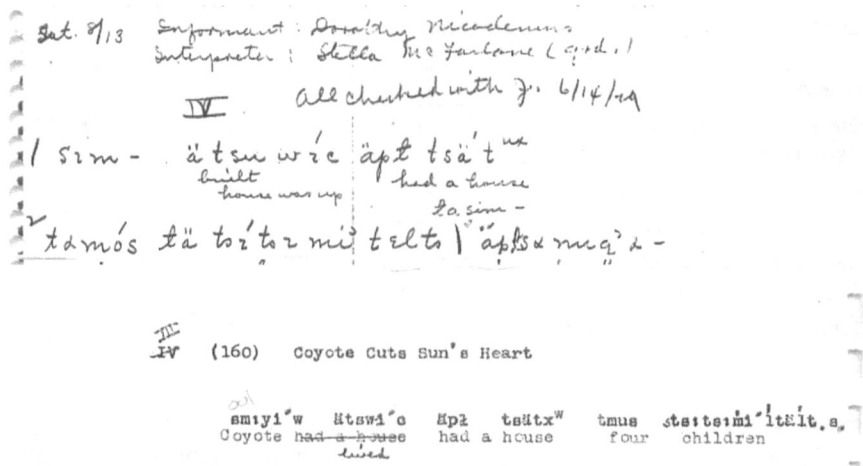

Figure 1: Screenshot of split-screen view of hand-written (top) and typed (bottom) field notes for narrative in the CAOLR

half (the hand-written notes) and the bottom half (the typed manuscripts) can be scrolled through independently, allowing the viewer to match the original and revised transcriptions of the texts. Both the hand-written fieldnotes and typed manuscripts often have editorial marks and hand-written comments, often the work of Reichard providing a glimpse of the collaboration among these scholars that occurred during the transcription and recording of the oral narratives collected. The CAOLR represented an impressive and important achievement – and in 2010 a new phase of the project was undertaken to review and revise the underlying infrastructure of the site, in light of emerging best practices for web-based language resource development, as these were beginning to be developed in, for example, Farrar and Lewis (2007).

The CAOLR provided a place for the storage of digital surrogates of historical documents, but did not in itself meet the definition of a "digital archive." We surveyed the available literature and found two key resources to guide our redevelopment of the CAOLR: Chang's (2010) TAPS Checklist – a resource that provides guidance in evaluating the trustworthiness of online language archives, and Bird and Simons' (2003a, 2003b) work on development of online language archives. Our goals were to:

– Ensure that the site, and the material it contained, was developed in a way that was trustworthy, durable, discoverable, appropriately expandable and sustainable;

100 years of analyzing Coeur d'Alene with the community — 205

- Regularize the site so that it was in line with best practices for modern web development generally, and online language archiving specifically;
- Secure the viability of the site through the near future, and make sure it could be repatriated entirely to the Coeur d'Alene community when the community believed repatriation to be feasible and appropriate; and
- Complete this work in a manner that was as consistent as possible with the "grassroots" model of development used by Bischoff and Yasin Fort (see Bischoff and Fountain 2013 for discussion of this model, and its consequences).

By 2013 this collaboration resulted in a new site, the Coeur d'Alene Online Language Resource Center (COLRC).[17] The COLRC meets the following best practices for web development and online language archiving, in addition to housing all of the content and features originally provided by the CAOLR:
- In all resources in the COLRC, complete and recognizable metadata records are provided in a standard format. We elected to follow the conventions of the Dublin Core Metadata Initiatives[18] (DCMI);
- All resources are stored in such a way that data is separated from presentation – data other than image files are stored and maintained in xml, the site's navigation and presentation are managed via css;
- The site utilizes html 5 standards for presentation, all non-textual resources (audio files, images) are stored in standard and durable formats (pdf, png, jpg, mp3 and wav); and
- The search functionality is expanded to allow simultaneous searching in any of the three supported orthographies across all searchable resources, and renders more resources on the site easily discoverable by users in the Coeur d'Alene and scholarly communities.

More important than these technical advancements, however, was the development of a clear and collaborative Mission Statement for the COLRC.[19] This statement articulates and commits the site to responsible development and management in collaboration with (and with leadership from) the Coeur d'Alene Tribe via the Language Programs office of that Tribe. The development of the Mission Statement required the team to grapple with difficult questions of sustainability, ongoing maintenance, and ongoing relationships among the various

---
17 The COLRC is available at http://lasrv01.ipfw.edu/COLRC/.
18 DCMI standards and guidelines can be found at http://dublincore.org/.
19 http://lasrv01.ipfw.edu/COLRC/home/mission.php

stakeholders in its development and use. These issues are difficult because they require the evaluation of long term goals and requirements in an environment of short term funding and rich and abiding uncertainty.

The development of the COLRC was undertaken with the support of the National Science Foundation's Documenting Endangered Languages (DEL) Program,[20] and was therefore subject to demands that the material in the site be accessible to scholars as well as community members (see Benedicto this volume for discussion of this issue). The history of work on Coeur d'Alene language has always been marked by collaboration between these two groups, however – we view the development, maintenance, and improvements of the COLRC as just another step in that history of collaboration.

4 21st century Coeur d'Alene collaborations – an academic and indigenous community scholar's perspective

hiskwist khwa Audra Vincent. chn te'l 'l'lkhwi'lus. Vincents le k'we'y tech tsi' biinwahulumkhw. chn schitsu'umsh. t'i's hinune' khwa Patricia Vincent. t'i's hnpipe' khwa Richard Vincent. t'i's hnqine' khwe Jessie Vincent. t'i's hnqhipe' khwe Stephen Vincent. t'i's hnchche'ye' khwe Betty Goudy. t'i's hisile' khwa Albert Goudy. schitsu'umsh khwa hnqine' hilhnqhipe'. Muckleshoot khwe hnchche'ye'. Yakama khwe hisile'.[21]

'My name is Audra Vincent. I am from Desmet, Idaho. Before that the Vincents were from the Benewah area. I am a member of the Coeur d'Alene tribe. My late mother was Patricia Vincent. My late father was Richard Vincent. My late paternal grandmother was Jessie Vincent. My late paternal grandfather was Stephen Vincent. My late maternal grandmother was Betty Goudy. My late maternal grandfather was Albert Goudy. My dad's parents were Coeur d'Alene. My mom's mom was enrolled Muckleshoot and my mom's dad was enrolled Yakama'.

My contribution to this chapter will be how the COLRC has helped in our program's efforts to learn and teach the language as well as its benefits to our language revitalization efforts. I got involved in this project when I was still finishing my M.A. I worked on the metadata, some proofreading of the site as well as

---

20 Award numbers BCS-1160394 and BCS-1160627.
21 Co-author Vincent has chosen to introduce herself and this section of discussion in Coeur d'Alene.

some presentations of the project at conferences. Now I am the Program Manager for hnqwa'qwe'eln (the Coeur d'Alene Language Program).

My career goals and life's work revolves around my love for my language. I did not grow up with my language though. I am from a generation that did not have access to our language like previous generations. My grandparents were from the boarding school era where the goal was to eradicate language and culture. They knew their languages but did not pass them on to their children. Because of this my parents did not know their language to teach me or my two siblings. My main language learning started in high school with Reva Hess who was a non-tribal member and her co-teacher Lawrence Nicodemus who was a fluent speaking elder. I took the classes offered at Lakeside high school and then took the college courses offered through North Idaho College, which Lawrence also co-taught. As a result of taking these classes and learning from Lawrence and Reva I developed a passion for language revitalization. I went to college with the goal of obtaining skills that would help in my goal of returning back home to work on revitalizing Coeur d'Alene. At the University of Washington I double majored in American Indian Studies and linguistics. I have recently received my M.A. in linguistics from the University of British Columbia.

The Coeur d'Alene language is a severely endangered language with only two fluent speakers who are in their 90s. Hnqwa'qwe'eln's mission is to create new speakers of the language to ensure that the language will continue to survive for future generations. We are working on developing a new speech community to use and pass on the language. Since Gladys Reichard's fieldwork in the 1920s there have been other researchers who have done field work on Coeur d'Alene as well. Lawrence Nicodemus learned linguistics from Reichard and did extensive language revitalization work up until his death. There have been elder interviews conducted in Coeur d'Alene by fluent speaker Lavinia Felsman in the 1980s with other fluent speakers. The Coeur d'Alene Language Program has been in existence since 1995. Starting in 2001 the Language Program has held weekly meetings to document language with the remaining fluent speakers. All of this research has given us a huge store of language documentation. A lot of our language documentation sits in an unusable format. The COLRC helps make some of this documentation accessible to community members as well as researchers.

We are in a state where we want the community to use the language and learn it. If we have resources the community members would use to learn language then we want to make them easily available to those people. There are also tribal members who live far distances from the reservation but desire a connection to the language who can benefit from this resource. The COLRC provides this opportunity.

Along with the loss of language in our community was also a loss of cultural knowledge. The COLRC contains access to Reichard's work on Coeur d'Alene stories. We used to have traditional story tellers in our community who passed down these stories orally but that is not the case anymore. Having access to these stories in a written format gives our people access to some of our cultural knowledge that otherwise would have been lost with the passing of the last story tellers. Maybe with this type of access storytelling could in the future be revitalized alongside language.

Access to the COLRC has been shared with the community but there are not a large amount of community members who use this as a resource yet. The main people who regularly use the COLRC are the same people involved in language and culture revitalization. This is a small amount of people. The Language Program and Culture Program use the COLRC daily and often many times throughout the day. This is a significant resource for the work in our programs. Before the COLRC the main resource we used was the print version of the Nicodemus (1975a, 1975b) dictionaries. Often times this is not enough to find what we are looking for. There are words that are listed in one volume but not the other. The COLRC search function is the most helpful for our daily language activities. The search function opens up different ways for us to find words or sentences. We are able to search pieces of words in English or Coeur d'Alene. With this we are able to narrow our searches by a specific morpheme type so we can find certain sentence types. If we want to figure out how certain affixes are used we can press the link in the list that will bring you to the relevant section in Reichard's grammar. Having easy access to Reichard's grammar also provides a place to look up information about words or structures we are currently researching. Also, since we no longer have the original print version of the Nicodemus (1975a, 1975b) dictionaries to give out to language learners we are able to direct them to the COLRC where they can search through the root dictionary.

We use the COLRC when we are planning lessons, when we are researching our language, and as a teaching tool within the classroom. We have a lot of use for the COLRC currently but we also see its potential for future revitalization efforts. There have been different communities who have lost their fluent speakers decades ago. Without fluent speakers these people have to rely on language documentation to re-awaken their languages. Some communities are more fortunate than others with the amount of documentation that they have available to them. It is a fact that sometime soon we will be a community with no first language fluent speakers of Coeur d'Alene. We will be fortunate though that we have access to a resource like the COLRC.

Besides the resources available on the COLRC we also have other publications, research and recordings available at the Language Program. It is a future goal that we add what we have available to the COLRC so that it is more easily accessible to our community of language learners. There is a lot of future potential for this site to be a one stop resource for all available resources on our language. Speaking as a tribal member, community member, language revitalizationist, and linguist, I am thankful that our community and language program has this available for our revitalization efforts now and in the future. *chi'limt* 'I am thankful.'

5 Conclusions

The conceptualization of CBR as a model for researchers to follow considerably antedates much of the work discussed in this paper. The work of the 20th century was conducted in an almost completely unacknowledged imbalance of power, in the 21st century these asymmetries could at least be noticed and analyzed – but they still exist. Reichard and Teit might be described in some respects as 'lone wolf' style linguists, in the parlance of Crippen and Robinson (2013), but we hope that this discussion problematizes that description and reinforces the kinds of complex interplay described by Bowern and Warner (2015) between academic and community goals. Rice (this volume) refers to the "four Rs" commonly used in CBR in the Canadian context: respect, relevance, responsibility, and reciprocity. We find at least some evidence that these values underlay the work of various researchers throughout the 100 years of collaborations in Coeur d'Alene, sometimes in unexpected ways.

References

Bird, Steven and Gary Simons. 2003a. Seven dimensions of portability for language documentation and description. *Language* 79. 557–582.
Bird, Steven and Gary Simons. 2003b. Extending Dublin Core metadata to support the description and discovery of language resources. *Computers and the Humanities* 37. 375–388.
Bischoff, Shannon T. 2001. Lynx: A morphological analysis and translation of Dorothy Nicodemus' Coeur d'Alene narrative. Missoula: University of Montana MA thesis.
Bischoff, Shannon T. 2007. *Functional forms-formal functions: an account of Coeur d'Alene clause structure*. Tucson: University of Arizona Ph.D. dissertation.
Bischoff, Shannon T. 2011a. Lexical affixes, incorporation, and conflation: the case of Coeur d'Alene. *Studia Linguistica* 65. 1–31.
Bischoff, Shannon T. 2011b. Formal notes on Coeur d'Alene clause structure. Cambridge: Cambridge Scholars Publishing.

Bischoff, Shannon T. and Amy V. Fountain. 2013. A case-study in grass roots development of web resources for language workers: The Coeur d'Alene archive and online language resources (CAOLR). In Shannon T. Bischoff, Deborah Cole, Amy V. Fountain and Mizuki Miyashita (eds.), *The Persistence of Language: Constructing and Confronting the Past and Present in the Voices of Jane H. Hill*, 175–202. Amsterdam: John Benjamins.

Bischoff, Shannon, Amy Fountain, John Ivens, and Audra Vincent. to appear. A bibliography of Coeur d'Alene with commentary revisited. *Northwest Journal of Linguistics*.

Bowern, Claire and Natasha Warner. 2015. 'Lone Wolves' and collaboration: A reply to Crippen and Robinson (2013). *Language Documentation & Conservation* 9. 59–85.

Brinkman, Raymond. 2003. *Etsmeystkhw khwe snwiyepmshtsn 'you know how to talk like a whiteman'*. Chicago: University of Chicago Ph.D. dissertation.

Chang, Debbie. 2010. TAPS: Checklist for responsible archiving of digital language resources. Dallas, TX: Graduate Institute of Applied Linguistics MA thesis.

Doak, I. G. 1992. Another look at Coeur d'Alene harmony. *International Journal of American Linguistics* 58. 1–35.

Doak, Ivy G. 1997. *Coeur d'Alene grammatical relations*. Austin, TX: University of Texas dissertation.

Doak, Ivy G. and Anthony Mattina 1997. Okanagan-lx, Coeur d'Alene-ilš, and Cognate Forms. *International Journal of American Linguistics* 63. 334–361.

Doak, Ivy G., and Timothy Montler, 2000. Orthography, lexicography and language change. In Nicholas Ostler and Blair Rudes (eds), *Endangered Languages and Literacy. Proceedings of the Fourth FEL Conference*. http://montler.net/papers/ OrthographyFEL22000.pdf (accessed 23 May 2017).

Crippen, James A. and Laura C. Robinson. 2013. In defense of the Lone Wolf: Collaboration in language documentation. *Language Documentation & Conservation* 7. 123–135.

Czaykowska-Higgins, Ewa. 2009. Research models, community-engagement, and linguistic fieldwork: Reflections on working within Canadian Indigenous communities. *Language Documentation & Conservation* 3. 15–50.

Falk, Julia S. 1997. Territoriality, relationships, and reputation: The case of Gladys A. Reichard. *Southwest Journal of Linguistics* 16 (1). 17–37.

Falk, Julia S. 1999. *Women, Language, and Linguistics: Three American stories from the first half of the twentieth century*. London: Routledge.

Farrar, Scott and Will Lewis. 2007. The GOLD community of practice: an infrastructure for linguistic data on the web. *Language Resources and Evaluation* 41. 45–60.

Frey, Rodney. 2005. *Landscape traveled by Coyote and Crane: The world of the Schitsu'umsh (Coeur d'Alene Indians)*. Seattle: University of Washington Press.

Lyon, John and Rebecca Greene-Wood (eds). 2007. *Lawrence Nicodemus' Coeur d'Alene dictionary in root format*. Missoula, MT: University of Montana Occasional Papers in Linguistics.

Himmelman, Nikolaus P. 2006. Language documentation: What is it and what is it good for? In Jost Gippert, Nikolaus P. Himmelman and Ulrike Mosel (eds). *Essentials of Language Documentation*. Mouton de Gruyter. 1–30.

Nicodemus, L. 1973. The Coeur d'Alene language project. *ICSL 8*. Eugene, OR.

Nicodemus, L. 1975a. *Snchitsu'umshtsn: The Coeur d'Alene language. A Modern Course*. Plummer, ID: Coeur d'Alene Tribe.

Nicodemus, L. 1975b. *The Coeur d'Alene language in two volumes: I The grammar and Coeur d'Alene-English dictionary; II English-Coeur d'Alene dictionary*. Spokane, WA: University Press.

Nicodemus, L., Matt, W., Hess, R., Sobbing, G., Wagner, J. M., and Allen, D. 2000a. *Snchitsu'umshtsn: Coeur d'Alene Reference Book Volume 1*. Plummer, ID: Coeur d'Alene Tribe.

Nicodemus, L., Matt, W., Hess, R., Sobbing, G., Wagner, M. J., and Allen, D. 2000b. *Snchitsu'umshtsn: Coeur d'Alene Reference Book Volume 2*. Plummer: Coeur d'Alene Tribe.

Palmer, Gary B. and Lawrence Nicodemus. 1982. Marking surfaces in Coeur d'Alene and universals in anatomical nomenclature. *Working papers for the 17th ICSNL*, 295–330. http://lingserver.arts.ubc.ca/linguistics/sites/default/files/1982_Palmer_Nicodemus.pdf (accessed 23 May 2017).

Palmer, Gary B. and Lawrence Nicodemus. 1985. Coeur d'Alene exceptions to proposed universals of anatomical nomenclature. *American Ethnologist* 12. 341–359.

Palmer, Gary B., Thomas E. Connolly, Armando M DaSilva. 1987. *Khwi' khwe gul schitsu'umsh = These are the Coeur d'Alene people: a book of Coeur d'Alene personal names*. Plummer, ID: Coeur d'Alene Tribal Headquarters; Las Vegas, Nev.: Dept. of Anthropology, University of Nevada.

Reichard, Gladys A. 1938. Coeur d'Alene. Franz Boas (ed) *Handbook of American Indian languages Part 3*. 515–707. New York: J. J. Augustin, Inc.

Reichard, Gladys A. 1939. Stem-list of the Coeur d'Alene language. *International Journal of American Linguistics* 10. 92–108.

Reichard, Gladys A. with Adele Froelich. 1947. *An analysis of Coeur d'Alene Indian myths*. Philadelphia: Memoirs of the American Folk-lore Society, v. 41.

Reichard, Gladys A. 1958–1961. A comparison of five Salish languages. *International Journal of American Linguistics* 24, 25, 26.

Rice, Keren. 2009. Must there be two solitudes? Language activists and linguists working together. In John Reyhner and Louise Lockard (eds), *Stabilizing Indigenous languages: encouragement, guidance, and lessons learned*, 37–59. Flagstaff, Arizona: Northern Arizona University.

Rice, Keren. 2010. The linguist's responsibilities to the community of speakers: Community-based research. In Lenore A. Grenoble and N. Louanna Furbee (eds.) *Language documentation: Practice and values*, 25– 36. Amsterdam: John Benjamins.

Rice, Keren. 2011. Documentary linguistics and community relations. *Language Documentation & Conservation* 5. 187–207.

Sloat, C. 1966. *Phonological redundancy rules in Coeur d'Alene*. Seattle, WA: University of Washington dissertation.

Teit, J. 1917. Coeur d'Alene Tales. Franz Boas (ed), *Folktales of Salishan and Sahaptian Tribes*, 119–128. New York: American Folk-Lore Society.

Teit, James. 1930. The Salishan Tribes of the Western Plateaus. In, Smithsonian Institution Bureau of American Ethnology. Franz Boas (ed), *Annual Report of the Bureau of American Ethnology to the Secretary of the Smithsonian Institution Volume 45*, 23–396. Washington D.C.: US Government Printing Office.

Vincent, Audra. 2014. *Coeur d'Alene aspect*. Vancouver, BC: University of British Columbia MA thesis.

Wickwire, Wendy. 1993. Women in ethnography: The research of James A. Teit. *Ethnohistory* 40. 539–562.

Wickwire, Wendy. 2016. Tiet, James Alexander (until 1884 he spelled his surname Tait), in *Dictionary of Canadian biography, volume 15*, University of Toronto/Université Laval, 2003–, http://www.biographi.ca/en/bio/teit_james_alexander_1884_15E.html (accessed 1 July 2016).

Natasha Warner, Quirina Geary, and Lynnika Butler
Creating learning materials and teaching materials for language revitalization: The case of Mutsun

Abstract: When a community is working to revitalize a language, especially a dormant one, community members must create opportunities for people to learn the language. It is easy to focus on written teaching materials as important resources for learners, and outside linguists often collaborate with communities by writing teaching materials such as word lists, coloring books with words in the language under the pictures, language textbooks, and audio-visual language lessons. There is a lot to know about how to produce effective teaching materials, and community members' pilot tests may reveal unexpected things about what types of materials the community prefers and finds effective. However, it is also important to consider how one creates opportunities for learning apart from producing paper (or audio-visual) documents. Creating learning opportunities also includes choosing times, settings, and topics that allow learners to practice open conversation, and teaching how to stay in the language when one does not know a word. The authors explore these issues by discussing their experiences with creating opportunities for learning the Mutsun language (Costanoan, California/USA), through traditional language teaching materials, language activities, and more open-ended settings. We argue that when linguists attempt to work with a community on revitalization, they should avoid restricting the focus to production of written teaching materials, and should think broadly about creating opportunities for language use.

Keywords: Mutsun, community revitalization, language teaching materials, language use

---

Natasha Warner, (all post correspondence), Department of Linguistics, P.O. Box 210025, The University of Arizona, Tucson AZ 85721USA, nwarner@email.arizona.edu
Quirina Geary, Amah Mutsun Tribal Band and University of California, Davis, quirina.geary@yahoo.com
Lynnika Butler, Unaffiliated scholar, lynnika@gmail.com.

https://doi.org/10.1515/9783110527018-012

1 Introduction

When doing language revitalization, a community needs to find ways for community members to learn the language. The first thing one thinks of doing for revitalization may be "We should make a little book with some vocabulary" (or some language lessons, or a community-oriented grammar, or a computer program with audio recordings and pictures, etc.). This may happen because an outside linguist wants to "give back to the community" in some way. However, teaching materials alone are not likely to create fluent speakers. This does not mean that it is pointless to make such materials, but rather that one should also create opportunities for learners to practice speaking and understanding the language beyond those materials (as discussed by Eschenberg and Saunsoci along with Miyashita et al. this volume, for language use in a classroom setting). We encourage linguists working with communities to think of creating opportunities for language usage as a revitalization method in itself (see Langley et al. this volume). The product of revitalization work may not be a booklet, but rather an unscripted conversation in the language or a setting for conversations to occur.

If one approach to revitalization work is to create language booklets or teaching grammars, the opposite end of the continuum must be the Master-Apprentice Program, which emphasizes creating situations for use of the language between a learner and a fluent speaker, with just enough structure to help the master and apprentice keep talking in the language (Hinton et al. 2002). Linguists of course recognize the importance of many hours of natural language input, such as Master-Apprentice provides, to language acquisition. Still, many linguists turn to developing written classroom language teaching materials that do not provide natural fluent input. In this article, we discuss our experiences with producing structured language teaching materials and in creating more natural spontaneous environments for language usage. The language we work with is Mutsun, a Costanoan/Ohlone language of the area where modern-day San Juan Bautista (California, USA) is located. The last fluent speaker of the language, Mrs. Ascension Solarsano, died in 1930. Her work with J.P. Harrington, along with work by some earlier linguists as far back as 1807, provides a large corpus of written information on the language. The Mutsun people now live in disparate locations in and outside of California, with no area where the majority of the population is Mutsun. This geographical situation makes revitalization more difficult (Warner et al. 2009). We have been working since 1996 (Geary, who is a Mutsun community member, since 1996, later joined by Warner and then Butler, who are linguists and not community members) on revitalizing the Mutsun language through learning from those materials.

2 Our experiences with making language teaching materials

2.1 Language textbooks

When someone begins teaching a Spanish course, there are any number of textbooks available. In a revitalization setting, if one wants a textbook, the teacher will probably have to write it. We have developed partial drafts of two textbooks for Mutsun. In 1999, two years after Geary and Warner began working together, Warner visited Geary at her house for several days and we wrote several chapters of a basic textbook. We did not consult the Second Language Acquisition (henceforth SLA) literature at that point for guidelines on textbook writing, because at that early point in the project, this was an attempt to plunge in and get any type of teaching material at all on paper during a brief chance to work together in person. The first chapter consisted of greetings. Each of the remaining chapters introduced a grammatical topic. For example, the second chapter introduced nouns and how to say *hinTis neppe?* 'What is this?' and *neppe___* 'This is a ___.' The fourth chapter introduced numbers 1–10 and the plural. The sixth chapter introduced transitive verbs and the object suffix.

Each chapter was centered around a grammar topic, not around a real-life situation. This textbook was written for community members with no knowledge of linguistics, without grammatical terms. For example, the chapter on transitive verbs and the object suffix was titled "Doing something to things," not "Direct objects." Each chapter consisted of a list of simple example sentences with their English translations and a very short grammar explanation. We made these sentences up in order to avoid grammar that had not been introduced yet; they were not taken from archival Mutsun documents. Chapters taught a few sentence structures as templates (e.g. "This is a ___" or "I see a ___"), allowing learners to fill a large number of words in to make many sentences quickly, although these might not be especially useful. Grammar explanations used minimal technical terms. For example, the explanation for plural was "If there is more than one of something, you put *–kma* or *–mak* on the end of the word. If the word ends in a consonant, put *–mak*. If it ends in a vowel, put *–kma*." This basic textbook contained no pictures, no activities, and no stories or conversations or songs. In some ways it was closer to a linguist's grammar of the language than to a textbook, although with more example sentences and less explanation. Hinton sometimes tells learners who are trying to work with a linguist's grammar that they should just read the example sentences and ignore all of the text in between them (2002: 81). Our early textbook was not so different from that approach. This textbook clearly shows that it was written partly by a linguist, and it does not follow the format expected for a textbook for a college Spanish class.

In approximately 2002, we began writing a new textbook for Mutsun with the assistance of student volunteers at the University of Arizona. We focused each chapter around a daily life communicative situation. For example, the third chapter is titled "Running into a friend at a restaurant." This textbook still uses few technical terms and provides readable explanations of grammar. However, it also includes games and activities that provide practice for specific structures, conversations and short stories (written by us), and some pictures. Conversations and stories are accompanied by a vocabulary list and a translation. Learners could have some natural language usage after fewer chapters than with the grammar-based textbook. This later textbook looks much more like a college language textbook, or at least like an unfinished draft of one. This textbook was also not based on the SLA literature on textbook design, but we did make use of our own knowledge of language textbooks we had studied from in writing it. One reason that we did not consult the literature or recruit someone with expertise in textbook design is that at this time period, the primary focus of the group was on developing the dictionary (Warner et al. 2016), which was very time-consuming.

Warner, a linguist with experience studying various languages as an adult from textbooks, expected that Mutsun learners would prefer the second textbook. However, this does not seem to be the case. Some of the activities have been helpful in workshops but overall, learners have preferred the early, basic textbook, despite or perhaps even because of its heavy emphasis on grammar. For an adult learner who approaches language analytically, learning how to use one suffix to make a lot of new words can be both rewarding and approachable; learning to read a whole conversation, even if it is simple, may be neither.[1] We have seen Mutsun learners greatly enjoy learning to use a few nominalizers and apply them to several verbs to quickly expand their vocabulary. This allows one to derive *tummeSmin* 'a cook,' *tummemsa* 'place where you cook (kitchen),' *tummen* 'thing one cooks,' and *tummes* 'thing you use to cook (stove?)' from the verb *tumme* 'to cook.' In the future, we hope to observe more about what makes a particular grammar-based lesson engaging, and to survey learners about their preferences. If this preference for a streamlined grammar-based textbook continues, it would also be convenient, since this type of textbook is much faster to write.

---

[1] See Skehan (1996) on preferences of analytic vs. memory-oriented learners, although this appears to describe learners at a higher level.

Geary and other community leaders taught monthly language classes for a year in 2000–2001, the first Mutsun language classes. The main resource was the early textbook, with one lesson per chapter. She supplemented with pictures and repetition and provided audio recordings to go with each lesson for participants to listen to during that month. 10–20 people attended each class. Later, Geary and other leaders tried a "language committee" approach, with a small core group of about 7 people (including Geary), in hopes of training teachers. They met for two 3-hour sessions per week. This group tried working with the later textbook, but after a few lessons, they decided to use the more simple looking first textbook. This group continued off and on for about two years, and also used the Mutsun *Green Eggs and Ham* book described below, and developed a major revision of the Mutsun orthography, without the help of any outside linguist. More recently, a group led by the tribal leadership has offered language classes in person at the University of California, Santa Cruz, and has streamed these over the internet. These classes also included the early grammar-based textbook.

2.2 Written free-standing teaching materials

We have developed a variety of written teaching materials that can be used independently, without a textbook. Most of these materials were developed by Geary (alone or in collaboration with other community members), and Warner only contributed by checking a draft for errors, at most. For example, a group of Mutsun community members translated Dr. Seuss' *Green Eggs and Ham* into Mutsun as their project at the Breath of Life workshops one year. This book is useful for language teaching for the same reasons it works well as an easy reader: words and phrases repeat frequently and build up gradually, and the rhythm makes it fun. It is very effective for teaching fluency on certain phrases (*ekwe-ka hiwsen...* 'I do not like...').

We have written a collection of short stories (1–2 paragraphs) in Mutsun to provide simple texts to read. A Mutsun community member with expertise in art, Kanyon SayersRood, developed a coloring book with Mutsun words accompanying the picture on each page.

One especially successful item was a set of index cards Geary developed. At a Breath of Life workshop, she wrote basic nouns, basic verbs, pronouns in subject and object form, and the object suffix and plural suffix each on a card. This required only a few minutes, so no preparation was required beyond buying index cards. Geary then showed several novice learners including two of her older children how to combine a noun, verb, noun, and object suffix to make a simple transitive sentence. She also showed them how to combine a noun and verb to make an intransitive sentence. The novice learners would line up cards on a table and then say the sentence. Soon the learners needed more things to practice, so Geary introduced more structures. Learners enjoyed teasing each other by making sentences with amusing or semantically unlikely meanings by rearranging the cards, e.g. *moT-me hiwsen amma penyekse?* 'Do you want to eat a cat?' instead of *moT-me hiwsen amma tooTese?* 'Do you want to eat meat?' The learners who tried this method at the workshop quickly learned to make, pronounce, and understand a large number of sentences.

2.3 Games, audio, and other non-written materials

We have developed several audio or audiovisual learning materials for Mutsun, as well as many games. Around 2004, we first developed a list of daily life phrases. Geary surveyed Mutsun community members, asking what things they say often, and added her own items to the list. Warner and Butler translated the sentences into Mutsun during a visit, and together we recorded the phrases and their English translations to circulate as an audio CD. The phrases included many things one might say to one's children, such as 'Clean your room' or 'It's time for dinner,' as well as greetings, asking the time, etc. In 2014, Geary and Warner made an updated version, re-checking Mutsun usage after the near-completion of the dictionary (Warner et al. 2016). This recording could be useful to learners, especially if they focus on a few sentences at a time. However, the phrases probably required too much grammatical complexity to serve as good language learning material.

We have also created a list of the Mutsun words and sentences needed in order to play the traditional *Tallik* stick-throwing game. Such games are very common in California Indian cultures, and Harrington recorded the cultural information about this game in his notes, along with the words for the two types of sticks used (throwing sticks and counters). We developed a list of sentences one would need in order to play the game (e.g. 'My turn,' 'You won,' 'How many counters?') and translated them into Mutsun. Geary made several sets of Tallik sticks with traditional decorations, and taught her children to play. This game seems to be an engaging way to use Mutsun for new learners, and it is culturally relevant. We also developed a Mutsun translation of the Hokey-Pokey, useful for teaching body parts and imperatives, and for providing a break during a long language workshop. Some additional games we have used as Mutsun teaching activities are Mutsun translations of Twister, Simon Says (as *mayan monse*, 'coyote says'), head-shoulders-knees-and-toes, and Go Fish, as well as a traditional ball game played with a *pakkuT* ball. We have also translated the English "happy birthday" song.

We have developed a few videos. We used one wordless cartoon video that we obtained online, wrote a Mutsun text describing the actions, and dubbed a Mutsun recording onto the video. More recently, at the 2014 Breath of Life workshop, Geary, two of her older children and another Mutsun participant, Warner, and a student with video editing skills dubbed a Bugs Bunny cartoon into Mutsun. Because of time constraints, Warner translated the English text to Mutsun. This project was carried out completely within the week of the conference, and the characters were voiced by learners who had little exposure to Mutsun before the workshop. Many of the sentences had to be re-recorded several times, the speakers were heavily coached on pronunciation, the intonation in the final recording was not ideal, and the dubbing was clearly not professional. However, we were able to produce an entertaining video that is easy to understand and voiced by learners within a week. The sentence structures within the video are too varied to teach how to make sentences, but learners could easily learn some vocabulary (e.g. *suksusu* 'duck' and *ceeyes* 'rabbit') from the video. This method has potential for involving teens more in revitalization work. This video contrasts with the one described by Miyashita et al. (this volume), which was created over a much longer time span, with more professional video techniques and considerable thought given to the language pedagogy of the content storyline. Unlike Miyashita et al.'s more sophisticated project, our goal with the Bugs Bunny video was to produce something usable within the one-week span of the workshop, involving early learners, and following the learners' choice of content.

Even though Mutsun learners have favored the early grammar-based textbook over the later one with integrated activities, songs, etc., we have found that it is important to make the learning fun, using simple games and songs. This creates the most relaxed learning environment and leads to sustained knowledge of Mutsun. Thus, the preference may be for basing lessons around a grammar-heavy textbook, but adding games and songs or activities such as creating a video as part of the class or workshop.

3 Our experiences with creating situations for talking in Mutsun

It is important to create chances for learners to use Mutsun productively and creatively, in conversation or story telling or other open-ended language use. At one Breath of Life workshop in approximately 2005, when Geary and Warner discussed at the beginning of the week what to do for the project, Geary stated immediately that she had made booklets and stories in the past, but next she wanted to be able to hold a conversation in Mutsun. Warner agreed that this was a good next step at that point. We were joined later that week by Butler. We began practicing holding unstructured conversations about daily life topics (e.g 'How did you sleep?' 'Are you hungry?' 'Did you eat/shower/other verb yet?' 'Let's go.' 'What do you want to do/eat/other verb?'). We spent as much time as possible during the week practicing conversations like this, and discovering what concepts or sentence structures we needed and did not know. For example, which of the many words glossed as 'wash' should one use with a reflexive to mean 'to shower'? We had to get from looking up individual words in the draft dictionary and laboriously piecing together sentences to generating sentences without looking anything up. We developed a strategy for how to stay in the language if one did not understand: one could say *oySo?* 'again?' to avoid saying "What was that?" in English. Part of practicing having a Mutsun conversation was learning to stick to topics we readily had the words to express, rather than going into abstract complex topics such as feelings about cultural revitalization.

At the end of the week, we stood in front of a large audience consisting of the joint attendance of the Breath of Life workshop and the Stabilizing Indigenous Languages Conference, and held an unscripted conversation entirely in Mutsun. That week was the first time Mutsun had been used in conversation since approximately 1915. Some attendees of the Stabilizing Indigenous Languages Conference whose languages have fluent speakers may not have grasped how significant this accomplishment was. Taking Mutsun usage from "let's make a textbook/coloring book/easy reader/video" to "let's just talk" was an important development.

Approximately a year later, Geary visited Warner's home for a week during Warner's spring break, so that we were both able to devote all our time to working on the language. We optimistically aimed to speak exclusively Mutsun. We did not succeed in that, but we did speak Mutsun perhaps a third of the time, which was far more than we had ever used it before. We were especially pleased during that week at two developments. First, while working with the archival texts on microfilm, we encountered a long text of connected Mutsun speech we had not known about. We were very pleased to find that we were able to read almost all of it easily even though it did not have a translation, and that the language usage and sentence structures sounded a lot like the sentences we were using in our own Mutsun. Since most of the archival records of Mutsun contain sentences out of context or individual words, and there are very few longer stretches of connected speech that seem to have been produced as a fluent discourse, we had had to learn Mutsun with little to no discourse context and few long, complex sentences. Finding this text and being able to read it easily confirmed that our method of learning was in some way successful. The second noteworthy moment during this week was of a different sort: at the end of the week, we walked into a coffee shop on the University of Arizona campus and hesitated, because we had been about to order coffee in Mutsun. Although this was a fleeting experience, it suggested we were making progress in making usage of the language natural.

In order to reach even that level of struggling semi-fluency, one must make the jump from constructing sentences bit by bit to using the grammar productively and more quickly. In Warner et al. (2009) we describe how Warner talked to her pre-linguistic son, gradually building more and more complex sentences around a single word as a starting point. This allowed Warner to practice using the syntax and morphology, and then to move to writing short stories in Mutsun, where writing allows time for checking one's work. Saville-Troike and Barto (2017: Ch. 5) discuss a case of a young child learning English as a second language similarly starting with a word and then building up a longer and longer sentence while talking to himself, to practice the language. The same work discusses the strategy of learning through writing, because writing allows time to puzzle out a sentence slowly, unlike conversation (2017: Ch. 6). Another strategy we used in our early attempts to start speaking was knowing phrases that often begin a sentence. For example, we would decide to tell each other about simple things that happened when we were children. By starting with a known phrase *koc-ka sinni* 'when I was a child,' we had a fluent starting point that could be followed by many short sentences (e.g. *koc-ka sinni, makke wattinis tisnilantak.*' When I was a child, we went to Disneyland.' *koc-ka sinni, Tawras makke materatka.* 'When I was a child, we lived in Madera.')

At the Breath of Life workshop in 2014, while working on the Bugs Bunny video described above and teaching newer learners, we did not spend as much time conversing in Mutsun. However, Warner found at the end of the week when she needed to write an email in a language she had not often used recently (Japanese) that she had Mutsun lexical items interfering with her Japanese, despite being overall much more fluent in Japanese. We take lexical interference from Mutsun into another language as a sign that the processing of Mutsun is becoming more natural.

Some opportunities to use Mutsun in an unstructured way may be written rather than spoken. There has been increasing use of Mutsun on Facebook in recent years, although the quantity of language usage is still small and much of it consists of a few words or set phrases (e.g. *miSte!* 'good!' *Sokwe!* 'great!' *muysin-ka-mes* 'I love you'). Some posts are on individuals' pages, others are on pages created as Mutsun community groups. We hope to increase usage of Mutsun through Facebook in the future, as many community members use this form of social media.

We feel at this stage that we (Geary and Warner) need to make a lot more opportunities to speak Mutsun, at least to (re-)gain better fluency ourselves so that we can teach others. After doing this, we could investigate what settings where Mutsun people live might facilitate people starting to use Mutsun. In Warner et al. (2009), we discuss the scattered geographical setting of Mutsun, and the impact this has on creating opportunities for language usage. Telephone calls are one obvious method. We have found it difficult to make the initial switch into Mutsun in a conversation. It is difficult to find appropriate topics that one is able to express and actually wants to say. We should perhaps revisit some of the methods discussed above.

4 Issues in using the methods above

4.1 Language materials and use based in traditional cultural material or not

When producing written and audiovisual language learning materials, we have created some materials based in the traditional culture, such as the phrases for the Tallik game. We considered developing a version of the *Green Eggs and Ham* translation using traditional foods like salmon and acorns instead of the eggs and ham of the original. However, we have also developed many materials that do not incorporate traditional culture, including stories about children going to school, stories with bicycles or cars, and translations of English children's songs (e.g. Itsy-bitsy spider, Hokey-Pokey). We have tried to strike a balance between integrating language teaching with cultural revitalization, and allowing Mutsun people to discuss everything they want to discuss, including their lives in modern houses and cities, in Mutsun. Learning the language is not the entire goal in itself, it is a means to cultural revitalization. However, whenever groups of Mutsun people or individuals have considered whether to create new words for items that did not exist when the language was documented, they have decided that they want to be able to discuss their modern daily lives in the language (e.g. "Give me a word for microwave!").[2] This also helps to reinforce that Mutsun is a living and modern language.

---

[2] This raises the question of who decides what word to create for such concepts. Thus far, Mutsun has not had a particular body that has the responsibility for creating new words. New words have primarily been developed by Warner and Geary in consultation with anyone working with them when a word is needed. Because Mutsun morphology is rather transparent and includes a large number of nominalizers, and the archival documents include some examples of how to use these to create more specific words (Warner et al. 2007), the decisions about how to create words for new concepts are often simpler than they might be in some other languages.

The same issue also applies to creating opportunities for conversation. So far, we have mostly attempted to use Mutsun in daily life conversation, which is not typically about traditional Mutsun culture. However, as we move forward it would be possible to plan to talk in Mutsun while doing a traditional activity such as collecting materials for basket making. Lisa Carrier notes that she, Geary, and other community members organized culturally relevant fieldtrips incorporating language material: "Our field trips (the campout included) to collect shells, sedge, willow, making regalia, tule boats – we always incorporated our language into those trips. So new cultural learnings and experiences were first introduced in Mutsun and not just English causing the language to stick." Hinton et al. (2002) give many suggestions for ways to continue one's conversation in the heritage language while doing both traditional activities and activities in the broader world (e.g. going to the grocery store, fixing a car). We have not yet attempted to visit a grocery store while speaking Mutsun. The number of lexical items one would need in order to cope with a modern American supermarket is staggering.

Finally, when trying to balance traditional culture and modern daily life in language use, one might keep in mind that a culture is not only basket making or what foods one eats. A culture is also how people treat each other, how one "does" politeness in the language, and what people think is right and wrong, to name just a few examples. For example, English speakers trying to give a command in Mutsun often find it rude to use a Mutsun sentence like *harat nuppi!* 'Give me that!' or *kiTray nuk!* 'Stir this!' where the verb simply takes an imperative suffix.[3] In English, most people might say "Could you give me that?" We have sometimes discussed with each other that it is not rude in Mutsun to just use a plain imperative verb form. We have very little information in the written record about what sounded polite or rude to fluent Mutsun speakers. However, we have found no evidence of an indirect command form like "could you..." and many examples of imperative verb forms in what appear to be polite settings.

We feel that language learning and cultural revitalization are more linked than people may think. To fully embrace the heritage language, we must have humility; to value the customs and beliefs for the sake of the Mutsun people, past and present, and not for display or recognition. One must ground oneself and get back to the heart of what makes one Mutsun. This is necessary in order to have the motivation to learn the language over a long timespan. It is important to immerse our culture into the lessons and learning. They go hand in hand for real impact.

---

[3] Our use of exclamation points to draw readers' attention to the imperative verb forms may exacerbate the problem.

4.2 The outside linguist as language learner

In our case, Warner is an outside linguist, not a community member, but she has been one of the people to undertake learning to speak Mutsun. Is it part of a linguist's work to actually learn to speak the language they are working with? In a typical fieldwork setting, doing language documentation while working with a fluent speaker, a linguist might eventually learn to speak the language reasonably well, or might only learn the structures of the language but not be able to conduct a conversation. In our specific case of language revitalization work, it seemed necessary for Warner and Butler to work on learning to speak the language along with Geary and other community leaders, because this provided more people to produce Mutsun language input for others to learn from, and it allowed us to spend more of our time together in Mutsun. A professional linguist may have an advantage in language acquisition because of past experience learning other languages as an adult, and because of familiarity with a range of possible phonological, morphological, and syntactic patterns in other languages. For example, the Mutsun plural suffix is -*mak* after a consonant-final stem and -*kma* after a vowel-final one, while the object suffix is -*e* after sonorants and sibilants and -*se* otherwise. A linguist may have a head start on remembering and applying patterns like this simply because the linguist has seen patterns like this in phonology problem sets before. Obviously, if an outside linguist can gain some fluency in the language, the purpose is to help teach community members, whether by providing spoken input in the language, or by teaching in a formal classroom or workshop setting. Generally, if there are currently no spheres of usage for the language, then perhaps the most obvious first sphere of usage to create is conversations between the people working on language revitalization, which may include an outside linguist. Furthermore, trying to learn the language may increase an outside linguist's commitment to and understanding of the community. An outside linguist collaborator is someone who may have already committed to years of work, and who may be useful as an additional partner for language practice. We also feel strongly that we cannot grasp what the community needs from us if we are not doing this work along with community members, trying to speak as well.

4.3 Grammar vs. language immersion

Perhaps one should teach and learn a language by immersion, and should not worry about teaching grammar overtly. However, when there is no community of fluent speakers who can produce large quantities of natural language input, it is hard to start producing sentences without studying grammar. Furthermore, many adults are analytical language learners who enjoy learning template-like structures they can use to make a large number of sentences. As described above, we have found that many Mutsun learners enjoy explicitly learning suffixes and sentence structures. Jumping directly into the varied sentence structures of open conversation is much more difficult. However, some learners may not do well with grammar explanation. We find that we need to keep an eye out for how much grammar and analysis a given group of learners wants. The method of teaching basic sentence structures by giving novice learners index cards with nouns, verbs, and suffixes on them and teaching them how to line them up to make basic sentences offers a way to teach grammar without giving abstract explanations. One can color-code nouns and verbs, for example, and tell learners to put one of the blue cards first, one of the red cards next, etc., rather than explaining nouns and verbs, subjects and objects.

4.4 Language goals

As we have written before (Warner et al. 2007, Bowern and Warner 2015), it is important to discuss what the language goals are. Possible language goals include becoming a fluent speaker of the language. However, there are also smaller goals like being able to greet one's children in the language, being able to recite a prayer in Mutsun (whether a more traditional one or a Christian prayer), teaching one's children a few words of Mutsun to identify with their heritage, etc. The Mutsun tribal leadership, with help from Warner, recently wrote a portion of a letter to the legal office of the Pope in Mutsun in the process of protesting the canonization of Junipero Serra (founder of the California mission system). Val Lopez also began a statement in Mutsun at the United Nations Forum on Indigenous Issues. Although no one at the Vatican or the U.N. can understand Mutsun, these uses of the language have symbolic value. Hinton (2001) discusses the value of uses of the language that do not require fluency, like reading a prepared prayer.

Both in creating structured language learning materials, and in creating opportunities for open-ended language usage, community members and linguists could discuss what the community's language goals are. We have discussed our goals at some times, as when Geary declared at the beginning of a Breath of Life workshop that she wanted to be able to hold a conversation. During a visit in 2014 we discussed "what's next" explicitly. Over the course of the almost 20 years we have been working together, we have probably more often jumped in and done something rather than planning what goal it might satisfy first. However, it has always been with either tacit or overt understanding that we at least want to become semi-fluent speakers and teach others. More discussion of language goals as part of the planning process might be helpful, but it is also hard to know what one's language goals might be before seeing what is achievable.

4.5 Why do people often focus on written language teaching materials?

Where does the focus on structured teaching materials as opposed to creating opportunities for open-ended speech come from? The field of Linguistics has made a shift in recent decades, so that graduate students now learn that there is an expectation of "giving back" to the community. Often, people focus on making materials that only teach lexical items, like labeled coloring books. The next step may be a language textbook. Crippen and Robinson (2013) repeatedly refer to "language primers," and Bowern and Warner (2015) discuss this focus on simple written materials that do not create fluency. The current authors have certainly emphasized creating such materials at some times, too. This was our starting point for several years.

Linguists who are not community members may focus on creating such materials because their understanding of "giving back" to communities is that one is supposed to create language booklets or a teaching grammar, and leave copies of them behind when one leaves (Miyashita et al., this volume). They may not have thought of community language planning and choosing language goals as part of revitalization. Community members may have a perception that the place where one learns languages is in a classroom, and therefore may look for classroom-style materials as the solution to revitalization. However, we know that fluent language learning happens through hearing large amounts of natural input, as in the home, and usually does not happen easily in the classroom.

Furthermore, for community members wanting to connect with their ancestors and heritage, it can be very rewarding to learn a few words of the language. Learning lexical items can give instant gratification, whereas learning to speak semi-fluently takes a long time. Learning to type a few words is easier than learning to pronounce them, and gives some way to connect with one's heritage and show that immediately. Facebook offers an excellent medium for this type of language use, although it is not restricted to it.

5 Conclusions

We believe that both outside linguists and community members often tend to focus on structured language teaching materials, sometimes to the exclusion of planning opportunities for less structured language use. Just as an endangered language with fluent speakers has spheres of usage (Fishman 2001), if a dormant language is to be revitalized, it needs to have spheres in which it is used. If the only sphere of usage is language textbooks and other structured teaching materials, this may not fulfil anyone's goals. We argue that both community members and linguists (whether they are community members themselves or not) need to plan ways to create opportunities for more open-ended, less structured language use. This does not mean that one has to jump straight into open conversation. Open-ended language use can also have some structure to it, as in our example above of taking turns telling stories about one's childhood by beginning the sentence with *koc-ka sinni...* 'when I was a child,' so that one knows how to start the first sentence and what kinds of topics to choose. This provides a chance to use the language productively and creatively. The Master-Apprentice approach (Hinton et al. 2002) also provides many suggestions for semi-structured open-ended language use. Overall, planning for spheres of usage is part of the language revitalization process, and creating opportunities for open-ended language practice is part of language learning and teaching. In the case of Mutsun, we believe that if we can create at least one functional Mutsun speaker, immersion is possible in the near future. We know it is possible. We just need to take the time.

References

Bowern, Claire, and Natasha Warner. 2015. 'Lone Wolves' and Collaboration: A Reply to Crippen & Robinson (2013). *Language Documentation & Conservation* 9. 59–85.
Crippen, James A., and Laura C. Robinson. 2013. In defense of the lone wolf: Collaboration in language documentation. *Language Documentation & Conservation* 7. 123–135.
Fishman, Joshua. 2001. Why is it so hard to save a threatened language? (A perspective on the cases that follow.) In Joshua Fishman (ed.), *Can threatened languages be saved? Reversing language shift, revisited: A 21st century perspective*, 1–22. Buffalo, NY: Multilingual Matters
Hinton, Leane. 2001. Sleeping languages: Can they be awakened. In Ken Hale and Leane Hinton (eds.), *The green book of language revitalization in practice*, 413–417. Leiden: Brill.
Hinton, Leane, Matt Vera, and Nancy Steele. 2002. *How to keep your language alive: A commonsense approach to one-on-one language learning*. Berkeley: Heyday.
Saville-Troike, Muriel and Karen Barto. 2017. *Introducing Second Language Acquisition*, 3rd edn. Cambridge: Cambridge University Press.

Skehan, Peter. 1996. Second language acquisition research and task-based instruction. In Jane Willis and Dave Willis (eds.), *Challenge and change in language teaching,* 17–30. Oxford: Heinemann.

Warner, Natasha, Lynnika Butler and Quirina Geary. 2016. *Mutsun-English English-Mutsun Dictionary: mutsun-inkiS inkiS-mutsun riica pappel. Language Documentation & Conservation* Special Publication no. 11. Honolulu: University of Hawai'i Press. http://hdl.handle.net/10125/24679 (accessed 24 May 2017).

Warner, Natasha, Quirina Luna, and Lynnika Butler. 2007. Ethics and revitalization of dormant languages: The Mutsun language. *Language Documentation & Conservation* 1 (1). https://scholarspace.manoa.hawaii.edu/bitstream/10125/1727/6/warner.html (accessed 24 May 2017).

Warner, N., Luna, Q., Butler, L., and Van Volkinburg, H. 2009. Revitalization in a scattered language community: Problems and methods from the perspective of Mutsun language revitalization. *International Journal of the Sociology of Language* 198 (2009). 135–148.

Raina Heaton and Igor Xoyón
Collaborative research and assessment in Kaqchikel

Abstract: This chapter examines the ethics of linguistic work in a situation where there is already a substantial amount of indigenous-led infrastructure for language documentation, description, and revitalization. It deals specifically with the Mayan context in the highlands of Guatemala and the collaborative language work both authors are engaged in. It begins with an overview of the collaborative research tradition in Guatemala and the complex reactions Maya scholars and activists have had to outside researchers. We then discuss recent developments with respect to language revitalization in the Kaqchikel area, and how this has opened up new opportunities for collaboration. The second half of the chapter looks at specific projects the authors have worked on together to do linguistically-informed assessments of children's progress in a Kaqchikel immersion school, with the aim of using the results to improve language proficiency. These projects exemplify the kinds of projects that can be mutually beneficial for academic researchers and community activists, without impacting the autonomy Maya have with respect to the language programming, planning, policy, and research which they have created out of the decades-long fight for the decolonization of Mayan languages and culture.

Keywords: Kaqchikel, Mayan, collaboration, assessment, revitalization

---

* We would like to thank the editors for organizing both this volume and the 2016 LSA symposium on this topic. We would also like to thank Carmen Jany, Julie Velásquez Runk, Lyle Campbell, and Judith Maxwell for their comments on an earlier version of this chapter. We would also like to give a special thanks to William O'Grady for providing the impetus for the line of research which has brought and continues to bring us into productive collaborations. We thank the teachers at Nimaläj Kaqchikel Amaq' for their instrumental help in coordinating and conducting the assessments, and finally we thank the broader Kaqchikel revitalization community for their dedication to the preservation of their language. The research for the assessment was funded by the Bilinski foundation, and the CLIP project is funded by the University of Hawai'i at Mānoa and the Smithsonian Institution. Any remaining mistakes are our own.

Raina Heaton, (post correspondence), University of Oklahoma, 860 Van Vleet Oval, Copeland Hall, Room 235, Norman, OK 73019-3119, rainaheaton@ou.edu
Igor Xoyón, Nimaläj Kaqchikel Amaq' School, Chimaltenango Guatemala *and* Maya Kaqchikel University, Comalapa Chimaltenango, Guatemala, melodyschool.chi@gmail.com

https://doi.org/10.1515/9783110527018-013

1 Introduction

There has been a long history of outside researchers[1] conducting linguistic research on Mayan languages in Guatemala. Constant Maya efforts, often in collaboration with outside researchers, to create an equal place for their languages and culture within the establishment has culminated in the development of numerous institutions, programs, and projects which address different aspects of language and culture revitalization. These programs are run predominately by Maya and disseminate information to the larger Maya community. While interactions with outside researchers have had a large influence in the creation of these programs, Maya scholars and activists have at various points questioned the ethics and validity of scholarship on Mayan topics by outside researchers (see Warren 1998: 79–83), and have demanded a larger voice in the formal representation of their languages and culture (Fischer and Brown 1996). The existence of Maya linguists and scholars, the extensive language revitalization/management infrastructure, coupled with this question about the ethicality of external research on Mayan languages, brings us to the point where we must ask, "how do non-Maya fit into an ethical research paradigm for Mayan languages?" If the goals of many collaborations between linguists and endangered language communities culminate in the creation of native linguists and infrastructure like those already available for Mayan (c.f. Czaykowska-Higgins 2009: 25), this question will likely become more and more important as more communities around the world reach this point.

This chapter deals with the relationship of the outside researcher to the type of community which has developed its linguistic resources to the point where Native activists and scholars are in control of language planning, description and dissemination. We can only offer our own solutions to this question (see sections 3 and 4), but we expect that just as with community-based research (CBR) in general, the answer will vary depending on the context and the nature of the relationships forged (cf. Holton 2009: 172; Rice 2011: 199). However, we do believe

---

[1] As far as we are aware, there is no consensus as to who might qualify as an "outside" or "foreign" researcher. Many researchers operating in the area are from the U.S., Europe, and Asia, and are certainly considered foreign outsiders, and expectations involving publishing in Guatemala and/or in Spanish are targeted at researchers in this category. As for researchers from within Guatemala, most of the linguistic work which has been done by Maya is with respect to their own language, so it is unclear whether a Q'eqchi' Maya, for example, working on K'ichee', would also be considered "foreign". In the opinion of Xoyón, Maya from other groups and Ladinos would also be considered "foreign" since they do not necessarily share the traditions, history, territory, experience, interests, etc. of that particular group.

that community-based collaborative projects involving outside researchers can yield results that benefit all parties. This chapter uses collaborative work on Kaqchikel, one of the larger Mayan languages, as a case study, although the context applies equally to all extant Mayan language communities. We first outline the long process of the decolonization of research practices in Guatemala, and the expectations Maya have of outside researchers in terms of ethical practices. We then look at the types of roles non-Maya linguists can have in new CBR projects such that the linguist maintains an active research agenda which complies with the standards set by Maya for decolonized research.

2 The decolonization of research practices in Guatemala

The foundations and expectations of collaborative research in Maya communities were established in the 1970s, well before many now working with Mayan languages were even born. This places the burden on younger researchers, activists, and those new to the area to understand the history of collaborative research in the region and the needs of the community, and then to interact with established expectations. This section provides background on Mayan collaborative research and revitalization, and contextualizes the stated expectations for outside researchers in Guatemala with respect to the decolonization of research practices. Some of the primary themes of CBR and ethical practices with respect to speakers and communities, especially in Native American communities, include training native speakers to document their own languages (cf. Grinevald 2003), equity and reciprocity, particularly in terms of sharing linguistic materials (cf. Dwyer 2006), issues of how knowledge about communities is created and disseminated (England 1992; Battiste and Henderson 2000), and the sociopolitical aspects of language work (cf. Cameron et al. 1992; Dorian 1993). In the Maya case, these types of ideas developed very strongly within the community as part of a cultural movement to situate Maya as the stewards of their own languages and history.

There are two very influential organizations in the history of Mayan language documentation and research, Oxlajuuj Keej Maya' Ajtz'iib' (OKMA) and the Proyecto Lingüístico Francisco Marroquín (PLFM). Both began work on Mayan languages in the 1970s, OKMA under the direction of Nora England and the PLFM's program under the direction of Terrence Kaufman. These organizations were pioneers in the execution of some of the CBR ideals above, particularly with respect to the training of native speaker linguists. Both organizations combined trained over 150 Maya linguists, who then went on to create grammars and dictionaries for their languages under the supervision of these organizations (see England 2003b: 734). Although these organizations are no longer active,[2] the work conducted by OKMA and the PLFM has formed the foundation for all of the subsequent work done on Mayan languages, and provided the expertise which allowed revitalization and planning efforts to operate on the scale that they currently do.

Although less than 1% of Maya receive university educations, there are an increasing number who have received *licenciaturas* (akin to bachelor's degrees) in linguistics or related fields from the Universidad Mariano Gálvez (which in the past few years has been expanding its indigenous language programs), Universidad Rafael Landívar and the Universidad San Carlos de Guatemala. There are also a growing number of Maya who have received masters and doctorates in linguistics from foreign institutions (e.g. at the Center for Indigenous Languages of Latin America at the University of Texas at Austin; see Woodbury and England 2004). These scholars, trained by OKMA, the PLFM, or universities, constitute a core of Maya linguists who have taken over the role of the outside linguist with respect to language description, and are also active in language planning and policy. Some are also involved in local and international academic discourse on Mayan languages and linguistics.

Many Maya linguists are now also in charge of various parts of the extensive infrastructure of support for Mayan languages, created through the efforts of those involved with the Maya movement. The Maya movement emerged in the 1980's to promote cultural, political, and socio-economic equality for Maya. The movement grew out of the aftermath of "La Violencia" (The Violence, as it is popularly termed, also known as the Guatemalan civil war), which caused the death of thousands of Maya. The movement has had many positive effects, including the promotion of Mayan language education, the creation of various organizations to support linguistic research, policy, and materials production, and the development of standardized versions of many Mayan languages (England 2003b: 735). Some of the most influential bodies that came out of the Maya movement include a Mayan languages academy (Academia de Lenguas Mayas de Guatemala, ALMG), which handles policy and planning issues for all Mayan languages; Editorial Cholsamaj, one of the primary Mayan printers which publishes most of the Mayan language educational and documentary material; and (for Kaqchikel specifically, but other such organizations exist for other languages) the Comunidad Lingüística Kaqchikel/Kaqchikel Cholchi', which is the local branch of the ALMG that employs native speakers to produce pedagogical and promotional materi-

---

[2] OKMA ceased operations around 2006/2007 due to issues of funding. The PLFM still exists, although it is no longer active in indigenous language training and documentation. It primarily offers Spanish classes to visitors, as well as one-on-one classes in several Mayan languages.

als in the language. They also provide language classes on request for Kaqchikel people interested in learning their heritage language. For a detailed history of Mayan language policy, organization, and progress see Maxwell (2004).

2.1 Expectations for outside researchers

Language work in Guatemala is now at a point where there are a number of well-trained Maya linguists, especially for the majority languages like Kaqchikel, K'ichee', Q'eqchi', etc., who are complemented by a larger number of language activists tasked with implementing the policies and tools made by the linguists, with various indigenous language institutions at their disposal. The Mayan case is therefore in many ways a success, particularly in terms of what many community-based language revitalization collaborations hope for: to arrive at that point where there are trained indigenous, native speaker linguists who help run a large number of language-related programs, governmental and otherwise, which promote indigenous language education and vitality on a large scale. This also extends beyond the community, with Maya linguists engaged in academic discourses about Mayan languages. This sort of community direction of research is the pinnacle of decolonization and self-determination (cf. Grinevald 2003; Woodbury and England 2004; Rice 2006; *inter alia*).

However, the point at which Native linguists can take over the linguistic work, at least that which the community is actively interested in, is also the point at which, potentially, the community stops needing (or wanting) outside linguists (c.f. Czaykowska-Higgins 2009: 25). The question is then, how are outside linguists useful to the field and to the community, while still staying within the decolonized, collaborative framework established in the region? England (1992: 34) makes the point that this applies to theoretical linguists just as it does to documentary linguists: all outside researchers should be training Maya to the level necessary to engage in and control Mayan linguistics.

The link that the Maya movement creates between language, politics, and the fight for social justice creates a complicated environment with respect to outside researchers, which defines the nature of collaborative relationships in the area. There is a pervasive worry in Guatemala about various types of neocolonial practices (see also Czaykowska-Higgins, this volume; Smith 1999), a sentiment not uncommon amongst peoples of the Americas, for obvious reasons. Even though Spain colonized Mesoamerica, the economic and political fallout from having the US as a northern neighbor has played a part in fostering skepticism of outsiders' motives and goals. While there are many objections Maya have made to outside research, two of the most tangible are (1) that work on Mayan languages needs to be accessible to speakers, which means their circulation in Guatemala and versions in Spanish or the Mayan language of study, and (2) statements about "helping" do not automatically counteract the implicit politics or control relationship in a given project (see Warren 1998: 80–81, Appendix 2). These hark on the common themes in the literature on CBR in the Americas related to control and access, i.e. the acknowledgement that knowledge is powerful, and in true collaborations all parties have both (c.f. Leonard and Haynes 2010; Yamada 2007). Relatedly, prior experiences with research having a tangible effect on daily life in Guatemala has led to a desire for greater control in how Maya are portrayed in scholarship. For example, Fisher and Brown (1996: 4) report that Ladino elites have used research on the violence between precolonial city-states to justify the brutal suppression of the "uncivilized" Maya. For Maya, controlling the narrative means mitigating such unintended negative influences, and it is also necessary for reversing the negative stigma associated with Mayan languages and people within Guatemala.

Lastly, in the view of many Maya, linguistics is "a bridge between language structure and language politics" (England 2003a: 39), as well as the broader Maya movement. For outside linguists, this creates an additional level of responsibility, since the relationship of language to identity and politics has made discussions even of specific grammatical phenomena inherently political (Barrett 2008: 278). The politicization of linguistic phenomena, which is also tied into the sociocultural goals of a movement reacting to systemic oppression, creates an environment where anyone working on linguistic issues may get tied to the other social, cultural, and political aspects of the movement as well. This moves beyond "language activism" in the sense that linguists are actively engaged in the movement to document and preserve endangered languages, and transitions into language advocacy, where language research entails involvement in the broader context which encompasses national politics, identity, ideology, spirituality, pedagogy, orthography, and social justice (Cameron et al. 1992; Dorian 1993; Florey 2008).

This distrust of the motives of outside researchers, the need to control the Mayan narrative, the strength of indigenous-run language institutions and the conflation of language and politics within the Maya movement has led to the general sentiment that outside (non-Maya) researchers are expected to consult, not direct (or at least relinquish some amount of autonomy in the research process), to train Maya linguists, and to demonstrate solidarity with Mayan socio-political concerns (Cojtí Cuxil 1997, 1990; England 1992; Warren 1998: 81). England (1992: 29) notes that the voicing of these sentiments came as a surprise to many linguists, including herself as the director of OKMA, that "…good will and good relations with the individual collaborators in our past research, and even instruction in literacy and linguistics on the part of many of us were not enough to avoid rather severe criticism of our role in Mayan linguistics." Although the sentiments underlined above are clearly based in some of the guiding principles of collaborative research, the mandate itself is minimally collaborative, since it implies that all parties do not have an equal say in the creation, execution and dissemination of the project. Only having the ability to consult and to train can be a difficult mandate for researchers who want to study aspects of Mayan languages which are not directly applicable within the existing Mayan language infrastructure, or also those less interested in being engaged in what is often a dangerous national political struggle. Regardless, this is an important precedent for all research done in Maya communities, and sets up expectations for the ways in which any new research on Mayan languages should proceed. These are the types of issues all outside researchers must understand and negotiate for themselves when working in this region.

3 New collaborations: Building on an existing framework

In terms of work on Mayan languages, the directive from section 2.1 above is a clear answer as to how outside linguists should interact with Maya communities: be a consultant. This is certainly one avenue, and frees up linguists interested primarily in the documentation of languages before they no longer have speakers to go work on other languages which do not (yet) have community or native speaker linguists. However, there are numerous non-Maya linguists who continue to work on Mayan languages in an academic capacity. The issue at hand is how do outside researchers, particularly those looking to enter the field, engage with the existing Mayan language infrastructure in a way that is maximally ethical and compliant with the directive in 2.1. In the case of the authors, productive and ethical CBR which benefits all parties involves forging into new areas of inquiry which happen to be immediately applicable to the goals of Maya activists as well as the academic community.

The ability to build on the framework laid out by Maya in 2.1 comes from the ever-evolving context of language revitalization and politics in Guatemala. The ALMG and the various formal institutions for language work were founded in the 1990s. Two decades later, Mayan languages have received considerable attention and federal recognition, most notably in the form of the *Ley de Idiomas Nacionales* [Law of National Languages] in 2003, and a subsequent mandate in 2011 that required local languages to be offered in primary schools in Guatemala. However, activists who were excited about these monumental steps toward equality and support for Mayan languages have been disappointed by the apparent stagnation in progress on all fronts. The government support for primary school indigenous language programs did not materialize, either in the form of quality pedagogical materials or training for teachers, Maya or non-Maya, in how to teach indigenous languages. In terms of the Maya movement, changes in the long-standing institutions (bureaucratic, financial, etc.) have caused activists to be dissatisfied with the progress that has been made in Mayan language revitalization, expressing that the materials which have been produced so far are not sufficient to offer real Mayan language-medium immersion instruction, and that centralized efforts are therefore not succeeding in actual language revitalization.

Groups of activists have therefore taken it upon themselves to come together and create grassroots Mayan language educational institutions in their own communities. Many of these efforts are collaborative efforts among different Maya communities, and have led to a number of new institutions just in the last several years. For example, 2013–2014 saw the creation of two new Mayan universities, one in San Juan Comalapa, and another in Santo Domingo Xenacoj. Although they are not officially recognized in Guatemala, they offer access to higher education to Maya who cannot afford to either live at or make the long commute to universities in Guatemala City. Not only does this lead to more Maya receiving higher education, it also offers them an education which supports rather than discriminates against their worldview, and gives them the training they need to be the next generation leading the Maya movement. Mayan language education is also being addressed at the primary level by Ruk'u'x Qatinamit, a consortium of schools in Chimaltenango, Tecpán, and Patzicía which develops and shares Kaqchikel language immersion materials. There are many other such primary schools working to offer language immersion classes, although to our knowledge they operate individually. There are also other groups that use Mayan languages in bringing ancient Mayan cultural practices into present time. These include music, dance and theater groups such as Sotz'il from Sololá and B'alam Ajpu' from the Tz'utujil area, as well as Sak Chuwen, a group of Maya hieroglyphists who trained with foreign glyph specialists like David Stewart and Nikolai Grube, and who now give traveling workshops which teach the ancient hieroglyphs to other Maya. They have also created an adapted glyphic system for writing Kaqchikel, which can be seen at the stela erected at the entrance to Iximché in Tecpán for the Oxlajuj B'aqtun ceremony on December 21st, 2012.[3]

---

[3] There are also a large number of currently active language-related programs which are run by non-Maya researchers and institutions (foreign and Guatemalan), and as such will not be discussed here. These include language programs funded by foreign institutions which primarily teach foreign students Mayan languages, e.g. Oxlajuj Aj, Kab'lajuj Ey, and a new program associated with the University of Maryland in Patzún; NGOs which provide services in Mayan languages such as Wuqu' Kawoq; the glyph workshop group Sak Chuwen mentioned above which bring

This new energy and resolve to provide meaningful language support in the Kaqchikel area has created the opportunity to form new collaborations with outside researchers as well. Many of the same expectations for outside research still exist, such as making all research accessible to the community and demonstrating solidarity with the sociopolitical goals of the Maya movement. As such, both authors regularly speak to Maya and non-Maya audiences about ways to face the uphill battle for Maya linguistic and social equality. However, as newer programs, there has been a willingness to accept input from outside projects, collaborations and ideas which will help achieve their goals of creating new speakers, especially since many do not feel supported by the local establishment. The edict with respect to linguistic research, at least as we have come to understand it for ourselves, is slightly different from the one in section 2.1: researchers should use their expertise to contribute directly and indirectly to the improvement of the existing language resources and programs; their involvement encourages Maya to be proud of their language(s) and culture.

There are three important components inherent in the above statement: first is the acknowledgement that the presence of an outside researcher often inspires additional interest in the project from the immediate community. Such outside interest in the language can encourage people to revalorize their language and combat the ideas that many of them learned in school, that their languages are not real languages, do not have modern relevance, etc. This is positive, as long as it is not a primary motivating factor (see Hofling 1996 on Itzaj). Second (and third) is the allowance for both direct and indirect applications for language research. Direct contributions to programs are those which fall more traditionally under the heading of collaborative research: linguists and activists work together, pulling from their respective strengths to create a research plan, the results of which will directly and immediately benefit revitalization programs. These projects come in innumerable forms, and many such collaborations are described in this volume, including one facet of our collaboration which is discussed in section 4 below.

However, there are also opportunities to make *indirect* contributions, by which we mean projects which contribute to knowledge about different aspects of the language which will at some point be useful, but may not have immediate

---

Maya together with foreign glyph specialists for the purpose of teaching Maya about Maya hieroglyphs; media programs which are aimed at Mayan issues and cultural popularization, but are Spanish-medium and as such do not directly contribute to language revitalization, e.g. various local radio broadcasts and the ALMG television channel; and also Guatemalan programs which promote Mayan languages but at any given time may or may not be headed by Maya, such as the Ministerio de Educacíon and the Mayan language programs at Guatemalan universities such as Universidad Mariano Gálvez.

applicability. There is active interest among those working on Mayan language pedagogy in projects which will help teachers understand and teach the language better. This often intersects with goals of linguists, particularly descriptive linguists, who are seeking to understand all of the complexities of various grammatical phenomena. The generalizations which such avenues of inquiry produce are likely too complex for the primary school classroom, but are instrumental when teaching adults or when giving grammar classes to future language teachers, linguists, and activists. There is therefore general support for language research which is not completely collaborative (in that it usually involves a line of questioning designed by the linguist), but which will produce results or information that will be shared with the community for their own future applications.

Notice that there is one aspect which is conspicuously missing from the revised set of expectations which was a key component of the earlier set of expectations: control. In this model there is no conflict about which party is in control of the research agenda, with either direct or indirect projects. Maya activists have their own goals and their own agendas, and are very passionate about and capable of progressing their vision for Mayan languages. In that way, they already have control of the agenda, and beyond certain established projects, outside researchers will always be ancillary to that vision. So there is less preoccupation with who initiated a given project, as long as the results are beneficial to the revitalization effort and there is no suggestion that the community is being exploited. Projects are free to be principally designed by either party or to be developed together, and involve what Czaykowska-Higgins (2009: 25) calls a "democratization of knowledge", where no party has the privilege of knowledge to the exclusion of the other. This situation, where the community is in control of the language agenda, such that they do not feel either threatened by or reliant on an outside linguist is perhaps the best scenario with respect to groups in the more advanced stages of language revitalization. The community serves to benefit from both internal and external expertise, and scientific inquiry into the finer points of these languages remains open to all invested parties, as long as the research is conducted in an ethical manner (e.g. per Dwyer 2006 and the LSA code of ethics) and respects the wishes of the community (e.g. per Cojtí 1990; England 1991).

4 Case studies: Current projects

This section discusses case studies of CBR in the Mayan context in which the authors have been or are currently engaged. They are meant to model some possible types of projects which are implementable in a situation where the language community already has extensive, Native-run language revitalization/management infrastructure. While both of the projects discussed in this section were initially conceived by outside linguists, they were designed with the help of the participating community members and produced concrete recommendations which immediately benefit the community and the field of linguistics.

One of the main goals of Maya activists is to move beyond simply the production of materials which support Mayan languages and actually revitalize Mayan languages by creating new, competent speakers. This means that there is a renewed interest in introspection and reflection on the progress that has been made in language programs, and in metrics which would provide some indication that revitalization efforts are bearing fruit. While foreign language programs are no strangers to assessment, systematic information on the progress made by indigenous language revitalization programs by and large has not been available. However, linguistically informed assessment of acquisition in indigenous language programs could yield essential information about the strengths and weaknesses of a program, which could then be applied to the improvement of the program to benefit the learners.

While linguistic studies of acquisition in indigenous language programs are still few, this is a growing area of inquiry within linguistics (e.g. Morgan 2016; Peter, Hirata-Edds, and Montgomery-Anderson 2008). This type of research is therefore an interesting niche, since these studies center around community revitalization programs and aim to directly benefit the revitalization movement, while at the same time contributing to a new and expanding linguistic subfield. In terms of research expectations, revitalization assessment studies are fulfilling community needs and helping to achieve the goals of CBR. These are collaborative projects which draw on the strengths of both sides—the pedagogical talents and teaching resources of the language program, and the linguistic knowledge and analytical skills of the linguist. Section 4.1 gives a brief overview of an assessment project orchestrated by the authors in 2014 (see Heaton and Xoyón 2015, 2016 for a more detailed discussion of the project), and section 4.2 discusses other related ongoing projects.

4.1 Nimaläj Kaqchikel Amaq'

Nimaläj Kaqchikel Amaq' (NKA) is a pre-primary through elementary school which is part of Ruk'u'x Qatinamit Kaqchikel school consortium, and serves approximately fifty ethnically Kaqchikel children in the city of Chimaltenango. Kaqchikel is spoken in the highlands of Guatemala, and, despite having several hundred thousand speakers, it is threatened by the sociopolitical dominance of Spanish and the growth of tourism in Kaqchikel territory. Intergenerational transmission has broken down in many Kaqchikel towns, particularly among upwardly mobile families. Kaqchikel has also been standardized, although there are a large number of dialects with strong local identities, some of which are quite linguistically divergent. Unfortunately, Kaqchikel as a language has been absent in Chimaltenango for two generations, so the children at NKA are not regularly exposed to Kaqchikel in either the home or in local public domains. While the school has been in operation for the past thirteen years, the Kaqchikel language immersion curriculum has only been in place for the past three. At the time of writing, NKA teaches students ages 3–10, which is pre-primary through fourth grade. They have been steadily expanding their Kaqchikel immersion curriculum with the goal of teaching all subjects (save Spanish) in Kaqchikel. They currently teach math, reading, physical education, art, computers, and Kaqchikel language classes in Kaqchikel. Since the school day in Guatemala is short, students are exposed to approximately 10–13 hours of Kaqchikel per week, provided by four teachers who are native Kaqchikel speakers from San Juan Comalapa.

The goals of NKA are very much in line with the goals of the Maya movement as a whole, and exhibit the same blurring of the lines between language, culture, and sociopolitical aims. These goals are:
1. To have students achieve fluency in Kaqchikel by the time they graduate from high school;
2. To strengthen Maya identity through the Kaqchikel language;
3. To create the future producers of literature, movies, and other culturally significant works in Kaqchikel, as well as future Kaqchikel teachers, leaders, and representatives for the Kaqchikel nation.

The goals of the linguist, in this particular instance, bring the needs and desires of the school together with the opportunities at the intersection of revitalization and language acquisition:
1. To help NKA create a successful language revitalization program, i.e. which creates new, fluent speakers of Kaqchikel;
2. To generally be as useful as possible to the fight for the equality and preservation of Mayan language and culture, in the present and in the future;
3. To be able to publish scholarly work based on collaborative efforts which contribute to the better understanding of language acquisition and revitalization.

The third goal, while sometimes a sticking point in other communities, has not been an issue in this case. All the results and products from the collaboration are seen and edited by both parties prior to dissemination.

Although the Kaqchikel language program at NKA is still quite young (and had only been fully active for 1.5 years at the time of assessment), we decided to test the students early on in their acquisition process to see what they had already keyed in on, and also to provide a baseline for future assessments. At the time, teachers reported that students seemed to understand what was going on in class and were able to respond to commands. Because their comprehension was reported to be better than production, we tested both comprehension and production using picture elicitation and identification tasks to get a well-rounded picture of the students' Kaqchikel capabilities. The other relevant aspect of the test was that while we only looked at very simple, frequent constructions (sequences of 3–4 morphemes), we specifically targeted categories and contrasts which are present in Mayan but lacking in Spanish. Not only is the acquisition of such contrasts necessary to becoming a competent speaker of Kaqchikel, but non-Spanish linguistic features also tie in to a key concern of the Maya movement, which is transmitting "pure" Mayan, which looks as little like Spanish as possible (cf. Maxwell 1996).

Some pertinent results of the tests included that children produced completely correct verb forms 26.5–47.12% of the time (there were no significant age effects), which is quite good considering that they had only 1.5 years of partial immersion at the time. When students did not produce the correct verb form, it was usually because they produced the imperative form (which is equally morphologically complex) instead of the third person form, which suggests that imperatives are disproportionally frequent in the input. Additionally, some students appeared to be at an intermediate stage in terms of their understanding of productive morphology, where they would apply third person prefixes to a fully conjugated imperative form.

Interestingly, the results of the comprehension test showed that students did not understand as much as their teachers expected. Seventeen students (32%) correctly identified singular and plural forms above the rate of chance, and only one student correctly identified intransitive positional forms vs. stative positional forms (the non-Spanish distinction) above the rate of chance. Difficulty with the positional system was also evident from the production test, where students had particular trouble producing stative positional forms. This indicated that even though the children are comfortable producing the intransitive positional forms, they do not yet understand the difference between the intransitive and stative positional constructions (in-progress motion vs. having achieved a particular shape/position).

As a result of the assessment, the school has made efforts to increase the amount of Kaqchikel input the students are exposed to on a daily basis, and also to find ways to incorporate a wider variety of inflected forms into classroom activities. Specifically, NKA has created additional series of games and activities which target verb conjugation, asked teachers to modify their methodology to limit the amount of time spent asking questions or reading as a group (so that students do not evade real learning by copying their peers), and re-imagined their approach to vocabulary learning via pictures in the classroom. Specific findings about the strengths and weakness of individual students have pointed teachers to which topics need more attention, and challenged them to specifically use and teach linguistic features which are not found in Spanish. Also, although it is still early, the school now knows that their efforts are indeed resulting in language learning. It is entirely possible that the methodology will require tweaking, and there is always room for improvement, but this program has certainly taken its first steps toward achieving its language goals. We intend to test the progress of the program again in coming years, once the Kaqchikel curriculum is more fully developed.

This type of study is a valuable contribution to pedagogy, as it gives linguistically sound feedback to revitalization programs. It also provides a valuable contribution to linguistics, as it adds to a growing body of research on language acquisition in indigenous immersion programs. Additionally, it complies with the established expectations for outside researchers in section 3 in that the efforts of the researcher contribute directly to the improvement of the existing language resources and programs. As such, engagement in these types of mutually beneficial CBR projects continues movement towards the decolonization of research practices on Mayan languages.

4.2 The Comparative Language Input Project (CLIP)

Studies like the one above target performance; they look at what children have acquired, and what that says about what still needs to happen for them to become competent speakers. However, performance is only one side of the story. We know from the language acquisition literature that how much children are ultimately able to acquire is limited by the quality and quantity of the input (e.g. Hart and Risley 1995). Some generalizations can be made about what children are hearing by looking at production (as in the NKA case above, where results suggest that children probably hear a disproportionate number of commands with respect to third person forms), but the ability of various programs to reach their goals in creating native speakers is reliant on the linguistic input they can offer their students.

The Comparative Language Input Project (CLIP) is a collaborative project between the University of Hawai'i at Mānoa and the Smithsonian Institution (P.I. William O'Grady) which is gathering information about the nature of the input children are receiving in indigenous language immersion programs. This information will be used to help establish benchmarks against which individual programs around the world can assess their progress in providing learners with the type and quantity of input needed to support language revitalization via the creation of new fluent speakers. This is a new project, so the first results are not expected until later this year.

NKA has been participating in the project in order to gain a better understanding of the frequency with which children hear particular forms. In addition to the analytics generated by CLIP, we also plan to look at the frequency of those features which are found in Kaqchikel but not in Spanish, as well as the more complex forms involving layers of derivational morphology. The findings from CLIP will also provide NKA with a more precise idea of how much more input is necessary for the program to begin to produce fluent speakers, which is a key goal of NKA.

The CLIP project is a much larger-scale project than that described in section 4.1, and involves coordination and a negotiation of the relationship between outside researchers and communities from very different parts of the world. As such, the desire of each group to participate (or not participate) was driven by their own goals, and by how they felt about sharing information about their programs with the global community, which includes those interested in the findings for academic reasons as well as members of other endangered language programs whom the results might benefit. While this project was initiated by linguists, the project is highly collaborative in that it involves a team of indigenous and non-indigenous researchers working together to produce mutually beneficial findings. The project has also provided training for community members in the relevant technology and analyses so that programs may generate comparable data for themselves in the future.

5 The fruits of collaboration

NKA continues to work with linguists to gather the expertise and data needed to assess the progress of their students and to provide targeted, specific advice on how to make their language program maximally effective. They also continue to gain international support for their endeavors (which is particularly important since they are not supported by the Guatemalan government or local establishments), which has potential for increasing their funding. From the linguist's perspective, not only are researchers able to make meaningful contributions to the field of linguistics, they are also able to help fulfill the goals of the community through collaborative investigation. This type of project, where the linguistic research directly addresses the needs and desires of a language community, defies the oft-felt separation between more formal language research and "community service" projects, which directly benefit the community but do not necessarily inform "real" linguistics (cf. Rice 2011: 191–192). The case studies presented here demonstrate that the goals of the two need not be mutually exclusive, as a single project can simultaneously address both formal linguistics research requirements and the language goals of the community. Such projects also do not impact the autonomy Maya have with respect to the language programming, planning, policy, and research which they have created out of the decades-long fight for the decolonization of Mayan languages and culture.

The overall feeling of many Maya activists about working with outside expertise is that we must all learn from each other. Often outside linguists bring experience from other parts of the world in which language revitalization has been successful. In addition to researchers from the US, NKA has worked with members of the Basque community and learned about their sixty-year long language revitalization effort, which has been extremely successful. The successes of programs like these demonstrate that an indigenous language can be used in all aspects of life in a modern world. This is inspiring for many Maya in Guatemala who have been conditioned to think that Mayan languages are part of the past, and success in the future requires languages like Spanish and English. And, while these stories of success are heartening, information about problems and failures which outside researchers, speakers, and programs have experienced are also extremely important. Learning about past failures and what has not worked helps everyone by saving precious time and effort in the fight for the vitality of indigenous languages.

References

Barrett, Rusty. 2008. Linguistic differentiation and Mayan language revitalization in Guatemala. *Journal of Sociolinguistics*. 275–305.
Battiste, Marie and James Youngblood (Sa'ke'j) Henderson. 2000. *Protecting Indigenous knowledge and heritage*. Saskatoon, Saskatchewan, Canada: Purich.
Cameron, Deborah, Elizabeth Frazer, Penelope Harvey, M.B.H. Rampton, and Kay Richardson. 1992. *Researching language: Issues of power and method*. New York: Routledge.
Cojtí Cuxil, Demetrio. 1990. Lingüística e idiomas mayas en Guatemala [Linguistics and Mayan languages in Guatemala]. In Nora C. England and Stephen R. Elliott (eds.), *Lecturas sobre lalingüística maya*, 1–25. Antigua, Guatemala: Centro de Investigaciones Regionales de Mesoamérica (CIRMA).
Cojtí Cuxil, Demetrio. 1997. *Ri Maya' Moloj pa Iximulew: El Movimiento Maya en Guatemala* [The Maya movement in Guatemala]. Guatemala City, Guatemala: Cholsamaj.

Czaykowska-Higgins, Ewa. 2009. Research models, community engagement, and linguistic fieldwork: Reflections on working within Canadian Indigenous communities. *Language Documentation & Conservation* 3 (1). 15–50.

Dorian, Nancy. 1993. A response to Ladefoged's other view of endangered languages. *Language* 69 (3). 575–579.

Dwyer, Arienne M. 2006. Ethics and practicalities of cooperative fieldwork and analysis. In Jost Gippert, Ulrike Mosel, and Nicolaus Himmelmann (eds.), *Fundamentals of language documentation: A handbook,* 31–66. Berlin: Mouton de Gruyter.

England, Nora. 1992. Endangered Languages: Doing Mayan Linguistics in Guatemala. *Language* 68. 29–35.

England, Nora. 2003a. Maya linguists, linguistics, and the politics of identity. In *Proceedings of the Tenth Annual Symposium about Language and Society* – Austin, April 12–14, 2002. Texas Linguistics Society 45. 33–45.

England, Nora. 2003b. Mayan language revitalization and revitalization politics: Linguists and linguistic ideologies. *American Anthropologist* 105. 733–743.

Fischer, Edward and R. McKenna Brown. 1996. Introduction: Maya cultural activism in Guatemala. In Edward Fischer and R. McKenna Brown (eds.), *Mayan cultural activism in Guatemala,* 1–19. Austin, Texas: University of Texas Press.

Florey, Margaret. 2008. Language activism and the 'new linguistics': expanding opportunities for documenting endangered languages in Indonesia. In Peter K. Austin (ed.), *Language Documentation and Description* 5. 120–135.

Grinevald, Colette. 2003. Speakers and documentation of endangered languages. In Peter K. Austin (ed.), *Language Documentation and Description* 1. 52–72.

Hart, Betty and Todd R. Risley. 1995. *Meaningful differences in the everyday experiences of young American children.* Baltimore, MD: Brookes Publishing.

Heaton, Raina and Igor Xoyón. 2015. An assessment of linguistic development in a Kaqchikel immersion school. Paper presented at the Fourth International Conference on Language Documentation and Conservation in Honolulu, HI, 26 February – 1 March.

Heaton, Raina and Igor Xoyón. 2016. Assessing language acquisition in the Kaqchikel program at Nimaläj Kaqchikel Amaq'. *Language Documentation & Conservation* 10. 497–521.

Hofling, Charles Andrew. 1996. Indigenous revitalization and outsider interaction: The Itzaj Maya case. *Human Organization* 55 (1). 108–16.

Holton, Gary. 2009. Relatively ethical: A comparison of linguistic research paradigms in Alaska and Indonesia. *Language Documentation & Conservation* 3 (2). 161–175.

Leonard, Wesley and Erin Haynes. 2010. Making "collaboration" collaborative: An examination of perspectives that frame linguistic field research. *Language Documentation & Conservation* 4. 268–293.

Maxwell, Judith M. 1996. Prescriptive grammar and Kaqchikel revitalization. In Edward Fischer and R. McKenna Brown (eds.), *Mayan cultural activism in Guatemala,* 195–207. Austin, Texas: University of Texas Press.

Maxwell, Judith M. 2004. Ownership of indigenous languages: A case study from Guatemala. In Mary Riley (ed.), *Indigenous intellectual property rights: Legal obstacles and innovative solutions,* 171–220. Walnut Creek, California: AltaMira Press.

Morgan, Juliette. 2016. Acquiring Chickasaw morphology through a master-apprentice program. Paper presented at the Society for the Study of the Indigenous Languages of the Americas in Washington DC, 7–10 January.

Peter, Lizette, Tracy Hirata-Edds and Bradley Montgomery-Anderson. 2008. Verb development by children in the Cherokee language immersion program, with implications for teaching. *International Journal of Applied Linguistics* 18 (2). 166–187.

Rice, Keren. 2006. Ethical issues in linguistic fieldwork: An overview. *Journal of Academic Ethics* 4. 123–155.

Rice, Keren. 2011. Documentary linguistics and community relations. *Language Documentation and Conservation* 5. 187–207.

Smith, Linda Tuhiwai. 1999. *Decolonizing methodologies: Research and indigenous peoples.* London: Zed Books.

Warren, Katy. 1998. *Indigenous movements and their critics: Pan-Maya activism in Guatemala.* Princeton, NJ: Princeton University Press.

Woodbury, Anthony and Nora England. 2004. Training speakers of indigenous languages of Latin America at a US university. In Peter K. Austin (ed.), *Language Documentation and Description*, vol. 2, 122–139. London: SOAS.

Yamada, Racquel-María. 2007. Collaborative linguistic fieldwork: Practical application of the empowerment model. *Language Documentation & Conservation* 1 (2). 257–282.

Julie Velásquez Runk and Chenier Carpio Opua
The collaborative process in a Wounaan meu language documentation project

Abstract: In this chapter, we argue for attention to process in collaboration. We carried out research as part of the Wounaan Oral Traditions Project, a four-year collaboration jointly planned by Wounaan authorities and storytellers and U.S. anthropologists and linguists that centered on the story genre from a 60 year corpus of audio recordings. We used participant observation, audio recordings, project meeting documents, and field notes as the basis of our analysis. Our aims are five-fold. First, we frankly share our experiences to contribute to the scant literature on international language documentation research that is developed collaboratively from initial planning to evaluation. Second, we distill characteristics to which we attribute our success: trust in the collaborative process and one another, flexibility in making changes, and regular and open lines of communication. Third, we reveal the opportunities—enhanced scholarship, wider social networks, and expanded administrative skills—that resulted from our work together. Fourth, we identify the managerial, publication, and subsequent funding difficulties that endured to the Project's end. Finally, we demonstrate co-writing as a means to integrate co-theorization as part of process, furthering collaboration as both relating to the study of knowledge (epistemology) and the study of reality (ontology).

Keywords: process, community-based language research, collaboration, Wounaan meu, Wounaan, co-theorization, co-writing

---

Note: A Documenting Endangered Languages collaborative grant, #BCS 0966520 and 0966046, from the National Science Foundation and National Endowment for the Humanities provided the financial support for this research and we received a supplemental grant for the Wounaan language experts, JVR, and ELK to participate in the American Indian Languages Development Institute. Funding for the initial collaborative proposal planning workshop was from a UGA Faculty Research Grant with travel support for ELK provided from the UA's Social and Behavioral Sciences Research Institute small grants program. A UGA Willson Center for Humanities and Arts supported a teaching release for JVR.

Julie Velásquez Runk, Department of Anthropology, Baldwin Hall, University of Georgia Athens, GA 30602-1619, julievr@uga.edu; Proyecto Tradición Oral Wounaan; Smithsonian Tropical Research Institute
Chenier Carpio Opua, Edificio #3456, Oficina A10, Calle Primera, Juan Díaz, Congreso Nacional del Pueblo Wounaan and Fundacíon para el Desarrollo del Pueblo Wounaan, Ciudad de Panamá, República de Panamá, cheniercarpio@hotmail.com; Proyecto Tradición Oral Wounaan

https://doi.org/10.1515/9783110527018-014

The collaborative process in a Wounaan meu language documentation project —— **247**

1 Introduction

Collaborative research, often referred to in linguistics as community-based research (CBR), has increasing importance in social science scholarship. In anthropology, collaborative research has a long genealogy, stemming from work by Franz Boas and his associates (Rappaport 2008; Lassiter 2005b). Once only a small part of anthropology and linguistics, changes in theoretical approaches have meant significant attention to community-based collaborative research. In particular, poststructuralist thought of the twentieth century's latter half emphasized the dynamics of power in social construction. Eric Lassiter's (2005a) *The Chicago Guide to Collaborative Anthropology* offers a historical review of collaborative thought and research practice. He describes scientists' greater recognition of how power and history shape the ethnographic process, which were underscored in the critique of anthropology's relationship to colonialism and academic privilege (e.g., Deloria 1969). Consequently, scholars turned toward feminist, postmodern, activist (e.g., Hale 2007), empowerment (e.g., Rice 2006), and indigenous approaches (e.g., Denizen and Lincoln 2010; Smith 2002) that sought to transform power relations with attention to reflexivity, multiple sites, a diversity of voices, and applied and public anthropology. One result was collaborative research.

Collaborative, community-based, or participatory action research emphasize collaboration throughout the investigative process (Czaykowska-Higgins 2009; Dwyer 2010; Lassiter 2005a; Rice 2011). It thus differs from more event-based participation, consultation, or other such "pseudo-collaborative designs" (Leonard and Haynes 2010: 273). Carried out from project conceptualization to fieldwork to writing, collaborative research is both deliberate and explicit (Lassiter 2005a). It moves the locus of research control from typically western-trained scientists to the collective of researchers, community members among them (Benedicto et al. 2007; Rappaport 2008). This results in collaboration as not only a moral choice, but a choice that

---

* We dedicate this chapter to hapk'ʌʌn Toño Peña Conquista and Tonny Membora Peña, advanced and apprentice language experts, respectively, on the PTOW who passed away during the writing of this chapter. Each contributed greatly to writing and teaching Wounaan meu, and the leadership of their people. Both also were extraordinarily kind and generous individuals. We remain in mourning of their passing and miss them tremendously. We are grateful to the PTOW team for their expertise, enthusiasm, and steadfastness: Ron Binder, Doris Cheucarama Membache, Elizabeth Lapovsky Kennedy, Bryan James Gordon, Chivio Membora Peña, hapk'ʌʌn Tonny Membora Peña, hapk'ʌʌn Toño Peña Conquista, Chindío Peña Ismare, and H. Roy Teucama Barrigón. We are deeply appreciative of Liz's initial manuscript review, helpful suggestions, and foundational commitment to decolonizing research without which this project would not have been possible. We also are thankful for two anonymous reviews. The Wounaan Podpa Nʌm Pömaam (Wounaan National Congress) and the Foundation for the Development of Wounaan People backed this research under sequential administrations and we are grateful for their support and counsel.

makes for good science (e.g., Holton 2009; Rappaport 2008; Rice 2011). This is not to say that it is comfortable, and Crippen and Robinson (2013: 131) have encouraged discussion of "negative outcomes" so that scientists do not get the false impression that collaboration always is easy and fruitful (Benedicto this volume; Rice this volume). Scholars have noted that much of the literature on collaborations, particularly linguistic ones (Dobrin 2008; Crippen and Robinson 2013), have focused on the U.S. and Canada. Rappaport (2008) has urged refocusing sights outside of the North American orbit to build new intellectual genealogies and nourish collaborative anthropology.

Researchers increasingly consider collaboration as more than a method, viewing it instead as a means of co-theorizing (Breunlin and Regis 2009; Rappaport 2008; Shulist 2013; Tallbear 2014). As a result, fieldwork shifts from data collection to co-conceptualization and co-analysis to theory building (Rappaport 2008). One such example was The Neighborhood Story Project in New Orleans' Seventh Ward. Through the collaboration among high schoolers, neighbors, community organizations, and academics, researchers found that discussions, fights, and creative energy that flowed among collaborators could create productive frictions, which both challenged the work and fed back recursively into the Project (Breunlin and Regis 2009). In recent language documentation work in Oregon and Oklahoma, Leonard and Haynes (2010) likewise illustrated new understandings of speakerhood via their collaborations. Rappaport (2008: 2) has urged such reflexivity, noting that little is written about how researchers come to learn through collaboration (see also Pérez Báez this volume).

This chapter is based on our experiences with a four-year collaboration among U.S. linguists and anthropologists and Wounaan indigenous authorities and language experts to document the Wounaan meu language via an existing corpus of Wounaan oral traditions. Language work was suggested by Wounaan authorities in 2007, collaboratively planned in 2008, and funded, jointly agreed upon, and re-planned in 2010 as the Wounaan Oral Traditions Project (PTOW, from the Spanish name). Yet, three months after project initiation, Wounaan authorities suspended it. After months of conversations and negotiations, the impasse was resolved, and led to a reconfiguration and continuation of the Project, until its successful completion in 2014.

In this chapter, we argue for a community-based research approach that emphasizes process in collaboration via our account of the Wounaan Oral Traditions Project. Because of the somewhat sensitive nature of the topic, our project colleagues asked that we, as the U.S. (Julie Velásquez Runk, JVR) and Wounaan (Chenier Carpio Opua, CCO) leads, author this chapter. We use participant observation, audio recordings, project meeting documents, and field notes to examine the PTOW. Our aims are fivefold. First, we frankly share our experiences to contribute to the scant literature on international language documentation research that is developed collaboratively from initial planning to evaluation. Second, we distill characteristics to which we attribute our success: trust in the collaborative process and one another, flexibility in making changes, and regular and open lines of communication. Third, we reveal the opportunities—enhanced scholarship, wider social networks, and expanded administrative skills—that resulted from our work together. Fourth, we identify the managerial, publication, and subsequent funding difficulties that endured to the Project's end. Finally, we demonstrate co-writing as a means to integrate co-theorization as part of process, furthering collaboration as both epistemological and ontological.

2 Contexts

2.1 Wounaan

Wounaan indigenous peoples live in Panama and Colombia, with approximately 7,279 adult Wounaan in Panama (Dirección de Estadística y Censo 2012) and 9,066 in Colombia (Departamento Administrativo Nacional de Estadística República de Colombia 2005). Wounaan live in Panama's eastern region, in Panama and Darién Provinces, and Colombia's northwestern area, particularly the Chocó Department. Historically swidden agriculturalists, hunters and gatherers, as well as renowned artisans, Wounaan, like other groups in Panama, have a rising proportion living in urban areas (INEC 2012). Authorities in two traditional and legal structures represent the seventeen rural Wounaan villages and urban areas, supporting the population to the Panamanian state: the *Wounaan Podpa Nʌm Pömaam*[W] or Wounaan National Congress (CNPW), founded in 1998, and its NGO established a year later, the Foundation for the Development of Wounaan People (FUNDEPW). This structure allows the Wounaan population to have both traditional and legal support in representation to the Panamanian state, which is increasingly important as youth migrate from rural areas to urban ones.

Wounaan speak the Wounaan meu language (the language of the people), one of two language groups, in the Chocó language family (Constenla Umaña 1991). Aside from Emberá whose languages also are in the Chocó language family, the remaining five indigenous groups of Panama are Chibchan speakers.[1] Almost all Wounaan also are Spanish speakers. Panama's constitution

---

[1] Scholars and indigenous authorities typically refer to seven indigenous groups in the country: Ngäbe, Guna, Emberá, Buglé, Wounaan, Naso Tjërdi, and Bri bri. Some indigenous peoples also self-identify as Bokota (Dirección de Estadística y Censo 2012). Residents, authorities, and scholars remain unclear, however, as to whether Bokota are a distinct group or a different dialect of Buglé (see Velásquez Runk et al. 2011:15–17).

guarantees the right to indigenous language and culture (República de Panamá 1972). Despite these guarantees, indigenous languages typically are not taught in schools. With the passage of Law 88 of 2010 the government has committed to bilingual intercultural education (EIB) in majority indigenous areas (República de Panamá 2010).

2.2 Wounaan Oral Traditions Project

The language documentation project subsequently known as the Wounaan Oral Traditions Project (PTOW) was co-conceptualized. During a 2007 meeting with JVR to discuss past and future research, authorities expressed interest in language efforts, recognizing "the importance of having the ancestral essences and spirituality that each story contained". They realized that four anthropologists or linguists had audio recordings of Wounaan stories in Wounaan meu, some over 60 years-old. They suggested repatriating the recordings, archiving them for permanence, and using them as source material for linguistic study. For Wounaan people, CCO states, the recordings had much value, for documenting both the language and the stories, and to have them as inheritance for new generations of Wounaan people. The holders of the recordings (JVR, Elizabeth Lapovsky Kennedy, Ron Binder, and the estate of Jacob Loewen) were pleased to donate them for research, repatriation, and archival deposit with access under Wounaan control.

In 2008 collaborative project planning began in earnest. In that year's National Congress meeting of all Wounaan villages, the plenary approved a workshop to develop a language documentation proposal. Six months later, the CNPW, FUNDEPW, JVR, and Lapovsky Kennedy coordinated the workshop over three days. This led to the submission of the first grant proposal in fall 2008, and a resubmission in fall 2009.

In late spring 2010, the National Science Foundation's (NSF) Documenting Endangered Languages Program committed to funding the University of Georgia (UGA) and the University of Arizona (UA) for the three-year project, which received a no-cost extension for a fourth year. The Project's objectives were to prepare and deposit to archives the sixty year corpus of stories, transcribe and translate at least 30 stories, produce a distributional analysis, draft grammar and Wounaan meu-Spanish dictionary, train native speakers in language documentation and computer skills, and disseminate the results. Another collaborative planning meeting was held in July 2010 before project initiation. In September 2010 the CNPW and FUNDEPW halted the Project. After repeated meetings, the Project was reinitiated with revisions in 2011. We incorporated a new objective: to coordinate with Panama's Ministry of Education to develop curriculum in Wounaan meu as part of the National Directorate of EIB. This would insure that the materials developed by the Project were officially recognized by the government for use in state schools. Additionally, FUNDEPW was added as a subawardee to directly administer the language experts in Panama. The final project[2] centered on a team of Wounaan in Panama: an appointed authority (CCO), a half-time administrator (H. Roy Teucama Barrigón), and five full-time language experts, two advanced (Toño Peña Conquista, Chindío Peña Ismare) and three apprentice ones (Tonny Membora Peña, Doris Cheucarama Membache, Chivio Membora Peña). The remaining project team members were in the U.S.: a linguist (Binder), two anthropologists (JVR and Lapovsky Kennedy), and a joint linguistics and anthropology graduate student (Bryan James Gordon).

The Project resulted in the archival deposit of 420 recordings of Wounaan stories and songs, transcriptions and translations of 70 stories in 539 digital files, a grammatical sketch, and 5,000 word Spanish – Wounaan meu dictionary, translation of state curricula in Wounaan meu, two trainings of Wounaan teachers, Wounaan meu keyboards for Macs and PCs, Wounaan meu alphabets for display in classrooms, and three conference presentations. Stories and documents were deposited at the CNPW, the Archive of Indigenous Languages of Latin America, and the Colombian NGO Woundeko under password protection, accessible only by CNPW and Woundeko permission for non-commercial purposes. The recordings, only, are accessible to the public at the National Library of Panama and the Colombian Institute of Anthropology and History. For Wounaan, it was a source of pride to have the quantity of stories documented in their own language and Spanish, and authorities promoted the work nationally and internationally.

3 Methods

All research was carried out with institutional review board approval, permission of the CNPW and FUNDEPW, and authorization by Wounaan villagers and authorities in National Congresses. The Project was discussed publically in multiple National Congresses: the initial collaborative proposal planning meeting approved in 2008, continued negotiations to restart the Project approved by

---

[2] Unfortunately, no researchers were available in Panama to join the research team. No local researchers were working closely with Wounaan, the University of Panama's undergraduate anthropology program had been closed down, and no linguistics program existed in the country.

village authorities (*chi pörnaan*[W]) in 2011, ongoing work summarized in narrative and financial reports in 2013, and final project achievements reviewed in 2015.

We used participant observation, project meeting recordings and documents and field notes as the basis of our analysis. JVR was involved in the Project from its initial brainstorming stage and CCO was named to coordinate during the Project revisions: each was a principal investigator (PI) for the reformulated project. Initially, we did not intend to study the collaboration itself, therefore early recounting is based on our recollections, audio recordings, minutes, and (for JVR) field notes. From the impasse to close, we used many project documents including audio recordings of meetings and National Congresses, meeting minutes, annual and final personnel and project evaluations, and field notes. These are complemented by conversations with authorities, former project staff, and villagers. This manuscript was initially co-authored as a talk that we co-presented in 2013 at the Panamanian Anthropology Congress, then developed together as a manuscript that JVR wrote, revised by CCO, and edited after review by JVR in consultation with CCO.

4 Characteristics for cultivating collaboration

We found that trust in the collaborative process and each other, flexibility, and regular and open lines of communication were the three key means by which the Project overcame challenges and improved its success. We address each below.

4.1 Trust in the collaborative process and one another

From its initial planning to final evaluation our trust in the process of collaboration and one another strengthened the Project. CNPW and FUNDEPW were grounded in egalitarian traditions of discussion and consensus, in spite of their hierarchical structures. Both organizations had worked the previous seven years with JVR in something of an indigenous work party format, meeting as a group to discuss issues, share opinions, and make decisions. The other U.S. team members, especially UA PI Lapovsky Kennedy, likewise shared a commitment to research that addressed Wounaan needs for documenting their language (Kennedy 2012).

The PTOW benefited from this shared approach: it was initiated in its earliest stages as a collaboration via the proposal planning workshop. During three days, national indigenous authorities, U.S. anthropologists and linguists, and rural indigenous leaders and storytellers made suggestions about interests, needs, preferred products, office site, hiring, and other language documentation topics. Notable were village authorities' and storytellers' interests in having their children learn the stories in school; they considered story transcription fundamental to formal education about Wounaan language and culture. Other topics included ones that we had and had not considered, such as what to do with bawdy comments in the recordings (a topic of continued discussion throughout the life of the Project), which of the hundreds of stories to transcribe, which language experts to employ, what linguistics research would be most useful for teaching native speakers, the intellectual property of stories known by many, but narrated by few, whether and how multiple versions of stories by different narrators would be registered with Panama's Indigenous Intellectual Property Rights Law (Law 20 of 2000), and whether the names of storytellers could be used (traditionally one did not mention names of the deceased, but it was resolved to use names). That workshop resulted in project objectives and the decision to apply to funding from the NSF.

During times of concern, we redoubled our collaborative efforts, trusting that the process of discussing intent, opinions, ambiguities, and plans was foundational to carrying out the Project together. This was most pronounced during the Project suspension, negotiation, and reformulation. To address that, it is necessary to summarize Project initiation. In retrospect, we rushed the Project opening. The NSF notified the PIs of funding in April 2010, but at a reduced budget. JVR addressed potential budget cuts with Wounaan authorities over the phone, and she and Lapovsky Kennedy trimmed the Project and budget. The NSF granted final approval in May. Due to reduced funding, in the first year only the advanced language experts, Peña Conquista and Peña Ismare, were to work developing transcription and translation protocols. All were worried that they would seek other employment unless the Project began soon, and so we had to begin in summer 2010 despite our desire for a January launch. The next two months were a whirlwind of establishing the Project. In the U.S. this was setting up University accounts, undergoing institutional review, and ordering and transporting equipment. In Panama, CNPW, FUNDEPW, and the U.S. team organized and held a two-day project planning meeting with national and village authorities, drafted a research agreement, and carried out linguistics and IRB training for the language experts. JVR established the labor contracts through the Smithsonian Tropical Research Institute (STRI), via her Research Associate status. Based in Panama, STRI was well acquainted with national labor laws, and their payroll firm charged a 10% administrative fee for that service. The Project was underway in August when the U.S. team left for their fall semesters.

From mid-September 2010 to August 2011, the Project underwent thorough revision during which trusting each other and the process of working together were tantamount. In Panama some authorities expressed concern about the absence of Wounaan project management, which were compounded by the Smithsonian running local payroll instead of FUNDEPW. Additionally, strong comments made by a Woun[3] about the difficulty of local management were later attributed to JVR. The result was a decision by CNPW and FUNDEPW to suspend the Project, which they did by sending JVR a formal resolution in Spanish, copied to her department head and university president. A stunned JVR immediately called Lapovsky Kennedy who was equally shocked. JVR made calls to Wounaan authorities and colleagues, trying to understand what had transpired. Encouraged by Wounaan colleagues and backed by her department, she wrote a formal reply urging a discussion of concerns. However, teaching responsibilities and other commitments kept the U.S. team members in their country until January. In Panama, some Wounaan began discussing the resolution as well. There, discussion focused on the rejection of funding for a project they wanted. In addition, some Wounaan adamantly argued that JVR never would have said the comments attributed to her. Wounaan also brought up a change underfoot in Panama that related to the Project: in November, 2010 the government passed Law 88 of 2010 Recognizing the Languages and Alphabets of Indigenous Peoples of Panama and Dictating Laws of Intercultural Bilingual Education. Wounaan authorities were enthusiastic about the new law, and hopeful of its promise to development curricular materials in their language.

Over the next months, the U.S. team members and indigenous authorities cemented their commitment to the collaborative process, meeting multiple times towards changing the Project to better meet Wounaan needs. From JVR and Lapovsky Kennedy's perspectives, if the original Project was deficient, then they wanted Wounaan authorities to revise it. Two aspects were key to changing the tenor of the discussion: the funding would have to be returned to the donor if the impasse was not resolved, and the Project could be revised to incorporate Law 88 of 2010. With recognition of these two points, all began to revise the Project. This led to a third point: that FUNDEPW could manage the language experts via a subaward once staff were trained on administration compliant with labor laws. In the late January 2011 meeting of the National Congress, village authorities voted for their national representatives to continue negotiating and revise the Project. As discontent continued in Panama about potentially maintaining a Project suspension, in February 2011 a quorum of FUNDEPW convened and voted in new members of their board of directors. Continuity was maintained via the previous president, and all other board members turned over, with CCO as vice-president.

---

3 Woun is an individual.

When the U.S. team members, CNPW, and FUNDEPW's new board of directors continued meeting in May and June a few initially wanted to cancel the Project. During the negotiations, Wounaan authorities gained trust in the Project and gave a green light to advance it under a formal document. We finalized Project revisions in August.

The reformulated project put a renewed emphasis on process. During the course of revisions, team members strengthened trust in one another via trust in the dynamic of open, forthright conversation among team members and authorities. This was aided by Wounaan authorities' naming CCO to be their lead in the collaboration. It was so important for the execution of the Project that the FUNDEPW, CNPW, and the Project team take issues into consideration and have consensus; so we worked to strengthen the authorities' unity and communication so that we could together carryout Project activities. We counted on the continuing need to address and revisit issues together. Together we further institutionalized such conversations, scheduling four, rather than two, annual collaboration meetings each year.

4.2 Flexibility in making changes

Implicit in the emphasis on collaboration as process is a marked embrace of flexibility. By flexibility we refer to a willingness to alter existing project plans given changes in priorities or needs. For example, in the 2008 proposal planning workshop, the University of Arizona institutional review board (IRB) required the reading of a lengthy research consent form coupled with each individual's recorded sanction. Since Wounaan consent for the workshop was granted via a formal resolution of the 2008 National congress plenary, there was irritation with the IRB protocol. During his recorded consent the CNPW President declared "When and if we as traditional authorities of the Wounaan people make agreements with people for our people, it is a need, a plea of our need, otherwise we would not do it." Another participant disagreed with the requirement not to use participant's names "If the names of participants is not direct or doesn't appear in the work, I think that all the work will result as if it were anonymous." With these statements in hand, we approached the U.S. human subjects committees to justify the retooling of administrative protocols towards mutually respectful norms for consent and participation.

We believe that the rushed project opening in summer 2010 masked flexibility. For example, the second planning meeting upon funding was not to *tell* Wounaan about the Project, but to review and alter it as needed for the collaboration, which may not have been as apparent in our haste. Upon project suspension, we recommitted not only to collaboration as process, but also explicitly and repeatedly to flexibility.

This flexibility is evident in the five key changes we made during Project revisions. First, we integrated the Project with Law 88 of 2010. This was aided by newly strengthened relationships with the Ministry of Education's (MEDUCA) National Directorate of EIB and its Woun employee. The Project was reformulated to hire another apprentice language expert to be the linguistic liaison with EIB (T. Membora Peña). In addition to coordination, T. Membora Peña would integrate translated stories into MEDUCA curricula, and, in consultation with other language experts, translate MEDUCA materials into the Wounaan language and cultural context. Second, we sought to register the stories with Panama's indigenous intellectual property rights law (Law 20 of 2000). Funds were budgeted to pay a lawyer one day per month to pursue registration of the stories. Third, we changed Project administration in Panama so that FUNDEPW managed payroll and received its 10% administrative fee. This reflected authorities' increasingly important preference for any Wounaan project to be administered by them. Although, as discussed in the early planning, the NSF only permitted that funds be awarded to U.S. institutions, FUNDEPW could receive a subaward. Together we re-worked the budget, creating a subaward to the Wounaan foundation. As the financial management arm of the CNPW, FUNDEPW would hire a half-time administrator to run payroll, and CCO would be the subaward PI. To operationalize this change, we budgeted training for FUNDEPW in Panama's labor laws and accounting. Fourth and fifth, as noted above, FUNDEPW named CCO as the local project coordinator and we programmed four annual collaboration meetings.

Enacting these changes also required administrative flexibility to carry them out. In June 2011 the CNPW and FUNDEPW gave a good faith vote of approval of revision until the legal documents put them into effect. The latter took time for university and NSF approval, as well as the creation of UGA's subaward to FUNDEPW. Once the subaward was in place, it required flexibility in working with and re-working administrative protocols, such as streamlining reimbursements.

4.3 Regular and open lines of communication

Our third means of improving the Project was through regular and open lines of communication. Within the Project team, we worked to foster open communication about everyday and technical topics, ranging from stocking toilet paper in the bathroom to how to transcribe suprasegmentals. We were aided by our institutionalization of internet and Skype at the CNPW and FUNDEPW, and assured that all team members had email accounts. When other commitments kept U.S.

team members from Panama during the frequently difficult to schedule summer months, they participated in meetings via Skype. In spite of such technologies, much communication remained by phone. JVR made it a point to call the Project team periodically, and it was through this means that she frequently found out about administrative difficulties, particularly when CCO was traveling as part of authorities' land rights work. CCO took care to call whenever possible, and he and JVR developed a system in which she would immediately return his calls, covering the cost of the expensive international communication.

With revisions, we further formalized communication. Authorities' naming of CCO to coordinate in Panama was helpful, centralizing and facilitating communication on administrative issues and thus relieving the language experts from the same. CCO's presence in Panama was fundamental: his knowledge of everyday concerns as well as his years of experience running a business (as a Wounaan art vendor) enabled his administrative role. We established twice monthly Skype calls on linguistics issues, with much administration addressed in separate calls. In addition, the FUNDEPW subaward required clear scopes of work for PTOW staff and given the changes to the Project, the U.S. team likewise defined their roles. Creating the scopes of work clarified responsibilities and facilitated open communication and improved management. We instituted annual evaluations of the Project team, which we carried out together aided by the scopes of work.

The everyday work of the Project team and the larger meetings with the team and Wounaan authorities allowed topics to be addressed recursively. For example, we counted on new ideas not being thoroughly discussed the first time they were brought up. Instead, we often raised a topic and held subsequent discussions of the same, allowing Project team members or authorities the time in between to converse about them with each other, family, and friends. Given that Wounaan traditionally avoid conflict, this recursive approach also indicated that opinions and discussion truly were desired. For sensitive topics JVR or CCO typically met with the Project team members individually, and then might bring up their concerns anonymously to the group, using such phrases as "I heard that" or "people are saying".

Together, we furthered a dedication to a work party-like ($junta^S$-like) atmosphere in regularized meetings of the Project team and Wounaan authorities. Our decision to hold four meetings annually was supported with funding, allowing underemployed authorities' participation and fostering continued open communication with the Project team. This also permitted the authorities opportunities to get to know Lapovsky Kennedy and Gordon a bit better. The more sustained communication within the Project team and recursive approach meant improved conversations in the meetings with authorities. Through these meetings, for example, the Wounaan language experts told us they needed more dedicated work space. They were using the back half of the FUNDEPW office, and daily transcription and translation was done with the background noise of meetings in the connected front room. We worked with the local complex to improve and move into the adjacent space, creating a place for the Project in what became the CNPW's office.

We also disseminated information about the Project as widely as we could. We intentionally talked about the Project with many Wounaan, disbursing information about it, which seemed especially important in the years in which a National Congress was not held. Additionally, we presented the Project at Wounaan National Congresses in 2011, 2013, and 2015. We also presented results of the Project at the American Indian Language Development Institute (AILDI) and UGA (2012), the Panamanian Anthropology Congress (2013), the Society for the Study of Indigenous Languages of the Americas (2014), at STRI (2015), and when we were repatriating the recordings to the Colombian Institute of Anthropology and History (2016) and the Colombian Wounaan NGO Woundeko (2016).

At the end of the Project, we held a week of evaluation and proposal planning meetings. The first four days were spent with just the Project team, with an open discussion of successes and failures, and addressed what a new project might look like. For the final day we invited Wounaan authorities to join in a summary. At the end of the day, we celebrated a traditional Wounaan meal with the Project team and their families. Together with Wounaan chief Rito Ismare Peña, we awarded certificates to all Project personnel for their service.

5 Collaboration as process

As shown above, even research collaboratively designed from its earliest stages can be challenging and we found that conceptualizing collaboration as process allowed us to work through those challenges. When we initially sat down to write this article, we struggled to identify what made the collaboration work when it might have failed. We found that we had returned again and again to trust in the process and each other, flexibility, and regular and open lines of communication. Others likewise have addressed the importance of trust (e.g., Guérin and Lacrampe 2010; Yamada 2007), flexibility (e.g., Czaykowska-Higgins 2009), and communication (e.g., Meyer et al. this volume) in linguistic collaborations, and here we integrate them into the process itself and trust of it. Breunlin and Regis (2009: 141) similarly have suggested that challenges are part of the process, the "building layers of trust so that you can do the harder work" (Breunlin and Regis 2009: 141).

Like those authors, we found that the recursive, rather than simply iterative, approach to process allowed us to return, improve, adjust, move forward, and return to a different point when necessary. This recursivity is reminiscent of the narration of Wounaan stories, in which the storyline of the principal narrator may be partially repeated and then enriched, adjusted, or taken down a different path by the assembled people listening and contributing to stories.

The focus on process implicitly embraces other forms of knowing and being in the world. Dobrin (2008) has addressed this point. She noted that much of the linguistic literature on collaboration is about a system of morality that is fundamentally western, but that situating research within culturally particular systems of meaning creates new and potentially more productive modes of collaboration that bridge difference. Tallbear (2014: 1) observed that this is demanding, how she is "figuring out how to seek out and articulate overlapping respective intellectual, ethical, and institution building projects—how to share goals and desires while staying engaged in critical conversation and producing new knowledge and insights." Conceptualizing collaboration as process means simultaneously embracing it as methodological or epistemological *and* ontological. Doing so integrates the idea that for many cultures knowledge is relational, that is, a community of people engages in the development of knowledge. From this perspective, networked sociality is part of the development of linguistic information, as well as a benefit of research for both academics and communities (Czaykowska-Higgins et al. this volume; Dobrin 2008; Velásquez Runk 2014). Such relational networks of exchange, as Dobrin (2008) noted, can be more empowering when it involves others from afar. Collaboration as process recognizes not only such reciprocity (Dobrin 2008; Eschenberg et al. this volume; Miyashita et al. this volume), but also redistribution (Velásquez Runk 2014), particularly related to often persistent concerns about economic profit (Holton 2009).

Perceiving collaboration as process opened up opportunities. Foremost amongst these was that collaborative research clearly enhanced our scholarship, which is a common theme among those who collaborate (Breunlin and Regis 2009; Czaykowska-Higgins 2009; Fitzgerald this volume; Hale 2007; Holton 2009; Junker this volume; Laborde 2013; Langley this volume; Lassiter 2005a; Leonard and Haynes 2010; Rappaport 2008; Rice 2011; Stenzel 2014; Tallbear 2014). Both U.S. and Wounaan team members improved their knowledge of Wounaan socio-linguistics and language. For example, in preparing for a scientific presentation we discussed difficult to translate words. The language experts suggested we highlight ideophones, and not simply the more apparent onomatopoeia. One such example was the Wounaan meu word for the velocity of a dugout based on the way the bow cleaves the water. Similarly, in preparing another presentation, advanced language expert Peña Conquista inquired aloud about their history of battles with Guna peoples given language family affiliations and oral histories and histories of residence. This resulted in a prolonged discussion with the language experts and JVR on language families, indigenous oral traditions, and historical records of indigenous movement. Other opportunities included taking linguistics classes at AILDI, improving the voiceover tracts to Lapovsky Kennedy's three newly digitized ethnographic films (from 1964–1966), and co-presenting scientific talks.

Through the collaborative process we built social networks. This is key to linguistic research, "at the very least a social act and not simply an isolated intellectual act" (Czaykowska-Higgins 2009: 34). For Wounaan knowledge is relational, so that by strengthening relationships among the Project team and Wounaan authorities we improved our linguistics work. In addition, intimacy, commensality, and conviviality is part of constructing personhood for many South American, particularly Amazonian, indigenous groups (Overing and Passes 2000; Santos-Granero 2012). So that relationality helped break down the traditional researcher-researched binary (Tallbear 2014), which was especially important for us, the co-authors, to manage the Project. We knew each other tangentially for years, yet it was through the Project that we built very open communication and a strong professional relationship. Dobrin (2008) likewise noted the importance of relationality in Melanesian languages research. We highlight this culturally important perspective, also, beyond the research team. Our networks included staff of Panama's National Library, an indigenous intellectual property rights lawyer, Guna scholars working on their own dictionary, MEDUCA officials, Panamanian and international scholars, the publics that came to our talks, and the scholars, activists, and Wounaan authorities that we met when we repatriated the stories in Colombia. This underscores Czaykowska-Higgins' (2009: 34) observation that "as a social act, doing research is political and cultural."

For the Congress and Foundation the Project was a great help for the organizations in general terms, and especially administratively and financially. In particular, CCO states, we learned how to manage a project: how to coordinate the team, develop quarterly financial statements, standardize communication, and contract human resources. FUNDEPW's training in labor law and accounting helped it and CNPW to pursue additional institutional support activities. Frustrations with running payroll also led to a renewed emphasis to improve it. The Project was not alone in this, as coordination with recent partner NGOs allowed us to combine efforts for Wounaan institutional strengthening needs. The improved office space for the Project and CNPW was helpful for both. Additionally, IRB trainings underscored research ethics, and norms of consent, confidentiality, and anonymity in research practice. This latter emphasis on consent was timely as Panama was addressing issues of free, prior, and informed consent in state-sponsored infrastructure developments (dams and mines) and climate change mitigation strategy in indigenous lands (Velásquez Runk 2012). We agree that all projects that have to do with the Wounaan community, specifically, and indigenous groups, more generally, must coordinate, communicate, and work with indigenous authorities and organizations.

Yet, we also were challenged by this collaboration. We perhaps were most tested by time: to carry out collaborative research requires significant time (Lassiter 2005a; Rappaport 2008; Stenzel 2014). Almost every aspect of the Project required lots of time—from planning to making decisions, obtaining financial reports, compiling data and distilling its patterns, having MEDUCA approve curricular texts, and registering stories as intellectual property. Project revisions elevated the role of FUNDEPW, yet for both authors created additional administrative responsibilities that required more time to complete. JVR had to administer a subaward and budget, fashioning more work as none of the UGA grants or accounting staff knew Spanish and none of the FUNDEPW authorities or Project administrator knew English. In Panama, CCO relied on FUNDEPW authorities to access any of the Project funds, which often required more time than his two paid days of work a month. One effect, for example, was in 2012 just before the university's winter holiday closing, when we learned that the language experts had not been paid prior to their month-long vacations. That year JVR gifted each team member monies wired from her personal bank account. Additionally, health insurance issues for the language experts remained a problem throughout the life of the Project. Overall, the Project's intensive time commitment was difficult given teaching and community obligations, the four-year funding cycle, the lead PI JVR's status as an untenured professor, the FUNDEPW PI CCO's need to earn income, and various health problems among the Project team (Rice 2006 relatedly has noted that a linguist's time of life might prevent full collaborative involvement). It felt as if we were just on a roll when the Project ended.

Some of the time crunch ultimately resulted in limited publication. In the Project reformulation the graduate student's quarter-time university research assistantship was eliminated (and summer travel and expenses maintained), since he could submit dissertation research grant proposals. Those funds were used to pay for the EIB liaison linguist and half-time administrator. The linguistics analysis work was stymied as a result, since the graduate student became a campus teaching assistant to earn income. As none of the PIs were linguists, the changes to the grant with the reformulated budget resulted in less linguistic analysis and peer-reviewed publication.

The lack of linguistics publications stymied funding for subsequent research. We applied for additional funding in 2012 and 2013, and the absence of linguistics publications was the prominent reason for the rejections of our proposals. Unfortunately, then, the Project retooling to meet Wounaan needs compromised our ability to win further grant support.

Reducing the Project's linguistics contributions to peer-reviewed articles diminishes its contributions. We accomplished the permanent archiving of over four hundred recordings that spanned sixty years, transcribed and translated 70 of them, safeguarded them nationally and internationally under access restricted by Wounaan authorities in three countries, drafted an impressively detailed dictionary (but one that linguists wanted to at least double in size for publication), and provided the only significant funding to Panama's EIB for Wounaan meu curricula and teacher trainings. Yet, despite these accomplishments, the development of peer-reviewed linguistics journal publications was not completed, making the Project appear less accomplished in the eyes of donors. At the same time, our research talks to international and national audiences were more in line with Wounaan oral traditions. This brings to bear Benedicto's (this volume) point about misalignment between academia and community desired research products. That said, we still hope to make bilingual educational books of stories for Wounaan children that MEDUCA might approve.

Writing up this chapter has allowed us a welcome occasion to reflect on results and the collaborative process. Scholars have honed in on writing (using principal consultants as readers and editors, employing focus groups, editorial boards, collaborative ethnographer/consultant teams, community forums, and creating co-written texts (Lassiter 2005a: 139)) as an oft-forgotten mark of collaborative research that may further such insights (e.g., Field 2008; Lassiter 2005b). Through the last several years, our work with colleagues on co-presenting and, here, on co-writing has formalized open conversation of our results, discussion of our opinions, and a synthesis of the same with the academic literature, creating occasions for co-theorizing. Analyzing the collaboration together enabled us to share different perspectives about the Project's contributions, its challenges and opportunities, and what we learned about linguistics and working together through it, much of which we have documented here (and some of which we cannot due to space restrictions). Importantly, it allowed us to interrogate the Project suspension, and take ownership of the missteps that caused it, as well as our corrections. Additionally, it furthered our discussions of Wounaan meu linguistics and where to invest our future research efforts. This underscores the observation that only some material from collaborations may result in scholarly or popular works; that much of what transpires may not be written, but may have a lasting impact in communities (Rappaport 2008).

6 Conclusion

In this chapter we have argued for community-based participatory research that emphasizes process. Doing so allows for collaboration to be both epistemological and ontological, harnessing the relationality of knowledge. Using our experiences in the Wounaan Oral Traditions Project, which was collaboratively developed from its earliest stages, we have underscored such a processual approach. We frankly addressed our early difficulties in the Project and attribute our successful community-based participatory research to trust in the collaborative process and one another, flexibility in making changes, and regular and open lines of communication. We found that the focus on the process of collaboration allowed us to reformulate the Project given Wounaan concerns, enhance our linguistics learning, build social networks, and strengthen Wounaan organizations. The work challenged us in terms of the time required to collaborate well, the funding required to do so, and scientific production in peer-reviewed journal articles, the latter in spite of creating other linguistic research products. Co-authoring this chapter, like prior co-presenting, has facilitated co-theorizing, formalizing opportunities to reflect on research results and process, and underscoring the relationality of knowledge.

References

Benedicto, Elena, Demetrio Antolín, Modesta Dolores, M. Cristina Feliciano, Gloria Fendly, Tomasa Gómez, Baudillo Miguel, and Elizabeth Salomón. 2007. A model of participatory action research: the Mayangna linguists' team of Nicaragua. In Maya Khemlani David, Nicholas Ostler, and Caesar Dealwis (eds.), *Proceedings of the XI FEL conference on 'working together for endangered languages - research challenges and social impacts'*, 29–35. Kuala Lumpur, Malaysia: SKET, University of Malaya and Foundation for Endangered Languages.

Breunlin, Rachel and Helen A. Regis. 2009. Can there be a critical collaborative ethnography?: Creativity and activism in the Seventh Ward, New Orleans. *Collaborative anthropologies* 2 (1). 115–146.

Constenla Umaña, A. 1991. *Las lenguas del area intermedia: introducción a su estudio areal*. San Jose, Costa Rica: Editorial de la Universidad de Costa Rica.

Crippen, James A. and Laura C. Robinson. 2013. In defense of the lone wolf: Collaboration in language documentation. *Language Documentation & Conservation* 7. 123–135.

Czaykowska-Higgins, Eva. 2009. Research models, community engagement, and linguistic fieldwork: Reflections on working withing Canadian Indigenous communities. *Language Documentation & Conservation* 3 (1). 15–50.

Deloria, Vine. 1969. *Custer died for your sins: An Indian manifesto*. Oklahoma City: University of Oklahoma Press.

Denzin, Norma K. and Yvonne. S. Lincoln. 2008. Introduction: Critical methodologies and indigenous inquiry. In Norman K. Denzin, Yvonne S. Lincoln and Linda T. Smith (eds.), *Handbook of critical and indigenous methodologies*, 1–20. Los Angeles: Sage Publications.

Departamento Administrativo Nacional de Estadística República de Colombia. 2005. DANE website. http://www.dane.gov.co (accessed 20 September 2015).

Dirección de Estadística y Censo. 2012. *Censos nacionales de población y vivienda: Tomo 3*. Panamá: Contraloría General de la República.

Dobrin, Lise. 2008. From linguistic elicitation to eliciting the linguist: Lessons in community empowerment from Melanesia. *Language* 84 (2). 300–324.

Dwyer, Arienne M. 2010. Models of successful collaboration. In Lenore A. Grenoble and N. Louanna Furbee (eds.), *Language documentation: Practice and values*, 193–212. Amsterdam: John Benjamins Publishing Co.

Field, Les. 2008. *Abalone tales: Collaborative explorations of sovereignty and identity in native California*. Durham: Duke University Press.

Guérin, Valérie and Sébastian Lacrampe. 2010. Trust me, I am a linguist! Building partnerships in the field. *Language Documentation & Conservation* 4. 22–33.

Hale, Charles. 2007. In praise of "reckless minds:" Making a case for activist anthropology. In Les Field and Richard G. Fox, (eds.) *Anthropology put to work*, 103–127. New York: Berg.

Herlihy, Peter H. 1986. *A cultural geography of the Embera and Wounaan (Choco) Indians of Darien, Panama, with emphasis on recent village formation and economic diversification*. Baton Rouge: Louisiana State University dissertation.

Holton, Gary. 2009. Relatively ethical: A comparison of linguistic research paradigms in Alaska and Indonesia. *Language Documentation & Conservation* 3 (2). 161–175.

INEC. 2012. *Diagnóstico de la población indígena en Panamá con base en los censos de población y vivienda de 2010*. Panamá: Instituto Nacional de Estadística y Censo

Kennedy, Elizabeth Lapovsky. 2012. An interdisciplinary career: Crossing boundaries, ending with beginnings. *Feminist foundations* 24 (3). 119–129.

Laborde, Sarah. 2013. A research practice like Escher's drawing hands: Reflections on crossing disciplinary boundaries on Lake como, Italy. *Collaborative anthropologies* 6. 290–306.

Lassiter, L. Eric. 2005a. *The Chicago guide to collaborative ethnography*. Chicago, IL: University of Chicago Press.

Lassiter L. Eric. 2005b. Collaborative ethnography and public anthropology. *Current anthropology* 46 (1). 83–106.

Leonard, Wesley Y. and Erin Haynes. 2010. Making "collaboration" collaborative: An examination of perspectives that frame linguistic field research. *Language Documentation & Conservation* 4. 268–293.

Overing, Joanna and Alan Passes. 2000. Introduction: Conviviality and the opening up of Amazonian anthropology. In Joanna Overing and Alan Passes (eds.), *The anthropology of love and anger: The aesthetics of conviviality in native Amazonia*, 1–30. London: Routledge.

Rappaport, Joanne. 2008. Beyond participant observation: Collaborative ethnography as theoretical innovation. *Collaborative anthropologies* 1. 1–31.

República de Panamá. 2010. Ley 88 de 2010 Que reconoce las lenguas y los alfabetos de los pueblos indígenas de Panamá y dicta normas para la Educación Intercultural Bilingüe [In recognition of the languages and alphabets of indigenous peoples of Panama and dictating norms for Intercultural Bilingual Education]. *Gaceta Oficial* No. 26669-A, 26 de noviembre de 2010.

República de Panamá. 1972. Constitución política de la República de Panamá [Political constitution of the Republic of Panama]. *Gaceta Oficial* No. 17,210, 24 de octubre de 1972.
Rice, Keren. 2011. Documentary linguistics and community relations. *Language Documentation & Conservation* 5. 187–207.
Rice, Keren. 2006. Ethical issues in linguistic fieldwork: An overview. *Journal of academic ethics* 4 (1–4). 123–155.
Santos-Granero, Fernando. 2012. Beinghood and people-making in native Amazonia: A constructional approach with a perspectival coda. *HAU: Journal of ethnographic theory* 2 (1). 181–211.
Shulist, Sarah. 2013. Collaboring on language: Contrasting the theory and practice of collaboration in linguistics and anthropology. *Collaborative anthropologies* 6 (1). 1–29.
Smith, Linda. T. 2002. *Decolonizing methodologies: Research and indigenous peoples*. London: Zed Books.
Stenzel, Kristine. 2014. The pleasures and pitfalls of a 'participatory' documentation project: An experience in northwestern Amazonia. *Language Documentation & Conservation* 8. 287–306.
Tallbear, Kimberly. 2014. Standing with and speaking as faith: A feminist-indigenous approach to inquiry. *Journal of research practice* 10 (2). N17.
Velásquez Runk, Julie. 2012. Indigenous land and environmental conflicts in Panama: Neoliberal multiculturalism, changing legislation, and human rights. *Journal of Latin American geography* 11 (2). 21–47.
Velásquez Runk, Julie. 2014. Enriching indigenous knowledge scholarship via collaborative methodologies: Beyond the high tide's few hours *Ecology and society* 19 (4). 37.
Yamada, Racquel-Maria. 2007. Collaborative linguistic fieldwork: Practical application of the empowerment model. *Language Documentation and Conservation* 1 (2). 257–282.

Pius W. Akumbu
Babanki literacy classes and community-based language research

Abstract: Most of the linguistic work on Babanki, a Central Ring Grassfields Bantu language of Northwest Cameroon has been for the scientific world and not directly beneficial to the community. Such work on the language include Hyman (1979, 1980), Menang (1981, 1983), Tamanji (1987), Phubon (1999, 2002, 2007, 2014), Brye (2001), Mutaka and Phubon (2006), Akumbu (1999, 2008, 2009, 2011), and Akumbu and Chibaka (2012). Community participation in the above projects has been limited to providing information while the linguists have analyzed and published the findings. Efforts to give back research products to the community have met several obstacles including the lack of interest in reading and unavailability of electricity. This study draws from experiences in recent language documentation projects on Babanki (Akumbu 2013, 2014) and argues that in addition to using modern information and communication devices where possible, literacy classes present the best opportunities for the Babanki community to utilize research products.

Keywords: Babanki, literacy classes, community-based, research

1 Introduction

If linguistic research on endangered languages does not arouse interest in maintenance and/or revitalization, or if research outputs do not actually reach the target language community, then the research has only been completed partially. This is exactly what happens when results end up as excellent publications in bookshelves and at best, stimulate further investigations and promote knowledge in the scientific world. The goal of this paper is to contrast, as a native speaker, the theoretical work that has been done on Babanki against work that involves and gives support to the community. Advances in language documentation in recent years have emphasized the need to shift from doing work on language that is of direct benefit only to the researcher, to design projects that would allow community

---

Pius W. Akumbu, Department of Linguistics, University of Buea, P.O Box 63, Buea, Cameroon, akumbu.pius@ubuea.cm

https://doi.org/10.1515/9783110527018-015

members to also benefit (Cameron et al. 1992; Dwyer 2006; Hinton and Hale 2001; Rice 2006; Handman 2009). While recent work (Storch 2011; Lüpke 2011; Good 2012) has clearly highlighted the African perspective, I adopt Czaykowska-Higgins' (2009: 24) definition of Community-Based Language Research cited in Good (2012: 29) as follows:

> Research that is *on* a language, and that is conducted *for*, *with*, and *by* the language-speaking community within which the research takes place and which it affects. This kind of research involves a collaborative relationship, a partnership, between researchers and (members of) the community within which the research takes place.

The Babanki (ISO 693-3 [bbk]) community is made up of approximately 39,000 people (Lewis, Simons, and Fennig 2016) living in two separate villages - Big Babanki and Babanki Tungo in Northwest Cameroon. The dialects spoken in the two villages have only a few phonological and lexical differences which, however, do not hinder mutual intelligibility. Close to 90% of the inhabitants of Babanki are farmers. With the exception of craftsmen, and those who live out of the village, 9 out of 10 people make their living from cultivating the land (Akumbu and Wuchu 2015). In addition, Babanki has an oral tradition and its members lack a reading culture. The society is also highly stratified such that during ceremonies women sit separately from men and each group gets involved in different kinds of activities. In particular, women would be busy cooking and making other necessary arrangements while the men are discussing and drinking palm wine. When food is ready they are served the best share and then the women themselves would have the rest. It should also be mentioned that the Babanki are mostly Christians although Islam is gaining grounds with the coming of Saudi Arabians to the village in 2007. That notwithstanding, some people still engage in the worship of various gods.

One of the ways to give meaning to the monumental research work on Babanki which has contributed immensely to the development of outstanding linguistic theories such as Autosegmental Phonology, Lexical Phonology, and Register Tier Theory (see section 2) and has produced excellent scholars, is to ensure that the Babanki people are given the opportunity to familiarize themselves with, and if possible, utilize the research products. Work on the language should involve the community so as to support the maintenance and revitalization of the language as well as increase its documentary capacity. This entails engaging community members in decisions about what to document, what to do with the outputs, as well as giving them updates on research activities. This is pertinent because "in the end, it is the community people, not outsiders, who maintain or abandon their language: it is their choice if and how to revitalize, maintain, and fortify their language (Dwyer, Brenzinger and Yamamoto 2003). Nevertheless, the researcher could, if possible, make their skills available during the conception, planning and implementation of revitalization activities.

As a native speaker working on the language, I observed that most of the existing materials have not had any impact on Babanki maintenance or revitalization.[1] This is essentially so because the results of the work never get back to the community. I therefore began to think of how my work could become useful in preventing the endangerment and death of the language. The most available channel is the involvement of the community of users at all stages of the research activities (Himmelmann 1998; Rice 2011; Crippen and Robinson 2013). The more people get actively involved and are made to own the output of the activities the more interest they would have in developing and using their language, thereby avoiding its extinction.

Getting involved in the multimedia documentation of the language offered me the unique opportunity to move away from collecting information from a few individuals, writing papers and publishing in Journals or writing books, to getting large numbers of people involved in determining what should be recorded, where and when and what we could do with the products. The people were motivated to participate because they understood, after sensitization that documenting the language would help preserve it. In this paper, I focus on the opportunity to bring the output of the documentation activities to more Babanki people in literacy classes. However, before doing that, I illustrate that most previous work on the language never got back to the community.

---

[1] I was born and raised in an ordinary Babanki family although my father was from the royal family. Like in most homes in the village, we grew up speaking Babanki, a scenario which has changed remarkably in the last 10–20 years due to the influence of Christianity and modernism which have ushered in Cameroon Pidgin, the lingua franca of North West Cameroon. Cameroon Pidgin is common among youth and students who also speak some English and to a lesser extent French. English and French are the two official languages of Cameroon. English is the language of education and administration in Anglophone Cameroon (Northwest and Southwest Regions) while French is used in the other eight Regions of the country (Francophone Cameroon). The Babanki people who have been to school and learned English (since it is the language of instruction) may speak it with each other whereas French is occasionally used by those who have been exposed to it by living in Francophone Cameroon or learning it in school as a foreign language. Babanki is not taught in school yet and Babanki children are not allowed to use the language in the school environment. The language is not favored since it is neither a language of education, work, nor business. However, the Cameroon government has had plans since 1998 with Law no 98/004 of 14 April 1998 on the orientation of education to introduce indigenous languages and cultures in school.

2 Linguistic work on Babanki

By the late 1970s researchers began to take interest in the study of Babanki and since then many linguistic analyses of the language have been done. Unfortunately, the studies have been useful to the authors and the scientific world but of little or no impact to the Babanki community itself. This is mostly due to the fact that academic linguists are constrained by the need to either obtain academic qualifications, satisfy funding agencies, or produce original publications and advance science. For these reasons, even linguists who are community members have tended to focus on their personal academic interests than on the general interest of the community.

Some "outside" linguists have collected and analyzed data from Babanki and have either published their findings as journal articles or submitted them to academic institutions to obtain qualifications. The most outstanding ones include Hyman (1979, 1980); Tamanji (1987); Brye (2001); and Mutaka and Phubon (2006). At the same time the following linguists who are Babanki community members have equally worked on the language for similar reasons like outside linguists. For example, Menang (1981), proposed an analysis of the language spoken by *Nakang* (a masquerade in Babanki). He illustrated the differences between this restricted dialect and the ordinary day-to-day language of the people and exposed some of the connotative meanings that arise from this special usage. Menang (1983) undertook an elementary study of word classes in Babanki paying attention to the nouns alongside their concord systems. The two works by Menang were not published and the manuscripts are no longer available even to the author (Thaddeus Menang, Personal Communication).

As a requirement to obtain a Master's degree in Linguistics, Akumbu (1999) identified and described phonological processes that occur within the nouns of Babanki. Using the generative approach, he captured changes that occur within the nouns in isolation, as well as at phrasal level. That work, like most of those that follow were done because the Cameroonian university system directs these community members towards theoretical work in order to earn a degree which would possibly enable them (later on) to get the support to do development work on their language. This strategy leads the community members to work on the language for their individual benefit rather than for the benefit of the community.

Phubon (1999) contains a study of the phonological system in Babanki done for her BA Long Essay. She laid emphasis on the phonological rules that relate postulated underlying forms to the phonetic forms. To obtain a Master's degree in Linguistics, Phubon (2002) attempted an identification and explanation of the phonological and tonological processes that occur within the verb in Babanki.

One of the major findings of the work is that the verb in this language exhibits two tonal levels, high and low. The other tonal melodies, mid, rising and falling are derived through tonological processes. Using the Lexical Phonology model, Phubon (2007) identified and explained some phonological and tonological processes that occur in this language in order to obtain a Diploma of Advanced Studies in Linguistics.

Akumbu (2009) identified and described the two grammatical categories in Babanki that are used for temporal specification (tense and aspect), and demonstrated in the paper that there is a co-occurrence constraint that operates between tense and the time adverbials they occur with. Akumbu (2011), unlike Hyman (1979), proposed a synchronic account of tone in the Babanki associative construction within the framework of Register Tier Theory, making use of only a few tone rules. He concluded that the behavior of tones in the associative construction is conditioned by the presence of a nasal in the onset position of the juxtaposed noun roots.

Akumbu and Chibaka (2012) provide a description of the grammar of Babanki in a way that it will be useful to the learners and teachers of the language, as well as to others interested in this and other Grassfields Bantu languages. The book was published in Germany because of the university requirement that researchers should publish high quality work abroad and also because the authors received financial support from the Asien-Afrika-Institut, University of Hamburg.

Phubon (2014) presented a PhD dissertation on the phrasal phonology of Babanki and argued that the phonological and intonational phrases are prosodic domains for the application of phrasal rules. She showed that there are some rules which are only sensitive to syntactic constructions and used the prosodic hierarchy theory to explain how rules operate in the different domains in which they apply.

The Babanki–English lexicon (Akumbu 2008) differs from the studies above in that (1) it was not a university project and (2) it got to the community. The lexicon of over 2000 entries serves as an introduction to Babanki words and phrases. This work had been initiated in 2002 by SIL Cameroon and some Babanki people. When I started working with the Cameroon Association for Bible Translation and Literacy (CABTAL) in 2006, I was encouraged to verify the existing data base and to augment the entries. After working on it for two years, the lexicon was published with funds from the Kay Williamson Educational Foundation[2] and 1,000 copies distributed to the community.

---

2 http://www.rogerblench.info/KWEF/KWEF/KWEF%20opening%20page.htm

There is therefore a lot of work done on the language but apart from the Babanki-English lexicon which was distributed among the Babanki people in the villages and cities of Cameroon, none of the other works listed above is available to the community. In most cases, the materials have been kept in university libraries in Cameroon or abroad. Even the Grammar book published in Germany has not reached the Babanki community due to lack of information on its existence and the high cost. The thirty copies I received as author from the publisher were insufficient for myself and my colleagues. This situation mirrors what Czaykowska-Higgins (2009) has described as "language research conducted by linguists for linguists." Even in cases where some published materials have reached the community, only a few educated and highly motivated individuals have read them because the Babanki are mainly farmers and are either not literate in English or lack a reading culture. Literacy classes offer the unique opportunity to explore some of these materials and make them useful to the custodians of the language.

3 Work done by SIL Cameroon and the Cameroon Association for Bible Translation and Literacy (CABTAL)

Unlike the work done by academic linguists for the scientific world, SIL Cameroon and CABTAL have been principally interested in working with and for the community.[3] The leading principle at the two organizations is that literacy and Bible translation must be locally owned and locally driven because such an approach fosters sustainable community development. While work by missionary linguists has come under criticism (Pennycook and Makoni 2005; Rehg 2004; Grenoble and Whaley 2005; Keane 2002; Dobrin and Good 2009; Handman 2009), I simply attempt to present the situation as it has been up until now. CABTAL believes in facilitating language projects so that the speakers (users) can take individual and corporate responsibility for the transformation of their communities in order to

---

3 Formerly called the Summer Institute of Linguistics, SIL International is a non-profit, scientific educational organization of Christian volunteers that specializes in serving the lesser-known language communities of the world. They further focus on the application of linguistic research to the literacy and translation needs of the minority language communities. SIL Cameroon (www.silcam.org) came into existence in 1967 and since then has worked on more than 130 Cameroonian languages.

foster lasting success. SIL Cameroon began work in Babanki in 1998 by sending a survey team there to make a preliminary evaluation, based on both lexicostatistics and on village based speakers' perceptions of the level of inter-comprehension within Babanki and between Babanki and adjacent languages. They were also to determine the feasibility of developing literacy materials in the Babanki language and to identify the attitudes of village residents toward the idea of reading and writing Babanki or any adjacent languages. The results of the survey reported in Brye (2001) pointed to the probable success of a program to develop literature in the Babanki language.

In 2004, CABTAL took over the work initiated on Babanki by SIL Cameroon and subsequently introduced literacy classes and the Bible translation project in 2006. It was then that the first ever orthography statement/guide was proposed for the language (Hedinger and Viwun 2004). By September 2006 there were six literacy classes going on in Babanki villages and the number soon increased as several protestant churches in the area began to encourage adults to read and write in their own language. In 2006, I joined CABTAL to work as a linguist responsible for the description of aspects of the Babanki language and the development of literacy materials.

Information from their website shows that CABTAL believes strongly that development is started and cultivated through literacy.[4] When a person learns to read, their eyes are opened to a whole new world of possibilities. Opportunity to see their life in a new light suddenly becomes a reality. New doors are blown open and positive change can begin to take root. They want to facilitate change, rather than implement and be responsible for change. Only when a community catches the vision and their own dream, does their development remain long-term. Literacy skills allow access to information on health, HIV/AIDS, agriculture, commerce, further education, community events, and government programs. Mother-tongue literacy transforms a culture, leading to the development of new skills and knowledge, fresh confidence, and the ability to function as full members of society. CABTAL considers this *functional literacy* giving that there is little incentive to read if what an individual learns is not applicable to their life. Through literacy and Bible translation, the bondage of fear is loosed, people transition simply from existing to thriving, and a community starts to plan for the future and the daily lives of oral language speakers improve significantly. The above views have not gone unchallenged as it has been pointed out that "Missionary literacy work can carry with it certain biases, prioritizing reading over writing and

---

4 http://www.cabtal.org/?page_id=86

approaching texts as inherently truth-bearing" (Schieffelin 2000 cited by Dobrin and Good 2009). Similarly, Dobrin and Good (2009: 621) have observed that:

> Cultural assumptions about how the very process of speaking works may be at odds with Christian views; for example, the alignment of speech with inner belief that is so valorized by Western Judeo-Christianity (being truthful, nonsecretive, and so on) is by no means universal.

This notwithstanding, CABTAL is involved in the preparation and production of literacy materials (alphabet charts, reading books, and teaching materials), training of teachers as well as writers who can create stories and books in their own language. CABTAL could serve as a foundation or starting point for what Czaykowska-Higgins (2009) identifies as a "Community-Based Language Research model which allows for the production of knowledge on a language that is constructed for, with, and by community members, and that is therefore not primarily for or by linguists." Literacy can therefore be the first step in developing a community-based language research model regardless of who (linguists or missionaries) helps bring literacy to the community and their motives. This is particularly so because it enables the community of speakers, specifically those who are participants in the classes, to gain greater agency in the documentation process.

4 Babanki literacy program

As noted earlier, CABTAL introduced literacy classes in Babanki in 2006 and started to operate in six protestant churches in different locations in the two Babanki communities. Up until today the classes are free of charge and are held once a week. The aim is to help the participants develop self-confidence, obtain a certain degree of literacy, systematize their existing knowledge in order to promote a detailed understanding of local issues affecting them, provoke critical thinking on daily issues surrounding their lives, and to challenge cultural myths that slow down their development. The classes are aimed at everyone who would like to learn to read and write Babanki. However, a majority of the participants are those who have had some formal education and are therefore literate in English. The classes are dominated by female adults and only a few children attend irregularly. By June there were 32 classes running in the two Babanki villages. While new classes are created, the number of participants has continued to increase even in existing classes over the years. The class with the smallest number of participants in June 2016 had four students while the largest had 53. When the literacy classes started in Babanki, we prepared the orthography guide and then the Babanki-English lexicon. While Babanki is not yet taught formally in schools, there are plans to do so following the new development in Cameroon to promote the use of indigenous languages in primary and secondary schools. When this eventually happens, such literacy materials emanating from this kind of work by CABTAL will help in the teaching and learning of the language.

The facilitators are encouraged to link teaching to the daily realities of the learners.[5] The aim is to make learning to be as interactive as possible so that the participants would contribute to their own learning. The facilitator's role is to generate discussions of interest to the learners and to guide the process. The materials for learning are to be generated by the learners.

Learning to read and write is known in the Babanki community and in many other parts of Africa to be a thing that happens in a formal school setting. It is also known to be something that happens in and about a different foreign, whiteman's language, English. Getting people to learn to write and read Babanki was at first an infeasible activity. To an extent, it could be imaginable among those who had at least been to school but rather undreamt of among adults who have never gone to school. This explains why in the six initial classes, there were 49 female participants who had been to primary school in the past, only 16 male participants who had also been to school and 11 children who were attending primary school. This was the kind of feeling at the time literacy classes were introduced in Babanki but the impressions quickly changed once the people began to understand that it was possible for them to write their own language to the extent that they could write and read their names. In 2014, 24 participants out of 146 in 22 classes said that they had never set foot in class before but are now able to write and read a few expressions in Babanki. It should be mentioned that emphasis in the literacy class is on reading and writing. In class, therefore, the facilitators mostly write out lessons on the blackboard and then guide the participants to read after which they are encouraged to write.

Most of the (illiterate) men are not used to sitting with women in the same setting. Due to this cultural fact, and for the reason that the literacy classes are linked to Christianity which attracts more women than men in Babanki, it has been quite difficult to get men to participate in the classes. However, along the years some non-Christian adults have joined the classes to experience what the others tell them. There hasn't been any attempt to set up separate classes for male and female learners.

---

[5] The teachers in the classes can either be male or female. In June 2016, seven out of 12 teachers were people who had completed elementary school while five had completed secondary school. Four were employed as Primary school teachers in the village while the rest were not formally employed elsewhere. The teachers live in the village and engage in farming like most other people and then teach once a week.

5 The role of language documentation projects

When I got funding to document Babanki oral literature, my desire was to make sure that the results of my work should be of benefit to the community.[6] The first project was to document the language of Babanki ritual performances which contains poetic forms, lexical items and grammatical structures not found in everyday Babanki speech and which are threatened by the strong influence of modernism and especially Christianity which have caused the number of people who still engage in ritual performances to drop drastically. Consequently, the Babanki cultural values inherent in the ritual performances are no longer cherished and transmitted to younger generations. The second project extended to the collection of riddles, folktales, farm work songs, spells, curative chants and myths. It was also meant to prepare Babanki people to continue the collection of their folklore themselves. By the very nature of the projects, therefore, I had the obligation to involve community members at all stages of planning and execution of activities as well as utilization of the documentation outputs. The projects were therefore community-based, since they allowed the production of knowledge on Babanki for, with, and by the community members.

The first project was approved in July 2013 and by the end of November 2013, we had set up a team of four men and six women to work as consultants. Before we finally started in January 2014 each consultant was sufficiently informed of the activities and time schedules of the project. In the course of the project, we made sure every decision on which activity to record, who would be involved and who would participate in the processing of the recording was taken only after consulting a majority of the consultants.

Everything went on as planned but we noticed that the materials we were recording were not really being useful to the rest of the community members to whom we shared. From the outset, we chose to store our recordings on micro SD cards which would be used with cell phones since only a few people own television sets, CD and/or DVD players. The situation was made more difficult because only about 10% of the territory has electricity and the rest of the village depends on personal generators or bush lamps and torches. The problem therefore arose

---

6 The *Multimedia Documentation of Babanki Ritual Speech* project (January 2014 – December 2014) was supported by the Endangered Languages Documentation Programme (ELDP) and the *Multimedia Documentation of Babanki Oral Literature* (December 2014 – November 2015) received funding from the Firebird Foundation for Anthropological Research. The second project is meant to continue the work started during the first and to ensure that a permanent team is put in place for the documentation of Babanki oral literature.

from the fact that it is difficult for a person to charge the battery of their cell phone and then run it down within a short time. This is so because as of 2016 it cost 200 FCFA (approximately 40 cents) to pay for a full battery charge in a locality where most people depend on their farm produce to make a living, using money from the sale of some of their crops only rarely to purchase what they cannot produce. People would therefore accept the micro SD cards but would prefer to answer or make calls with their phones rather than run down the battery by playing a ritual performance. However, whenever we decided to gather people and show them something we had recorded, they turned out in large numbers. This forced us to begin to think of a better way of dissemination since one of our major objectives was to raise awareness and encourage the use of the language. It is at this moment that we thought of the literacy classes as a possible avenue for dissemination.

In a literacy class, there is need for teaching aids that foster the understanding and use of the language while engaging participants' emotions. Watching a performance by familiar people in a familiar context involving everyday experiences of participants inevitably enhances learning and creates value in the language. Participants quickly realize that their language is equally important and can be recorded and stored in different media that people can watch or listen to. In watching such activities and listening to the use of language they also discover the beauty and wealth of their cultural values. All the above help to motivate and encourage them to continue learning to read and write but above all to intensify speaking.

The only time participants in the CABTAL course (most of whom do not have television sets) had the opportunity to watch performances either on TV or on a projector was when we arranged for a projection in their class. They watched with excitement and expressed the desire to have more projections, suggesting that the videos were particularly interesting. This probably explains why enrolment in classes in 2015 increased drastically to 262 from 102 in 2013.

The recorded resources undoubtedly offer the best materials to use in the classrooms for promoting language and culture. In addition, this is the only setting where participants make the effort to read textbooks that are available in the language. For example, nearly all of them own a copy of the Babanki-English lexicon and report that they turn to it regularly especially when confronted with spelling difficulties in Babanki.

The participants eventually pass on the knowledge and experiences they gain in the classroom to their family members. Since most of the participants are mothers, their children have a greater exposure to the language and language resources. The younger participants equally carry the information to their parents and friends thereby motivating other community members to develop interest in the literacy classes. This probably explains why the number of classes continues to grow and the participants per class increase.

6 Conclusion

Babanki literacy classes offered us the unique opportunity to bring the results of our documentation work to the community members. This is particularly so because no matter the day-to-day contents of the classes and their syllabus, they undoubtedly provide a forum for community members to come together and consume research results created with or by them. By going through the literacy classes, we reached directly to those who took part in the classes including both facilitators and participants. In addition, we indirectly reached out to their family members as they carried their knowledge and experiences home and shared them. It was also observed that the classroom setting was the most likely place where the community members could make use of published materials in the language such as the Babanki-English Lexicon and the pedagogic grammar of Babanki. While other publications could not be useful to the participants because of their scientific nature, letting them know that so much work has been done on the language and published either in Cameroon or abroad encouraged them to know that their language is worthy and should be used and transmitted to younger generations.

This experience leads to the understanding that while researchers conduct research, publish, and archive their findings using up-to-date technology, they should figure out a way to disseminate the results, i.e., take them back to the people of the study area. It is evident that in the case of a community like Babanki which is primarily dominated by the oral tradition, giving people an opportunity to watch or listen to products of research could have a greater impact than reading would have; the challenges with reading being at least two-fold. First, the number of literate people in English is small, and secondly, the published materials rarely get back to the community. While a few people would play the SD cards in their cell phones and some would play the DVDs, a majority can best be reached through literacy classes. Since the classes are currently going on, every researcher who conducts research on any aspect of the Babanki language can pass through the classes to reach out to the community and make the results of the research available and useful to the people in the study area. This solution is most likely to work in other Cameroonian communities with ongoing mother-tongue literacy classes. This is feasible because the number of such classes has continued to increase throughout communities where CABTAL and SIL Cameroon are present.

In a whole, this paper represents an African voice talking about endangered African languages and proposing ways by which linguistic research in Cameroon can be both collaborative and community based.

References

Akumbu, Pius W. 1999. Nominal phonological processes in Babanki. University of Yaounde MA thesis.
Akumbu, Pius W. 2008. *Kejom (Babanki) – English lexicon*. Ga'a Kejom Development Committee. Bamenda: AGWECAMS.
Akumbu, Pius W. 2009. Kejom tense system. In Tanda, Vincent, Pius Tamanji and Henry Jick. (eds.), *Language, literature and social discourse in Africa: Essays in honor of Emmanuel N. Chia*, 183–200. Buea: University of Buea.
Akumbu, Pius W. 2011. Tone in Kejom (Babanki) associative construction. *Journal of West African Languages*. Volume 38 (1). 69–88.
Akumbu, Pius W. and Evelyn F. Chibaka. 2012. *A pedagogic grammar of Babanki*. Köln: Rüdiger Köppe Verlag.
Akumbu, Pius W. and Cornelius Wuchu. 2015. *Kejom (Babanki) linguistic practices in farming economies*. Kansas City: Miraclaire Academic Publications.
Brye, Edward. 2001. Sociolinguistic survey of Babanki. (824) Yaounde: SIL.
Cameron, Deborah, Elizabeth Frazer, Penelope Harvey, M. B. H. Rampton and Kay Richardson. 1992. *Researching language: Issues of power and method*. London: Routledge.
Crippen, James A. and Laura C. Robinson. 2013. In defense of the lone wolf: Collaboration in language documentation. *Language Documentation & Conservation* 7. 123–135.
Czaykowska-Higgins, Ewa. 2009. Research models, community engagement, and linguistic fieldwork: Reflections on working within Canadian Indigenous communities. *Language Documentation & Conservation* 3 (1). 15–50. http://scholarspace.manoa.hawaii.edu/bitstream/handle/10125/4423/czaykowskahiggins.pdf?sequence=1 (accessed 24 May 2017).
Dobrin, Lise M. and Jeff Good. 2009. Practical language development: Whose mission? *Language* 85 (3). 619–629.
Dwyer, Arienne M. 2006. Ethics and practicalities of cooperative fieldwork and analysis. In Jost Gippert, Nikolaus P. Himmelmann and Ulrike Mosel (eds.), *Essentials of language documentation*, 31–66. Berlin: Mouton de Gruyter.
Dwyer, Arienne M., Matthias Brenzinger and Akira Y. Yamamoto. 2003. Safeguarding of endangered languages: Report on the project of the intangible cultural heritage section of UNESCO. *The Endangered Language Fund Newsletter* 7 (1).
Good, Jeff. 2012. 'Community' collaboration in Africa: Experiences from Northwest Cameroon. *Language Documentation & Description* 11. 28–58.
Grenoble, Lenore A. and Lindsay J. Whaley. 2005. Review of language endangerment and language maintenance, and language death and language maintenance. *Language* 81. 965–974.
Handman, Courtney. 2009. Language ideology and Christianization. *Language* 85 (3). 635–639.
Hedinger, Robert and Andrew Viwun. 2004. Ga'a Kejom orthography statement. Yaounde: The National Association of Cameroonian Language Committees (NACALCO).
Himmelmann, Nikolaus. 1998. Documentary and descriptive linguistics. *Linguistics* 36. 161–95.
Hinton, Leanne and Kenneth Hale (eds.). 2001. *The green book of language revitalization in practice*. San Diego: Academic Press.
Hyman, Larry M. 1979. Tonology of the Babanki noun. *Studies in African Linguistics* 10. 159–178.

Hyman, Larry M. 1980. Babanki and the Ring Group. In *L'Expansion Bantoue*, 225–258. Paris: SELAF.
Keane, Webb. 2002. Sincerity, 'modernity,' and the Protestants. *Cultural Anthropology* 17. 65–92.
Lewis, M. Paul, Gary F. Simons and Charles D. Fennig (eds.). 2016. *Ethnologue: Languages of the world*, 19th edn. Dallas, Texas: SIL International. http://www.ethnologue.com (accessed 24 May 2017).
Lüpke, Friederike. 2011. Orthography development. In Peter K. Austin and Julia Sallabank (eds.), *The Cambridge handbook of endangered languages*, 312–336. Cambridge: Cambridge University Press.
Menang, Thaddeus. 1981. A special language for a special speaker. Ms.
Menang, Thaddeus. 1983. Word classes in Ga'a Kejom. Ms.
Mutaka, Ngessimo and Esther Phubon. 2006. Vowel raising in Babanki. *Journal of West African Languages* 33 (1). 71–88.
Pennycook, Alastair and Sinfree Makoni. 2005. The modern mission: The language effects of Christianity. *Journal of Language, Identity, and Education* 4. 137–55.
Phubon, Esther. 1999. Aspects of Babanki phonology. University of Buea BA long essay.
Phubon, Esther. 2002. Phonology of the Babanki verb. University of Buea MA thesis.
Phubon, Esther. 2007. Lexical phonology of Babanki. University of Yaounde 1 DEA thesis.
Phubon, Esther. 2014. Phrasal phonology of Babanki: An outgrowth of other components of the grammar. University of Yaounde 1 dissertation.
Rehg, Kenneth L. 2004. Linguists, literacy, and the law of unintended consequences. *Oceanic Linguistics* 43. 498–518.
Rice, Keren. 2006. Ethical issues in linguistic fieldwork: An overview. *Journal of Academic Ethics* 4. 123–155.
Rice, Keren. 2011. Documentary linguistics and community relations. *Language Documentation and Conservation* 5. 187–207. http://scholarspace.manoa.hawaii.edu/bitstream/10125/4498/1/rice.pdf (accessed 24 May 2017).
Schieffelin, Bambi B. 2000. Introducing Kaluli literacy: A chronology of influences. In Paul Kroskrity (ed.), *Regimes of language*, 293–327. Santa Fe: School of American Research Press.
Storch, Anne. 2011. *Secret manipulations: Language and context in Africa*. Oxford: Oxford University Press.
Tamanji, Pius N. 1987. Phonology of Babanki. MA thesis, University of Yaounde.

Web Resources
http://www.cabtal.org/?page_id=86. Accessed on 11 January 2015.
http://www.drussa.net/index.php?option=com_content&view=article&id=1501%3A. Accessed on 16 February 2015.
http://www.silcam.org/. Accessed on 26 January 2015.
SIL 2008 Annual Report http://www.silcam.org/documents/AR08.pdf

Philip Mutaka
Exploring new research perspectives on African cultures through language documentation

Abstract: The chapter indicates new avenues of research that would be of interest to local populations in sub-Saharan Africa and that would be enhanced by documentary linguistics. The chapter has two parts. First, the author proposes a new way of devising a dictionary that would meet the interest of the local population with respect to learning or revitalizing culture. Elements of such a dictionary are developed in the Kinande-English dictionary (N. Mutaka and Kavutirwaki 2011) as well as in its French version, where some specific lexical entries contain material that encapsulates basic elements of the Kinande culture. A similar conception of such a dictionary is found in Melis (2004) for the Masa language. Secondly, the author pleads for a type of research that would help Africans understand who they really are as the so-called revealed religions (Islam and Christianity) have tended to convince them of the non-existence of the spiritual world. Yet, there are so many manifestations of the interaction of the spiritual world with the world of the human beings, often with mind-boggling events, for example, human beings changing into animals, communication with animals and trees, and travelling supernaturally. This is an area avoided by Western science (although the notion of haunted houses with similar manifestations is not strange to the Western world). Illustrations of such manifestations are given in the chapter in a bid to invite the scientific community to also probe this area. In the chapter, the author presents what is feasible within documentary linguistics, with the hope that other researchers will step in to investigate these manifestations and provide an explanation that helps understand the human being from an African perspective. Such ethnographic material could be reported in dictionaries either as extensive comments for some lexical entries as in Melis (2004) or as separate articles as in N. Mutaka and Kavutirwaki (2011). A potential consequence of the exploitation of such ethnographic material is that this will help societies understand religious ideologies in the modern world.

Keywords: strange phenomena, African culture, supernatural, lexical entries, testimony, spiritual world

---

Philip Mutaka, Department of African Languages and Linguistics, University of Yaounde 1, P.O. Box 755 Yaounde, Cameroon, pmutaka@gmail.com

https://doi.org/10.1515/9783110527018-016

1 Introduction

Apart from suggesting ideas based on the Kinande dictionary (Kavutiraki and N. Mutaka 2012; N. Mutaka and Kavutirwaki 2011) and the Masa dictionary by Melis (2004) for innovative ways likely to be of interest to the local communities and to revive their respective cultures, the second part of the chapter will consist mostly of strange phenomena that I have been made aware of here in Cameroon and that I know are symptomatic of sub-Saharan Africa. Most of those phenomena are so baffling, and yet, one has the impression that they are either ignored by modern science or then that they are occulted because they are believed to be related to the supernatural world. Yet, these phenomena are part of our world. They create anxiety in some of us and they often influence our day to day behavior. Some of them often impact us. We need to assuage our fears and wish that some cogent explanation of their manifestation be given. In this chapter, I will first give a body of data consisting mainly of stories I have gathered from my sociolinguistics students from the University of Yaounde 1, here in Cameroon. This is an important part of the chapter in that it makes the reader aware of the existence of such strange phenomena. I will then propose ways that such phenomena could be documented with the help of documentary linguistics so as to provide a stronger foundation for various researchers, not necessarily linguists, to attempt an explanation. My ultimate belief is that, if we are able to decrypt the networks that the initiates who often belong to secret societies have with the spiritual world, one possible consequence is that we may succeed to better understand religious ideologies in the modern world.

2 Revitalizing cultures through cultural dictionaries

Although it is commonly accepted that a dictionary and a grammar book are basic documents that contribute to the learning of a language and that they are therefore useful literacy tools for foreign language learners, from the point of view of native speakers of African languages, particularly peasants who are mostly illiterate and who form the majority of people in need of literacy materials, it is not clear that dictionaries and grammar books as we know them today are ever useful to them. If we take seriously the idea that literacy can enhance development (whether cultural, economic, or social), it is imperative that researchers render their dictionaries more attractive to these communities by addressing their real needs of learning, and hopefully, of reviving their languages and cultures. To meet such challenges, I wish to draw the readers' attention to ideas that are implemented in

Melis's dictionary of Masa (Melis 2004), and also N. Mutaka and Kavutirwaki (2011) and Kavutirwaki and P. Mutaka (2012) and that, if fully exploited in the elaboration of cultural dictionaries, could really prove useful in reviving our African cultures.

Because dictionaries basically consist of a list of lexical entries organized in an alphabetical order, it may prove useful to expand on the contents of certain lexical entries to introduce cultural material specific to an ethnic community. The best inspiration comes from Melis's dictionary. For a lexical item in the dictionary main entries, Melis foresees a frame of five subtopics in which he inserts his cultural comments whenever possible. These are: food, medicine, daily life activities, religion, and oral literature. Thus, to give an idea of what he writes under religion in his comments on the **cóʔón-dá** *Balanites aegyptica "savonnier"*, a tree species, the following is an excerpt from that section of his comments:

> [...] En cas de manque de pluie, on sacrifie une brebis au pied de cet arbre. Le savonnier est utilisé par le lignage Baha pour faire l'ordalie. [He then describes the ordeal (ordalie) and he will then include the prayers that are done during that ordeal as follows:] Quand commence la deuxième partie, séquestration dans les huttes (gúɗuk-ŋà) après l'imposition du nom, le chef de l'initiation fait une offrande d'œuf à Matna et Bagawna avec l'invocation suivante: Celui qui cherche les jeunes initiés et voudrait les perdre, Matna ! Bagawna ! J'ai pris l'œuf, et vais jeter l'œuf pour toi Bagawna, et que cet homme tombe devant moi. A la sortie de l'initiation, il y a une libation de bière avec offrande d'œufs: La‚ata ! L'homme qui viendrait chercher les jeunes initiés pour les perdre, [et montrer ainsi que] mon initiation n'est pas bien faite, ils [les enfants] sont perdus au cours de l'initiation d'un tel, cet homme, La‚ata, veuille le perdre [=le tuer] ! Que la prochaine saison des pluies ne le trouve pas [en vie]. Autrefois, quand on faisait encore les grandes chasses collectives, un grand sacrifice à Bagawna était nécessaire, pour étourdir (túwúr) le génie et permettre aux hommes de chasser.
> (Melis 2004: 300–301)

> [...] In case of a lack of rain, a sheep is sacrificed at the foot of that tree. The savonnier is used by the Baha lineage to perform the ordeal (ordalie).

> When the second part starts, sequestration in the huts (gúɗuk-ŋà) after the imposition of the name, the head of the initiation makes an egg offering to Matna and Bagwana with the following invocation: The one who is looking for the young initiates and who wants to lose them, Matna! Bagawna! I have taken the egg, and I will throw the egg for you Bagawna, and may that man collapse in front of me. At the exit of the initiation, there is a libation of beer with an offering of eggs. The man who would come to look for the young initiates to lose them, [and show thus that] my initiation has not been done well, they [the children] are lost during the initiation of such a person, that man, La,ata, may you lose him [= kill him]! May the next rainy season not find him [alive]. In the past, when they used to do large scale collective hunting sessions, a big sacrifice to Bagawna was necessary, in order to confuse (túwúr) the genie and allow men to hunt.
> (Melis 2004: 300–301)

Notice the richness of the cultural comments the author makes in the lexical entry of "savonnier." He is able to document the practice of the "ordalie," give samples of traditional prayers used during the "ordalie," give information on what happened to the people when they used to do collective hunting and how they would deal with the god of hunting to let him allow the hunters to hunt in the forest.

Whenever possible, Melis (2004) also presents pictures that reflect the culture of the Masa, for example to illustrate their villages, their clothing, fishing nets, baskets, and musical instruments with relevant comments to allow the reader to understand how they are used by the Masa.

The same idea is also exploited in Kavutirwaki and N. Mutaka (2012) in that they wanted the dictionary to also serve as a tool for Nande speakers to learn more about their culture. In addition, this dictionary contains other articles that the authors believed to be more culturally significant for the native speakers. These articles include: phrasal expressions, personal names, a section on medicinal plants that includes the terminology of medicinal herbs known by the Nande, the terminology of diseases in Kinande and the treatment of certain diseases with medicinal plants, elements of Kinande culture through a sample of pictures (which can be viewed on the Afranaph website[1]), additional notes on the Nande/Konzo from a Konzo perspective, and a chapter on the Bakonzo traditional beliefs in medical and curative values derived from herbs by Stanley Baluku.

In the second part of this chapter, I report on strange phenomena related to the spiritual world that community-based dictionary compilers could be reporting either as part of lexical entries as in Melis (2004) or as separate articles in the dictionary as in N. Mutaka and Kavutirwaki (2011).

3 Exploring strange phenomena

I wish to be precise from the outset that most of these strange phenomena are somehow related to witchcraft. But, what is witchcraft? As noted in Njolle, Medzogo, and P. Mutaka (2011), the concept of witchcraft is normally treated as a cultural ideology, a means of explaining human misfortune by blaming it either on a supernatural entity or a known person in the community (see also Bloomhill 1962; Parrinder 1958; Middleton and Winter 1963; Debrunner 1959; Mbiti 1985; Evans-Prichard 1963). Since these are phenomena that take place in our world that is submitted to the same physical laws, why do we always have to consider

---

[1] Cf. http://www.africanabaphora.rutgers.edu/Kinande-dictionary. See also the French version of the dictionary at www.africanmuseum.be/museum/research/publications/rmca/online/online-kinande.pdf

them as strange? Is it not because we do not understand them and that there is a need for the scientific world to try to understand their underpinnings in order for them to no longer appear strange to the informed mind? As will be observed through their descriptions, their manifestation often results from the use of, or rather the combination of, certain natural elements. The rest of this chapter contains (a) excerpts that better explain them and (b) suggestions on how to obtain additional data from documentary linguistics that might help explore them better. My ultimate hope is that with such enriched data, other researchers will step in and endeavor to explain them.

3.1 The concept of the Mwankum among the Mbo and the Bakossi

I wish to first of all make an observation of what I have found baffling here in Cameroon about certain beings. This is the country where I learned about the word "juju." I have been made to understand that it is usually a human being wearing a mask that makes him look like a masquerade and who becomes endowed with supernatural powers. I have heard of another type of "juju." It has never been clear whether it is a human being or a spiritual being who is able to intervene in the life of people. What is extremely curious is that this being is usually identified with a specific ethnic group. Such is the case of the Mwankum who is a supernatural being dealing specifically with the Bakossi and the Mbo ethnic communities. The following excerpts taken from Nkunde Ewanoge (2016), a Bakossi speaker, better describe him:

> To the Bakossi people, Mwankum represents justice in the traditional society especially in the resolution of mysterious matters like witchcraft. His mystical nature permits him to transcend human perception. He is the highest executive in the land. He punishes the dissident and recalcitrant members of the community. This juju appears only when there is a very serious issue at hand that was beyond the members of the community to handle. His presence is besought in difficult situations such as the mysterious disappearance of children or someone who went to a farm by day and never returned. Here he acts like a searchlight that gets to the root of what happened and tries to bring them back home if they are still alive. If they are dead, he's the one who carries out such burials, since corpses of such mysterious circumstances are not brought to the community. They are buried there in the forest where they died.' [....] Sɛ́ Mwǎnkumɛ́ (i.e., Mwankum) is a peaceful juju who is on the side of the oppressed and stands for peace. He doesn't shed blood no matter the gravity of the offence committed, he restores peace by ostracizing the culprits or pronouncing fines on them. Like we mentioned above, he mostly appears when invoked or when he sees the need to come to the aid of a people in bondage or in distress. He then disappears without notifying anybody. He is the custodian of peace and tranquility in the Bakossi communities that accept him. He is the traditional arm of justice.

The following, also from Ewanoge Nkunde (2016), is an example of what he is able to do.

> More so, in a village near Manjo, there was a malicious old woman who caused the nine-year old son of her neighbor to disappear. When they started looking for this child, no one suspected the old woman, nor did they imagine that his disappearance was mysterious. It was not till dark that the elders decided that the "juju" should be invoked because the situation had gone beyond human comprehension. As soon as he appeared, his shout was heard at the end of that village by a stream. He brought out the boy from the middle of that stream on a stone where the old woman had mysteriously transferred him, waiting for things to die down before sacrificing him. She was at once disproved and banished from the village and the boy restored to the parents.

3.2 The Mbombog at the Basaa's

While the Bakossi and the Mbo have Mwankum, the Basaa derive their protection from a group of initiated elders who wield supernatural powers (see also Bassong 2011). The following excerpt from Kigwe Ricarda (2016) better explains the concept of Mbombog. (Her original text is in French. The translation is mine.)

> "Mbombog" is a panther human being and he is a legislator for acquiring the fundamental knowledge related to the animal, plant, and mineral kingdom and to the laws that govern the two faces of the universe, that is, the visible and the invisible, to the mastering and handling of language, to the signs and symbols and the exclusive possession of the ancestral relics and thus its sublimation that entails the sublimation of the candidate.
>
> [...] For the Basa'a, the NGAMBI has various formulas. The most important one is called Ngambi-Si;[2] it associates a natural living element through which the reincarnated ancestor through a trap-door spider makes communication with the human beings.
>
> The Mbombog is the guardian of history, science, arts, and tradition. For that purpose, he must know the cosmogony myths, the historical, genealogical, and geographical origin of his people, the main events of the past that crucially influence the present and the future. He must also know the main elements nature derives from, their properties, and the laws that preside on their composition. He must be clearly informed on all the specialized practices that take place in his sphere of regulation. He is the guardian of rites and noble traditions inherited from the ancestors and he is the guarantor of their perpetuation according to the established forms. He schedules (rhythms) the social time that is sacred or secular

---

2 Following an explanation in Bassong (2011:202), Ngambi is a secret society that serves as the means of communication between the visible and the invisible world. It has access to the most secret truths, in the present time or in the future, thanks to its ability to communicate with the ancestors through signs and dreams.

of the cultural and civil celebrations. He must master the art of making the ointments, the powders, the perfumes, the luster solutions [...] destined to combat evil within its various forms: physiological, psychological, sociological or metaphysical and those likely to attract the favors of the divinities onto his people.

[...] Language in the visible world derives its power from the *Ndombol*, the power of words of the ancestors; thus, all that had been consigned in the form of blessing, law, taboo, social prohibitions called *mben basogol* by the *basogol*, « ancestors » remains efficient today and for eternity despite the fact that they are invisible in our eyes of the layman; the belief wants them to be present in everything that exists: the wind that blows, the water that flows, the stone that is inert, the leaves that are under our feet, [...] because the dead are not dead, they have simply changed on the vibratory plan, they have transmuted, reincarnated [...]

3.3 The totem phenomenon

The totem phenomenon is a situation in which a human being has an animal as his double (i.e., his proxy). At times, he may change into an animal. To better explain this, let me convey it to you in the words of Mouebong Mbebi Geraldine (personal communication).

The « totem » phenomenon is the power that certain individuals have to change themselves into an animal, most particularly a dog, a bird, a tortoise, a lion, a panther, a gorilla, a boa, and an ant. Once someone is aware that he has a totem, he acquires the characteristics of that animal. If it is a lion, he becomes ferocious, speedy, choleric, and he acquires a certain agility; even his voice undergoes modifications. Some people change themselves often at night to disturb their neighbors. This is often the case for people who have mice as their totem as a way to come and steal food, money, and even jewelry; others go at night to steal in the farms or to eat the game (animals) that have been caught in the traps. To give a concrete example, I have a neighbor in the village who, at nine years old, was initiated by her grandmother and her totem was a bird. Her job consisted of following women to their fields and after they have sown, the little girl who had changed into a bird used to come and dig out the seeds and eat them, so that, at the harvest time, only their fields would yield good harvest.

3.4 Phenomena related to witchcraft

In many sub-Saharan African societies, sorcerers are known to do extraordinary deeds such as removing a corpse from its tomb without digging the grave. Recently, a colleague university professor told me that, in her Basaa culture, after the burial of a corpse, the grave has to be guarded for 9 days as it is estimated that, after 9 days, the corpse will be completely spoilt and could no longer be used for witchcraft purposes. She told me that she personally knows a university teacher in Yaounde who was waylaid by secret society members to belong to their group. They invited him to participate in their meetings. They then told him that he had to share their special food which would empower him to be able to accomplish feats of digging out corpses from a distance. They also threatened him with secrets that he should never reveal, otherwise, he would die mysteriously.

Another story accomplished by the sorcerers is the one Gounou Pulcherie reports in a manuscript entitled "The Koogan dance" that appears in a *Evanescent African cultures* (N. Mutaka, 2016). It is the following.

> One day, in a village called Batié, one man was coming back from his errands. On his way back, he was waylaid by thugs who stopped him, beat him, stripped him of all his belongings, tied him, and introduced a cloth in his mouth and threw him in the bush. However, one of them somehow felt guilty and came back to untie him. As he was a member of the Koogan secret society, he put a drum in the stomach of each of the thugs and only left out the one who had untied him. All of these thugs died because of the pain the drum caused to them.

Other stories have to do with the handling of a corpse. There are times a corpse seems to impose its will to the people who carry it. The following story reported by Mefire Armand Marius (personal communication) is a good illustration of such a phenomenon and it also explains how supernatural phenomena related to a dead person are usually related to pacts the deceased might have concluded with the spiritual world while still alive.

> The Bamoun always bring back the corpse to the native land for its inhumation. However, what might happen is that, while going there, the car breaks down for no reason at all, whether mechanical, electrical. At other times, an accident may occur. In such a case, the driver of the car says that everything in front of him turned black, that he could not see the road, or that a ferocious animal threatened him.

> Note that to drive a car that has a corpse requires a special driver who is well prepared. Those accidents and breakdowns are explained by certain acts that the deceased most probably undertook when he was still alive and which are now manifesting after his death. Such acts are mostly: (a) the will of the deceased, (b) the pacts and forbidden things (c) his affiliation to a secret society (d) the possession of mystical powers [...] In general, it is the mystical power that someone has while still alive which is freed at his death and which causes such phenomena. One can foresee or avoid such phenomena when they know the deceased's intimate life. People need to respect his will, search the deceased to take away any talisman, cut the spell and the pact before proceeding to his inhumation. For the Bamoun, to communicate with the spiritual world implies to decode these phenomena, and then to proceed to rituals or to speak to that deceased who will listen and is in need of being venerated, re-assured, and understood.

The following testimony, told by Donfack Sonfack Diane (personal communication), shows why the Bamileke ethnic communities are so attached to their dead parents, partly through the cult of the skulls,[3] because they believe that the dead intimately intervene in their lives.

> The following story is something that I live in relation to my father who is already dead. We have a particular history after his death. I was living with his brother. After the burial, life became very difficult, and each time I faced a difficult situation, he came to speak to me at night. He has often warned me on some of my choices and he has protected me from the mystical attacks that my other brothers used to undergo and which have never reached me. For example, when I had to pay a book or that I had no food, he would tell me to wake up early and go to the road where I would find a package and that was mine. And each time I found the amount of money that I needed. Sometimes when I made a bad decision, he warned me against it. My mother became seriously sick these last few weeks. And there was a stone that she had rubbed on my father's head at his burial and that we preciously keep. She took it and talked to him through it saying these words: "you have left me in charge of your children and now, I feel threatened. Help me." At night, he said to my mother: "I am your shield, no one will harm you." We began the prayers and my mother has recovered. The dead are not dead. My father is in front of me and I can feel his presence through his help and counsels.

3.5 Strange phenomena related to twins

One thing that I have learned here in Cameroon is that twins or the child who is born immediately after the twins wields special powers. I have had several students who were twins and who have recounted supernatural adventures in which they were involved. One girl for example told me that, at times, she would go to a party with her brother in an astral location. They would dance there and eat and when she came back home, she would not eat because she was full. Another one told us in class that his twin brother once asked him to accompany him to the States and that they would fly mystically. He refused. His brother went there nevertheless and when he came back, he somehow had an accident that manifested in his speech. The following is another such story about twins reported by Ngono Mougbay Khadhija (personal communication) from what her relatives from her village told her.

---

[3] The Bamileke communities in Cameroon are known to revere their ancestors through the cult of the skull. This simply means that, in their houses, they have a special place where they keep the skulls of their ancestors. They regularly bring them food, and whenever they have an important decision to take, like marrying a daughter or travelling abroad, they consult their ancestors by talking to these skulls and asking for their blessings. They consider their ancestors as intermediaries between God and them as living human beings.

There is a strange phenomenon that occurred at Foumban during a marriage ceremony among the Bamoun. In that village called Funtain, there are two young twins who usually gave authorization for an event to take place in the village. Somehow, the married couple did not contact the twins before their marriage and this caused compromising situations. While the women were busy in the kitchen, the twins blocked the fire so that the women could no longer cook. The women who were in the kitchen lit the fire. The fire was lit with strong visible flames but it could not cause the pots to heat up and the food could not cook. Despite all the efforts of these women, the pots simply did not heat and the food did not cook, and this occurred for several hours until the married couples went to see the twins. The twins requested two white roosters. Once they were given those roosters, they flew towards the sky and their legs no longer touched the ground. They did some incantations and two minutes later, they took a handful of salt that they threw in the fire, and from then on, the food began to cook.

3.6 The magic ripening of a banana tree

This phenomenon took place in the Department of Nde in a Bazou village, as reported by Baga Kemkeu Elvire Daniela (personal communication). It runs as follows: The chief of the village comes with a banana trunk, most of the time with a plantain. He puts it in a traditional basket, makes it germinate at the same instant, makes it grow, the fruit comes out of it, the leaves fall down, which is a way to tell that the plantain is ripe. They put it in fire, and once it is cooked, they eat it right there. All this happens within 20 to 30 minutes.

This phenomenon conveys above all the power of the village chief, his superiority to his subjects and his notables. It is also a way of showing the people that food could never lack in the village; famine could not affect them or affect the entire kingdom. The phenomenon also conveys the ability for the chief to take care of his people, to care about their wellbeing so that there is nothing that they can lack and that they should know that they could always count on him in case they become desperate for getting food.

3.7 Other strange phenomena

The other strange phenomena I wish to discuss are the ones published in N. Mutaka and Lenaka (2001) and Mutaka (2011). In Mutaka and Lenaka (2001), Flora Bolima, a former student of mine reports on how, when she was a child, she experienced the phenomenon of having "four eyes," that is, she could see what normal people could not see such as how a newly dead person would pass away on a special road, how witches could congregate at a bridge without being visible, how a witch could sit on the roof of a house without being visible, and so on. In Mutaka (2011), there is this fabulous report by Manbossia in his paper entitled "How animals and things can speak and communicate in the Yambassa culture"; in this report, he tells how old animals, more specifically, a dog, a duck, a cat, and a hen would regularly communicate with the chief, to inform him on events that took place in the village. There is also this story by Njolle et al. in their paper entitled "Glimpses into a mystical world: reflections on the attitude the modern African could adopt" that tells of children who reported how, through witchcraft, they were old people and how they attacked their victims. The other story in this paper is of a witch who was caught at her home while she was half human being and half animal. To force her to reveal her witchcraft practices, she was beaten and was made to reveal that she was a witch. At first she did not want to utter a single word. Then they tickled her with the taro leaves (called macabo in Cameroon), as they knew that no witch can resist revealing her witchcraft practices if she is tickled with such leaves. She thus revealed that she was a witch and that, among witchcraft practices, witches and wizards can change into hedgehogs, owls, tigers, panthers, or mice to destroy people's harvests and that, at times, they travel at night, using groundnut chaff, old sardine cans, shoes, and brooms as airplanes.

4 Prospective research venues to these strange phenomena

The various excerpts in the preceding section aimed at providing data on unusual phenomena which, at present, are not readily explainable by scientific reasoning. These phenomena are, by the way, not the only ones. Before zeroing in on some of the phenomena I wish modern science should further investigate, I would like to briefly recapitulate them by categorizing them.

First, I believe most of these strange phenomena have to do with the existence of a spiritual world that some human beings have access to. In order to access this spiritual world, these people have to either belong to a secret society whose members know certain products, plants, concoctions they have presumably swallowed and also songs, drum beats, and magical utterances that enable them to communicate with the spirits or that can induce such spirits to manifest themselves in human, animal, vegetal, or mineral form. This is what would explain the magical power that not only traditional chiefs and some of their notables purportedly have but also the evil power that sorcerers are able to manipulate. Here, I arrange the stories mentioned in the preceding section about the Mwankum, the Mbombog, the communication with animals and trees, and also the worshiping of the skulls or the stones as replacement for the skull in the Bamileke culture.

Secondly, I believe some people are able to perceive or be sensitive to peculiar energy that radiates through a range of vibrations normal human beings are insensitive to but that some animals, and maybe some vegetation are able to capture. This may be difficult to conceive but I wish to explain why I came up with such an idea. The people who allegedly have "four eyes" and also such animals like the dogs and the cats which react or see what is invisible to the common people are probably sensitive to special vibrations. In order for elements of nature to also react so as to produce rain, wind, thunder, probably that some kind of vibrations are emitted by phenomena that have to do with spiritual beings and that set into motion these elements of nature.

Thirdly, I believe that there are intermittent material bodies born out of the power of ideas that link the human world to the spiritual world as Iyari, one of my sociolinguistics students, once suggested to me. (See, however, a more coherent interpretation he gives of these strange phenomena in the second part of our joint paper (N. Mutaka and Roosevelt Iyari to appear). This is an idea that might be difficult to accept. But consider the following facts that led me to conceive such an idea:

(a) The notion of phantom bodies. Very often, when someone dies, there are people who report that they saw such a person around their houses or that they met him on the road.
(b) The bodies allegedly resurrect. Although I have not given any examples in the excerpts above, I wish to draw the reader's attention to the firm belief in the resurrection of bodies among the Bayangi of the Manyu division in Cameroon (see Tabe 2013). Ayuk's manuscript that will be published in *Evanescent African cultures* (N. Mutaka, 2016) provides convincing evidence of this phenomenon.
(c) The so-called totems in the form of animals or trees. To my mind, natural laws cannot explain how a human being has his double in an animal. These animals or trees that are totems are presumably the result of a spiritual being that manifests itself in the human world in the form of an animal or a tree in order to fulfill an idea, namely, of providing some form of protection to a human being when he is in the forest. In the case of witches who change for example into mice or birds, the idea is to enable them to cause harm to their neighbors in a camouflage body. Note that, in certain cases, witches have been accused of using some other person's real body to manifest themselves. Children who are witches and wizards and who travel supernaturally using cans as airplanes also fit in this category of people who are able to change into their spiritual beings in order to accomplish evil deeds.
(d) The idea of angels is also linked to this concept of intermittent material body. I know that in the Christian religion, angels are often depicted as having wings.

However, the way this term is used in the African context is the equivalent of someone whose identity is completely unknown but who manifests himself in the life of someone in order to help him. After accomplishing the mission, he disappears completely. Although I did not give any excerpt on angels, I wish to refer the reader to an individual mentioned in P. Mutaka (2012): this is a person who came to Mevoutsa's place to inform her mother that they should bring Mevoutsa to a traditional witch doctor. Curiously enough, even the witch doctor said that he did not send that individual and he did not know him. No one knew him in fact.

(e) The existence of "Mami wata," that is, human beings whose upper part is human and the lower part fish. These are allegedly at times sighted along the ocean in Duala. I also wish to state that students have told me stories where they say that they have met beautiful girls in bars in a city like Maroua but who are not normal human beings. Another student told us that, in Chad, taxi drivers have been sighted with feet in the shape of tree trunks and that such taxi drivers could not have been normal human beings.

Given the existence of these strange phenomena, and assuming that they are not merely a world view of the reality by some specific African communities, the question is to know whether they can be explained by natural laws and thus be subjected to scientific scrutiny. Another important question is whether they are worth investigating if it is true that they belong to the spiritual world as I have assumed. I believe these phenomena are simply a challenge to science and will need to be accounted for scientifically sooner or later. As I consider the various problems sub-Saharan Africa presently faces, I suggest that there are two areas worth investigating as I believe the fruits would be beneficial to most African individuals. First, there is this area of protecting a specific ethnic community against witchcraft and all sorts of evildoers as has been pointed out for the Mwankum as the protector of the Bakossi and Mbo communities. Secondly, it would be nice to find out how to neutralize evil that some human beings possess as a result of their dealings with the spiritual world, or, as is commonly thought, as a result of witchcraft.

Assuming that these are worthy motivations that could lead scientists to investigate these strange phenomena, the question is: where to start? What are the crucial data they should access? Notice that, many people dealing either in witchcraft or with spiritual worlds are constrained by the rule of secrecy. Once you are initiated into a secret society and know the elements that give supernatural power, you are required to keep the information secret, otherwise you face instant death. Because this paper is meant to solicit the linguistic community its contribution to provide data likely to be exploited by researchers from other fields to account for these strange phenomena, I believe, the right way would be to start gathering information that gives an inkling on what these secrets might be. In other words, we should be able to obtain indirect evidence that might lead scientists to ultimately discover the formulas that enable certain individuals to communicate with the spiritual world, acquire supernatural power, and neutralize the evil deriving from witchcraft.

This is where I wish to propose the contribution of documentary linguistics and community-based research. Because many governments are genuinely interested in the revitalization of their cultures, I believe young researchers should be encouraged to record data and ultimately exploit it following their specific interests. Several papers in this volume give leads that could be fruitfully exploited for enabling researchers to produce language materials likely to encourage local communities to actively revitalize their languages and become proud in promoting what they consider as positive aspects of their cultures, (e.g., Péres-Báez, especially her ethnobotany project; Bischoff, Fountain and Vincent; Warner, Geary, and Butler for creating revitalization learning materials) Among cultural data that might be explored are the following:

(a) Any cultural ceremony or ritual as it will inform who does what, the deities that might be invoked, the songs, the words and utterances used in such ceremonies;

(b) The cultural lore of the community in terms of tales, legends, songs, lullabies, etc. As for the exploitation of this material, the researcher may take notes of the different items that are used and what they represent for the communities. Eventually, the researcher might try to obtain explanations from the guardians of the tradition, such as the notables or the traditional chiefs. Since we already know that, in certain rituals, certain plants, animals, and seeds are used, the researcher could try to know why they are used in such rituals and thus gather specific information related to them. More generally, the cultural knowledge of a community is usually represented, if not veiled, through their tales, legends, riddles, etc.; and

(c) Data collection in the form of interviews from people who have either undergone the strange phenomena or from those who have witnessed them. Such people will not necessarily reveal the information that is considered secret in their societies, either because they do not know it or because they are afraid to get chastised mystically by the gatekeepers of their traditions. But the information they will reveal will likely lead scientists to figure out where to look to explain the underpinnings that lead to the manifestation of these strange phenomena.

Notice also that it is by closely working with the native speakers that one can discover the richness of the culture hidden behind the contextual use of certain words as demonstrated in Franchetto (2006: 183–212) and that, in order to not betray the community whose language is being investigated, one will know whether it is appropriate to disclose certain findings that may be considered sacred for such a community (see Hill 2006: 113–128 for a similar problem where the native speakers were angry because her husband had published a dictionary on their language and by so doing, he was providing knowledge on their culture that was not supposed to ever be provided).

As for the initial publication of findings related to the cultural richness of a community, they would fit as extensive comments on certain specific lexical entries of the type of community-based dictionaries as in Melis (2004) or as a separate article included in such a dictionary as in N. Mutaka and Kavutirwaki (2011).

As to the question how this research could ultimately be beneficial to the native speakers, suppose scientists were to discover how a "juju" like the Mwankum finds out the evil doers in a community and goes to threaten them and eventually punish them, this knowledge could be used in modern times to better understand religious ideologies.

5 Conclusion

To conclude, if we take seriously the idea that research should benefit local communities, there is a need to re-orient the writing of dictionaries so as they may take into account their needs that are not necessarily those of the scientific communities. As advocated in this paper, such dictionaries should contain cultural material associated to certain lexical items or featuring papers that directly address the needs of those communities. The major part of the chapter advocates the need to explore new research avenues related to strange phenomena many people witness in sub-Saharan Africa and that seem to have been largely avoided by modern science because they are related to the spiritual world. Documentary linguistics and community-based research could serve as a tool to gather indirect evidence that researchers of various fields would then further exploit to account for such phenomena. The initial findings that would be obtained through a close collaboration of the researchers with the community would be reported as comments on some lexical entries in the kind of community-based dictionary advocated in this paper. Knowledge about the underpinnings of these strange phenomena could ultimately result in a better understanding of religious ideologies.

References

Bassong, Paul Roger. 2011. Cosmogonie Basa'a-Egypte Pharaonique. In Ngessimo Mutaka (ed.), *Glimpses of African cultures/Echos des cultures africaines*, 197–204. Paris: L'Harmattan.
Bloomhill, Greta. 1962. *Witchcraft in Africa*. Cape Town: Howard Timming.
Debrunner, Hans Wener.1959. *Witchcraft in Ghana*. Accra: Presbyterian Book.
Evans-Prichard, Edward Evans.1963. *Witchcraft, oracles and magic among the Azande*. London: Oxford University Press.
Franchetto, Bruna. 2006. Ethnography in language documentation. In Jost Gippert, Nikolaus Himmelmann, and Ulrike Mosel (eds), *Essentials of language documentation (Trends in linguistic studies and monographs 178)*, 183–211. Berlin: Mouton de Gruyter.
Hill, Jane H. 2006. The ethnography of language and language documentation. In Jost Gippert, Nikolaus Himmelmann, and Ulrike Mosel (eds), *Essentials of language documentation (Trends in linguistic studies and monographs 178)*, 113–128. Berlin: Mouton de Gruyter.
Kavutirwaki, Kambale and Ngessimo Mutaka. 2012. *Dictionnaire Kinande-français suivi d' un index français Kinande*. http://www.africamuseum.be/museum/research/publications/rmca/online/online-kinande.pdf. Accessed 20 May 2017.
Kigwe, Augustine Ricarda. 2016. Dieu et la religion chez les bantu : cas des Basa'a du Cameroun. In Ngessimo Mutaka (ed.) *Evanescent African cultures*. University of Yaounde 1. Manuscript.
Mbiti, John S. 1985. *African religions and philosophy*. London : Heinemann
Melis, Antonino. 2004. Dictionnaire encyclopédique du Masa. France: Université de Tours dissertation.
Middleton, John and Edward H. Winter (eds). 1963. *Witchcraft and sorcery in East Africa*. London: Routledge
Mutaka, Ngessimo M. 2011. *Glimpses of African cultures / Echos des cultures africaines*. Paris: L' Harmattan.
Mutaka, Ngessimo. M. (Ed.). 2016. Evanescent African Cultures. University of Yaounde 1 manuscript.
Mutaka, Ngessimo M. and Ngoran Loveline Lenaka .2001. The magic world in the Nso culture: An ethnomethodological study. *Working Papers*, Centro Piemontese di Studi Africani.
Mutaka, Ngessimo and Kambale Kavutirwaki. 2011. *Kinande/Konzo-English dictionary with an English-Kinande index*. Trenton: Africa world Press.
Mutaka, Ngessimo and Iyari Roosevelt. To appear. Contact with the invisible world: Life experiences in Cameroon. *Evanescent African Cultures*.
Mutaka, Philippe. 2012. *Divine bud*. Mankon: Langaa Research and Publishing Common Initiative Group, Lightning Source, UK.
Njolle, Cecilia, Sylvain Medzogo, and Philip Mutaka. 2011. Glimpses into a mystical world: Reflections on the attitude the modern African could adopt. In Ngessimo Mutaka (ed.), *Glimpses of African cultures/Echos des cultures africaines*, 118–120. Paris: L'Harmattan.
Nkunde Ewanoge. 2016. The Mwankum "juju"and the Mwankum secret cult in the Bakossi land. In Ngessimo Mutaka (ed.) *Evanescent African cultures*. University of Yaounde 1. Manuscript.
Parrinder, Edward G. 1958. *Witchcraft*. London: Faber and Faber.
Tabe Oben, A. E. Florence. 2013. Defining attitudes towards traditional beliefs among the Manyu people of the South West Region of Cameroon. In Pierre Fandio (ed.), *Popular culture and representations in Cameroon: The journey across the Mungo River*, 163–181. Kansas City: Miraclair Publisher.

Joshua R. Meyer, Nicholas Kloehn, Andrew Carnie, Diana Archangeli, Ian Clayton, Muriel Fisher, Michael Hammond, Adam Ussishkin, Natasha Warner

The field is not the lab, and the lab is not the field: Experimental linguistics and endangered language communities

Abstract: The scientific ideals of experimental/laboratory linguistics which uses large scale subject pools, statistics, carefully constructed controls and expensive equipment can run into conflict when working with an endangered language community. The questions raised by experimental linguistics are not necessarily those of most interest to the community and endangered language communities are not necessarily well-suited to support the requirements of experimental linguistics methodologies. In this chapter, we report on our experience working with speakers of Scottish Gaelic on the Isle of Skye in Scotland. We address questions of study design and how we had to modify our research methodologies for working in partnership with this community and we consider how our work was received by the community. We finally present feedback we received from study participants and sketch what we think are best practices for using experimental methodologies in collaboration with an endangered language community.

Keywords: Gaelic, Celtic, Laboratory, Phonetics, Psycholinguistics

---

* All authors are affiliated with the University of Arizona, with the exception of Clayton who is at the University of Nevada Reno. We would like to thank the community of speakers that we have worked with in Scotland, whose dedication to supporting and revitalizing their language is an inspiration to us. Thanks also to Carmen Jany, Shannon Bischoff, Colleen Patton and an anonymous reviewer for helpful comments and suggestions.

Joshua R. Meyer, joshuameyer@email.arizona.edu, **Nicholas Kloehn,** kloehn@email.arizona.edu, **Andrew Carnie,** carnie@email.arizona.edu, **Diana Archangeli,** dba@email.arizona.edu, **Muriel Fisher,** murielf@email.arizona.edu, **Michael Hammond,** hammond@email.arizona.edu, **Adam Ussishkin,** ussishki@email.arizona.edu, **Natasha Warner,** nwarner@email.arizona.edu: Department of Linguistics, P.O. Box 210025, The University of Arizona, Tucson AZ 85721USA
Ian Clayton, University of Nevada Reno, Department of English (0098), 1664 N. Virginia Street, Reno, NV 89557 iclayton@unr.edu

https://doi.org/10.1515/9783110527018-017

1 Introduction

As experimental equipment becomes more compact, accessible and portable, incorporating experiments into field research becomes increasingly plausible for linguists everywhere (see for example, Whalen and McDonough 2015). Experiments constitute a subset of the tools available to the linguist, and within almost every subfield of linguistics, the use of such methods has been established. However, when working with an endangered language community, adopting such methods entails adapting to a unique set of concerns. Working with an endangered language requires that not only are the experiments going to produce fruitful results, but they also must have clear benefits for the community (see Rice 2010, 2011, and this volume for discussion of the relationship between research and community service, and Czaykowska-Higgens, this volume, for an elaboration on how one might measure outcomes in such partnerships).

This paper is a reflection on the authors' experience using experimental techniques[1] with speakers of Scottish Gaelic on the Isle of Skye in Scotland. In what follows, we describe our experiences working with Scottish Gaelic, and come to outline specific considerations we feel are required on the part of the linguist in approaching an endeavor similar to ours. In order to do so, we describe the nature of our research group, the aims that we hoped to achieve regarding our research questions, and the ways in which our group was connected to the endangered-language community. We discuss the challenges of transferring to

---

1 A reviewer rightly points out that by definition all scientific linguistic work is experimental in the sense that it includes hypothesis testing. That includes of course traditional pen and paper elicitation or in more modern techniques of documentary linguistics (see for example many of the other chapters in this volume, e.g. Fitzgerald's paper). We do not mean to diminish the importance of the scientific method in traditional field methodologies. We are using the term "experimental" here as a shorthand, commonly found in the discipline, to refer to instrumental methodologies, psycholinguistic methodologies, and other techniques that require statistical analysis of speakers who participate in a controlled study. These are the techniques traditionally viewed as "lab" based linguistics and have largely been restricted to more widely spoken languages like English or Spanish. A similar observation can be made about our use of the term "theoretical linguistics" later in this paper. We do not intend to suggest that traditional field methodologies do not involve theories (nor, for that matter, do we mean that experimental methodologies do not use theories). We are using the term as it is commonly used among practitioners to refer to formal structural approaches (including but not limited to Generative Grammar). Rightly or wrongly, the terms "experimental" and "theoretical" are commonly used in these ways in the discipline and we adopt that usage while recognizing that they could be confusing and probably misleading.

the field the experimental techniques that would answer our research questions. We also describe the particular challenges of working with the Scottish Gaelic speaking community. Finally, we describe the feedback we received from the experiment participants and outline where we can improve our approach in the future.

2 Research agenda, methodologies and community connections

At the University of Arizona, we have a research team that has collaborated on four National Science Foundation Grants researching Scottish Gaelic syntax, phonetics, phonology, and morphology and has recently begun a new research grant into the phonology of Welsh.[2] The Scottish Gaelic part of the team consists of five faculty (Archangeli, Carnie, Hammond, Ussishkin, Warner), a native speaker (Fisher), a post-doctoral fellow (Clayton, now faculty at the University of Nevada), 16 graduate students and graduate alumni, including the two first authors of this paper, and a number of undergraduate research assistants. Our research has used elicitation, computational techniques from corpus linguistics, and experimental methodologies – the latter being the focus of the present work.

We selected experimental methodologies to focus on some of the typologically rare phonological properties of the Scottish Gaelic language[3] such as apparent nasal fricatives, a unique palatalization pattern, morphologically triggered initial consonant mutation, epenthesis, hiatus, and preaspiration, among others. The wide variety of tools allowed us to investigate each phenomenon from different perspectives. Our questions were of three types: the phonetic realizations of the phenomena in question, the psycho-phonological representation of alternations, and native speaker perception of these phenomena. We elicited three classes of responses from native speakers:
(a) Physiological articulation (tongue movement or nasal airflow), using ultrasound machine and an oral/nasal airflow measurement system.

---

[2] NSF Grants numbered: BCS11443818, BCS0921685, BCS0639059, BCS1453724
[3] We also did one experiment on the production of Gaelic-influenced English.

(b) Reaction times and response choices (from button presses) to an auditory or visual stimulus, testing materials involving gated and other modified speech as well as masked-priming.
(c) Written or spoken responses to a prompt.

A list of the published research emerging from this group is found in Appendix A.

3 Ethical principles for experimental work with endangered-language communities

We would like to start this paper with an observation that also has important practical implications: Experimental work on an endangered language is not appropriate in all situations. For many languages, doing experimental field work would be a waste of time and would squander limited resources (see Dixon 1997 for more on this observation). Languages that either lack sufficient basic documentation (such as a grammatical description or dictionary) or do not have sufficient speakers to do a statistically valid experiment should be investigated through other means. If the community needs help with construction of pedagogical tools or in language planning then an experimental approach to language description may well be a poor use of resources.

In our research on Scottish Gaelic we have been lucky. Despite being endangered, the language has a long descriptive tradition with numerous dictionaries and grammars and has a significant literary tradition. The language also has many pedagogical resources and has both political and media support systems in place. Thus for us, while we continue to do traditional elicitation, documentation, and description, we are able to do experimental work as well. This might not be possible in other communities.

With this in mind, there are a number of prerequisites to beginning an experimental research program with an endangered language. (1) The researcher must have access to a sufficient amount of descriptive work on the language, and (2) a sufficient amount of language documentation materials to provide a basis for experimental stimuli. (3) There must also be sufficient community interest for the proposed experimental research, and ideally the community should have (4) a pre-existing revitalization infrastructure. In our experience, having a revitalization infrastructure, is needed for fostering collaboration with the speaker community. It may be the case that the experimental research is purely academic (i.e. theory-driven) and researcher-focused in nature. As such, if there is no revitalization infrastructure, even with the interest of the community it is unclear how the linguist will be of benefit to the community, cf. however Perez Báez, this volume. The first two requirements (description and documentation) are necessary for constructing valid experiments, whereas the last two (interest and infrastructure) ensure that the linguist is working in accordance with the community goals.

4 Developing community relationships and the importance of the community linguist

Linguistic research done with communities that speak endangered languages has implications outside the scope of the research itself. Research often brings along with it funding and resources for equipment, research assistants, and—in both direct and indirect ways—the community of speakers. Along with these funds may come such issues as who benefits from the funds and who does not. As such, the broader context of research cannot be ignored if the linguist hopes to conduct ethical research.

In addition to taking precautions to minimize broader negative effects of research on a community, linguistic research should only be conducted when the community is open to the research taking place. This may seem obvious, but there exist many levels of interest that can be characterized by involvement and collaboration. The experimental research on which this chapter is based is researcher-focused in nature, but developed as a fully collaborative documentation project. In short, researcher-focused projects need not always be dispreferred. This type of work is one way to meet the needs of all involved parties (Czaykowska-Higgins 2009, this volume; Bowern and Warner 2015; Fitzgerald, this volume; but cf. Crippen and Robinson 2013). For linguists and communities of endangered languages, it may be impossible to design a study that reflects the interests and needs of both parties.

In the case of our research on the Isle of Skye, Scotland, our affiliation with Sabhal Mòr Ostaig (SMO), the Gaelic-medium College, was crucial when it came to providing space to run experiments, participant recruitment, and credibility to the community. The authors' experimental and theoretical research subsequently spawned a documentation project in collaboration with the Media Studies unit at SMO. Without our existing affiliation with SMO, such a project would not be possible. The primary goal of this new project is to develop an audio-video corpus of vernacular Scottish Gaelic. The corpus consists of high quality digital audio and video recordings of interviews with native Gaelic speakers. The interviews address a variety of topics, but are focused on traditional occupations, oral history, folklore, and personal narratives. The collected material will be provided with time-aligned transcriptions in the original Gaelic, morpheme-by-morpheme glosses, and English translations. No such corpus has been previously available, and as such the audio-video corpus will be a major boon to both the research and local communities. This project has also received financial support from the National Science Foundation [#BCS 1500620 and BCS 1500220].

The success of our research in the community is largely to due to the fact that we are collaborating with a native speaker with deep community ties. Muriel Fisher, who won the 2014 Community Linguist award from the Linguistic Society of America, is a native speaker of Gaelic from the village of Glendale on Skye. While she currently resides in Tucson and teaches Gaelic at the University of Arizona, she has maintained strong connections with her home. She returns each summer to Skye to teach summer courses at SMO. She has a wide network, not only of native speaking friends and relatives, but also of language experts who work at SMO. This has allowed us to have unique access not only to speakers who can serve as consultants in our experiments but also access to expertise in the grammar and dialectology of the language, which was invaluable in constructing the stimuli for our experiments.

Fisher's own work in pedagogy is an important bridge between our more theoretically-oriented work and the needs of the community. As a teacher she has created a four-level textbook with audio material in the language. She also has developed some unique and popular courses at the Gaelic college, including a refresher course for native and heritage speakers who would like to brush up their Gaelic. Since she started collaborating with us, she has learned a lot of linguistics —she is a natural at language description and scientific observation—and now incorporates many of the insights of linguistics and our research into her own teaching. For example, our work on vowel epenthesis and stress has helped her explain to students one of the more baffling aspects of the Scottish Gaelic orthography.[4]

While Scottish Highland culture is similar in many ways to American culture, there are many surprising and challenging differences. These come in every way from the norms of politeness to negotiating complex agreements. Take, for example, helping elderly native speakers to be comfortable with a potentially scary instrumental set up like our ultrasound machine. While the speakers are familiar with ultrasound technology from their doctor's offices, it brings to some the special anxiety associated with a medical procedure. Another source of anxiety relates to

---

[4] In particular, epenthetic vowels are not written, yet are predictable based on the orthographic consonants. A sonorant followed by a non-homorganic obstruent (excluding voiceless stops) following a stressed vowel, is consistently followed by an epenthetic vowel even though it is not written.

language attitudes: whether they are "doing the task right" or "misrepresenting their language." This is particularly acute in a community like Skye, where Gaelic has long been viewed as a second-class language and until recently all schooling was done in English. Speakers often express concern that they "don't really know Gaelic properly" because they didn't go to school in the language, or they don't know all the words that their grandparents did, etc. As such they are often reluctant to participate in studies where it appears the stakes are high (because we are either using fancy equipment, or they are surrounded by a group of people that includes university professors). Fisher has been critical in mitigating these issues. For instance, when consultants first arrive at our study sites, they are greeted by Fisher, who sets them at ease by greeting them in Gaelic, offering them tea and biscuits, and gently talking them through the demographic questionnaire, consent documents and the experimental procedure. As a community insider, she was acutely aware of the anxieties study participation can bring out in speakers. She was able to joke with the consultants and relax them. She also sat with the participants if they were nervous and talked to them in Gaelic to help them feel more relaxed.

The novelty of an experimental setting can potentially put community members in an uneasy state. Uneasiness compounded with a seemingly endless barrage of experimental items could easily end badly. Fisher was able to tell us when the experiment was too long and which pieces of equipment would be too uncomfortable or intimidating. American undergraduate participants are accustomed to sitting in front of a computer screen for hours, whereas for many speakers of endangered languages this is not the case. Under Fisher's supervision, all of our experiments were developed in a way to be as comfortable as possible for participants. For example, one of our tasks called for participants to listen to real and nonsense words in Gaelic and then judge which words were real and which were fake. After we had compiled a list of candidate words, she worked with us to discard any words that were archaic or had negative connotations. Without a native speaker community member as part of our design team, we may have inadvertently asked participants to listen to words that were taboo or vulgar. After the stimuli had been approved and our experiments were in a testable state, Fisher performed the task as if she were a participant. Based on her feedback, we made adjustments to ensure that the experience would not be stressful or awkward. This included adding extra pauses into the experiments and rewriting our briefing scripts to better explain procedures. Another example has to do with the production of the stimuli for one of our speech perception experiments. Most gating experiments gate to white noise or a square wave to avoid adding perceptual artifacts. Fisher found this too irritating in pilot testing, so we gated to silence instead, which avoids irritating beeps. The cost in potential perceptual artifacts has turned out to be not a problem.

Fisher also helped mitigate one of the biggest challenges we had in recruiting consultants to participate in our experiments. The University of Arizona institutional review board (IRB) has a template for a very comprehensive and lengthy subject consent form that we were required to have each consultant complete. The consent form is of course for the protection of the speaker, but it is a challenge for many Gaels, who remember that complex legal documents were once used as tools to evict Gaelic speakers from their ancestral lands. Speakers are very concerned about signing such documents, but are happy to offer their consent once given an equivalent oral description of the experimental procedure and their rights as participants. Fisher's sensitivity to this issue led to fruitful discussions with our IRB over whether such a detailed form was necessary with this speaker community, and subsequently we were able to bypass the written consent form while still ensuring that our native speakers were appropriately informed about what the experiments entail and what their rights were.

Another potentially awkward and difficult part of conducting experiments in the field is the question of compensation. On one hand, we want to recognize the expertise and linguistic prowess of the participant. This means paying more than we might to an undergraduate doing a 20 minute experiment in a typical linguistics lab, but it also means doing it in a way in which the speaker will not feel compelled to participate if they don't want to or if they are embarrassed about taking money, especially if this might cause upset elsewhere in the community. Best practices in compensation will vary by the community a researcher is working with. In our case, under the advice of Fisher, we did not cast our compensation as a "payment", but instead as a "thank you gift", which was given to the consultant in a sealed thank you card signed by all the field team. This exchange was done in private by Fisher as part of the intake. In our case, taking cash out of a pocket and directly handing it to the participant would have been seen as very offensive. Otherwise it would have been likely that speakers would refuse the money and may have taken offense that we would try to "pay" them.

Dropping twelve excited foreign researchers down in the middle of a relatively quiet rural island environment brings with it the challenge of ensuring the community will accept our work and invite us back. Fisher was critical to our success in this as well. Knowing us all personally, but also knowing her community, she was able to coach us in basic social niceties that would ensure we were viewed as welcome partners of the community rather than scientific interlopers who were looking to examine the natives under microscopes. This coaching was in everything from the dress of our research group, which was too informal and in some cases too revealing for the community standards, to the personal conduct of the research group from the minute a speaker-consultant walked into the space where we were performing the research. Fisher had us repeatedly rehearse and practice our patter and our manners as we conducted the experiments so that it helped the native speakers feel comfortable and made us a more accepted part of the local community.

Most importantly, Fisher has been critical to helping us explain our sometimes esoteric research questions to native speakers and help them understand what kind of impact our work would have on the language community. She also helped us shape our questions in ways that would better serve the community. As an example of the former, we are interested in the mental representation of the morphologically triggered phenomenon of initial consonant mutation (lenition). Traditional Gaelic pedagogy requires the student to learn a set of rules for the alternations[5] and memorize a heterogeneous set of morphological environments in which it occurs and the exceptions to those environments. The mutation phenomenon is a challenge for classroom learners. Our research has exposed one or two facts that might be relevant to how mutation is taught. First, our research shows that even taking into account dialect and age, there is actually widespread variation among speakers in where they apply the rules and when they apply the exceptions – apparently with little effect on comprehension. This means that with the exception of a couple of cases where the mutation is the unique marker of a morphological contrast (such as in the past tense of verbs), instructors may instead want to model the mutation in their own speech and writing rather than spending a great deal of time on prescriptive instruction, allowing learners and lapsed native speakers to acquire the contrasts through exposure. Second, although the results are still not fully clear, some of our data may be consistent with the idea that native speakers simply store both allomorphs of a word (lenited and unlenited) rather than applying an online phonological rule (Green 2006; Warner et. al 2013). As such teachers of the language may simply want to have students learn both forms from the beginning rather than teaching one "underlying" form and a set of principles for deriving the lenited form. Here our research can inform instructional practice, while the perspective of community language teachers helps us shape our research question.

It is in no way an exaggeration to say that without Fisher, this project would not have been feasible. At least one community member should be in close consultation during the planning of any such experimental work, to help the researchers to avoid any cultural or practical pitfalls

---

[5] In Gaelic lenition, the following changes occur, leaving aside details about palatalization: /p/ → [f], /f/ → ∅, /m/ → [v], /b/ → [v], /t/ → [h], /d/ → [ɣ], /s/ → [h], /k/ → [x], /g/ → [ɣ].

5 The Challenges of Experimental Design

The construction and administration of experiments when working with an endangered language community brings its own unique challenges (Clemens et al. 2012; Norcliffe et al. 2015). For example, the resources for building the experiments are more limited and the population we study is both smaller and more diverse. This creates situations unfamiliar to many experimental linguists who expect greater statistical and instrumental power than may be available in the field context.

5.1 Stimuli

Building experimental stimuli relies on having access to resources such as dictionaries, word lists, corpora and grammars. Even though Scottish Gaelic has a number of different dictionaries (Dwelly 1902–1912; MacFarlane 1912; Mark 2003), these reference materials bring with them their own special challenges. As inherently conservative tools, dictionaries for languages like Gaelic, which have a long literary tradition, often contain many words that are archaic, dialect specific, or generally unfamiliar to native speakers. This is exacerbated in cases like that of Scottish Gaelic, where there is universal bilingualism (with English) and there is a tendency to only use Gaelic for basic day-to-day communication. Many Gaelic speakers don't have technically specialized vocabularies and tend to switch to English when discussing more technical matters. So we found that many of the words and forms we selected from the dictionary were of no use in our experiments, as speakers simply didn't know them. Here again, Muriel Fisher was a critical factor in our success, since only she could identify which words speakers were likely to know and which they were not. We were also able to directly draw on her native-speaker knowledge of the language to find the right items (e.g. "Can you think of a one syllable word that begins with an f that rhymes with bat?" or "we need a word that sounds like X", etc.)

For example, in one of our studies, we asked participants to read aloud words off a screen while ultrasonic images of their tongue's movement were recorded. The goal was to compare tongue movement in words with lenition versus words without lenition. The two categories of words needed to be as similar as possible in all respects besides the lenition. That is, all words should be equally common, equally long, have similar syllable structures, etc. To hold these various aspects constant, we needed a large and representative corpus of Scottish Gaelic. If our corpus were a collection of 18th century literature, we may have presented words that were unknown to the participants, even if all the relevant aspects were controlled. Similarly, if we had too small a corpus of modern Gaelic, we would not have enough data to reliably control all stimuli, even if the participants knew all the words. For these reasons, the documentation from which stimuli are drawn should be both *large* and *representative* of the speaker's knowledge. For our corpus, we combined three smaller corpora into one. The first two corpora were pre-existing (MacBain 1911; Pike and Maolalaigh 2013) whereas we created the third by compiling online publications from the Scottish Gaelic language BBC (BBC Alba). With this combination of resources, we were able to develop stimuli for our experiments.

5.2 Participants

In a university setting, experimental linguistics often involves large numbers of undergraduate participants. Such participants are relatively easy to come by. An announcement to a university's psychology or linguistics department will usually suffice to bring in enough students to fill out an entire study. Moreover, there is such access to participants that some may be excluded from the analyses based on non-standard experimental performance. We can legitimately discard an undergraduate participant's results, for instance, because she has been studying German since she was 5 years old, her vowel perception does not pattern with other participants, or she has an under 80% accuracy rate on some task. Researchers often expect to exclude participants based on such exceptions or technical problems, and so recruit more students than are needed for a study. This is not the case with endangered languages. This kind of participant is not who we get when we go into the field. When working on an endangered language, every drop of data is precious. This cannot be changed, and so other aspects of an experiment might have to be altered to work successfully in the field. For instance, to increase statistical power, more items per community member may be appropriate. However, too many experimental items may lead to boredom, stress, or fatigue. In our case, we had to redesign a typical lexical decision experiment by adding in extra resting periods. Lexical decision is a task in which real words and non-words are presented to the participant, and the participant must decide which words are real and which words are invented. In a university, such studies have been conducted with up to 480 words (Bentin et al. 1985). We wanted to present as many words as possible to each participant, but the more we added, the more stressful the task would become. A compromise was made—extra breaks (a total of four, where just one is normal) were inserted during the task, and a total of 160 words were used. Fewer words and more breaks resulted in a less stressful task.

However, there are some aspects of the population that cannot be controlled in the field setting. In university settings, the fact that we are drawing from the student body means that we are already controlling numerous aspects of our sample population. But in the field, it may be much harder to control or balance a participant pool for age, dialect, socio-economic status, frequency of target language use, or education. All of these add variation into the sample and potentially experimental error into the data. Community members of differing ages will have varying levels of hearing, vision, and exposure to computers. In a language like Gaelic, different speakers have different levels of competency with the language. Some speak it all the time. Others learned it as children. Some use it in their work or school. Others only use it to talk to their grandparents. Some have university-level education in the language. Others are only literate in English. Some were monolingual in Gaelic until school age; others have been functionally bilingual since starting to speak. All of these factors will influence their performance. When working with a small community of speakers, whose time and resources are limited and whose members live at considerable geographic distances, these differences simply cannot be avoided. The more variation between participants, the harder it will be to find a statistically significant effect. For these reasons, even when using sophisticated statistical techniques such as linear mixed regression, researchers may encounter resistance in the peer review process because of potential confounds and small subject pools. While we expect that such complaints mostly come from researchers who work on larger more widely spoken languages where such factors can be easily controlled for, we also recognize the scientific concern of such researchers as clearer more definitive conclusions are always better than more tentative ones. It is important to recognize that there is more value in conducting this work with a less clear set of results than not conducting it at all, which is the only other alternative. If one wants a broader view of language beyond that available from more widely spoken languages, then one has to make accommodations in this regard. The results and conclusions may not be as clear-cut as those in more traditional experimental work, but it is better to have some results than nothing, especially when the language may not be spoken at all in the future. The broader impacts of this kind of research may well make up for any minor deficiencies of experimental power.

The actual conduct of experiments with this diverse body of participants is also different from that in traditional linguistics labs. With community-based experimental work it is important to pay special attention to each person's needs, comfort, and background. For example, many of our native speaker consultants were elderly and had hearing or vision problems. When we conducted experiments that entailed listening to modified gated speech, these speakers often had trouble hearing the stimuli. Similarly, we conducted a nasal airflow study in which speakers were asked to read from a printed list of words. Unfortunately the shape and position of the nasal mask prevented speakers from wearing glasses (or forced them to wear them at odd angles). This is not only uncomfortable for the participant, but it means that they may not be correctly seeing the prompts. Accommodating these kinds of obstacles requires careful forethought and attention and may require some on-the-fly improvisation on the part of the experimenter (e.g. writing out the stimuli in a larger print size). Careful attention on intake can also help. When we discovered that one of our extremely fluent speakers never learned to read or write in the language (although she was literate in English), we were able to save the consultant a great deal of embarrassment by not having her do experiments that relied on reading or writing in Gaelic orthography. Instead we redirected her to recording some stories and histories with our native speaking collaborator. Even though she did not participate in the experiments we were able to gain some valuable data for our other documentary projects, while also recognizing the consultant's knowledge and understanding of the culture and history of the island and respecting her language knowledge.

Other non-trivial differences distinguish speakers of an endangered language from undergraduate students. These two groups have different expectations of the researcher, different attitudes towards the languages they speak, and different levels of familiarity with experimental settings. For these reasons and others, it is misguided to expect that research in experimental linguistics can be directly transplanted from a university laboratory into the field, wherever that may be. One major difference between typical experimental participants and community members relates to their expectations of the researcher. Speakers of an endangered language who are willing to participate in such research are often proponents of revitalization efforts themselves, and so have a vested interest in the outcomes of the research. As such, it is possible that participants feel under pressure to perform well on the experimental tasks because they want to aid the researcher. Monolingual undergraduate participants probably do not have these attitudes towards experimental research and are less likely to be upset by certain experimental tasks. For example, if a task contains a training phase in which the participant is given feedback on their mistakes, this may not be stressful at all for the undergraduate. However, for a speaker of an endangered language this may very well feel like intense judgment on their linguistic abilities. The structure of almost any experimental task can be reinterpreted as a test, and tests can be stressful as well as shaming if one is insecure about one's ability in the target language. It is of utmost importance that community members are very clearly briefed before all experiments that these tasks are in no way a measure or judgment of their language abilities. This is especially true in the context of an endangered language community, where speakers are often not confident about their linguistic ability.

For example, after finishing a task we frequently heard speakers say things like "Oh dear, I didn't do very well on that. I wish you could have tested my mother. She was a much better speaker of the language than I am. I hope I didn't ruin your experiment." After a few instances of this kind of response, we quickly adjusted our explanations of the tasks and tried to make it clear that we weren't testing their competence in the language and that we expected variation (as well as some errors since everyone makes errors in speaking); indeed, variation and errors were in some ways more interesting to us than what they learned in school.

5.3 Summary

It should be obvious from all the considerations discussed in this section that experimental work done in collaboration with an endangered language community is very different from experimental work done in a lab. There are unique challenges in constructing the experiments and in building a participant pool. Resources for constructing balanced and controlled experiments are less available and the selection of materials may require much more work than that required when working with a majority language. The participant pool is more heterogeneous than that normally found in the lab and is likely much smaller. There are different expectations of the participants, which shift the way experiments are conducted. These considerations are all critical to successful conduct of experimental work with an endangered language community. We also note that the scientific community must also be prepared to have different expectations for the outcomes of such research.

6 Community evaluation of our research

During our 2014 and 2015 visits to Scotland, we invited participants to respond to a questionnaire about what they thought about our work. The questionnaire posed various questions about participants' (1) opinions on the research (such as its usefulness and impact on their language), (2) comfort during the experiments, and (3) understanding of the research. The main use of these surveys was to try to understand where we had room for improvement and which of our design decisions played out well. Since we ourselves conducted the survey, we can expect that the results are likely to be biased in our favor. Even though we made the questionnaires anonymous, consultants are unlikely to give us critical feedback since they knew we would be reading them. This is especially true since we made an effort to engage with them and participate in their community. Because we were their guests, they were highly unlikely to give us serious critiques. Quite expectedly then, the responses to our survey were overwhelmingly positive. For example, we learned that our preparation was largely successful with respect to participant comfort. While pleased by this, we focus here on those areas where the consultants gave us specific critical responses.

Many participants replied that they did not fully understand the research. This result was not terribly surprising given that some of our experiments were investigating very technical topics. One artifact of this is that some of the native speakers felt that we did not take advantage of their unique knowledge of the structure, history and culture in the language. This is not a satisfactory result for us. In response, working closely with Muriel Fisher, we have developed one-page handouts written in lay language to be distributed at SMO and to future participants. These handouts concisely review the methods and theories with which we are working and use language that is not laden with terminology. We hope that these pamphlets will help community members better understand the research we are conducting. We also attempted to provide an explanation of why the questions we were addressing might be relevant to not only our understanding of the Gaelic language, but also to their community efforts.

Participants' overall opinions on the merit of the research fell into two major categories. Either people said that the research is important in that it (1) adds to the status of the language or (2) may hopefully be used in pedagogy. The former group expressed sentiments such as "[...] more understanding of the language will hopefully lead to more respect/appreciation of it", and that the research helps the community "[...] realize that we do have a worthwhile culture/language."

For the participants who hoped that our research results can be incorporated into pedagogy, we had responses such as "I would hope that this would help being able to teach Gaelic in an easier way for learners", and "The research findings could be helpful in informing future teaching and learning". The main goal of our research was linguistic rather than pedagogical, and as such these opinions are worth noting as they reflect our intuition that our work must have clear broader impacts.

7 Conclusions

For both the experimentalist hoping to work in the field and the community linguist hoping to incorporate new techniques, experimental work on endangered languages is a new and challenging task. Special attention has to be paid to experimental design and the relationship with the community. A running theme in this chapter is the importance of having a community member involved in the project from the beginning. Without this kind of invaluable assistance, experimental work within endangered language communities is highly likely to encounter serious problems. With active community engagement, we could feel much more confident that our research led to a net positive effect for all parties involved. Our initial theoretical work opened up doors for collaboration on a documentation project, and the participants found the overall experience interesting and enjoyable.

Appendix A

Papers and presentations based on the research described here
Archangeli, Diana, Jeff Berry, Andrew Carnie, N. Hunt, Sunjing Ji, and Keisha Josephs. 2011. ATR in Scottish Gaelic Tense Sonorants: A preliminary report. In Andrew Carnie (ed.), *Formal Approaches to Celtic Linguistics*, 283–306. Newcastle upon Tyne: Cambridge Scholar's Press.
Archangeli, Diana, Samuel Johnston, Jae-Hyun Sung, Muriel Fisher, Michael Hammond, and Andrew Carnie. 2014. Articulation and neutralization: a preliminary study of lenition in Scottish Gaelic. *INTERSPEECH*. 1683–1687.
Archangeli, Diana, S. Johnston, Jae-Hyun Sung, Muriel Fisher, Michael Hammond, Andrew Carnie. 2014. Svarabhakti vowel articulation in Scots Gaelic. Paper presented at the 14th Confrerence on Laboratory Phonology, Tokyo Japan, 25–27 July.
Brenner, Daniel, Andrea Davis, Natasha Warner, Andrew Carnie, Muriel Fisher, Jessamyn Schertz, Michael Hammond and Diana Archangeli. 2011. Can you say [ṽ] or [x̃]. aerodynamics of nasalized fricatives in Scottish Gaelic. *Journal of the Acoustical Society of America*, 130 (4). 2550.
Brenner, Daniel, Andrea Davis, Natasha Warner, Andrew Carnie, Muriel Fisher, Jessamyn Schertz, Michael Hammond and Diana Archangeli. 2011. Can you say [ṽ] or [x̃]. aerodynamics of nasalized fricatives in Scottish Gaelic. Paper presented at the Acoustical Society of America annual conference, San Diego, 30 October–4 November.
Chen, Yan, Elise Bell, Michael Hammond, Andrew Carnie, Adam Ussishkin. in prep. A modern corpus of Scottish Gaelic constructed from on-line BBC Alba website. University of Arizona manuscript.
Clayton, Ian. Forthcoming. Revisiting Hebrides English. To appear in *English World-Wide*.
Clayton, Ian. 2017. Preaspiration in Hebrides English. *Journal of the International Phonetic Association* 47 (2). 155–181.
Davis, Andrea, Michael Hammond, Diana Archangeli, Andrew Carnie, Muriel Fisher, Natasha Warner, Collin Gorrie, Lionel Mathieu, Jessamyn Schertz. 2011. Perceptual and judgment-based experiments on Scottish Gaelic Svarabhakti. Paper presented at the 14th International Congress of Celtic Studies, Maynooth Ireland, 2–5 August.
Hammond, Michael, Andrea Davis, Natasha Warner, Andrew Carnie, Diana Archangeli, Muriel Fisher. 2014. Vowel insertion in Scottish Gaelic. *Phonology* 31. 123–153.
Hammond, Michael, Yan Chen, Elise Bell, Andrew Carnie, Diana Archangeli, Adam Ussishkin, Muriel Fisher (2017) Phonological restrictions on lenition in Scottish Gaelic. *Language* 93.2: 446–472. DOI: https://doi.org/10.1353/lan.2017.0020
Schertz, Jessamyn, Diana Archangeli, Andrew Carnie, Jae-Hyun Sung, Lionel Mathieu, Michael Hammond, Natasha Warner, Brenna Ward, Chelsea Milburn, Peter A. Brown, Daniel Brenner, Collin Gorrie and Andrea Davis. 2011. The articulation of epenthetic vowels in

Scottish Gaelic. Paper presented at the 14th International Congress of Celtic Studies, Maynooth Ireland, 2–5 August.

Sung, Jae-Hyun, Diana Archangeli, Ian Clayton, Daniel Brenner, Samuel Johnston, Michael Hammond, and Andrew Carnie. 2014. The articulation of lexical palatalization in Scottish Gaelic. Poster presented at the 167th Meeting of the Acoustical Society of America, Providence, RI, 5–9 May.

Sung, Jae-Hyun, Diana Archangeli, Daniel Brenner, Ian Clayton, Samuel Johnston, Michael Hammond, and Andrew Carnie. 2013. The articulation of Scottish Gaelic plain and palatalized consonants. Paper presented at Utrafest VI, Queen Margaret University, 6–8 November.

Warner, Natasha, Andrew Carnie, Daniel Brenner, Micaya Clymer, Lionel Mathieu, Jae-Hyun Sung, Jessamyn Schertz, Michael Hammond, Diana Archangeli, Muriel Fisher, and Collin Gorrie. 2011. Nasalization and frication in Scottish Gaelic. Paper presented at the14th International Congress of Celtic Studies, Maynooth Ireland, 2–5 August.

Warner, Natasha, Andrew Carnie, Muriel Fisher, Jessamyn Schertz, Lionel Mathieu, Collin Gorrie, Michael Hammond, and Diana Archangeli. 2011. The timing of perceptual cues in Scots Gaelic. Paper presented at the annual meeting of the Acoustical Society of America, San Diego, 30 October–4 November.

Warner, Natasha, Daniel Brenner, Jessamyn Schertz, Andrew Carnie, Muriel Fisher, and Michael Hammond. 2015. The aerodynamic puzzle of nasalized fricatives: Aerodynamic and perceptual evidence from Scottish Gaelic. *Laboratory Phonology* 6 (2). 1–44.

Warner, Natasha, Daniel Brenner, Jessamyn Schertz, Andrew Carnie, Muriel Fisher, and Hammond, Michael. 2014. The aerodynamic puzzle of Scottish Gaelic nasalized fricatives. Paper presented at Dag van de Fonetiek, Utrecht, the Netherlands, 17 December.

Warner, Natasha, Daniel Brenner and Andrew Carnie. 2012. Nasalized fricatives vs. approximants in Scottish Gaelic. Paper presented at the Celtic Linguistics Conference 7, University of Rennes II, 23 June.

Warner, Natasha, Ian Clayton, Andrew Carnie, Muriel Fisher, Daniel Brenner, Michael Hammond, Diana Archangeli, and Adam Ussishkin. 2013. Perception of Scottish Gaelic alternating (leniting) consonants. Paper presented at the annual meeting of the Acoustical Society of America, San Francisco, 2–6 December.

Warner, Natasha, Ian Clayton, Daniel Brenner, Andrew Carnie, Michael Hammond, Muriel Fisher. 2014. The effect of Gaelic initial consonant mutation on spoken word recognition. Paper presented at the Celtic Linguistics Conference 8, Edinburgh, 6–7 June.

Warner, Natasha, Ian Clayton, Daniel Brenner, Andrew Carnie, Michael Hammond, Muriel Fisher. 2014. The effect of Gaelic initial consonant mutation on spoken word recognition. Paper presented at the annual meeting of the Linguistic Society of America, Minneapolis, MN, 2–5 January.

Warner, Natasha, Jessamyn Schertz, Andrew Carnie, Muriel Fisher, Lionel Mathieu, Collin Gorrie, Michael Hammond and Diana Archangeli. 2011. Timing of perceptual cues in Scots Gaelic. *Journal of the Acoustical Society of America*. 130 (4). 2573.

Warner, Natasha, Jessamyn Schertz, Andrew Carnie, Muriel Fisher, Diana Archangeli, Michael Hammond, Lionel Mathieu and Collin Gorrie. 2012. Timing of perceptual cues in Scots Gaelic sound distinctions. Paper presented at the Celtic Linguistics Conference 7, University of Rennes II, 23 June.

Ussishkin, Adam, Natasha Warner, Ian Clayton, Daniel Brenner, Andrew Carnie, Michael Hammond, and Muriel Fisher. 2017. Lexical representation and processing of word-initial morphological alternations: Scottish Gaelic mutation. *Laboratory Phonology: Journal of the Association for Laboratory Phonology*, 8 (1). http://www.journal-labphon.org/article/10.5334/labphon.22/ (accessed 25 May 2017).

References

Bentin, Sholomo, Gregory McCarthy, and Charles C. Wood. 1985. Event-related potentials, lexical decision and semantic priming. *Electroencephalography and clinical Neurophysiology*, 60 (4). 343–355.

Bowern, Clare, and Natasha Warner. 2015. Lone wolves and wollaboration: A reply to Crippen and Robinson (2013). *Language Documentation & Conservation* 9. 59–85. https://scholarspace.manoa.hawaii.edu/bitstream/handle/10125/24634/bowern_warner.pdf (accessed 25 May 2007).

Clemens, Lauren E., Jessica Coon, Peter Graff, Niclás A. López, Adan Morgan, Pedro M. Pedro, and Narua Polinsky. 2012. Experimental design for field linguists. Paper presented at the annual meeting of the Linguistic Society of America, Portland OR, 5–8 January.

Crippen, James A., and Laura C. Robinson. 2013. In defense of the lone wolf: Collaboration in language documentation. *Language Documentation & Conservation*. 7. 123–135. https://scholarspace.manoa.hawaii.edu/bitstream/10125/4577/1/crippenrobinson.pdf (accessed 25 May 2017).

Czaykowska-Higgins, Ewa. 2009. Research models, community engagement, and linguistic fieldwork: Reflections on working within Canadian indigenous communities. *Language Documentation & Conservation* 3 (1). 15–50. https://scholarspace.manoa.hawaii.edu/bitstream/10125/4423/1/czaykowskahiggins.pdf (accessed 25 May 2017).

Dixon, Robert M. W. 1997. *The rise and fall of languages*. Cambridge University Press.

Dwelly, Edward. 2001. [1902–1912]. *Illustrated Gaelic-English dictionary*. Edinburgh: Birlinn.

Green, Anthony D. 2006. The independence of phonology and morphology: The Celtic mutations. *Lingua* 116 (11). 1946–1985.

MacBain, Alexander. 1911. *An etymological dictionary of the Gaelic language*. University of Stirling dissertation. http://www.ceantar.org/Dicts/MB2/index.html (accessed 25 May 2017).

MacFarlane, M. 1912. *The School Gaelic dictionary*. Stirling: Eneas Mackay. https://archive.org/details/cu31924026841043 (accessed 25 May 2017).

Mark, Colin. 2003. *The Gaelic-English dictionary*. London: Routledge.

Norcliffe, Elisabeth Alice C. Harris, T. Florian Jaeger. 2015. Cross-linguistic psycholinguistics and its critical role in theory development: Early beginnings and recent developments. *Language Cognition and Neuroscience* 30. 1009–1031

Pike, L., and Maolalaigh, R. Ó. 2013. Faclair na Gàidhlig and Corpas na Gàidhlig: New Approaches Make Sense. E-prints. http://eprints.gla.ac.uk/119406/7/119406.pdf (accessed 25 May 2017).

Rice, Keren. 2010. The linguist's responsibilities to the community of speakers: Community-based research. In Lenore A. Grenoble and N. Louanna Furbee (eds.) *Language documentation: Practice and values*, 25–36. Amsterdam: John Benjamins.

Rice, Keren. 2011. Documentary linguistics and community relations. *Language Documentation & Conservation* 5. 187–207.

Whalen, Doug and Joyce M. McDonough. 2015. Taking the laboratory into the field. *Annual Review of Linguistics* 1 (1). 395–415.

Margaret Florey
Transforming the landscape of language revitalization work in Australia: The Documenting and Revitalising Indigenous Languages training model

Abstract: This paper explores the motivation underpinning the creation of the Documenting and Revitalising Indigenous Languages (DRIL) Training Program, a locally responsive and highly flexible grassroots training model that was developed in Australia by the author and launched in 2010. DRIL is overtly political in its orientation and was designed to serve the expressed needs of Indigenous language activists. It aims to create a transformative social impact through building skills in linguistics and language revitalization strategies alongside a greater sense of agency so that Aboriginal and Torres Strait Islander people can develop, run and control their own language projects themselves. In the eight years since its inception, over 550 Indigenous people representing 114 different languages from all Australian states and territories have taken part in DRIL workshops. The DRIL model has now expanded to incorporate several different strands of training including the foundational flexible mode, a professional development program, and two nationally recognized qualifications. We are beginning to see transformation taking place as the participants build their linguistic skills, move with greater confidence into leadership roles in language projects, develop new partnerships with linguists in which community members retain control, and start creating their own community-accessible materials.

Keywords: DRIL, RNLD, training, agency, revitalization

---

* First and foremost, my deep thanks go to the people across Australia who have participated in this program and who are working with great dedication and determination to breathe life and strong voice into their languages. I gratefully acknowledge the support of the Indigenous Languages and Arts program administered by the Australian Federal Government's Department of Communication and the Arts. Grants from the ILA program have permitted RNLD to develop and run the Documenting and Revitalising Indigenous Languages Program since its inception in 2009. I also thank former DRIL Trainer Jessica Solla for discussions that have contributed to this paper.

Margaret Florey, Resource Network for Linguistic Diversity, Box 9, 19–21 Argyle Place South, Carlton, Victoria 3053, Australia, margaret.florey@gmail.com

https://doi.org/10.1515/9783110527018-018

1 Introduction

This paper explores the trajectory of the development of the Documenting and Revitalising Indigenous Languages Training Program (DRIL)—an innovative model that was developed in Australia to offer grassroots training to Aboriginal and Torres Strait Islander people and increase their sense of agency to develop, implement and control their own language documentation and revitalization projects. DRIL is a program of the Resource Network for Linguistic Diversity (RNLD Inc.), an Australian-based not-for-profit organization that was founded in 2004. Margaret Florey, one of the co-founders, first applied for and received Australian Federal Government funding for the RNLD in 2009.[1] This marked a critical turning point in the development of the organization and its programs. Florey was able to shift the focus of her work from the university sector to the RNLD and begin developing the DRIL training model. The RNLD thus entered a new phase, moving from being an online knowledge and information sharing hub run primarily by volunteers to becoming a key national organization delivering grassroots training to Indigenous people across Australia. The DRIL program is now the cornerstone of the RNLD's work, and its positive impact is widely felt on language revitalization activities being undertaken by Aboriginal people across the country.

This paper discusses the motivation for the creation of the DRIL model and how it has grown over just eight years from a small program delivering flexible grassroots training to a larger program offering several different strands of training including national qualifications. Over 550 Indigenous people have taken part in DRIL workshops through this time, and we are beginning to see transformation taking place as the participants build their linguistic skills, move with greater confidence in to leadership roles in language projects, develop new partnerships with linguists in which community members retain control, and start creating their own community-accessible materials.

2 The DRIL training program: motivation, background and goals

The development of the Documenting and Revitalising Indigenous Languages training model grew from the confluence of several socio-political factors. First, it

---

[1] The Federal Government grant scheme that is the primary funder of Indigenous language work in Australia was first known as the Maintenance of Indigenous Languages and Records (MILR) program and later become the Indigenous Languages Support (ILS) Scheme and then the Indigenous Languages and Arts (ILA) Program.

is well known and widely reported that linguistic diversity is challenged in every corner of the globe, and that scenario is reflected in the papers in this volume. Australia's Indigenous languages have been heavily impacted by processes similar to those that are threatening Indigenous languages worldwide. The vast majority of Australia's 250 or more Indigenous languages are highly endangered and in urgent need of both language documentation and language revitalization activities. For example, Marmion et al report in the Second National Indigenous Languages Survey (2014: xii) that "Examination of the NILS2 data allows us to make the assessment that there are now only around 120 languages still spoken. Of these about 13 can be considered strong, five fewer than in NILS1."

Second, Aboriginal and Torres Strait Islander people press for the right to reclaim, speak and transmit their languages. These rights continue to be contested in Australia despite a deepening understanding of the link between Indigenous languages and identity, health and wellbeing, and a growing body of research evidencing these links (see AIATSIS and FATSIL 2005, and Whalen, Moss and Baldwin 2016). Australia did not become a signatory to the 2007 United Nations *Declaration on the rights of Indigenous peoples* (UN 2007) in which Articles 13 and 14 offer recognition and rights for Indigenous languages. Through the last fifteen to twenty years, calls have increased for constitutional recognition of Australia's First Peoples along with recognition that Aboriginal and Torres Strait Islander languages were this country's first languages. The Australian Parliament set up a Joint Select Committee on Constitutional Recognition of Aboriginal and Torres Strait Islander Peoples in 2012 that recommended that Australians vote in a referendum to alter the Australian constitution on these issues.[2] Reconciliation Australia launched the Recognise campaign in 2013 to press for recognition on these two matters. While the issue has gained some support, several consecutive parliaments have deferred setting the date for a referendum out of concern that it will not succeed.

Third, despite the high level of language endangerment, the urgent need for actions to redress this situation, and the clear desire on the part of Aboriginal and Islander people to reclaim and speak their languages, there continues to be a lack of control by Indigenous people over strategies and programs to document and revitalize those languages. Very few Indigenous people in Australia are working in the field of linguistics, and language documentation activities in this country continue predominantly to be undertaken and led by non-Indigenous linguists. This of course is not unique to Australia: for example, Czaykowska-Higgins (2009: 20) notes that in Canada "primary linguistic research or fieldwork on Indigenous

---

[2] http://www.recognise.org.au/about/expert-panel-report/

languages in the last 100 years has been led by researchers who are not members of the language-using community."

These three factors were all central to the creation and development of a new training model that is overtly political in its orientation. At its inception, the primary aim of the Documenting and Revitalising Indigenous Languages training program was to create a transformative social impact through building a greater sense of agency so that Aboriginal and Torres Strait Islander people could develop, run and control their own language projects themselves. This remains the core mission of the program, and achievement of this social impact is intrinsically linked to increasing the pool of trained Indigenous linguists through delivering grassroots, community-centered training in linguistics and language documentation and revitalization methods.

3 Identifying the barriers

Concern has been expressed nationally and internationally about the gap between the aspirations of Indigenous people to lead language revitalization and documentation projects and their engagement with such projects. In order to work towards the goals of the DRIL program, it was necessary first to identify the barriers that are implicated in hindering the aspirations of Indigenous people in this field and then second to develop a training environment in which those barriers could be addressed.

The first barrier to be identified was that formal education was only meeting the needs and goals of very few members of Indigenous communities who were seeking to study linguistics and participate at a higher level in documentation and revitalization activities with their languages. Many Indigenous Australians continue to feel alienated from an educational system which has failed them and which does not feel safe. This perspective has been discussed by Yorta Yorta environmental advocate Lee Joachim, who is passionate about education. He is vocal about changes that need to be made to develop ways that Indigenous and non-Indigenous people can learn from each other and work out how to walk forward together (see Bowra nd.). Yet Joachim expresses a strong concern that "formal education is oppressive and tormenting" (pers. comm. 2016) and that universities are culturally and emotionally not safe places for Indigenous people who are living between two worlds. This perspective accords with the experience of linguist Lesley Woods, who points out that being part of a largely non-Indigenous university system can be both undermining and isolating for Indigenous linguists in Australia. Woods says that "At times I have been appalled at the way the literature fails to acknowledge that in fact Indigenous people themselves might at some point study, read the literature and take issue with the research methodologies" (pers. comm. 2016). She highlights the critical need for different models and an effective support network that would also allow challenging issues and experiences to be addressed openly and safely. Ofelia Zepeda has also made a powerful contribution to these topics in discussing the challenges she faced in mediating between her intimate language and cultural knowledge, the requirements of a collaborative research project, and the (often negative) responses of members of her community to her dual roles as a researcher and language teacher (Zepeda and Hill 1998).

The wider resonance of these personal reports about alienation from the formal education system became apparent and could be quantified in the results of a survey that was administered in June 2016 to participants in RNLD's Professional Development strand. The participants were asked to respond on a 10-point scale[3] to 43 questions in three sections on 1) Training and language work, 2) Training and daily life, and 3) Training and the future. In Section 3, the responses to "I want to continue learning more about language work" averaged 9.6 and to "I would like to study in a Certificate program" averaged 9.1. This provides clear evidence of this group's enthusiasm about continuing study when they are able to access courses that are culturally appropriate and take place in a safe learning environment, as is the case for RNLD's Certificate programs (described in Section 5 below). In contrast, the participants' ambivalence to the university environment is clearly seen in the responses to "I would like to study at university" which averaged just 5.3. This response was the lowest in the survey, and it is stark against the average of 8.2 for the other 42 questions in the survey. It supports the oral evidence that universities continue to feel unsafe, alienating and oppressive to many Indigenous people and that this is an ongoing barrier to participation in higher education.

In the Australian context (and more widely), the second barrier requiring attention was that very few Aboriginal and Torres Strait Islander people are working in the field of linguistics in Australia. In her PhD thesis, Jo Caffery[4] analysed thirty years of courses and graduates of linguistics training that had been specifically designed for Australian Indigenous adults within the Center for Australian Languages and Linguistics (CALL) at Batchelor Institute of Indigenous Tertiary Education (BIITE).[5] Caffery interviewed 98 participants and found that "graduates of linguistics training specifically designed for remote Indigenous

---

[3] 1=strongly disagree, 5 = neither agree or disagree, 10 = strongly agree
[4] Caffery was formerly Coordinator and Senior Lecturer at the Center for Australian Languages and Linguistics.
[5] CALL is now the Australian Center for Indigenous Knowledges and Education (ACIKE) — a collaborative partnership between Batchelor Institute of Indigenous Tertiary Education (BIITE) and Charles Darwin University.

adults are not working in the field or are achieving limited language documentation and maintenance outcomes" (2008: iii). At the same time, linguists and lecturers Margaret Carew and Gail Woods from the BIITE were also exploring and writing about models for training Indigenous people in language work and teaching skills in Central Australia. They noted that "In order to retain control of their languages, it is becoming increasingly important that the speakers or descendants of speakers have the necessary linguistic skills to be employed in their communities to do the language work in these areas" (2008). However, Carew and Woods identified the challenge that very few employment opportunities for Indigenous people trained in linguistics and language work exist outside of schools and language centers. Such opportunities often involve working in a language consultant capacity for projects funded through grants. Linguist Jeanie Bell takes up this point, discussing the powerlessness that can be experienced by Aboriginal people involved in linguistics projects: "Aboriginal people working in language teams on collaborative research projects or revival and maintenance language programs, may feel powerless because of a lack of experience, training, knowledge or understanding of linguistic concepts" (Bell 2010: 84).

Looking at this issue from another angle, Florey, Penfield and Tucker (2009) (building on the earlier work of Penfield, Flores and Tucker 2007, Penfield 2008, and Florey 2008) examined in some depth the highly stereotyped use of the terms "linguist" and "language activist" in the literature on documenting and revitalizing endangered languages. They found that

> [A contrast between these terms] demarcates respective roles in the language documentation and conservation enterprise. The distinction assumes that the core activities of language documentation and description are undertaken by a linguist: that is, typically someone who is non-Indigenous, external to the language community and formally trained in linguistics. In contrast, the core activities of language revitalization and maintenance will be undertaken by a language activist: that is, typically someone who is Indigenous, internal to the language community and who lacks (higher level) formal training in linguistics.

This contrast is also apparent in the literature on community-based language research (CBLR). Czaykowska-Higgins (2009: 19), for example, writes that "I will simply assume very broadly that there are two types of participants in linguistic fieldwork research: outsider linguists and members of a language-speaking community, however that community may be constituted." As Florey, Penfield and Tucker (2009) note, the stereotyped role assigned to Indigenous participants in language projects perpetuates an "outdated assumption that members of language communities are not involved in, or do not aspire to be involved in the activities of language documentation and description." It reinforces the perception that is widely held amongst Indigenous language activists in Australia that linguistics is primarily the business of non-Indigenous people.

4 Creating a flexible training model

The identification of the barriers outlined above led us to ask what changes needed to and could be put in place to bridge the gap and better meet the aspiration of Aboriginal people to control and run their language programs. A series of questions arose. What models for training in linguistics would facilitate this field becoming less alienating and more open to Aboriginal people? Was it possible to create a safe environment for learning that would build a strong set of skills in linguistics and support the leadership goals of Aboriginal people aiming to control and deliver their own language projects? This exploration was not taking place in isolation and, as outlined below, these questions were being investigated from a range of perspectives by Indigenous and non-Indigenous linguists and educators in different parts of Australia and internationally. The successful and long-standing North American training programs such as AILDI, NILI and CILLDI provided a potential starting point for creating the DRIL model in Australia.

The American Indian Language Development Institute (AILDI) is the oldest of the North American institutes (McCarty et al. 1997, 2001). Created in 1978, AILDI's mission is to provide critical training to strengthen efforts to revitalize and promote the use of Indigenous languages across generations.[6] For almost forty years, three weeks of workshops have been held each summer at the University of Arizona. Zepeda (2011) notes that AILDI "is one of the longest running and most successful training and education models for Indigenous educators working in the area of language education, research, maintenance, revitalization and documentation." It has inspired several sister institutes.

The Northwest Indian Language Institute (NILI) was created at the University of Oregon in 1997. NILI offers a two-week summer institute in linguistics, an indigenous language, teaching methods, and language activism. NILI staff also work with tribes and organizations on various short and long term projects.[7] The Canadian Indigenous Languages and Literacy Development Institute (CILLDI) was also modelled on AILDI.[8] Now in its sixteenth year, CILLDI is a three-week-long intensive summer school held at the University of Alberta (see S. Rice et al 2009).

---

6 See http://aildi.arizona.edu/
7 See http://pages.uoregon.edu/nwili/
8 See http://www.cilldi.ualberta.ca/

CILLDI also now offers a six-course Community Linguist Certificate that is delivered over three summers. S. Rice (2011) reported that 41 students representing eight languages from the Athapaskan/Dene, Algonquian, and Siouan language families had completed the Certificate by 2011.

In providing training that is targeted towards Indigenous people and that strengthens a network between the trainees, the institutes in part provide an example that directly speaks to the Australian setting and needs. They demonstrate that intensive training in linguistics and language teaching can create powerful outcomes. However, structurally and socio-politically the intensive summer program model didn't address some of the changes that we felt were needed for the Australian context. Carew and Woods (2008) had demonstrated the value of community-based training. Their successful project-based model was delivered on-site in communities, giving more flexibility in delivery and allowing training to be "integrated into the social and cultural framework of the community" (2008: 3). Caffery's analysis of the Batchelor Institute courses had also found that "changes are needed in (i) curriculum development and delivery methods, (ii) the policy and practices of educational institutions, particularly with respect to literacy and student numbers, and (iii) access to regional language centers to help negotiate cultural and project support issues in remote communities" (2008: iii).

The influence of the international institutes and the Central Australian experiences can all be seen in the development of DRIL. The core features of the DRIL program have been created to directly address and respond to the issues and needs discussed above. In the sections that follow, I outline those features in more depth, beginning with the training model that was first envisaged and that began to be developed in 2009. This is now known as the *Flexible DRIL* program to distinguish it from the several other program strands that have since been created.

4.1 Building trust

The DRIL model was designed to be highly flexible and responsive to the very diverse training needs identified by language communities across Australia, encompassing strong language, revitalization, and reclamation language situations. Two factors are key to the success of the model. Although we make people aware of the availability of the DRIL program, trainers do not actively seek out training sites or participants but rather work only in response to requests for workshops. Those requests have come from individuals, family groups, community groups, language teams, staff of Aboriginal Language Centers, art centers, traditional owner organizations and other Indigenous organizations. Second, prior to the commencement of each workshop, a participation agreement is signed by the trainers and the participants. This confirms a) that the participants wish to take part in the workshop and b) that "the Resource Network for Linguistic Diversity will not have any rights to store, use or distribute materials that are made as part of this training workshop unless a separate agreement is negotiated." This protocol was put in place in the pilot phase of the DRIL model to counter earlier negative experiences of linguists removing materials or not sharing their recordings and publications resulting from linguistic research.

There is no set training program that is used across each location. Rather, a different program is tailored in negotiation with each particular training site. Over a series of phone or Skype calls, the trainers come to understand the broader goals and the specific project that the participants wish to undertake. We then map out a suggested program for a workshop that usually runs over three days. The draft program typically includes three or four of the training modules that are described in the next section below. The program remains flexible throughout the workshop in the sense that it may be modified several times based on the needs and the responses of the participants. The trainers typically carry a range of equipment to workshops in order to be able to change the program responsively.

Trust builds quickly in this intensive and responsive environment. Trauma is a common experience and deep hurts from loss are often triggered by language activities. We emphasize in our workshops that all emotions are welcome and we are privileged to hear and witness deeply moving stories of the experiences of the participants—in regard to their histories, their family lives, and their language work. Again, as appropriate, these stories can be woven into the training and transformed into part of the revitalization activities.

4.2 On-site training

A critical issue faced by many Aboriginal people living in small and isolated communities or the more distant rural towns is the lack of access to training opportunities. To counter this, from the outset DRIL workshops have always been delivered on-site regardless of the remoteness of the community or the Indigenous organization requesting training. In order to ensure that a sense of familiarity and safety is built into the training program, we ask the participants to find a location for the workshop. Generally, the location is only restricted by the training topics and whether they involve the use of technologies and will thus require access to electricity. With families and community groups, we have trained on people's traditional lands (by rivers and billabongs), in community centers, church halls, people's homes (in kitchens, porches and back yards), parks, public libraries and

Indigenous organizations. About a third of our work is undertaken in Aboriginal language centers and these workshops have tended to include a mix of work indoors in the center and outside in various environmental settings. Very few of our workshops have been held in schools as earlier negative educational experiences mean that they are often not felt to be safe places.

Following this grassroots model, 123 DRIL workshops have been delivered since 2010 in 37 locations across Australia including six sites in New South Wales, six in the Northern Territory, nine in Queensland, six in South Australia, one in Tasmania, three in Victoria and six in Western Australia. These workshops have encompassed a wide range of different language scenarios and have been requested by Aboriginal language centers, Indigenous organizations, community groups, and schools.

4.3 Participants

Up to the time of writing, 550 Indigenous adults have taken part in Flexible DRIL workshops. We aim to limit the number of participants in a workshop to 15–20 people in order to be able to work intensively and flexibly with people from very different backgrounds. There are no formal enrolment processes or entry requirements for the Flexible DRIL workshops and no particular educational background is expected or required. The training method largely involves oral delivery and is available and accessible to participants regardless of their level of literacy. There are also no age restrictions for DRIL workshops. Approximately 10% of the participants have been children aged 16 or younger, and the adult participants cover all age groups from teenagers to the very elderly.

The on-site training model has also been crucial in providing much wider access to our workshops. Participants do not have to travel away from family responsibilities and they are often able to negotiate with their workplaces to attend. The community setting means that people can linger around the edge of a workshop during the first day and watch to see how it works and what might be expected of them. When it feels safe, they can begin to join in. A typical example comes from a recent workshop held in a small northern Victorian town. A boy of about eleven came to the workshop with his mother. He was struggling at school and had taken the day off. At first, he sat back from the group and played on his phone. Gradually, his attention was drawn to the training. He watched for a while, and then moved his seat closer and began first to listen and then to participate. He was excited to join a group of men in some practical language exercises. The next day, his older sister also came to the workshop. This family is now working together to practice the language skills that they are learning.

4.4 Training topics

Over the last seven years, the Flexible DRIL training program has grown organically to include some 41 modules (or subjects) within the eight topic areas outlined below. Some of the modules were part of the initial curriculum framework developed by the author, including those focused on linguistics, making and editing recordings, searching for and retrieving archival resources, and sharing skills. Other modules, such as those in the *Developing a Language Project* cluster, were first requested by the staff of Aboriginal language centers to support the ability of language workers to develop their own language projects. Yet other modules were added in response to the specific needs of community members in a particular site. These include the Master-Apprentice immersion language learning methods, making animations, digitizing recordings, and developing dictionaries. In all cases, the training is very hands-on and quickly moves from theory to practice.

Developing a Language Project: these six modules cover all stages of planning and developing a language project, from choosing the topic and goals of the project, to considering ethical and cultural issues and setting up protocols, creating a language team, writing a grant application for funding, finding existing information and resources about the language, and developing partnerships and networks.

Using Technologies: the seven modules in this topic begin with the basics of using computers and the internet. This topic also covers making and editing digital audio and video recordings, creating metadata, and learning to digitize heritage recordings. Participants can also learn to search online archives and other web-based resources to find and retrieve language materials.

Master-Apprentice Language Learning Program: these six modules focus on the skills included in developing and running a Master-Apprentice team in the home, community or workplace. They begin with an overview of the Master-Apprentice principles and move on to learning and using a range of language learning methods that develop communicative ability in the target language, planning sessions, and keeping a journal of progress and challenges faced by the team.

Models for Language Revitalization: this cluster of four modules assists in understanding different models that can be used to revitalize or reclaim a language, and in going through a process to select an appropriate strategy for a particular language situation.

Creating Language Resources: this topic cover the skills needed to produce language resources ranging from print to audio, video and animations. The dictionary module helps learners to understand about different types of dictionaries, to choose the kind of dictionary they want to create, and the best software program for the project.

Linguistics and Language Documentation: ten modules are currently offered in this topic area. They begin with an introduction to the core areas in linguistics and the kind of work that linguists do. Learners can then choose topics in phonetics, morphology, and syntax and more advanced topics are offered in language documentation and transcription.

Public Awareness: this module develops the ability to publicize Indigenous language issues in the wider world. Participants learn about public awareness strategies, how to use PowerPoint, create a media campaign, make a presentation, and write about their language.

Sharing and Applying Skills: the three modules in this topic focus on sharing skills more widely in the community and workplace, and planning for work and further study.

4.5 Number of workshops

The number of workshops we deliver varies from site to site and is dictated both by the needs of the community or organization and also by the capacity of our small training team. In some cases, only one or two workshops are needed for the participants in the site to be able to continue with their own work. This is exemplified by the Tasmanian Aboriginal Center in Launceston. Much knowledge about the languages of Tasmania was lost due to the widespread loss of life in that state during the early colonial era. Aboriginal Tasmanians are working with great determination to bring their language back through Palawa Kani, a composite language reconstructed from the remaining materials. The community is highly motivated, very organized, and strongly independent. To date, we have run just two workshops at the request of the TAC in 2014–2015. Each workshop has focused on specific skills that are designed to strengthen the abilities of the team of Palawa Kani teachers. The group then confidently continues applying the skills with their language work knowing that they can contact us for further training as the need arises.

In contrast, between 2012 and 2015, eight workshops were delivered at the Woorabinda community in Central Queensland. There are two Traditional Owner groups on Woorabinda country and approximately fifty other language groups that were forcibly removed from their own land first to Taroom mission and then to Woorabinda from across Queensland in the early twentieth century. This extremely complex site has been the subject of great trauma and loss. Very few people speak their heritage language and the DRIL workshops permitted people to begin working with archival materials to start learning their language.[9] Community elder Anthony Henry says "There are many people like me, whose language and culture was virtually taken away. I grew up not understanding my status as an Aboriginal, with this need to make myself whole again. In the process of losing our language, we have been lost as people. But I have now found speakers of my mother's tongue [Barada] and I am using words salvaged by linguists many years ago. It's very powerful" (Burdon 2016). This site has required more training workshops to allow participants to work at their own pace as they uncover and process the trauma of their past.

4.6 Follow up and support

The vast majority of the sites in which we have trained have requested additional training and to date we have delivered on average four workshops to each site. DRIL trainers also continue to be available to training participants between workshops. With some participants, we have had weekly or fortnightly phone calls or Skype meetings to follow up with progress and to brainstorm strategies and activities. An online DRIL Resource Room provides resources to participants, including worksheets and study notes and a series of *how-to* videos covering topics such as downloading and using Audacity to edit audio recordings, transcribing with ELAN, digitizing heritage recordings, and using PowerPoint.

5 Nationally accredited certificates

The DRIL model has been constantly evolving through the past eight years. Through the early years of developing the model, we had argued that the flexible delivery was a key defining feature of DRIL and that our training program was designed to meet the needs of people who wanted to build a specific set of skills and were not seeking a qualification. We felt that as people were nurtured in learning within this safe informal educational environment, they would potentially gain the confidence to move on as desired to formal education to continue their studies in linguistics or language teaching. Indeed, we designed a module that was intended to provide the information and support to help them make this transition. It is easier in retrospect to see that this was naïve. As

---

9 Some of the historical background to Woorabinda is reported in Burdon 2016, who also discusses the language work that RNLD has done with members of the community.

the training program began to gain a strong, positive reputation in communities and organizations, DRIL participants were keen to continue learning in an environment in which they were flourishing and we began to receive requests for qualifications in language work.

In 2012, we were asked by our Federal government funding agency to investigate the possibility of accrediting our training modules and providing qualifications. This met with some initial reluctance, flowing primarily from concerns about remaining true to our mission and also about our capacity to undertake this step. However, we could see the value of qualifications to the people with whom we were working, and we agreed to take up this challenge. We now find ourselves excited by the new pathways that we are able to offer. At the same time, it is important to note that alongside the Certificate programs we are continuing to offer the Flexible DRIL program. This program is crucial in building relationships and the safe learning environment that makes it possible for some people to continue on to Certificate programs. It is also clear that not all of our participants wish to attain a qualification. Some people want to build very specific skills to undertake a particular project, and we will continue to work to meet these needs.

Australia's Vocational Education and Training (VET) sector is complex, and it has been a steep learning curve to understand the requirements of the Australian Skills Qualification Authority that oversees the process of accrediting certificate courses. It has been a slow process for the staff of our small organization to create the certificates while also continuing to deliver Flexible DRIL workshops. We added a Training Support Officer to our team to manage the paperwork involved with accreditation and record-keeping. VET courses include Certificates I–IV, Diploma and Advanced Diploma qualifications. The complexity and level of difficulty of the courses (including hours of training, assessment items, and literacy requirements), increases from the lowest level of a Certificate I through to the diplomas. Typically, Certificates I and II provide basic skills often undertaken under supervision and assessment can be oral. Certificates III and IV require more independent work and are designed to build a pathway to further learning.

5.1 Certificate III in Aboriginal Languages for Communities and Workplaces

In 2013, we began developing a Certificate III in Aboriginal Languages for Communities and Workplaces and in January 2015, the RNLD succeeded in gaining national accreditation for this course (assigned the national code 10541NAT). This Certificate III takes place in three one-week blocks with some work to be undertaken between blocks. It includes thirteen core units[10] that cover a range of skills. The Certificate III has been designed to provide a foundation in Aboriginal languages and linguistics. It develops knowledge of the Australian language family and the relationships between languages, and introduces core concepts in linguistics and methods to revitalize Aboriginal languages. The certificate also includes basic skills in computing and use of the internet, and covers methods for making and editing recordings and digitizing heritage recordings. Students undertake a unit in raising awareness about Aboriginal languages, and learn to create publicity materials and make presentations.

Delivery of the Certificate III was launched in April 2016. It was piloted in two Aboriginal language centers in Western Australia that have been part of the DRIL program since it first began in 2010: Wangka Maya Pilbara Aboriginal Language Center in South Hedland and Mirima Dawang Woorlab-gerring Language and Culture Center in Kununurra. Eleven participants representing seven different languages joined the course at Wangka Maya, while ten participants from two language groups took part in Kununurra. Seventeen of the twenty-one participants in the two sites graduated with their Certificate III in October and November 2016.

Holding true to the principles underpinning our programs, the Certificate was delivered on-site at the language centers. We have worked hard to ensure this course is accessible to people across a range of literacy skills. The materials are written in plain English, and were further modified as necessary throughout the pilot workshops. Our delivery mode remains largely oral and very hands-on.

It was very exciting to work with the students in the first two cohorts. We could not have predicted the pride and very high level of motivation that the students displayed in working towards this qualification. The twenty-one students ranged in age from 31 to 57. Few of them completed high school—indeed, most only reached Year 10—and only two or three have any post-school qualifications. Most of these people are engaged in their language work on a day-to-day basis, including those employed in the language center or in a school. One of the greatest areas of excitement was seeing the students gain a deeper understanding of linguistics and an awakening awareness that this could open or advance a career path for them.

5.2 Certificate II in Master Apprentice Language Learning Program

At the same time that the Certificate III was being processed for accreditation, we began developing a Certificate II in the Master Apprentice Language Learning Program. The RNLD had helped to launch the Master Apprentice Program in

---

10 See http://www.rnld.org/CertIII

Australia in 2012 when we organized two national workshops that were led by a US training team from the Advocates for Indigenous California Language Survival (AICLS), including Leanne Hinton, Nancy Steele and Stan Rodriguez. Thirty-six Indigenous people from thirty-one language groups across Australia took part in these workshops. This model has had to be adapted to the Australian model to allow for the many locations in which there are not fluent speakers who can act as Master speakers in Master-Apprentice teams (see Florey and Olawsky 2013). These adaptations have been built into the Certificate II course.

National accreditation for 10124NAT Certificate II in Master Apprentice Language Learning Program was achieved in October 2015.[11] Students in this course are required to take eight core units, six of which focus on building skills in the Master Apprentice method, and two of which provide foundational skills in computing and use of the internet. The Master Apprentice units build the foundation for and practice in this model. Students are trained in immersion language learning methods, they form a Master Apprentice team, and learn to create resources and plan sessions for members of the team. The course includes a twenty-week practicum in which students undertake a minimum of seven hours of immersion language learning in their team. The Certificate II was launched in February 2017 at the Far West Languages Center in Ceduna, South Australia, and the first cohort completed the certificate in August 2017.

5.3 Certificate IV in Documenting and Revitalising Indigenous Languages

The next stage in building our suite of qualifications is to return to the development of a Certificate IV in Documenting and Revitalising Indigenous Languages. The Certificate IV course will continue from the Certificate III and will focus more intensively on higher-level skills in linguistics. It will be the capstone of our Certificate programs and will provide a critical qualification for Indigenous staff in Aboriginal language centers. We plan to negotiate a pathway for articulation to university entry for the Certificate IV graduates.

5.4 Partnership RTO agreement

In the Australian context, accredited certificates can only be delivered by a Registered Training Organization (RTO). The RTO requirements are onerous and not reasonably achievable by a small organization such as the RNLD at this stage in

---

[11] See http://www.rnld.org/CertII

our development. Further, we continue to work towards the goal of the certificate programs being delivered by Indigenous trainers under the umbrella of an Indigenous RTO. To this end, the RNLD began negotiating a partnership agreement with the Australian Indigenous Leadership Center (AILC) in 2015. The AILC is a leading Indigenous organization that delivers Certificate II and IV training in leadership and governance. The partnership RTO agreement that was signed in December 2015 opens exciting opportunities for cross-fertilization between both organizations. Our certificate programs were brought on scope with the AILC in early 2016, allowing us to begin delivery of the courses.

6 Professional development program

In 2014, the RNLD was offered the opportunity by our Federal Government funding agency to create a Professional Development Program. This was a targeted program envisaged by the funding agency as a means of furthering the careers of Aboriginal people employed in language centers. The RNLD was asked rather broadly to "provide training opportunities to Indigenous language organizations for professional development of language workers." We interpreted this brief as an opportunity to address the following goals:
- increase the professional capacity of Indigenous people engaged in language work,
- strengthen the participants' knowledge of linguistics, language documentation, and language revitalization methods,
- develop the capacity of Indigenous language activists to become trainers and share skills with other people in families, communities and workplaces, and
- help to build a professional network amongst Indigenous language activists.

Eleven participants were invited to join the first Professional Development workshop that ran over eight days in November 2014. The participants came from eight sites across Victoria, South Australia, Western Australia and the Northern Territory, and represented eleven different languages. All participants had previously taken part in DRIL workshops, and were selected because of their high motivation, drive to lead language revitalization projects, and their growing interest and skills in linguistics. Over the course of the eight days, they explored the grammars of their languages and deepened their understanding of linguistic structures and terminology. In their final presentations, they talked movingly about their language journeys, what it meant to begin studying linguistics, and what they want for their languages.

This group came back together for a Stage II workshop in July 2015. In this eight day workshop, the participants moved on to more advanced topics in linguistics and began to write creatively in their languages. This time, their presentations included a puppet play, an audio story in a language that had not been spoken for an estimated 135 years, a poem reflecting on the process of working to revitalize a language, an exploration of onomatopoeia in bird names, an animation about learning linguistic terminology, and a lively language teaching session.

A second grant permitted us to build on this success and invite a second cohort of participants to join the Professional Development program in November 2015. This time, the thirteen participants came from 11 sites in New South Wales, Queensland, Western Australia, South Australia and Victoria. They represented fifteen different languages, only two of which are spoken fluently while most are the target of reclamation programs. With our experience from the first cohort of PD participants, we were able to accelerate the program of linguistic study for the second group. One participant who has been deeply frustrated for a decade by her inability to understand and use the grammar of her own language explains her experience thus: "It was a week of immersion in linguistics and language. By the time I left there I was all over transitive/intransitive, finally got "regressive assimilation", and actually really understood the uses of ergative/instrumental suffixes, locative/temporal suffixes, perlative, ablative, allative and causal suffixes too. There was the luxury of asking and asking and asking until you got it. It was a huge turning point and I learned that it is possible, for those that have the desire, patience and knowledge, to explain even the most complex of linguistic concepts so that they could be understood by the layperson" (Sharon Edgar-Jones, pers. comm.). This cohort came back together in June 2016 for a Stage II workshop that continued their intensive training in linguistics.

Fourteen of the participants from both cohorts were invited to come together in late May 2017 for our first Stage III professional development workshop. This focused on the theme of *Building Indigenous leadership in language work*. Linguistic sessions were also included on Project planning, Complex sentences, Historical linguistics and language change, and Semantics (word creation).

In 2016, RNLD also developed a new project with five of the Professional Development participants, drawn from both cohorts, who planned to work together to create a community-driven framework for creating language learner's guides. This project derived from the deep frustration that the participants (and many other community members) feel about grammars and dictionaries that have been written by non-indigenous linguists that aren't accessible to indigenous communities. One participant captured the feelings of many people when she wrote in a letter supporting the grant application that such resources "alienated would be learners with [the] uncompromising use of jargonistic terms and actually inhibited grass roots community efforts to revitalize language." Unfortunately, the project has not yet succeeded in attracting funding. We plan to continue to work with the group to seek other sources of funding because of its importance to their communities and also to the team members. It will take their skills to the next level and see them apply their growing linguistic knowledge to the writing of learner's guides for their own languages. It will also put them in mentoring roles with other communities as they support the wider implementation of their framework.

7 Linking up: Partnerships between linguists and trainees

A further important program that has been developed by the RNLD through the past five years (re)links members of communities with linguists who have worked on the documentation of their languages. Crucially, the power in these newly formed relationships remains with the community members. The link is established only at their behest and supports the trainees in further developing and applying their linguistic skills. We are finding that this program is powerful in building or supporting new relationships that are beneficial to all parties.

In 2012 and 2013, linguist Gavan Breen returned with DRIL trainers to Woorabinda community in Central Queensland. As noted earlier, Woorabinda has been the site of massive dislocation and trauma through the past ninety years and community members estimate that approximately fifty different languages are represented in this community. In the 1960s and 1970s, Breen built an extraordinary database of materials for some 51 languages across western Queensland, South Australia and the Northern Territory.[12] It was very moving to be part of the workshop in which he returned to the community members recordings that he had made with their family members some fifty years earlier (see Burdon 2016). Very warm relationships have grown between the community and Mr Breen, who, now in his eighties, continues to work to produce materials that are useful to a number of language groups in their language revitalization work.

New relationships have also been forged between Dr Luise Hercus and a family group in northern Victoria who are reclaiming the Madhi Madhi and Wadi Wadi languages. Dr Hercus played a central role in the documentation of languages of northern Victoria, New South Wales, and South Australia. In 2015, she returned to Swan Hill with a DRIL training team and with linguist Dr Stephen

---

[12] In 2014, RNLD ran a project to scan, digitize and archive Gavan Breen's extensive collections of handwritten field notes for these languages. See http://www.rnld.org/BreenDonaldson

Morey, with whom she had co-authored *The Mathi Group of Languages* (Blake et al 2011). Hercus and Morey worked intensively with the family group over several days, building on the strong foundation that the men had already developed in understanding the linguistic structures in their languages through DRIL workshops and their own determination. Both of these languages had been silent for a long time. Indeed, Morey suggested that it might have been 135 years since Wadi Wadi was last spoken. That weekend, new stories and songs were created and recorded in both languages in a productive and moving partnership between the family members and the linguists.

Morey (pers. comm.) later noted that, "It is really significant that they had read through the book very comprehensively, and that [the men] are regularly asking perceptive questions that have led to (a) identifying errors in the book, (b) identifying gaps in the analysis and things that we could have said more about, or (c) identifying those gaps in the data that didn't allow us to say anything about that aspect of the language." Hercus later emailed to say that "It was a wonderful experience, and probably the most successful and inspiring few days I have ever experienced" (May 12, 2015). What is very apparent here is that all parties have felt both personal and research-oriented benefits from the connections that they are making. The men have since twice been to Canberra to continue working with Dr Hercus and were able to be at the celebrations for her 90th birthday in January 2016.

Stephen Morey is also working in close partnership with RNLD staff member and trainee linguist Ebony Joachim, who is a member of the Yorta Yorta Nation of northern Victoria. Morey was a co-author of *The Yorta Yorta (Bangerang) Language of the Murray Goulburn, including Yabula Yabula* (Bowe and Morey 1999). This respectful working partnership is also proving mutually beneficial. Joachim is delving deeply into her language to understand verb paradigms from the quite limited extant materials. As she identifies gaps, Morey is reopening his investigations of the historical documents to try to unearth additional data. This is a project that is seeing Joachim's linguistic skills rapidly develop while Morey is challenged to revisit some of his earlier analyses. Joachim writes, "It has been a great way to understand what was written in the book. Stephen has been assisting me in working more closely on my language. He is very conscious of the issues with the grammar and is very keen and happy to continue mentoring me in building my skills further wherever he can" (pers. comm.).

A further partnership in this program is now beginning to develop between Pitta Pitta man Aaron James, who is participating in the RNLD's Professional Development program, and Professor Barry Blake, who wrote a sketch grammar of Pitta Pitta (Blake 1979). James is highly motivated to understand Blake's materials and to rework them in a format that will be useful for his own language learning and for his community.

These projects all highlight the value of building a bridge that can facilitate linguistic and language revitalization work that is done directly by community members in a mentored partnership with linguists. The power in these relationships, and ownership over language work and any materials that are produced, remains with the community. It is also important to note that all of the linguists who have participated in these linking-up programs have felt a deep benefit themselves in the work and in the new relationships. They are able to see the outcome of their linguistic research in a new light, while also seeing the great value in collaborating to make such materials more widely accessible to community members.

8 DRIL and the community-based language research model

In outlining the training strands and allied activities that have been developed by RNLD and the DRIL program since 2009, it is useful to reflect briefly on whether and how these activities fit into the community-based language research (CBLR) model outlined by Yamada 2007, elaborated by Czaykowska-Higgins 2009, and further discussed by authors such as K. Rice 2011 and in this volume (esp. Czaykowska-Higgins et al. and Rice). The CBLR model primarily focuses on the collaborative working relationships developed in a linguistic research project between a linguist (usually identified in the relevant literature as external to the language community) and members of the language community. On this basis, it could be argued that the DRIL model sits outside of the CBLR model as it currently conceived. The core activities of the DRIL program do not involve linguistic research but rather focus on the transmission of skills to support Indigenous people in controlling and running all aspects of their own language programs themselves. An exception to this is our Linking Up program, which does bring external linguistic researchers together with community members to serve the interests and needs of communities. This branch of the RNLD's activities exemplifies CBLR in action, with a carefully negotiated collaboration between all parties.

It may then be tempting to make the case that the DRIL program fits within the earlier Advocacy or Empowering research models outlined by Cameron et al (1992) and reviewed by Czaykowska-Higgins (2009: 22–24). The DRIL program and indeed the broader RNLD organization actively advocate for the rights of Indigenous people to speak and transmit their languages, and for the maintenance of Indigenous languages. This paper has also pointed to the empowerment goals of the DRIL training program. However again, these models are premised on a research relationship in which the (non-Indigenous) researcher is the expert and largely retains the power. DRIL actively supports the goals of Indigenous people in countering this power relationship and shifting control back to the language community. In this sense, the training program fits more closely into the paradigm of advocacy outlined in Hill (2002).

CBLR is an important model that is positively influencing the relationships that are being built between community members and linguists, and is resulting in research and outcomes that benefit all parties. Rather than reject the applicability of this model to DRIL and indeed to other allied training models, the training programs provide an opportunity for the CBLR framework to be expanded so that it overtly recognizes and is inclusive of Indigenous linguists working on their own or other Indigenous languages. This space is no less fraught and no less deserving of our attention. As Zepeda and Hill (1998) amply demonstrated almost twenty years ago, an insider linguist may still be viewed as an outsider by members of their own community when they take on the nontraditional role of researcher. This reconception or expansion of CBLR will mean confronting and reframing current stereotyped notions of *insider* and *outsider*, rethinking who the partners are in a collaboration, and what negotiations will be needed for a research project to proceed and serve all parties. This can only be of advantage to the field of linguistics and to the shared enterprise of documenting and revitalizing Indigenous languages.

9 Next steps

The ability of the RNLD's DRIL program to continue growing and become sustainable is now contingent on its capacity increasing. This small organization has just ten part-time staff (equivalent to 5.6 full-time staff), including four trainers. We are at the limit of our ability to meet the growing demand for our programs. We now deliver Flexible DRIL workshops, two Certificate courses, and a Professional Development program, and are creating another certificate. The DRIL training program has already expanded far beyond the original vision of just one person. These strands now reflect the skills, experiences and ideas of many people, essentially including the hundreds of participants and the members of the DRIL training team. Crucially, each of our programs remains true to the original goal of increasing the ability of Indigenous people to develop and run their own language programs themselves and to drive the revitalization of their own languages. Despite the challenges we face, DRIL is demonstrating the impact that alternative, community responsive pathways can have. From its humble start, it is beginning to transform the landscape of language revitalization work in Australia.

References

Australian Institute of Aboriginal and Torres Strait Islander Studies, and Federation of Aboriginal and Torres Strait Islander Languages. 2005. *National Indigenous languages survey report 2005: Report submitted to the Department of Communications, Information Technology and the Arts*. Canberra: DCITA.

Bell, Jeanie. 2010. Language and linguistic knowledge: a cultural treasure. *Ngoonjook: Journal of Australian Indigenous Issues* 35. 84–96.

Blake, Barry. 1979. Pitta Pitta. In *Handbook of Australian Languages Volume 1*. Edited by R.M.W. Dixon and Barry J. Blake. Canberra: Australian National University Press.

Blake, Barry, Luise Hercus, Stephen Morey and Edward Ryan. 2011. *The Mathi group of languages*. Canberra: Pacific Linguistics, School of Culture, History and Language, College of Asia and the Pacific, Australian National University.

Bowe, Heather and Stephen Morey. 1999. *The Yorta Yorta (Bangerang) language of the Murray Goulburn, including Yabula Yabula* Canberra: Pacific Linguistics, Research School of Pacific and Asian Studies, Australian National University.

Bowra, Matilda. nd. "Lee Joachim is an agent for change." Interview in *Dumbo Feather* blog. http://www.dumbofeather.com/conversation/lee-joachim-is-an-agent-for-change/ (accessed 25 May 2017).

Burdon, Amanda. 2016. Speaking up. *Australian Geographic*. 28 April. http://www.australiangeographic.com.au/topics/history-culture/2016/04/speaking-up-australian-aboriginal-languages (accessed 25 May 2017).

Caffery, Josephine. 2008. Linguistics training in indigenous adult education and its effects on endangered languages. Charles Darwin University dissertation.

Cameron, Deborah, Elizabeth Frazer, Penelope Harvey, M.B.H. Rampton, and Kay Richardson. 1992. *Researching language: Issues of power and method*. New York: Routledge.

Carew, Margaret and Gail Woods. 2008. Angkety kalty-anthem, angketyek kalty-irrem, anwern aparlp-ilekerr (Teaching and learning languages so we don't lose it): Own language work training in Central Australia. In: *Warra Wiltaniappendi: Strengthening Languages: Proceedings of the Inaugural Indigenous Languages Conference [ILC] 2007*, 24–27. Adelaide, SA: University of Adelaide.

Czaykowska-Higgins, Ewa. 2009. Research models, community engagement, and linguistic fieldwork: Reflections on working within Canadian Indigenous communities. *Language Documentation & Conservation* 3(1). 15–50.

Florey, Margaret. 2008. Language activism and the "new linguistics": Expanding opportunities for documenting endangered languages in Indonesia. In *Language Documentation and Description* 5. 120–135.

Florey, Margaret and Knut Olawsky. 2013. Developing a regional Master-Apprentice training network in Australia. Paper presented at the 3rd International Conference on Language Documentation and Conservation (ICLDC). University of Hawai'i.

Florey, Margaret, Susan Penfield, and Benjamin V. Tucker. 2009. Towards a theory of language activism. Paper presented at the 1st International Conference on Language Documentation and Conservation (ICLDC). University of Hawai'i.

Hill, Jane. 2002. "Expert rhetorics" in advocacy for endangered languages: Who is listening and what do they hear? *Journal of Linguistic Anthropology* 12 (2). 119–133.

Marmion, Doug, Kazuko Obata and Jakelin Troy. 2014. *Community, identity, wellbeing: the report of the Second National Indigenous Languages Survey*. Canberra: Australian Institute of Aboriginal and Torres Strait Islander Studies.
McCarty, Teresa L., Lucille J. Watahomigie, Akira Y.Yamamoto, and Ofelia Zepeda. 1997. School-Community-University collaborations: The American Indian Language Development Institute. In Jon Reyhner (ed.), *Teaching Indigenous Languages*, 85–104. Flagstaff: Northern Arizona University.
McCarty, Teresa L., Lucille J. Watahomigie, Akira Y. Yamamoto, and Ofelia Zepeda. 2001. Indigenous educators as change agents: Case studies of two language institutes. In Leanne Hinton and Ken Hale (eds.), *The green book of language revitalization in practice*, 371–383. San Diego: Academic Press.
Penfield, Susan, Emilia Flores, and Benjamin Tucker. 2007. The role of the language activist in documentation and revitalization. Paper presented at the Conference on the Endangered Languages and Cultures of Native America, Utah, Salt Lake City.
Penfield, Susan. 2008. Revitalization and language activism. In ELAP Workshop: Issues in Language Revitalization and Maintenance. SOAS, London, 9 February 2008.
Recognise: http://www.recognise.org.au (accessed 25 May 2017).
Rice, Keren. 2011. Documentary linguistics and community relations. *Language Documentation & Conservation* 5. 187–207.
Rice, Sally. 2011. Delivering linguistic training to speakers of Endangered languages: CILLDI (University of Alberta) and the Community Linguist Certificate Program. Paper presented at the Consortium on Training in Language Documentation and Conservation Panel at the 2nd International Conference on Language Documentation and Conservation, University of Hawai'i, 11–13 February.
Rice, Sally, Benjamin V. Tucker, Christopher Cox, Bruce Starlight, and Gary Donovan. 2009. Linguistic Training in an Endangered Language Community. In Conference on the Endangered Languages and Cultures of Native America. Utah, Salt Lake City.
United Nations. 2007. *Declaration on the Rights of Indigenous Peoples* https://www.humanrights.gov.au/publications/un-declaration-rights-indigenous-peoples-1 (accessed 25 May 2017).
Whalen, Doug, Margaret Moss, and Daryl Baldwin. 2016. Healing through language: Positive physical health effects of indigenous language use. F1000Research 5. 852 https://f1000research.com/articles/5-852/v1 (accessed 20 May 2017).
Yamada, Racquel-Maria. 2007. Collaborative linguistic fieldwork: Practical application of the empowerment model. *Language Documentation & Conservation* 1 (2). 257–282.
Zepeda, Ofelia. 2011. The American Indian Language Development Institute: A special training & education model for Indigenous People. Paper presented in Consortium on Training in Language Documentation and Conservation Panel at the 2nd International Conference on Language Documentation and Conservation, University of Hawai'i, 11–13 February 2011.
Zepeda, Ofelia and Jane Hill. 1998. Collaborative sociolinguistic research among the Tohono O'odham. *Oral Tradition* 13 (1). 130–156.

Index

Aboriginal 314
Aboriginal Tasmanians 325
academia 46
academic 1, 41
academic linguist 32
academic product 42, 43
academic scholars 195
academic work 48
accessibility 25
accountability 69, 80, 86
accreditation 327
accredited 326
action-oriented 2, 14, 22, 24, 34
activists 11
activity 189
Africa 9
AILDI 320
Algonquian 178
Algonquian Linguistic Atlas 171
animation 178, 182, 331
anthropologists 11
application 178, 186
Archive of the Indigenous Languages of Latin America 52
archiving 203
– requirements 62
audience 56
audio 185
Australia 314
authorship 46, 47

Bakonzo 283
Bakossi 284
Bamileke 288
barriers 317
Basaa 285, 286
Bayangi 291
benefit 67, 69, 73, 74, 84
bilingual intercultural education 249–250
binary distinction 201
Blackfoot 176, 177
– New Blackfoot 184
– Old Blackfoot 184
Breath of Life workshop 219

British Columbia 68
broader impacts 58

CAOLR 204
capacity building 4, 89, 94, 169
Central Queensland 325
certify 47
challenges 28, 29, 191
Cherokee, 104
CILLDI 320
CITI training 46
classroom 181
Coast Salish 68, 70
Co-authoring 263
Coeur d'Alene 194
Coeur d'Alene Online Language Resource Center 205
collaboration(s) 117, 206
– academic-tribal 96
– inside/outside classroom 153, 155
collaborative 2, 21, 24
collaborative partnership 198
collaborative process 246, 249, 252, 258, 259, 260, 263
collaborative websites 164
Colombia 249
communication 67, 80, 187, 246, 248–249, 252, 256, 257, 258, 260, 263
community 10, 19, 266, 267
– efforts 310
– evaluation 309
– interest 299
– language teachers 304
– membership 10
– relationships 300
community-based language research 68, 334
community-based research 13, 14
– CBR 2, 201
– emergence of 119
– ideology 2
– methodology 2
– orientation 2, 32
– philosophy 32

https://doi.org/10.1515/9783110527018-019

community-based research (*continued*)
- practice 2
- tool 2
community-centered 95
community collaborators 25
community driven 95, 133, 331
community investment and ownership 132
community involvement 2
community linguist 300
Community Linguist Certificate 321
community members 1
community-of-practice 20
community-oriented 24
community researcher 28, 33
community setting 17, 20
community situated 2, 16, 34
Comparative Language Input Project 241
compensation 303
confidential 51
consent 50, 60
consultation 76, 77, 78
- meaningful 67, 68, 75, 76
continuum 202
control 67, 69, 72, 74, 84
copyright 203
corpus 300, 305
countable outputs 3
co-writing 246, 248–249, 262
Cree 6
cultural 182
- issues 324
cultural comments 282
cultural revitalization 221
cultural sensitivity 137
cultural values 160
culturally relevant 42
curriculum 188
curriculum development 321

daily life conversation 222
Darrell Kipp 179
data 50
data management plans 61
decolonization research practices 230
decolonizing 67, 69, 87, 89, 90
democratization knowledge 77, 81
descriptive work 299

dictionary 202, 280, 281, 283
- cultural dictionaries 282
- dictionaries 305
- Kinande 281
- Masa 281
differences 301
digital access 202
digital infrastructure 164
digital resources 6, 194
digital technologies 164
Diidxazá (Isthmus Zapotec) 113
discourse markers 183
discoverable 205
diverse 15, 321
documentation 5, 9, 71, 83, 85, 266
- a community-driven language 138
- knowledge 120
- language documentation materials 299
- multimedia 275
Documenting Endangered Languages
    Program 61
dormant 212
DRIL 314, 315, 321
- training program 315–317
dual roles 318
Dublin Core Metadata Initiatives 205

economic power 59
educational 182
educational system 317
elders 68
empowerment 72, 73, 74
Endangered Languages Documentation
    Programme 58
engagement 43
equal collaborators 151
equality 74
ethical 324
ethical principles 299
ethical research 34
ethnobotanical research 122
ethnographic sketch 197
expandable 204
experimental 297
experimental linguistics 296
experimental methodologies 298

Index — 341

experimental techniques 297
experimentation 5
expertise 67, 69, 77, 81
external researchers 40

FERPA 54
field 296
fieldwork 33
flexibility 246, 249, 252, 255, 256, 258, 263, 321
formal education 317, 326
format 45
four eyes 289
free-standing teaching materials 216–217
full-immersion 144
functionally bilingual 307
funding institutions 57

geography 11
goals 15, 40
– explicit 23
governance 75
grammar 48, 202
grassroots
– model 323
– training model 314

healthcare professionals 11
Hul'q'umi'num', 70

identity 11
ideology 56
immersion 223
impact 304
imperfective 181
indigenizing 67, 69, 87
indigenous
– educators 320
– language activists 314
indigenous community scholars 195
indigenous intellectual property 260
indigenous intellectual property rights 253
indigenous knowledge 73, 85
indigenous-led infrastructure 228
informal educational environment 326
information and communication technologies 166, 173

Innu 6
insider 335
institutional review board 52
instruction
– prescriptive 304
intangible cultural property 85
intangible outcome 3, 44, 67, 87–89
intangible results 103
intellectual property 71, 85, 86, 261
intellectual tradition 39. See also Junker this volume
interactive 187
Intercultural Bilingual Education 254
interdisciplinary 190
intermittent material body 291
inverse 183
Isle of Skye 297

judgment 308
Junker this volume 145, 259

Kinande 280
knowledge 44, 46, 56
Koasati Language Project 132, 139
Konzo 283

Lab 296
language
– activist/activism 319, 320
– endangerment 316
– history and culture in 310
– record of 198
– status of 310
– unique knowledge structure in 310
language abilities 308
language attitudes 301–302
language community 39
language documentation 137, 198
language maintenance 6
language work 16
Latin America 49
Latin-American 48
leaners 188
lexical decision 306
lexical entry 282
linguist 319
linguist-focused research 112, 114

linguist-speaker relationship 151
linguistic hierarchy 49
linguistic ideology 49
linguistic subfields 1
linguistically-informed assessments 228
Linking Up 334
literacy 266, 268, 270, 271, 272, 273, 281
– classes 274, 276, 277
– materials 274
– mother-tongue 272
long-term commitment 15

Madhi Madhi 332
maintenance 266, 267
management 67, 71, 72, 74
Masa 280
master apprentice 324, 328
Maya for Maya 8
Mayan 8
Mbo 284
Mbombog 285
meaningful consent 42
meaningful consultation 66
meaningful products 6
memorandum of understanding 85
metadata 205
methodologically appropriate 53
misalignments 3, 41, 45, 57
Montana 178
morphosyntactic 183
multimedia documentation 268
museistic 62, 64
Mutsun language 212
Mwankum 284
myths 197

Nande 283
National Ethnobotanical Herbarium Online 123
National Science Foundation 58
Native American 186
Native American Languages Lab 100
natural linguists 47
negotiation 322
NILI 320
nontraditional role 335
Northwest Cameroon 9

obstacles 157
obviation 183
Oklahoma Native Language Association 98
Omaha Tribe of Nebraska 152
online dictionaries 172
onomatopoeia 331
on-site 322
orientation 10, 23, 201
orthography 135, 272, 301
outcomes 33
outsider 335
overtly political 317
ownership 67, 69, 75, 78, 84

Panama 249
PAR 40
participant pool 307
participant variation 307
participants 306–309, 323
participation 118
participation agreement 322
partnership(s), 66, 68, 82, 84, 86, 332–334
– successful 26
passion 34
patience 34
pedagogical 177
pedagogical materials 29
pedagogical resources 199
pedagogy 304, 310
perseverance 34
persistence 34
phantom 291
philosophy 4, 7, 10, 201
phonetics 298
phonology 298
physiological articulation 298
Piegan Institute 179
– Cuts Wood School 184
Pitta Pitta 333
policy experts 11
political 314
politicians 11
power 56, 77, 81, 84, 86
power and linguistic rights 40
power imbalances 24, 31, 57, 62
practical 18

practical relevance 17, 18
preservation 59
principles 41
principles of respect 74, 75, 78, 79
process 255
product 10, 44, 45
product of research 45
professional development 318, 330–332
protocols 69, 74, 77, 84, 322
publication(s), 261, 262

qualifications 327

reaction times 299
reciprocal 15
reciprocal involvement 22
reciprocity 34, 69, 74, 87
reclamation 321
reconceptualizing 201
reconciliation Australia 316
relevance 24, 34, 87
religion
– religious ideologies 280, 294
remoteness 322
research
– community-driven 145
– leadership 126
– linguist-focused 116
– university-driven 145
researcher-focused 300
resources 15
respect 15, 34, 87
responsibility 34, 87
responsive 321
results 73, 74, 75, 84
revitalization 5, 59, 178, 199, 208, 266, 267, 268
– infrastructure 299
right of return 53, 54
RNLD 315

Scotland 296
Scottish Gaelic 296, 297
self-publishing 142
selling 44
SENĆOŦEN 70, 71
service 43
service-learning 101

severely endangered 207
sharing 75
short-term funding 28
small subject pools 307
Snchitsu'umshtsn 194
social action 77
social change 77
social responsibility 31
sociolinguistic landscape 112
software 28
solidarity 11
spiritual world 281, 287
Stimuli 305–306
storytelling 208
strange phenomena 281, 292
structured language teaching materials 226
study design 296
subject consent form 303
supernatural 281, 283
supernatural phenomena 287
supernatural powers 284
sustainable 204
sustainable models 94, 107
syllabic characters 169

taboo 302
talking dictionary workshops 102
tangible outputs 87
Tasmania 325
teachers 11
teaching materials 143
technological divide 7
technologist 11
technology(ies) 6, 202, 324
theoretical linguistics 297
theoretical work 202
time 261, 263
Torres Strait Islander 314
totem 286
traditional academics 47
traditional cultural material 221
traditional cultural values 151, 162
traditional publication 45
training 95
– program 324
– topics 324–325

transformative 317
trust 15, 76, 78, 79, 246, 249, 252, 255, 258, 263, 322
trustworthy 204
twins 288
two-way training 21

Umoⁿhoⁿ (Omaha) 152
understandable 25
university-driven research 133
university researchers 20
university setting 20
unpublished 203
URACCAN 44

Vancouver 66
variation 304
varied 32
venue 56

viable opportunities 5
video 180

Wadi Wadi 332, 333
Welsh 298
Western science 280
western-style academic 40
western values and ethics 162
witchcraft 283, 286
Woorabinda 325, 332
word lists 305
workshops 323
worldview 15
Wounaan 8
written 56

Yambasaa 290
Yorta Yorta Nation 317, 333

www.ingramcontent.com/pod-product-compliance
Lightning Source LLC
Chambersburg PA
CBHW030605230426
43661CB00053B/1848